"Mysticism is not mystifying at all, but simple, always available, and utterly clarifying. Carl McColman's much-needed book will allow you to experience this for yourself! Christians and all Seekers will find both meat and dessert in such a full meal."

—**Richard Rohr, OFM, author of** *The Naked Now:*
Learning to See as the Mystics See **and**
Everything Belongs

"A wise and supportive guidebook for those going deeper on the Christian mystical path. This book is grounded in sound scholarship and thoughtful reflection, but what makes it sing is the authenticity of the author's own contemplative journey."

—**The Rev. Cynthia Bourgeault, author of** *Centering Prayer and*
Inner Awakening **and** *The Wisdom Jesus*

"If you identify as Christian, make this book a new Gospel. If you are not, read it as a catalyst to finding the mystic heart of your own spiritual identity."

—**Rabbi Rami Shapiro, author of** *Perennial Wisdom for*
the Spiritually Independent

"Comprehensive, accessible, and dynamic, Carl McColman's *New Big Book of Christian Mysticism* is a masterpiece! Offering a rich mix of history, clear explanation, attention to the social dimension, inclusivity, community, and resources for further learning, *The New Big Book of Christian Mysticism* leads us gently into the deeply ordinary, very human, keenly subversive and joyful activity we simply call contemplation. A must-read for every spiritual seeker!"

—**Carmen Acevedo Butcher, translator of** *Practice of*
the Presence **by Brother Lawrence and**
The Cloud of Unknowing, **and author of**
Hildegard of Bingen: A Spiritual Reader

"Carl McColman's *The New Big Book of Christian Mysticism* is accessible for those brand new to mysticism and a deep dive for those who have been studying it a lifetime. In this new edition, McColman explores mysticism's direct connection to topics like embodiment, social justice, eroticism, and sexuality, inviting the reader into mysticism's aliveness."

—**Cassidy Hall, award-winning filmmaker, podcaster, and author of *Queering Contemplation: Finding Queerness in the Roots and Future of Contemplative Spirituality***

"A mystic is one whose eyes are open to seeing the Eternal in every fleeting moment of human life on this earth, and whose heart is open to the Love that permeates each and every thing in this universe. This new volume lays out more of the rich treasures of the Christian tradition for those aspiring to awaken their mystic heart."

—**Ruben L. F. Habito, author of *Be Still and Know: Zen and the Bible* and *Living Zen, Loving God***

"Bringing mysticism and contemplation out of the clouds and down to earth, Carl provides everyday mystics and spiritual seekers with a portal to embrace the Presence unceasingly. In this extraordinary contribution, Carl ushers the discussion into contemporary times by noting the ongoing impact of Christian mysticism on struggles for liberation and human dignity. I believe the timeless wisdom contained in this volume will feed and enlighten those who follow in our footsteps."

—**Lerita Coleman Brown, professor of psychology emerita, spiritual companion, and author of *What Makes You Come Alive: A Spiritual Walk with Howard Thurman***

"With *The New Big Book of Christian Mysticism*, Carl McColman has reawakened in me that deep, radical, relational tenderness that first called me into the practices and lineage of Christian mysticism. This book offers helpful definition without ceasing to dance, and makes present both the mystery of Presence and the wonderful companionship of those who have gone before us."

—**Alana Levandoski, singer-songwriter whose albums include *Behold, I Make All Things New* and *Hymns from the Icons***

"*The New Big Book of Christian Mysticism* is a must-read for anyone wanting to deeply explore the riches of the Christian contemplative tradition. Carl McColman is a trustworthy guide and teacher who beautifully synthesizes the wisdom of the Christian mystics and invites us to experience the new frontiers of interspirituality. Additionally, McColman's work includes vital, yet often overlooked, contributions of BIPOC mystics. This book is truly a gift!"

—**Adam Bucko, author of *Let Your Heartbreak
Be Your Guide* and coauthor of
*The New Monasticism***

"In this wonderful book, Carl McColman reveals the essence of Christian mysticism in an eloquent, inspiring, and powerful narrative. A master teacher, McColman artfully weaves tales from the Bible together with the lives and insights of ancient and modern-day mystics to reveal the mystical paths of yesterday, today, and tomorrow. In doing so, he invites us into the heart of the Mystery, that which gladdens our hearts and manifests God's Love for all of us. A beautiful journey awaits!"

—**Rev. SeiFu Singh-Molares, executive director of
Spiritual Directors International**

"Carl McColman's *New Big Book of Christian Mysticism* is a grace-filled, invaluable resource and a practical handbook that invites us into a life more attuned with the Holy, enabling us to live into who we are meant to be as contemplatives-in-action. I will be recommending it to all my 'anam charas'—my soul friends on the journey to fullness of life in God's Love."

—**Caroline Oakes, author of *Practice
the Pause: Jesus' Contemplative Practice,
New Brain Science, and What It Means
to Be Fully Human***

"An amazing resource! If you want a sense of the varieties of the Christian spiritual life and insight into the mystical way, this is a necessary read."

—**James Ishmael Ford, author of *If You're Lucky, Your Heart
Will Break: Field Notes from a Zen Life* and coeditor of
*The Book of Mu: Essential Writings on
Zen's Most Famous Koan***

"*The New Big Book of Christian Mysticism* is a true gift! This revised and expanded edition draws us deeper into the heart of the divine, and Carl McColman is a skillful and trustworthy guide on this journey. He offers ancient and modern examples that both inspire and instruct the reader on how mysticism can be a part of our everyday lives. I am so grateful for this book. I know I will turn to it again and again!"

—**Kate H. Rademacher, author of *Reclaiming Rest:***
The Promise of Sabbath, Solitude, and
Stillness in a Restless World

"This is not only a *big* book of Christian mysticism; it is also an extraordinarily *accessible* book. In clear and engaging prose, McColman lays out what is distinctive about the Christian mystical path, but in a way that also calls Christians to learn from the mysticism of other traditions. He describes Christians as 'little Christs' who can truly share in Jesus's awareness of oneness with the God he called 'Abba.' Highly recommended for anyone seeking to understand and practice the mystical foundations of Christian faith."

—**Paul Knitter, Paul Tillich Professor Emeritus**
of Theology, World Religions, and Culture,
Union Theological Seminary, and
author of *Without Buddha*
I Could Not Be a Christian

"*The New Big Book of Christian Mysticism* is an invitation to reclaim the mystical heart of Christianity. Written with the depth of a scholar and the soul of a pilgrim, it is accessible, challenging, heartfelt and practical. With clarity and passion, Carl McColman urges us to recognize how relevant mysticism is for our time."

—**Colette Lafia, author of *The Divine Heart***
and *Seeking Surrender*

"In this generous theoretical and practical exploration of Christian mysticism, we are offered a compelling Christ-shaped vision of how each of us can live uniquely in the mystery of God's love. In his usual accessible and down-to-earth writing style, Carl McColman deepens our longing both to know this Great Love for ourselves and to make it more real where we live and work. This labor of love will be a treasured gift for God's children from all backgrounds."

—**Trevor Hudson, minister of the Methodist Church of Southern Africa and author of** *Seeking God: Finding Another Kind of Life with St. Ignatius and Dallas Willard*

"Before I heard about *The Big Book of Christian Mysticism*, I had been thinking about how such a book has been needed for a long time. Now, having read it, I'm glad we waited for Carl McColman to come along to write it. It's accessible, human, well-informed, balanced, broad . . . just what we needed."

—**Brian D. McLaren, author of** *A New Kind of Christianity* **and** *A Generous Orthodoxy*

"McColman's book on Christian mysticism is a masterpiece of scholarship and wisdom. This author obviously earned his understanding of mysticism through years of research as well as his own personal spiritual journey and there is no more powerful combination for inspired writing."

—**Caroline Myss, author of** *Entering the Castle* **and** *Anatomy of the Spirit*

"With his "Big Book" McColman has pulled off a tour de force: a work on Christian mysticism that is broadly accessible, but deep; scholarly but not pedantic; reverent, but judicious; thorough, but a good read; an excellent introduction to the subject for the general reader, but with plenty of meat for the specialist. Highly recommended for the neophyte, the informed, and the expert alike."

—**The Rev. Robert D. Hughes III, author of** *Beloved Dust: Tides of the Spirit in the Christian Life*

"In *The Big Book of Christian Mysticism*, Carl McColman offers us a thorough and engaging exploration of Christian mysticism which he defines as a form of alchemy – that is, transformation through the Source of all Love. His wise and clear writing takes us on a wide journey through both classical and contemporary mystic guides. Ultimately he invites us to catch a glimpse of the heart of Mystery through concrete suggestions for mystical practice and be transformed ourselves."

—**Christine Valters Paintner, author of** *Water,* *Wind, Earth, & Fire: The Christian Practice* *of Praying with the Elements*

"If you are looking for both a primer on Christian mysticism as well as an in-depth treatment of this oft-misunderstood aspect of the spiritual life, here is your book. Readable, useful, well-researched, Carl McColman's *Big Book of Christian Mysticism* helps both the novice and those already well along on the journey toward a deeper relationship with God to see that mysticism is ultimately not at all a mysterious quest, but a human— and possible—one."

—**Paul Wilkes, author of** *Beyond the Walls:* *Monastic Wisdom for Everyday Life*

"A brilliant contribution from a clear, concise and articulate author! Carl McColman's *Big Book* deepens the conversation as he explores the paradoxes of the mystical/traditional approaches, outlines the bias against cultivating an interior life and illuminates the reader on practices to embrace in order to relate to a dynamic Living God.

—**Lauren Artress, author of** *Walking a Sacred Path*

"McColman's book is wise and wonderful, deceptively simple! Are you interested in having a relationship with something that's ultimately unknowable? Me too. It's not easy, but dig in, here!"

—**Jon M. Sweeney, author of** *Almost Catholic* **and** *The St. Francis Prayer Book*

"In this delightfully accessible book, Carl McColman dispels the notion that Christian mysticism exists somewhere in the ether, and reveals its solid, earthy roots. If you want a rich, nourishing life of faith, and virtues that flourish like wildflowers, read Christian Mysticism, and let the good news in it transform you."

—**Claudia Mair Burney, author of** *God Alone is Enough:* *A Spirited Pilgrimage with St. Teresa of Avila*

"Mysticism is at the heart of faith, whatever religious or denominational flag we raise. Thoughtful, well-written doorways into these mysteries, such as this one, matter a great deal to all of us who seek communion with the Mystery Itself."

— **Robert Benson, author of *In Constant Prayer***

"Carl McColman's new book is truly a work of art as well as a spiritual guide for those who want to know more about Christian mysticism. Writing for a broad audience of readers, Carl wants everyone to become aware of that rich history and its potential meaning for today. He writes in a lively, engaging style, but his work comes out of deep wells of spiritual wisdom. Appealing to both head and heart, his book not only makes the history of Christian mysticism accessible, but also provides for readers guidance in prayer, contemplation, and transformation itself."

—**Ed Sellner, author of *Wisdom of the Celtic Saints*
and *Finding the Monk Within: Great Monastic
Values for Today***

In Loving Memory:

"Carl McColman has both studied and practiced the Christian mystical tradition, stressing its earthiness and 'ordinariness.' Like Thomas Merton, Michael Ramsey, and others, he holds that mysticism is not an esoteric realm reserved for the very holy, but is what all Christian life is about. I strongly commend this book."

—**Kenneth Leech (1939-2015), author of *Soul Friend*
and *Prayer and Prophecy***

"Charmingly and conversationally written, but also rich in nuance and thorough in its coverage and its attention to detail, *The Big Book* is, as its name suggests, a big—even an enormous—contribution to our current literature on the subject. Highly recommended."

—**Phyllis Tickle (1934-2015), author of
*The Great Emergence: How Christianity is
Changing and Why* and *God-Talk in America***

The New Big Book of Christian Mysticism

CARL McCOLMAN

THE NEW BIG BOOK OF
CHRISTIAN
MYSTICISM

An Essential Guide to
Contemplative
Spirituality

Broadleaf Books
Minneapolis

Library of Congress Cataloging-in-Publication Data

Names: McColman, Carl, author.
Title: The new big book of Christian mysticism : an essential guide to
   contemplative spirituality / Carl McColman.
Other titles: Big book of Christian mysticism
Description: Minneapolis, MN : Broadleaf Books, [2023]
Identifiers: LCCN 2023004856 (print) | LCCN 2023004857 (ebook) | ISBN
   9781506486840 (paperback) | ISBN 9781506486857 (ebook)
Subjects: LCSH: Mysticism—Christianity.
Classification: LCC BV5082.3 .M34 2023 (print) | LCC BV5082.3 (ebook) |
   DDC 248.2/2—dc23/eng/20230303
LC record available at https://lccn.loc.gov/2023004856
LC ebook record available at https://lccn.loc.gov/2023004857

Print ISBN: 978-1-5064-8684-0
eBook ISBN: 978-1-5064-8685-7

Contents

PART II: The Contemplative Life

Truly, your God is God of gods and Lord of kings
and a revealer of mysteries.
—King Nebuchadnezzar (Daniel 2:47)

There is nothing concealed that will not be revealed,
nor secret that will not be known.
—Jesus (Luke 12:2 NABRE)

The Christian of the future will be a mystic or will not exist at all.
—Karl Rahner

The deeper we get into any reality, the more numerous
will be the questions we cannot answer.
—Baron Friedrich von Hügel

Preface to the New Edition

Love is real, God is love, and God dwells in your heart.

And this God-who-is-Love wants nothing more than for you to realize what is already yours: the limitless joy of union with divine love as you behold the eyes of infinite compassion—and allow that compassion to guide your own life into care and service for others.

In the Christian tradition, mysticism is the spirituality of such union with God—union that comes through Jesus, God made present in human form: the Christ, who is the sacrament of God; the Holy Spirit, given to us by Christ, is the very breath of God, poured into our hearts.[1]

Christian mystics from ancient times have proclaimed that these three faces of divinity, the transcendent Creator, the immanent Christ, and the indwelling Spirit, are in fact one, although a oneness that still holds the diversity of three persons: for love becomes manifest through relationships, and so God the Creator and God-in-Christ and God the Holy Spirit together form one God, and oneness in God—and yet they remain three distinct persons, so that the love that is the very ground of their being may flow between them, to and from them, and within them, and through them to all their beloved creation.

This divine love is the source of all life, your and my life, and the lives of all we know and love. Divine love is poured into your and my hearts and knits all beings together, making us not only related to God, but in the words of the apostle Peter, "partakers of the divine nature."[2]

To partake in the divine nature is to dwell, here and now, in heaven. Jesus calls us to *embody* a heavenly life here and now (not merely to "get to heaven" after our death). When musicians like Donovan sang "Wear Your Love Like Heaven" or Jon Anderson of Yes chanted "We Have Heaven," they perhaps subconsciously illuminated the heart of mystical spirituality.

WHAT IS MYSTICISM?

This vague and multivalent word, *mysticism*, functions like a kind of Rorschach inkblot of the interior life: we see, or imagine we see, many diverse things in it and within it. Different people concoct all sorts of various and even contradictory ways of talking about it, understanding it, and living it.

No book on mysticism can offer you any kind of definitive statement about the subject. The best this (or any) book on mysticism can do is simply offer an invitation, a contribution to a conversation that has been formed for centuries and will no doubt extend and continue its formation long after you and I have passed into the silence of eternity.

Among the many things that we can say about mysticism, it implies a spirituality that is embodied, visceral, experiential—a here-and-now spirituality even as it calls us into the splendor of eternity. Put more simply, mysticism encompasses the *adventure* of spiritual living.

When we talk about *Christian* mysticism, we talk about that adventure as it is embodied in the wisdom teachings of Jesus of Nazareth, teachings that have been amplified and illuminated by further insights from Jesus's many followers through the ages, from the writers of the New Testament down through mystical and contemplative writers of every century since.

How can this claim to be a "big" book on Christian mysticism? On the one hand, the title is simply a way to differentiate this book from a book of quotations from the mystics that I curated called *The Little Book of Christian Mysticism*. By comparison, this is the bigger book. On another level, this title captures my hope to offer a meaningful introduction to what is in fact an immensely vast topic. Meaningful, but not comprehensive—after all, no single book can contain all the wisdom and treasures of mystical spirituality. This is a "new" big book—fully revised, updated, and with additional material added, with the goal of presenting a more inclusive and universal picture of this beautiful tradition. Reading this book will *not* give you everything you need to know about the topic, but may it give you a longing to read more, learn more, and—most important of all—seek those hidden places in your own heart where the silent gift of love resides, even now.

CHRISTIAN MYSTICISM IS MANY THINGS

Mysticism is Christianity's best-kept secret. It is a distinctive way to approach God and Christ and spirituality. It is an ancient and venerable wisdom tradition, a lineage of spiritual teachings that can be traced back to Jesus of Nazareth and his teachings as found in the earliest Christian writings—a tradition that promises to transform the lives of people who seriously and sincerely apply its wisdom to their own life circumstances.

Christian mystics understand and apply the wisdom of Jesus in a manner unlike that of ordinary religious belief or observance. The mystical life allows room for profound doubt and insistent questioning. It does not ask you to check your mind at the door and submit your will to some sort of external authority—whether that be a church, a priest or minister, or a book. Rather, Christian mysticism assumes that any respect you might pay to external authority can emerge only from a profound inner recognition or conviction that God is real and present, and that it is both possible and plausible for the average person to have a truly embodied and conscious relationship with God.

By *secret*, I do not mean to suggest that Christian mysticism is completely foreign to formal institutions and "religious" Christianity. Religion, at its best, is simply spirituality expressed in social and communal ways. Since Christianity involves loving God and loving our neighbors, Christian mysticism encourages an optimistic, positive outlook toward other people, despite everyone's human failings. But it is the mystical dimension of Christianity that can help us find joy in relating to God, ourselves, and others—in any context, even in organized religious settings like your neighborhood church (but it's not limited to just such settings).

The stories about Jesus and the first Christians include many tales of miracles and wonders, and some of the great saints and mystics of the Christian tradition have likewise reported the occurrence of supernatural visions and voices, or profound charismatic experiences that seem miraculous in nature and extraordinary in scope. For mysticism is all about possibility. It's fair to say it includes the possibility of mind-expanding and ecstatic encounters with God.

I do not wish to understate the richness of this spiritual tradition. But in its oldest and purest form, mystical Christianity is surprisingly humble, a wisdom path anchored in values like simplicity, trust, compassion, and serenity. The mystical life can be completely ordinary, utterly down-to-earth, and entirely naturalistic. You can be a mystic without ever seeing visions or experiencing ecstatic wonders or receiving direct messages from God. In fact, some of the greatest Christian mystics, like John of the Cross, felt that supernatural phenomena tended to be a problem, because they could so easily arise from nonmystical sources, like the human ego's need to feel important or special.

Christian mysticism invites us to look at God, Jesus, the church, our own souls, and our understanding of religious concepts like sin, repentance, or holiness in new and sometimes surprising ways. Mysticism, Christian or otherwise, need not contradict traditional religious teaching, but neither is it constrained by the institutional church. In many ways, however, it represents an element of Christianity that transcends human logic or reason—and that understands spiritual wisdom not as a closed system of unalterable truth, but as an organic circle of ever-expanding love, and therefore, possibility.

It has the potential to help us see everything in new and different ways— especially all of our cherished beliefs, sacred cows, and dogmatic illusions. It undermines all of our settled ways of looking at things, not because it seeks to cause chaos, but rather because it helps us open our hearts and minds to something that cannot be captured in ideology, or dogma, or theology, or philosophy.

That secret, that "something," cannot be put into words. Perhaps the word *God* is as good as any other. On the one hand, mystical spirituality will invite you to rethink everything you think you know about God—but when all the old images and ideas of God fall away, and you are left with a deep, unfathomable mystery that cannot be put into words (but may yet be encountered through love), to the mystic, that limitless mystery is as much "God" as anything else.

THE PARADOX OF MYSTICAL EXPERIENCE

When it comes to Christian mysticism, the more it reveals, the more it conceals. Mysticism calls us into the heart of mystery—spiritual mystery. Such mystery cannot be captured in words or concepts. Therefore, any book on the subject will, of necessity, be incomplete, paradoxical, and, at times, confusing or ambiguous.

Indeed, that confusion is rooted in the transrational nature of mysticism itself. Mystical spirituality opens you up to the love of God, yet insists you give up all your limited ideas and concepts about God, discarding them all as mere mental idols. The deeper you go, the more elusive God becomes. Yet the deeper you go, the more you realize you are a living embodiment of divine love.

The Christian mystics show us ways to take that interior journey, and the primary tools of the mystical trade are prayer, meditation, and contemplation.

When you begin to explore mysticism through such spiritual practices, you embark on a journey by which you slowly respond to that elusive mystery we call God. The mystical way always calls us into the present moment; it's not about what is going to happen tomorrow, or next year, or in the next life. It is about learning to live here and now in joy, about transforming consciousness, about becoming holy. The wisdom of the Christian mystics directs us to spiritual practices and exercises that can help us cultivate the spiritual dimension to our lives—yet the moment you focus your attention on practice, no matter how worthy or pious or spiritual it may be, you run the risk of getting lost in the judgmental dungeon of performance and measurement.

Perhaps you associate Christian mysticism with cloistered nuns chanting in monasteries, or hermits sheltered in the silent desert, or sages isolated on remote mountaintops, sheltered from the noise of the world. In these antiseptic settings, we imagine these mystics partake of sweet communion with God. Yet the renowned twentieth-century mystic Howard Thurman found one of his most life-altering encounters with the mystery not in a monastery but at a train station. The great fourteenth-century mystic Julian of Norwich received her "showings of divine love" not while she was alone in a hermitage, but during an illness as she lay suffering in a room surrounded by loved ones. Others have reported that their most amazing encounters with God have occurred while working hard to alleviate the suffering of the poor, the sick, or the dying. Mysticism isn't about keeping your hands clean and hiding in a separate life or community. Rather it impels you to get those hands dirty—always in the service of love.

Many people associate Christian mysticism with experience—the experience of union with God, or of the presence of God. But mysticism is also about a spiritual reality that can undermine experience itself, deconstructing all our masks and self-defenses and leaving us spiritually naked and vulnerable before the silence of the inexpressible mystery. This is a spirituality of bringing heaven to earth, and of going through hell while here on earth in order to get to heaven.

So, what does Christian mysticism mean *today*? How can we apply the wisdom of the mystics, and the insights that come from contemplation and Christian meditation, to our current circumstances and situations? These are the questions that have inspired me to write this book, and I hope these are the questions that will accompany you as you read and reflect on the pages to come. Mysticism (Christian or otherwise) is never just a topic you can learn about in some scholarly, abstract way. To explore mystical spirituality is to place yourself into the hands of the living God. If your heart is truly open, it will change your life.

I am conscious that readers of this book will come from many different religious and cultural backgrounds. I do not assume that readers will share my spiritual beliefs, church affiliation, race, gender identity, or political values. Having said that, much of the inner logic and coherence of mystical Christianity begins with the assumption that the Christian mystic, or student of such mysticism, accepts the teachings of Jesus and is, on some level, a follower of Jesus. This book would quickly become tedious if I tried to explain every basic point of Christian doctrine or belief, or if I continually tried to reassure those who do not accept such teachings that they, too, are welcome to explore this path. So let me apologize in advance if my poor skills as a writer have resulted in me saying anything that you cannot in good conscience agree with or intuitively accept.

If you come to this topic from another religious tradition or as an interspiritual or spiritually independent seeker, and you seek more background materials, I would encourage you to supplement the reading of this book with time spent reading the Bible, especially the Gospels (the stories of Jesus) and the letters of Paul and other early Christians. These foundational writings will provide you with important background information to the ideas and philosophy of mystical Christianity. And whether or not you ultimately accept the teachings of the mystics, I hope you will meet their wisdom with an open mind and an open heart. I believe this is wisdom for everybody.

This book is divided into two parts, "The Christian Mystery" and "The Contemplative Life." Part 1 is essentially an extended exploration on what mysticism is—where it comes from, how it is experienced and understood, and why it matters. Part 2 is more practical, and considers how mystical spirituality can be made a part of our ordinary, everyday lives—as well as seeing what implications that has for us as we seek to grow spiritually. Mystical Christianity is, in effect, a way of responding to divine love; the contemplative life consists of all we do to undertake such a response and how this, in turn, forms and shapes the balance of our lives.

As you read this book, you will find that I return to specific themes, images, Bible verses, and quotations from the great mystics, again and again. Mysticism is like a kaleidoscope: it's colorful and prismatic, forming endless images of beauty and wonder out of a small number of ordinary objects. Likewise, the basic elements of mystical theology and spirituality are surprisingly humble and earthy. Like a kaleidoscope, the same basic bits and colors continually reappear, forming new patterns of beauty as they tumble together in different ways. A monk once told me that the monastic life is all about repetition—indeed, monks chant and pray the same basic psalms and canticles day after day, week after week, decade after decade. Mysticism likewise has its own rhythmic, cyclical quality to it, so I encourage you to notice the recurring themes, ideas, and allusions as we journey together, ever deeper into the mystery.

CONCERNING LANGUAGE AND EQUALITY

We live in a time when we have come to recognize that our very language is often embedded with social and cultural systems of privilege and power. For example, Christianity teaches that God is beyond human categories of gender, and yet traditional God language is almost entirely masculine: God the Father, Christ the King, and so forth. Meanwhile, even language that may seem to be innocuous to some can actually harbor biases that can be exclusionary or even demeaning to others. An example here is the sections of the Bible labeled "Old Testament" and "New Testament"—divided by whether the writings in question are from the Jewish Bible or the earliest Christian writings. Does "old" here mean "outdated" or "inferior"? Unfortunately, especially in our consumer/throwaway culture, that assumption is too easy to make. And given the long history of anti-Semitism in Christianity, it's easy to see how this can be a problematic description. In addition to sexism, racism, or religious discrimination, our language can also sometimes convey ideas or values that are discriminatory toward LGBTQ+ persons or persons with disabilities.

As a writer whose ancestors are European, who is white, and who was assigned male at birth, I am aware that I do not always see when my words might be defaulting toward the systems of privilege that benefit white/male persons at the expense of others. As much as I try to be conscious of these issues, I recognize I still make mistakes.

In writing the *New Big Book of Christian Mysticism*, I'm trying my best to avoid language that is coded with messages of power, privilege, or exclusion. My editors and early readers have helped me to try to keep the language of the book as radically egalitarian and inclusive as possible (but any mistakes are, of course, my responsibility). I humbly ask for forgiveness if readers still find terminology that is harmful, exclusionary, or oppressive.

Meanwhile, as we try to foster language that includes rather than excludes—not only in this book, but in our lives—sometimes this means using words, nouns, pronouns, and so on that may feel novel or unusual. For example, in this book I refer to the two sections of the Bible as the "Hebrew Scriptures" and the "Christian Scriptures" rather than perpetuating the old/new dichotomy. I'm also trying to avoid using gendered pronouns in regard to God (although I do use such pronouns to refer to Jesus). If a sentence like "We trust that God loves God's creation because God said so" strikes you as clunky or awkward, please receive it in the spirit in which it is offered: as an attempt to bring a conscious sense of responsibility to our language, where inclusivity, equality, and fairness matter more than outdated ideas of what sounds proper or familiar.

PART I

The Christian Mystery

For human beings this is impossible,
but for God all things are possible.
—Jesus (Matthew 19:26 NABRE)

God became human so that humans might become God.
—Athanasius

Jesus sets before us a vision of the destiny of humankind, the
full realization of our human potential. . . . Since Jesus was fully
human, he was one of us. He understood our possibilities as well as
our human frailties and limitations, and he was directing us toward
our highest potential. The standard he used was not our intellectual
and social achievements, but the depth of his own self-giving love
and compassion, his total identification with suffering humanity.
—Pauli Murray

Everything sacred, that wishes to remain sacred,
clothes itself in mystery.
—Stéphane Mallarmé

CHAPTER ONE

The Transfiguring Moment

For everything there is a season, and a time for every matter
under heaven. . . . A time to keep silence, and a time to speak.
—Ecclesiastes 3:1, 7

The goal of life is vision.
—Clement of Alexandria

Recently, I was one of several guests on a podcast devoted to mysticism. Each
represented a different faith. Others included a Sufi Muslim, a Kabbalistic
Jew, and adherents of other wisdom traditions such as Advaita Vedanta or
Zen. The host had invited me as a representative of Christian mysticism.
So naturally, she asked me if I could explain what is unique and distinctive
about Christian mysticism.

"Well, there's a lot of things you could say about Christianity or Christian mysticism in particular," I began, "but the bottom line for Christian
mysticism is that it is anchored in the wisdom teachings of Jesus. To be a
Christian means to be a follower of Jesus, therefore a Christian mystic is
one who embodies the presence of God through the wisdom of Jesus."

"Was Jesus a mystic?" the host rejoined.

In response, I recounted two brief stories, one about Jesus, and the other
about one of Jesus's followers, almost two thousand years apart. I told the
podcast host, "I think these stories will shed light not only on how Jesus was
a mystic, but also on how the mysticism of Jesus lives on in the spirituality

of the Christian mystics. Each of these stories involves what we could call a transfiguring moment."

So I'll recount those same stories here, to get this chapter rolling.

Jesus, who lived during what we would now call the first century of the Common Era, developed a reputation and a following as a rabbi, or spiritual teacher, and also as a healer and wonder worker. He experienced opposition from many of the established religious leaders in his community. After Jesus created a public disturbance in Jerusalem by disrupting merchants operating inside the temple—the center of Jewish worship—he was arrested, flogged, and killed by the painful method of crucifixion. The faith of Christianity insists that this was not the end of the story—for Jesus's disciples proclaimed that on the third day following his death he rose from the dead, and they and others were witness to his resurrected appearances.

But my story focused on a moment that took place some time prior to Jesus's death.

One day, Jesus took three of his closest friends—Peter, James, and his brother John—and led them up a high mountain to pray. As they were praying, Jesus became transfigured before them: the appearance of his face changed, so that it shone like the sun, and his clothes became dazzling white, whiter than anyone on earth could bleach them. That must have been remarkable enough, but then suddenly he was joined by the prophets Moses and Elijah, who appeared glorious in their own way. They spoke with Jesus about the events that would later take place when he went to Jerusalem.

Jesus's three companions witnessed this numinous, extraordinary turn of events. Feeling terrified by the glory, they did not know what to say. Finally Peter blurted out, "Teacher, how good it is for us to be here! Perhaps we should install three tabernacles here, one for you, one for Moses, and one for Elijah." But hardly had he gotten these words out when they were all overshadowed by a bright cloud, which elicited an even deeper sense of awe. The cloud engulfed them, and from within it boomed a voice, speaking, "This is my Son, the Beloved; my chosen, with him I am well pleased; listen to him!" At the sound of this voice the disciples fell to the ground, overcome by their fear. But Jesus approached them and touched them, saying, "Get up and do not be afraid." When they dared to look up again, they saw no one except Jesus himself alone.

As they walked together down the mountain, Jesus instructed them to tell no one about this vision until the events that would transpire in Jerusalem. They kept his instruction and remained silent, telling no one about the remarkable things they had seen until after the resurrection.

Stories like this strike people in many ways. For some, this is remarkable evidence of Jesus's divinity, the favor that Jesus received directly from God and the care he took to prepare his closest friends for the traumatic events that were soon to come. But for others, this story seems more like a myth or a legend—it is human nature to concoct larger-than-life stories about heroes or heroines people admire, so perhaps Jesus's transfiguration is just that: something that only happened in the imagination of his followers.

Whether you find the story of the transfiguration inspiring or incredible, I invite you to keep it in the back of your mind as we look at another story, this one involving a twentieth-century mystic named Thomas Merton, a Trappist monk who lived in rural Kentucky. Like most monks of his time, Merton devoted his life to a continual rhythm of prayer, meditation, and contemplation, balanced by the work he did to contribute to the welfare of the monastery. Monks in those days rarely left the monastery grounds unless there was an important reason; on this March day in 1958, Merton had to go to the nearest big city, Louisville, for a matter concerning monastery business. In the city, he was walking in the downtown area and came to a street corner, the corner of Fourth and Walnut,[1] when in his own words, "I was suddenly overwhelmed with the realization that I loved all those people, that they were mine and I theirs, that we could not be alien to one another even though we were total strangers."

Writing about this in his journal—and later in a book, *Conjectures of a Guilty Bystander*—Merton describes this falling-in-love like waking up from a dream. At this point, he had been living in the monastery for over sixteen years, devoting his life to following Christ and seeking union with God. But in this moment of falling in love, it was almost as if "the whole illusion of a separate holy existence is a dream." He realized that merely being human, he was already more intimately united to God than all the efforts of his religious monastic striving could ever have hoped to achieve.

He continued to muse on this insight, revealing just how powerful his street corner vision was: "As if the sorrows and stupidities of the human condition could overwhelm me, now I realize what we all are. And if only everybody could realize this! But it cannot be explained. There is no way of telling people that they are all walking around shining like the sun." After further reflection on that moment, he concludes with the insight, "The gate of heaven is everywhere."[2]

How fascinating that, over 1,900 years after the earthly life of Jesus, a random and entirely unexpected moment of insight on a bustling street in an American city would result in a mystical vision of people "shining like the sun"—and, as a consequence, with Merton experiencing a sense of falling in love with them all. It's as if whatever happened to Jesus on that mountaintop so many centuries ago happened again—at least in Merton's eyes—to all the ordinary people walking along the street.

Jesus proclaimed of himself, "I am the light of the world," but he also told his followers, "*You* are the light of the world."[3] Perhaps the transfiguration represents an embodiment of Jesus-as-light, while Merton's experience of everyone "shining like the sun" is an example of how all people are the "light of the world." The light that transfigured Jesus's face and even his clothes is the same light that Merton saw shining out of everyone—a light that could only elicit the response of love. This light is truly a "gate of heaven" and it is indeed everywhere, in everyone. And forms the heart of Christian mysticism.

This light belongs not only to Jesus, or to mere mortals like you and me. Another great mystic, the Spanish Carmelite nun Teresa of Ávila, tells of a vision of an angel who also seemed to embody "the light of the world." Teresa wrote, "I saw an angel in bodily form standing very close to me on my left side. . . . He was quite small and very beautiful. His face was so lit up by flame brilliantly lit that I thought he must belong to that highest order of angels who are made entirely of fire." Teresa goes on to describe her encounter with this radiant angel in ways that some find inspiring, others frightening, and others even erotic in its implications.

> He held a great golden spear. The end of the iron tip seemed to be on fire. Then the angel plunged the flaming spear through my heart again and again until it penetrated my innermost core. When he withdrew it, it felt like he was carrying the deepest part of me away with him. He left me utterly consumed with love of God. The pain was so intense that it made me moan. The sweetness this anguish carries with it is so

bountiful that I could never wish for it to cease. The soul will not be content with anything less than God.[4]

An angel of light with a spear of fire, penetrating the heart and soul of an enraptured woman, leaving her moaning with love for God. Teresa would subsequently become one of the most important religious figures of her generation, a reformer in her Carmelite order, and the author of several books that are now regarded as classics of mystical Christian spirituality.

In the Hebrew Scriptures is a book of Wisdom literature called Ecclesiastes. In it are these familiar words: "For everything there is a season, and a time for every matter under heaven. . . . A time to keep silence, and a time to speak."[5] Transfiguring moments, like the three we have examined here, always seem to have a quality of silence about them. Even when Peter prattles on about building tabernacles for Jesus and Moses and Elijah, he is speaking nervously, breaking a silence that would have been better off without his words. When we truly, really, in an embodied way encounter the light, the fire, the love of God, the moment leaves us silent (think of the mute button on your television remote: *mute* and *mysticism* both come from the same Greek word that carries a sense of closing the mouth).

But then comes the time to talk about what has happened. Even when Jesus cautioned Peter and his companions not to talk about the transfiguration, he basically said, "Don't speak about it *yet*." Jesus knew that the time would come for the story to be told. Likewise, the time came for Teresa of Ávila and Thomas Merton and so many others who have embodied these transfiguring moments to tell of their experience as well.

MYSTICISM IS A STORY

Mysticism is a story that begins in silence and only takes on the form of language and narrative after the fact. We say that mysticism involves experience: the experience of union with God, or of the presence of God, or something as extraordinary as Teresa's encounter with the angel or Merton's street corner lovefest. But experience is not the entire story, either. The problem with experience is that it can be driven by the human ego, a self-directed phenomenon that can too easily become self-absorbed. Mysticism affirms the mystery of God more than mere experience. Sometimes God chooses to encounter us deep beneath the horizon of our awareness. That's one of many reasons why we call this type of spirituality "mysticism"—it ushers us into mystery, deeper than what our minds or even our hearts can comprehend.

All human beings, not just religious believers, have experiences related to God. We experience God, and we experience God-as-absent. We imagine God, and we imagine emptiness where we think God could or should be. We might embody a sense of longing for God, or an intuition of God-as-mystery, or a nagging feeling that nothing anyone says about God is ever truly adequate. And with each passing generation, it seems that more and more people have begun to believe that God cannot exist, and therefore any experience of God is merely a figment of the imagination. But even figments of the imagination can be a source of meaningful, powerful, and even life-transforming experience.

Actually, the insistence that "God does not exist" is not necessarily something mystics would be bothered by. No human being can fully comprehend God; therefore anything we say about God must be incomplete, limited and limiting, and perhaps even betrays God. Any God that we can comprehend can never fully represent the one true God. Therefore, in a very real way, any "God" you can imagine must ultimately *not* exist—for God can only fully exist far beyond or deeper than our limited abilities to know or even wonder.

Perhaps one difference between a mystic and an atheist is that the atheist sees the emptiness of God as proving a negation, whereas the mystic, in open-minded and heartful seeking, avoids making any such proof statement, instead seeing the emptiness of God as simply an invitation into an ever-deepening mystery of pure being itself, including the mystery of silence and life and love.

Silence has always been associated with mystical spirituality and contemplative practices. Silence helps us to notice and name our experience of God, but also can paradoxically undermine and subvert any experience we might have. Silence gently helps us to see that any experience of God is limited and incomplete, no matter how eloquently it could be put into words (or kept in silence).

Whatever else one might say about mysticism, begin with this: we encounter mysticism (Christian or otherwise) through language and silence. Silence is reliable, yet also is mysterious; language is graspable yet also subject to interpretation and misinterpretation, so in an absolute sense, it cannot always be trusted. Mysticism is a story that continually deconstructs itself. If you are looking for certainty or absolute incontrovertible "truth," mysticism will continually frustrate you and disappoint you. This is because mysticism centers more on God's incomprehensibility than in our human lust for certitude; mysticism celebrates the truth on God's ultimately-beyond-us level rather than "truth" in a finite, limited, humanly understandable way.

Because we cannot neatly boil mysticism down to a set of principles or propositions or logical forms, it is easy to ignore. Human beings like to be in control, so it only stands to reason that we secretly desire a way of understanding God that is more "controllable." Some people try to control God by rigid, fundamentalist theology; others try to control God by refusing to believe in God. The story of mysticism offers an alternative to either of those closed-systems approaches. This story invites you to be immersed in its wisdom, and seek to apply that wisdom to your own life. If you do, just be prepared to be amazed and unsettled by paradoxical ambiguity and its various plot twists and surprises.

Any book about mysticism cannot be the same thing as an embodied encounter with the mystery of God. Why bother reading such a book? Because we need the time for speaking just as we need the time for silence. We embody the encounter, and then we tell the story—if not the stories of our own encounters, then the encounters of others, as I have just done, recounting the tales of Jesus and Merton and Teresa. We recount these stories to remember them, to learn from them, to be inspired and, in turn, to inspire others by them. We draw principles and meaningful ideas from the stories of the mystics, and we regard those as teachings and as wisdom.

Sometimes, such wisdom teachings can become codified as doctrines or dogma. Dogma has become a dirty word in our culture, because we think of dogma as restricting and restrictive top-down beliefs. But that perspective is responding to the shadow side of dogma, how dogma can be abused, or dogma that has become obsolete (like the idea that God created all things in only seven days).

Mysticism helps us to avoid the shadow side of dogma by calling us away from the abstractions of theoretical doctrines and back into the embodied reality of a direct relationship with God. But it's a good idea to remember that dogma, at its best, can remain a useful tool to help us to learn more about the mysteries of mysticism. Take, for example, "God is love"—a solid dogma of Christian belief, but no one reacts against it because it is so true and real and necessary, and it is the opposite of "obsolete."

But what about the extraordinary, legendary, perhaps mythical tales that get attached to mystics (for example, Teresa of Ávila was said to be able to levitate when lost in rapt ecstasy)? Many stories about the mystics may be hard to swallow, more the province of folklore and myth than of literal history. Visions, locutions, levitations, apparitions, stigmata, all sorts of weird and extraordinary phenomena. Should we approach these stories with a skeptical eye? Or should we be skeptical of skepticism itself, and dare to believe that infinite wonders truly are possible? For now, I'll say this: just as myths and legends and folklore (not to mention the best novels) often contain wisdom and truth that may or may not correlate with an objective "this actually happened" reality, so the most fascinating and amazing stories of Jesus, the saints, the angels, and the mystics often have a lot to teach us, regardless of whether the stories have a historical basis in reality. Maybe the apostles just imagined the transfiguration, and maybe Teresa of Ávila just imagined the angel and Merton just imagined that people were shining like the sun. And maybe something extraordinary really did happen, who knows? Either way, these imaginal moments still transfigured the people involved, even if only in "interior" ways. And sometimes an interior change can have world-transforming exterior consequences. So as you explore the world of Christian mysticism, try not to be too attached to interpreting the stories of the mystics in any one particular way. Look for the spiritual meaning, no matter how believable you think a story is (or isn't).

I invite you to discover the stories of the mystics, as well as the ways the mystics have interpreted and made sense of their stories. Some of them will show up in the pages to come, although this book is not so much a book of history or theology as it is a book of spirituality. History tells us the story of the past. Theology helps us to make sense of teachings related to God (therefore, "mystical theology" involves the teachings related to the encounter of God-as-mystery). This book of *spirituality* invites us beyond the abstract limitation of stories and teachings and back into the embodied encounter with the hidden and mysterious presence of God.

Some mystics would argue that it's a mistake to divide theology and spirituality. Indeed, St. Teresa of Ávila referred to mysticism not as spirituality but as "mystical theology."[6] To truly enter into mystical wisdom, we need to balance an appreciation for spirituality with an understanding of both theology and history. We need it all: we need the stories; we need the ways we interpret the stories and the ways our communities interpret these stories. And we need to discover for ourselves the silence that inspired the stories of the past, and that can continue to inspire meaningful new stories today.

HIDDEN IN PLAIN SIGHT

If you stood on a street corner and asked twenty passersby to define mysticism, many people would laugh and say they have no idea what it means, and the ones who were willing to try to define it would all have something different to say about it. One person might guess that it's a synonym for Eastern spiritualities like Zen Buddhism or Advaita Vedanta; another would see it as a code word for New Age, Neopagan, or Wiccan spirituality. An atheist might dismiss it altogether as the kind of fuzzy thinking that makes religion a problem; and more than one Christian might tell you it's something that monks and nuns and saints do, but most would say it's far removed from the life of "ordinary" people.

Eventually it becomes obvious that mysticism is a vague word that can be used in a variety of ways to mean different things. This is not just because human beings can be sloppy and like to use words in imprecise ways—although that's probably part of the problem. But at its heart, mysticism as a word or concept is impossible to define because it is linked to *mystery*, to spirituality and inner experience—all notoriously squishy subjects. To unlock the mystery of Christian mysticism, we need to explore both the *story* of mysticism—by savoring the wisdom of the great mystics from more than two thousand years of Christian history and the scholars who have written about them—and also the *practical ways* in which mysticism can enlighten our spiritual lives today.

The story of mystical Christianity includes a wide array of colorful and sometimes eccentric characters who have much to teach us, not just about Christianity and mysticism, but about life in general. You've already met Howard Thurman, Thomas Merton, Julian of Norwich, and Teresa of Ávila; more will show up in the pages to come. When we take the time to understand their lives in a way that honors their wisdom, we begin to find ways to apply that wisdom to our own lives. Mysticism (Christian or otherwise) is far more than just an interesting philosophical concept—it is a powerful process for transforming our minds, hearts, and souls.

The Christian mystics tell us that their wisdom can help us to embody union with God—or at the very least, give us such a powerful sense of God's presence that it can revolutionize our lives. The purpose of such transfigured lives is not so much to achieve some spiritual goal (like getting enlightened or finding ecstatic bliss), but rather to participate in the dynamic ongoing activity of the Holy Spirit —to embody the flowing love of Christ, love that we in turn give back to God as well as to "our neighbors as ourselves."

The mystical tradition exists throughout Christian history, beginning in the stories of Jesus and his first students and friends, and still going strong today. Mysticism is not the only "flavor" of Christian spirituality, and there are tensions between mysticism and some forms of Christianity. You can be a Christian without being a mystic, and you can be a mystic without being a Christian. To embrace mystical Christianity implies being immersed in the distinctive spiritual lineage that began with the radical teachings of Jesus of Nazareth, and developed over the centuries to become a sublime expression of the human capacity to receive, give, and be transformed by divine love.

MORE THAN PHILOSOPHY, MORE THAN EXPERIENCE

It's easy to get sidetracked when exploring Christian mysticism. One detour I touched on earlier is to become so immersed in the scholarly study of mystical history and theology that the spirituality of mysticism—the embodied practice of interior transformation—gets lost in the process. Another detour involves becoming so entranced with the idea that mysticism means experiencing God that ultimately the *experience* starts to matter more than *God*.

To place too much emphasis on having mystical experiences or cosmic consciousness or secret visions, we run the risk of forgetting that Christian spirituality is grounded in the love of God—a love that leads to healing, transformation, and growth of the whole person (and the entire human family).

In other words, Christian mysticism is never an end to itself. The point behind mysticism is not to dazzle ourselves with ecstatic wonders, but to foster real and lasting changes, for the purpose of becoming more like Christ, which is to say, more compassionate, more forgiving, more committed to serving others and making the world a better place. Ultimately, experience is really just a small part of the overall package of what Christian mysticism is truly about.

Likewise, students of Christian mysticism can lose their way if they get too caught up in quests for secret knowledge, or hidden teachings that are supposedly the key to higher realities, that somehow have been lost (or suppressed) by church authorities. I'm willing to go with the idea that many of the key principles of Christian mysticism have been marginalized, ignored, or even rejected by many followers of Jesus, but when conspiracy gains traction, it often diverts attention from something deeper: the keys to Christian mysticism have for millennia been hidden in plain sight. The "mystery" of Christian mysticism is not about secret knowledge that has been locked away in a vault somewhere, but rather about the freely available wisdom that nevertheless stretches our minds and hearts beyond what can easily be put into words.

It's beguiling to speculate that some sort of secret knowledge has been squirreled away in the Vatican or in a monastery somewhere on the Sinai Peninsula for the past 1,500 years. But in reality, the mystical tradition in Christianity is much broader and deeper than that. The mystics were (and are) people who receive powerful encounters with the presence of God, who embody the joy and insight of nondual union with God, who undergo amazing and beautiful transformations of consciousness, and live by the teachings of Jesus—without getting lost in an arcane or esoteric fantasy world.

Another unhelpful idea that can detour us away from the wisdom of the Christian mystics is a fanciful notion that the only "real" mysticism comes from the East, from venerable wisdom traditions such as Vedanta or Zen. Therefore, Christian mysticism is merely Hinduism or Buddhism with a little bit of Jesus mixed in. Ironically, this idea is most often voiced by Christians who are both ignorant of their own history and fearful of other religions. Yet mystical Christianity has its own history, lineage, wisdom and spiritual practices, all of which emerged within the Jesus tradition, with roots in Jewish tradition and the Hebrew Bible. Like many Christians,

I admire mystical and contemplative traditions in all of the world's faiths, from the Eastern spiritualities mentioned above, to Sufism and Kabbalah, African religions and shamanism, and many others. And like many Christians, I understand the value of an *interspiritual* approach to mysticism, and know such an approach is meaningful for many people, of all religious identities. And it's been my experience that mystical or contemplative Christians tend toward an openness to the wisdom of other religions; however, this openness remains—at least for Christians—rooted in the central wisdom teachings of Jesus, the Bible, and the Christian mystics. Contemplative Christians explore the wisdom of other faiths not to dilute or weaken the wisdom teachings of Jesus, but to strengthen and deepen our appreciation of those teachings.

Since this is a book about *Christian* mysticism, allow me to set aside the question of interfaith or interspiritual mysticism for now (we'll come back to this topic in chapter 9). First, we'll focus on Christian mysticism and its beginnings and how Christianity has fostered its own longstanding homegrown mystical tradition with its own distinct practices, wisdom, and values.

From its origins in the words of Jesus, Christian mysticism is rooted in a beautiful and coherent body of wisdom teachings. Great saints, monks, nuns, theologians, philosophers, and artists throughout the centuries have made contributions to the faith that include their experience as mystics. Francis of Assisi, Hildegard of Bingen, Bernard of Clairvaux, Evelyn Underhill, John of the Cross, Caryll Houselander, Howard Thurman, Edith Stein, Meister Eckhart, Desmond Tutu, and Catherine of Genoa are just a few of the many Christian spiritual geniuses, down through the centuries, who lived by and taught the wisdom of encountering and embodying the mysterious, life-giving, love-infusing presence of God. Many of these names may be unfamiliar to you. Among other reasons, this is because mystics have a tendency not to draw attention to themselves or their experiences. Again, Christian mysticism is, in a very real way, hidden in plain sight, a simple, humble, down-to-earth spirituality that has slipped unpretentiously across the stage of history. The problem is not that mystical teachings are secret, but rather that so few people bother to learn the principles of Christian mysticism, much less apply them to their own lives for healing themselves and the world.

Some writers and scholars, who might humbly deny identifying them-selves as mystics, nevertheless have contributed much to our understanding of mystical theology, philosophy, and spirituality. In our time, scholars like Bernard McGinn, Louise Nelstrop, Barbara Holmes, Mark McIntosh, Grace Jantzen, Andrew Louth, Joy Bostic, Michael Battle, Amy Hollywood, Denys Turner, Michael Casey, and many others have contributed immensely to our common knowledge about Christian mysticism and contemplative spiritu-ality. Anyone who wants to become immersed in the mystical way would benefit from the scholarly writings of these authors. However, this brings us back to the problem of getting so caught up in the *study* of mysticism that we never get to the *practice* of contemplative Christianity. As much as scholarship can benefit us, it does not always make mysticism come alive in an intimate, practical way, which is work that takes us beyond the pages and deep within. An important question to ask for our own practice is how and why the wisdom of the mystics, ancient or modern, can be relevant today. How can we take the authentic mysticism of Christian history and tradition, and apply it to our own spiritual lives, here and now?

THE SEARCH FOR AUTHENTIC SPIRITUALITY

Jesus of Nazareth taught his followers radical new ways of loving one another and forming a beloved community. In the centuries following his life and teachings, others have carried the message forward, amplifying it, com-menting on it, applying it to new circumstances, and exploring the mysteries deep within that message. Every generation receives the message of Jesus in new ways, applying to their own unique hunger for divine love and the presence of God.

My inspiration to write this book came from my own desire for God, and I suspect most of you who will read this book have your own sense of deep divine longing. We live in a culture that, more than any other time in history, has access to countless ideas, teachings, and traditions designed to help us make sense of our hunger for God and our yearning for healing, purpose, and mission. The Christian mystics point us to Jesus—and to the powerful message proclaimed by Jesus and his follow-ers. Christian mysticism, therefore, invites us to begin our journey into the heart of God by engaging with the revolutionary and transfiguring teachings of Jesus.

Topics like repentance, holiness, sacrifice, and prayer all prove necessary for understanding the way of the Christian mystics. And for Christians and non-Christians alike, these can be difficult and fraught, made more complicated by the fact that different Christian traditions interpret these core concepts in different ways or have weaponized such concepts to cause harm, especially to people on the margins. Depending on your own background, these concepts may seem confusing because they are entirely new to you, or might make you uncomfortable because of how religious Christians have sometimes used these ideas. As we explore mystical Christianity, I encourage you to keep an open mind, and a willingness to view every aspect of this tradition through a contemplative lens. If you do so, you are more likely to find the splendor of mystical Christianity's deep affirmation of divine love.

One of the liberating gifts of Christian mysticism is the way it can take the truths of the gospel stories and transform them into exciting, spiritually luminous principles by which we can ignite our lives into a profound experience of God's love and healing presence. Even if you are devout and feel like you already know and accept the core teachings of Christian faith, I likewise ask you to approach mysticism with an open mind. Mystical spirituality does not change the wisdom teachings of Jesus. But it does shine an entirely new light on those teachings in ways that help us see what has always been there in powerful and exciting new ways.

Authentic Christian mysticism reflects and reinforces authentic Christianity. Conflict between mysticism and religion arises only when something has gone awry with one or the other. When Christianity is true to itself as a liberating faith in the radical teachings of Jesus, and Christian mysticism is true to itself as the Christ-centered encounter with the awesome mystery of God, they flow together beautifully and harmoniously. Thus, while it is helpful to draw a distinction between Christianity the religion and Christian mysticism, it's important not to divide what is meant to be unitive or overstate the difference, as if "Christian mysticism" were an entirely new or different religion.

The mystics have consistently emphasized that in order to enjoy union with God, one must engage with the social and communal dimensions of the Christian faith. For them, this engagement can take many forms: from hermits in wilderness solitude, to monks and nuns cloistered away from the world, to activists working hard to alleviate the suffering in our world. There is no one way to be a mystic, and no one way to be Christian, but to be a Christian mystic means bringing both of those spiritual dimensions together, in creative, life-affirming, and love-infused ways.

Mysticism fosters a transformational alchemy that integrates Christianity's promise of new life in Jesus with mysticism's promise of embodying the unitive presence of God. This allows something to emerge that is greater than the sum of its parts; it illuminates a path by which you can open yourself to what the apostle Paul calls letting "the same mind [consciousness] of Christ be in you" and what the apostle Peter calls being "participants of the divine nature."[7] Christian mysticism invites you to do more than just know *about* God, or Jesus, or spiritual transformation. It invites you *into* God, *into* Christ, *into* the Holy Spirit—and into the embodied transformation that comes about through the love and grace of God. It's intimate; it's heartful and mindful; it's oriented toward making a real, powerful, profound, and lasting difference in your life, your relationships, the world you inhabit.

CHAPTER TWO

The Mute Mystery: Making Sense of Mysticism

For my thoughts are not your thoughts,
nor are your ways my ways, says the Lord.
—Isaiah 55:8

What, then, is time? I know well enough what it is,
provided that nobody asks me; but if I am asked what it is
and try to explain, I am baffled.
—Augustine of Hippo

Mysticism, whether Christian or otherwise, can never adequately be put into words. Although there are many different dimensions to mysticism and many different ways to tell the story of the mystical life, this stubborn fact—this inability to describe it adequately with words, in other words, the *ineffability* of mysticism—holds true in all the stories and all the dimensions. So, with a spirit of gentle humility, we must begin our discussion of mysticism with an honest recognition that it can never be fully described or precisely defined.

LOVE IN A BOTTLE

Trying to define mysticism is like trying to put love in a bottle. It just can't be done.

To begin with, love is not something that can be pinned down to a specific point in space and time. Love is a spiritual reality that can never be defined, enclosed, or captured.

Mysticism, the spirituality of the embodiment of divine love, likewise cannot be quantified or classified. Its essence simply cannot be contained in human language—indeed, not even by the most sublime reaches of human thought. We can use language to evoke mysticism—to allude to it, to point to it, to create poetic metaphors or analogies about it that ring true—but these linguistic interpretations are ultimately like attempts to empty the ocean with a teaspoon. Like *God* or *spirituality* or *heaven*, mysticism takes us beyond what the most eloquent and poetic language can ever express. It pushes you to the limits of your imagination and then says, "Take another step." And another, and another.

Mysticism invites us beyond the normal boundaries of human thought, logic, rationality, and knowing. It takes us beyond the limits of philosophy, theology, psychology, and science. This may sound like a flight of fancy, a kind of spiritual make-believe; but mysticism points to something that countless witnesses, in cultures all across the world and in every age from the dawn of recorded history, insist is utterly real—maybe even more real than the universe and consciousness we inhabit without a second thought.

It doesn't take an expert in etymology to figure out that the word *mysticism* is related to the word *mystery*. Perhaps we can use our earthly language to catch tiny glimpses of that heaven-sent something—that mystery—that the great visionaries and saints describe as an embodied relationship with God. Maybe your heart will register a thrill of recognition as you read their writings, giving you some sense of what mysticism is. But, like love in a bottle, as soon as you try to put it into your own words, mysticism unfolds itself into a variety of paradoxes and seemingly contradictory truths that leave you as confused and befuddled as ever.

"Mysticism is the awakening of the soul to the reality of the presence of God," according to the Russian spiritual writer Valentin Tomberg.[1] In other words, mysticism—at least, Christian mysticism—means having a relationship with the God who is present. Indeed, this is its bedrock principle. But when it comes to some non-Christian forms of mysticism like Zen Buddhism or Taoism, God is not part of the equation at all. In these traditions, it is possible to be a mystic and an atheist—or at least, an agnostic. Then again, even some of the most profound Christian mystics talk about how unknowable God is. How can you have a relationship with something or someone who is fundamentally unknowable? And yet, that is where mysticism takes you.

When we talk about mysticism, we can use words that try to make sense of the mystery—"God," or "the Absolute," or "the Ultimate Mystery"—until the words themselves fail us. Then we are left with only silence, facing the mystery again, and perhaps scrambling to find new words, new concepts, and new ideas.

Even within a single religious framework like Christianity, mysticism has an unnerving tendency to contradict itself and deconstruct itself in bewildering and playful ways. As a dynamic spiritual force that has been at work in the lives of contemplatives throughout Christian history—and that continues to show up in surprising and unexpected ways among the faithful even today—mysticism remains perplexing and uncontrollable. God cannot be controlled; neither, apparently, can the spirituality of embodying God's presence.

The mystics themselves have long recognized the ultimate "unknowability" of this indefinable thing we call mysticism. But if we are tempted to just give up on trying to make sense of mysticism, we run the risk of abandoning an opportunity to get to know God better—and to get to know ourselves in relationship with God. So while it might be a fool's errand to try to explain mysticism, I'm going to give it a whirl. I will most certainly fail at this, but as a follower of Jesus, I know that grace is always present, even in the midst of our failures. I write about mysticism, not because I have it all figured out (I don't), or because I think my book will help you figure it all out (it won't), but because I hope my attempt to explore this inexplicable topic may contain some small glimmers of insight or encouragement that you can use on your own journey into the heart of the mystery that Christians call God.

EXPLORING THE UNKNOWABLE

If someone wonders, "What is mysticism?," how can it be defined briefly? Here are a few possibilities:

- *Mysticism is the art of union with God.*
- *Mysticism is the encounter with the presence of God.*
- *Mysticism is the experience of ultimate truth or reality, whereas religion is an organized and communal assembly of rituals, beliefs, and codes of conduct that are derived from that encounter with the ultimate.*
- *Mysticism is the heart of spirituality where all religious differences are resolved and we find unity in the Sacred.*

Each of these statements is useful, as far as it goes. In writing these brief definitions, I have tried to include room for both Christian and non-Christian mysticism, and both theistic (God-centered) mysticism and nontheistic mysticism.

The problem with these concise definitions is that they leave all the major problems, paradoxes, and seeming contradictions of mysticism unexplained. How can mysticism be about God when even Christians don't all agree on who or what God is or how knowable God is? Can we really say that mysticism is about "experience," when there are some mystics (like Jean-Pierre de Caussade) who insist that our feelings are unreliable when it comes to spiritual growth? And what's all this about resolving religious differences? Is that really what mysticism is about, or is that just wishful thinking on the part of those who try to gloss over real and intractable differences between religions? So each of these attempts at understanding mysticism ultimately seems to create as many questions as answers.

Let's expand this conversation with a few more definitions worth considering. The first comes from a contemporary English dictionary; the others from writers and thinkers who have wrestled with this mystery.

- *Mysticism: "Immediate consciousness of the transcendent or ultimate reality or God."*—American Heritage Dictionary
- *"In Greek religion, from which the word [mysticism] comes to us, the* mystæ *were those initiates of the "mysteries," who were believed to have received the vision of the god, and with it a new and higher life. When the Christian Church adopted this term it adopted, too, its original meaning. The Christian mystic therefore is one for whom*

God and Christ are not merely objects of belief, but living facts experimentally known first hand; and mysticism for him becomes, in so far as he responds to its demands, a life based on this conscious communion with God."—Evelyn Underhill[2]

- "For our purposes then, mysticism is defined as the response of the individual to a personal encounter with God within his own spirit."—Howard Thurman[3]

- "Christian mysticism is a way of life that involves the perfect fulfillment of loving God, neighbor, all God's creation, and oneself. .... It is an ordered movement toward ever higher levels of reality by which the self awakens to, is purified and illuminated by, and is eventually fully united with, the God of love."—Harvey Egan, SJ[4]

- "The first question students almost invariably ask is: 'So what is mysticism?' When the only answer they receive is 'Wait and see. You need to make up your own mind!' they think we are being deliberately obtuse."—Louise Nelstrop[5]

- "If we take spirituality as a broad term signifying the whole range of beliefs and practices by which the Christian church strives to live out its commitment to the Spirit present in the Risen Christ, then we can understand mysticism as the inner and hidden realization of spirituality through a transforming consciousness of God's immediate presence."—Bernard McGinn[6]

With the exception of the dictionary entry, all of the above definitions come from within a Christian context and referring to Christian mysticism. Now to make things more interesting, here are a few ideas about mysticism that come from non-Christian sources, or sources that are not exclusively Christian:

- "Mysticism is concerned with the possibility of personally encountering a spiritual reality which is hidden from our normal awareness like the sun behind the clouds. It is not concerned with propounding a philosophy that may be believed or doubted. The mystics tell us that higher consciousness is available to everyone, and by setting out on our own journey of spiritual exploration we can experience it for ourselves."—Timothy Freke and Peter Gandy[7]

- *"Mysticism is that point of view which claims as its basis an intimate knowledge of the one source and substratum of all existence, a knowledge which is obtained through a revelatory experience during a rare moment of clarity in contemplation. Those who claim to have actually experienced this direct revelation constitute an elite tradition which transcends the boundary lines of individual religions, cultures and languages, and which has existed, uninterrupted, since the beginning of time."—Swami Abhayananda*[8]
- *"Mysticism is a manifestation of something which is at the root of all religion and all the higher religions have their mystical expressions."—F. C. Happold*[9]
- *"Mystical experience is the direct, unmediated experience of what Bede Griffiths beautifully describes as the presence of an almost unfathomable mystery.' . . . This mystery is beyond name and beyond form; no name or form, no dogma, philosophy, or set of rituals can ever express it fully. It always transcends anything that can be said of it and remains always unstained by any of our human attempts to limit or exploit it." —Andrew Harvey*[10]

If you find yourself shaking your head as you attempt to fit together all these differing and frankly contradictory ways of describing mysticism, I assure you: you are not alone. When I first sat down to write this chapter, my goal was to come up with a soundbite-worthy definition of mysticism, that could easily be shared on your favorite social media platform. But after writing and rewriting and revising, my goal became much more modest: instead of pinning mysticism down, now I merely hope to evoke the complexity and diversity of this mysterious dimension of spirituality.

ORIENTING GENERALIZATIONS

While it may be tempting to look at these divergent approaches to mysticism and decide that it is an impossible topic to comprehend, we can try to build bridges between these various perspectives. Philosopher Ken Wilber writes about the connections between religion and science, between Eastern and Western spirituality, and about other broad areas of human knowledge.

In his book *A Brief History of Everything*, Wilber argues that the best way to approach large and complex topics is to begin by looking for patterns of similarity between the different elements of the material being investigated. We can apply this same principle to the complex and ineffable topic of mysticism.

Wilber uses the term *orienting generalization* to describe a broad, basic way of speaking about a difficult topic or complex issue. Even when experts can't find complete agreement on a particular definition, he notes, their perspectives may have enough commonality that orienting generalizations can be drawn from their differing viewpoints.

So what are the orienting generalizations of mysticism? We can make at least these initial observations based on the material we've looked at thus far:

- *Mysticism concerns a higher reality.* Different religions and philosophies call this by different names; the traditional Christian name for this reality is "God."
- *Mysticism involves an embodied encounter with, or conscious awareness of, this higher reality.* Precisely because this reality is "higher," however, there is that unavoidable and inexhaustible element of mystery surrounding it as well. In other words, mysticism seems to be grounded in experience, but simultaneously is something other than mere experience. It involves consciousness, but also transcends it.
- *Mysticism is often connected with religion.* By religion I mean the various social and cultural ways in which people relate to each other's common desire for contact with the Higher Mystery. This connection between mysticism and religion, however, includes real differences and tensions. Certainly it is possible to be religious without exploring mysticism; and some expressions of mysticism may not require a religious setting. And since community is such an important element within Christianity, Christian mysticism is more overtly religious (communal) than other forms of mysticism. In fact, while mysticism in general is often connected with religion, one could say that genuine Christian mysticism must always have some sort of communal dimension to it. Even the

hermits of the desert practiced hospitality, welcoming guests to their wilderness abodes.

- *Since religion concerns values, beliefs, ethics, teachings, and rituals, these things all have an impact on mysticism, at least in its religious forms.* Christian mysticism therefore can incorporate the more explicitly "religious" elements of Christianity, such as worship, the sacraments, and the ethical teachings of Jesus. It's important to remember that no religion is monolithic, and neither is mysticism. Just as religion includes many different ideas and values about God (some clearly paradoxical, if not apparently contradictory), so too mysticism entails a rather dizzying array of ideas, beliefs, and values, among which many paradoxes and tensions can be found.
- *Mysticism is more than just a spirituality of personal experience and consciousness—it is a way of life.* People who pursue the mystical life often do some pretty unusual things, including trying to live in a holy or sanctified manner, or (at the very least) embracing a regular practice of prayer, meditation, or contemplation. Such spiritual exercises are believed to foster or support the desired experience of intimacy with, union with, or even simply the felt presence of God.

In his book *Integral Spirituality,* Wilber suggests that the word *spirituality* can be understood in four distinct ways. He notes that many people regard spirituality as a rather vague, if not meaningless, concept and suggests this is because the word has a variety of meanings. It's not a question of which meaning is the "right" one—as they are all correct, depending on the context in which the word is used. Only when we start taking these distinctions seriously do we begin to recognize the beauty and value of spirituality. Moreover, it becomes easier to communicate about it in meaningful and effective ways.

Wilber gives four orienting generalizations about spirituality that can be applied to mysticism as well. Although spirituality and mysticism are not synonymous—all mysticism is spiritual, but not all spirituality is mystical— these generalizations can aid our understanding of mysticism.

1. Mysticism can refer to a particular type of experience—a "peak" experience of God/the Ultimate Mystery, which can also be called a "peek" experience in that it provides a glimpse of previously unimagined possibilities. The Bible has numerous examples of such experiences, which in traditional religious language are called "epiphanies." Among the most dramatic are the transfiguration of Christ, which we considered in chapter 1, and also the conversion of Saint Paul, which followed an encounter with the risen Christ on the road to Damascus.[11] Many, if not all, of the great Christian mystics experienced epiphanies of their own.

2. Mysticism also refers to a particular level of consciousness. This altered or heightened state—which has been known by many names, including enlightenment, holiness, sanctification, nondual awareness, and the unitive life—is not an isolated event, but rather represents a fundamental shift in awareness to a higher/holier state. As Saint Paul put it, "Let the same mind be in you that was in Christ Jesus."[12] Unlike an epiphany, which is transitory in nature, mysticism as heightened consciousness suggests a more or less permanent or longer-lasting change in awareness or knowledge of the ultimate mystery (God). While a mystical experience may involve having a glimpse of God's presence, mystical consciousness may mean an ongoing sense of divine union—of being one with God.

3. Mysticism may also refer to a particular type of ability—what Wilber calls a "developmental line." Just as some people are naturally gifted at music or sports or mechanics, so mysticism is a particular aptitude for which a person may exhibit a greater or lesser degree of innate skill. This suggests that a "mystically gifted" person has an innate ability, not only to experience the presence of the Ultimate Mystery, but also to manifest extraordinary spiritual abilities—to heal, to prophesy, to teach or influence others through a deep spiritual charisma, to live a holy or sanctified life. Of course, such mystical ability, like all other aptitudes, exists on a continuum. Just as you can enjoy music or literature or sports even if you are not a John Coltrane or a Virginia Woolf or a Michael

Jordan, you don't have to be a mystical genius to have some capacity for the mystical.

4. Mysticism refers to a particular attitude that has more to do with values than with experience, consciousness, or ability. In this sense, being a mystical person may mean nothing more than being serious about your belief that God is real and at work in your life, or having a clear conviction of the world as operating in harmony with God's plan, or consistently being more forgiving than judgmental about others' failings. Whereas the previous generalizations all seem to indicate that mysticism is something largely outside of your control (either you're born with a mystical ability or you aren't), a mystical attitude rests more on the choices and intentions you make. If you immerse yourself in mystical wisdom, if you are deeply engaged in the life of faith, if you choose to pray and meditate on a daily basis, you are cultivating a mystical heart even though you may have never enjoyed an extraordinary experience, or heightened consciousness, or any kind of supernatural ability. This may not be as dramatic a view of mysticism, but it has the virtue of being within the reach of the average person. Many Christian mystics, in fact, understood the spiritual life, not as something awesome and extraordinary, but as something humble, down-to-earth, and in many ways very simple and small.

In addition to Wilber's four orienting generalizations, I propose a fifth:

5. Mysticism refers to the inner dimension of religion. The world's great contemplative and mystical wisdom traditions typically emerge from within a larger and more "ordinary" religious or philosophical culture. Christian mysticism emerges within Christianity; Vedanta within Hinduism; Kabbalah within Judaism; Zen within Buddhism; Sufism within Islam. This generalization, however, may be more useful for Western than for Eastern religions. In the East, the line separating mysticism from religion seems fuzzier—although, even in the East, a distinction is drawn between the perfunctory performance

of religious rituals and a more heartfelt inner experience. In other words, you can burn incense to the Buddha every day for years and not necessarily experience awakening or enlightenment, just as a Catholic may go to Mass day after day and not necessarily have a mystical experience or enter into mystical consciousness. Even so, these religious practices might help you be far more open to mystical experience than if you never bother with religious exercises at all.

To make sense of these differing definitions of mysticism, I encourage you to simply accept the fact that there are paradoxes and tensions contained within them. I once asked an elderly Trappist monk how he defined mysticism. "A mystic is someone who exhibits extraordinary phenomena," he said. "They have visions, they hear locutions, they levitate, or something along those lines." Thus, he understood mysticism almost exclusively in terms of ability. Not surprisingly, he rejected the idea that mysticism can mean nothing more than a spiritual attitude or a religious sensibility. "Everyone is not called to be a mystic," he argued. "Everyone is called to holiness." For him, mysticism is therefore reserved for truly supernatural experiences or phenomena, although ordinary people still have the opportunity to cultivate a sense of connection to God in their lives.

Wilber's orienting generalizations and these five different approaches to mysticism can help us to appreciate mysticism as a broad and inclusive "container" for spirituality that can manifest in a variety of ways. Rather than worry about which one is right (or "the most" right), I encourage you to reflect on which of these ways of understanding mysticism make the most sense to you. That might give you a clue to *your* unique way of responding to God's love in your life.

THE PARTICLE AND THE WAVE

One of the most famous mysteries to perplex scientists was whether light, at its most foundational level, is composed of particles or of waves. The answer, it appears, is, "It depends." In fact, the properties of light may actually be influenced by those who observe it. Likewise, mysticism.

Is mysticism about specific experiences of God, or rather a more lasting consciousness of God? Is it an irresistible gift from God, or must an aspiring mystic make a choice in response to God's grace and out of desire for God's love? Are all these ways of understanding mysticism the same thing, or are they really as different as a wave and a particle? Or perhaps all of these different ways of understanding mysticism simply reveal the imprecision of language. Perhaps what some people call "mysticism" really could go by a different name—like ecstasy, contemplation, esotericism, or holiness.

Does mysticism involve something that happens as a specific event, at a specific moment and location in space and time, like Saint Paul's conversion on the road to Damascus? Or is it an ongoing state of mind, a way of seeing and thinking that may not involve particular extraordinary experiences, but rather points to a blessed and holy way of life? We are all more likely to encounter the mystery at the heart of mysticism if we remain open to all its paradoxes and possibilities.

TWELVE METAPHORS AND SEVEN INSIGHTS

Many seekers find that metaphors are especially helpful for understanding and appreciating the mystical life— sometimes metaphors can convey more insight than a more prosaic attempt at defining mysticism. The beauty of a metaphor is that it invites us to use our imagination to understand one thing by relating it to something else. It's not a literal or concrete relationship—metaphor is more the province of poetry than engineering. But hopefully these imaginative and symbolic images and ideas can deepen your appreciation of how mystical spirituality takes shape in peoples' lives. I'll keep my commentary on each of these metaphors brief, and invite you to reflect on the ones that particularly jump out at you.

- *Mysticism is a journey.* Imagine Moses leading the people to the promised land, or Paul traveling through Europe to share the message of Jesus. A journey involves movement through time and space, and often changes the traveler forever.
- *Mysticism is a love affair.* "We love because [God] first loved us," promises the apostle John.[13] There is mutuality, desire, and

affection available to those who seek intimacy with the divine mystery.

- *Mysticism is a school.* Monks have described the monastery as a "school for God's service," or a "school for charity." Mysticism is also a school: a school for the divine mystery we are called to dwell within. The curriculum lasts a lifetime, and "graduates" often devote themselves to helping others.

- *Mysticism is a metamorphosis.* One of my favorite children's books (for kids of all ages) is Trina Paulus's *Hope for the Flowers.* Like a caterpillar becoming a butterfly, mystics are invited to our own deep inner transformation.

- *Mysticism is a death and rebirth.* Like the caterpillar in its cocoon—or like Jesus following the crucifixion—we all must face the mystery of death someday. Mystics die to themselves so that they might rise to new life, which Christianity proclaims comes to us through Christ.

- *Mysticism is a desert.* Moses, Elijah, Jesus, Paul, the desert mothers and fathers . . . again and again, our spiritual tradition speaks of those who encountered God in wilderness places. If you don't live near a desert, you might still find a "deserted" place in your heart, where God awaits.

- *Mysticism is a mountain.* From Dante to John of the Cross to Evelyn Underhill, many mystics have compared the spiritual life to climbing a mountain. It's hard work and takes time, but the view is magnificent.

- *Mysticism is a castle.* This metaphor comes from Teresa of Ávila, who compared the human soul to what she called the "interior castle." God, of course, reigns at the heart of the manor, and we are called to dwell in the light of God's love.

- *Mysticism is a marriage.* An extension of the "love affair" metaphor, this metaphor reminds us that it's about more than just excitement and passion: it's love for the long haul anchored in fidelity, commitment, and an affection that slowly deepens over the years.

- *Mysticism is a cloud.* This also comes from a particular mystical classic, a book on contemplative prayer called *The Cloud of Unknowing.* In the cloud, the human mind is surrounded by the mists, but the heart takes the lead, for it can direct us through the cloud to the God who is Love.

- *Mysticism is a dark night.* This metaphor comes from John of the Cross, who wrote a sublime poem about encountering the love of God in a dark night. Like in the cloud of unknowing, within the dark night the heart leads the way.
- *Mysticism is an alchemical transformation.* This one is explored by Evelyn Underhill in her classic book *Mysticism: The Nature and Development of Spiritual Consciousness.* God will transform us just like the philosopher's stone can transmute base metals into gold.

If these metaphors don't fully resonate as a way to understand mysticism, here are seven other quick insights into how we can make sense of Christian mysticism: think of these as doorways leading to the mystical life:

- *Mysticism is embracing the mystery of God.* God is not a mystery to be solved (in an Agatha Christie sense), but rather a living invitation into a place beyond the limits of human reason. Mysticism says yes to that invitation.
- *Mysticism is the flowering of spirituality.* We think of a blossom as the most beautiful part of a plant. Mysticism, with its emphasis on divine love and the embodiment of union with God, is the flower that adorns Christianity (or any faith tradition).
- *Mysticism is intimacy in prayer.* How do we interact with the God who is present in our hearts, who seeks transforming union with us? Prayer is the means of communication: not prayer in a transactional, help-me-pass-this-test sort of way, but rather prayer as an ever-deepening process of fostering intimacy with God.
- *Mysticism is the exaltation of consciousness.* Jesus's first teaching was a call for *metanoia*—a Greek word that suggests both taking one's life into a new direction and a sense of interior transformation—of taking your consciousness to a new level. Ultimately this points to the highest possible dimension of

consciousness: conscious union with God. Mysticism shows the way.

- *Mysticism is the embodiment of loving union.* That "higher consciousness" is more than just a head trip. At its fullest, it must be a "heart trip"—an immersion of the entire self, body, mind, and spirit, into the bracing, healing, exalting presence of love divine. To be a mystic is to become one with love.

- *Mysticism is the realization of God's nonduality.* We live in a world of dualities: good and evil, right and wrong, justice and oppression . . . but the love of God invites us to a place beyond our mortal tendency to react to the world with love and hate, trust and fear, anger and judgment. Jesus's message is clear: love everyone (even your enemies). The wisdom of the mystics helps us to enter into that nondual love.

- *Mysticism is the compassionate service of God-in-our-neighbors.* Jesus was arguably the greatest mystic of all time, but he gave his life to serving and healing others. Likewise, no matter how exalted or ecstatic our experience of the mystical life might be, as followers of Christ we are called to ground that experience in generous, compassionate care of others. More than one mystic has suggested that the real measure of spiritual attainment is the degree to which we cheerfully serve each other.

AN ONGOING JOURNEY

A few years ago I was speaking at a conference, and during the Q&A period someone asked me if I could offer a brief definition of mysticism. I answered spontaneously and intuitively, "Mysticism is living in the mystery of the love of God." That's probably as graceful (and concise) a definition as any other I could come up.

As I wrap up this chapter, I am keenly aware of how incomplete this, or any, definition of mysticism is—and how immense mysticism is in all its aspects. But I encourage you to continue this journey of exploration, trusting that no one needs to intellectually understand all the details of mystical spirituality—but we *are* all invited to find our unique way to live in the mystery of the love of God. I hope the material in this chapter has helped you to at least make a start. Hopefully in the pages to come you will find additional insights for your unique expression of the mystical life.

CHAPTER THREE

To Play in Ten Thousand Places: Christ as the Center of Mystical Christianity

The heart of mysticism is Jesus.
—Ruth Burrows

Think of us in this way, as servants of Christ
and stewards of God's mysteries.
—Paul (1 Corinthians 4:1)

We've seen that mysticism is not a uniquely or specifically Christian concept. The word itself only dates back about three hundred years or so, which means it's not in the Bible or in the writings of most of the great Christian thinkers throughout history—including those we now think of as the great mystics— except within the last century or two. So twentieth-century Christians like Howard Thurman or Evelyn Underhill wrote about mysticism, but Teresa of Ávila, Julian of Norwich, Meister Eckhart, or Bernard of Clairvaux (among many others) had never heard of the word.

If we want to understand Christian mysticism we have to think not only about mysticism in a general sense but also about what is distinctive about the Christian expression of mysticism. That, of course, is the purpose of this entire book, but right now we need to consider the foundation of this path. That means looking at Jesus of Nazareth, whom Christians believe to be the Messiah, the anointed one (in Greek, Χριστός or *Christós*, from which we get the word *Christ*).

Immediately we face a problem, for Jesus has been understood, revered, and interpreted in many different ways over the centuries. In the words of poet Gerard Manley Hopkins, "Christ plays in ten thousand places"— which to my mind means there are almost as many ways of understanding Christ as there are people who follow Jesus. So as we seek to explore Jesus of Nazareth as the first and greatest of the Christian mystics, one of our tasks will be to set aside some of the unmystical ways we are used to thinking about him.

Too many Christians have weaponized Jesus—which is to say, they have misrepresented Jesus as a figure to fear, rather than as one who initiates us into the mysteries of God. One (very big) example of this adorns the ceiling of the Basilica of the National Shrine of the Immaculate Conception in Washington, DC. Built in the twentieth century, it's a beautiful church, with amazing mosaics and splendid art. But in the north apse of the main sanctuary of the church, a giant mosaic of Jesus—one of the largest mosaics of Christ in the world—hovers above the altar, representing Jesus as a remote figure of supreme power, watching over the interior of the church like a penny-pinching businessman watching over his employees, eager to catch them doing something wrong. There are many inaccuracies with this mosaic, not the least of which is how Jesus is depicted as a European (Caucasian) man, rather than a Middle Eastern Jew. But as bad as this white-skinned, blond haired, blue-eyed Jesus might be, what strikes even the most casual observer is how *angry* he looks. Seated in judgment over the world, his face seems filled with wrath; his brow is furrowed, his expression serious, completely devoid of gentleness or warmth.

If this is how you see Jesus, all of the mystical talk about *union* with him will seem weird and bizarre, if not downright terrifying. Who in their right mind would want to open their heart and soul to a deity who appears to be seething with rage?

To put the Christ in Christian mysticism—to truly embrace and celebrate Jesus as the anointed one, the Messiah— we have to begin by letting go of all the images of Jesus that have come down the ages, that represent him as angry, wrathful, mad, furious, judgmental, and apparently hell-bent (pun intended) on condemning those he deems unworthy. This might be the Jesus of too much religious Christianity, and of popular culture, but it's *not* the Jesus of the Bible—or the mystics.

To be clear, both the Bible and the mystics do show Jesus getting angry— usually due to something he sees as unjust or unfair. Jesus is not afraid to stand up for what is right, and to the extent that such a stance involves being angry at what *isn't* right, Jesus doesn't back down. But it's a different kind of anger, and one that's healthy, such as like any mature human being would feel when dealing with something that is unfair or oppressive.

Meanwhile, Jesus proves capable of showing incredible tenderness and mercy, of expressing forgiveness to those who have made mistakes, of healing those who are sick, making sure those who are hungry are fed, and even on occasion exhibiting a dry sense of humor (Christians often do a poor job of understanding Jesus as witty, but theologians like James Martin, Henri Cormier, and Elton Trueblood have written about this often overlooked dimension of Jesus's personality).

In addition to reclaiming a more well-rounded, three-dimensional sense of who Jesus was, we also need to take a look at his teachings. Christianity as a religion has often focused more on what Jesus *did* (he was a healer, he gave us the sacramental meal known as the Lord's Supper or Holy Communion, he died for our sins, he rose again) rather than the radical message found in what he *said*. I don't mean to belittle his actions, which often were motivated by great love and compassion. But those actions are more meaningful when understood in the light of the teachings. And when we really grapple with his teachings, we find that Jesus truly is, in the words of the Franciscan contemplative teacher Richard Rohr, the first major nondual teacher in the West.

Nonduality is a philosophical concept that emerged particularly in Eastern systems of thought like Advaita Vedanta. In essence, it is a recognition that there is a fundamental unity to all things that is deeper and more real than the apparent dualities and multiplicities that meet the eye. On the surface, it's easy to divide the world into categories like good and bad, material and spiritual, sacred and profane and so forth. Nonduality does not deny the existence of these kinds of divisions. But it acknowledges that there is a deeper unity that we are not always consciously aware of, a unity that can reveal the love and justice of God, even in all the seeming differences.

I like to think of it this way: when a person is standing at the north pole, to take a step in any direction is to move south. At the north pole, one cannot go any further north, and even the notions of east or west simply do not apply. Everything you see is to the south.

Now, imagine you are one with God. Everything you see, in any direction, is something, someone, God has created—and therefore, God loves. Because God loves all, you (being one with God) also love all. Even people who harm others (or themselves) you still love. You do not condone their hurtful actions, you grieve for the harm their actions cause, and if possible you work to stop their harmful behavior, but you never abandon the love you hold for them (and for all people, indeed all things).

Jesus is famous for instructing his followers to "be perfect" like God is perfect. It's tempting to interpret that as "don't ever do anything wrong." But the message is far more radical than merely a dualistic commandment to always be good and never be bad. Here's the full teaching, from Jesus's Sermon on the Mount.

> You have heard that it was said, "You shall love your neighbor and hate your enemy." But I say to you, Love your enemies and pray for those who persecute you, so that you may be children of your God in heaven; who makes the sun rise on the evil and on the good, and sends rain on the righteous and on the unrighteous. For if you love those who love you, what reward do you have? Do not even the tax collectors do the same? And if you greet only your brothers and sisters, what more are you doing than others? Do not even the gentiles do the same? Be perfect, therefore, as your heavenly God is perfect.[1]

The sun and the rain do not discriminate against those who are good or evil, nor is there a distinction between those who are righteous and those who are not. Like the weather, God sends love and mercy and forgiveness to all, for *in God all are one.* That's the key to Jesus's teaching—to why he's recognized as a "nondual" teacher—and why he is the epicenter of the Christian mystical life.

Jesus taught love, radical love. Love everyone, even your enemies. Forgive everyone. If someone hurts you, respond with compassion, not revenge. Be a force for good in the world. Be an agent for healing and reconciliation.

But Jesus also taught two essential ideas that form the headwaters of Christian mysticism. First, that he (Jesus) is one with God, and second, that we (human beings) are, or at least can be, one with Jesus.

Consider these verses from the Gospel of John. They express in different ways Jesus's understanding of the nondual unity that Jesus enjoyed with God—and with humanity.

- "God and I are one."
- "On that day you will know that I am in God, and you in me, and I in you."
- "I pray for those who will believe in me through their word, that they may all be one, just as you, God, are in me, and I in you, that they also may be in us, so that the world may believe that you have sent me. The glory that you have given me I have given to them, that they may be one even as we are one, I in them and you in me, that they may become perfectly one, so that the world may know that you sent me and loved them even as you loved me."
- "I am the vine, you are the branches. Those who abide in me and I in them bear much fruit, because apart from me you can do nothing."[2]

At its heart, Christian mysticism is the mystery of this divine union. Jesus is one with God, and we are one with Jesus, which means of course, we are all one in God.

Jesus represents the foundation and apex of Christian mysticism also by the template of spiritual initiation he gave to us in the final days of his earthly life. The story goes that, after running afoul of both the religious and political leaders of his day, Jesus was killed by the torturous method of crucifixion (being nailed to a cross and then left to die). Christians believe, following the testimony of Mary Magdalene, Peter and John, and the other apostles, including Paul, that on the first day of the week following his crucifixion, Jesus rose from the dead, and continued to teach and minister to his followers for forty days, before ascending into heaven—not leaving us bereft, but sending the Holy Spirit to live in the hearts of Christians and to guide them until the end of time.

Many people struggle with the story of Jesus's resurrection and ascension. Indeed, the apostle Paul admits even in the Christian Scriptures that it's a difficult story to accept.[3] But mysticism invites us to approach the story of Jesus's death, resurrection, and ascension not merely as a *matter of belief* but even more so as a *template for the spiritual life*. Look at it this way: everyone sooner or later dies—and most of us will undergo multiple metaphorical "deaths" before our eventual physical demise. We experience death when a relationship ends, when a conflict disrupts our lives, when we suffer a health crisis or a significant change in our life circumstances. All of these "deaths," no matter how painful or devastating they can be, are also potential doorways to "resurrection"—a new chapter in life—and even "ascension": a change that is not only different, but even better than what came before.

Jesus offers us a template for how to live. When we face a significant loss, we can retreat into fear, anger, depression, or chaos—but we are also given the choice of meeting that loss with profound trust that new life beckons us from the other side of the "death." And what we experience spiritually in the normal course of life, through Jesus we can trust that resurrection is available to us even after physical death.

The pattern of Jesus's death, resurrection, and ascension is called the "paschal mystery," from the Hebrew word for Passover, which was the Jewish festival that coincided with the timing of Jesus's death and resurrection. *Mystery,* as we have already seen, is a root word for mysticism. Jesus, therefore, invites us into the mystery (the mystical reality) of new-life-emerging-after-death. He shows us the way. The anointed one's initiation into death, resurrection, and ascension is now available for all of us.

This does not erase the fact that we will all die, and we will all suffer and experience loss. None of that changes. But the paschal mystery invites us to understand and experience loss and death from a place of deep trust and faith, rather than despair, anxiety, or fear. The mysticism of Jesus is a spirituality that invites us into an entirely new way of relating to death (both physical and spiritual/metaphorical). And once we revolutionize our relationship with death, we are empowered to an entirely new relationship with *life* as well.

This short chapter has barely begun to explore the depths of how and why Jesus matters as the key figure (sometimes called the "cornerstone") of the Christian mystical life. We have much more ground to cover in the pages to come, but I hope you will continue to bear in mind that both the radical teachings (anchored in love and non duality) and the life-affirming actions (including healing the sick, forgiving those who have made mistakes, and ultimately rising from the dead) of Jesus are essential to what Christian mysticism represents—and invites us into.

CHAPTER FOUR

Of Prophets and Philosophers: The Sources of Christian Mysticism

Anyone united to God becomes one spirit with God.
—Apostle Paul (1 Corinthians 6:17, adapted)

The Christian religion is primarily about a transformation of consciousness. This takes spiritual practice and the cultivation of wisdom. In another time, this was called cultivating the super-natural organism, what Paul called "a new creation." So the main thing is to be transformed into God, what the early church called deification, theosis, divinization.
—Thomas Keating

HOW DID CHRISTIAN MYSTICISM ORIGINATE?

It is not my intention to chart the history of Christian mysticism. Other writers, from Evelyn Underhill to Rowan Williams to Bernard McGinn, have already done a fine job covering the story of mysticism through the ages.[1] But still it makes sense to consider the sources of mystical Christianity, since it is part of any spiritual tradition to honor the wisdom of the past. Far from being a new or recent development within Christianity, the mystical and contemplative streams of Christian spirituality can be traced back to three significant sources.

First of all, just as Jesus and his earliest followers were Jewish, the origins of Christian mysticism can be traced back to Judaism, and especially to the mystical wisdom found in the biblical writings that form the Hebrew Scriptures, what Christians have called the "Old Testament." From the earliest encounters with God reported by figures like Jacob or Moses, to the mystical spirituality associated with the temple in Jerusalem, to the emerging wisdom articulated by prophets like Isaiah and Ezekiel, mysticism has deep roots in the Bible.

Then, there is the contribution from Greek culture. The Christian Scriptures were written in Greek, and the deeply spiritual wisdom of pagan philosophers from Plato to Plotinus was embraced by early Christian theologians and spiritual teachers like Clement of Alexandria in the late second century and Augustine of Hippo two hundred years later. This intellectual marriage between Greek philosophy and early Christian spirituality helped to create the language of the mystics, a language of transcendence, ecstasy, and interior transformation, that has set the stage for how Christians have experienced the presence of God—and told the story of that experience— ever since.

Finally, there is the unique contribution of Jesus and the earliest Christians. We have already looked at how Jesus himself was a mystic, and how his teachings convey mystical wisdom. His earliest followers, like the apostles John and Paul, expanded on Jesus's teachings and set the groundwork for Christianity's unique mystical tradition.

Most historians of Christian spirituality would probably accept the idea that mystics have been present in the Christian world from the first centuries. But in the first thousand years of Christian history, mysticism generally involved a more intellectual approach to faith—for example, mystical theology (a concept that emerges around the year 500 CE) refers to teachings that emphasizes God's hiddenness and our inability to speak about God in a definitive way. The earliest sense of a mystical dimension to Christianity often had to do with how Christians interpreted the Bible (the "mystical" sense of the Bible referred to hidden or oblique ways in which the Bible, especially the Hebrew Scriptures, pointed to Jesus) while the sacraments were understood as "mysteries" because they had a hidden dimension (for example, the real presence of Jesus, hidden within the bread and wine of Holy Communion).

From the time of Jesus, it would take a thousand years or more for mysticism to flower into the kind of poetic writings we associate with renowned mystics like Julian of Norwich, John of the Cross, and Teresa of Ávila. But even in the words of the earliest Christian mystics and spiritual masters— the desert mothers and fathers, the Celtic saints, and obscure but spiritually wise figures like Gregory of Nyssa, Pseudo-Dionysius, and Maximus the Confessor—we find hints of the contemplative wisdom to come.

THE JEWISH MATRIX: SEEKING THE FACE OF GOD

Christianity has a long and troubled history with Judaism, the faith of Jesus and his earliest followers. Spiritually speaking, we cannot fully appreciate the beauty and wisdom of Christian mysticism without first appreciating the splendor of the Jewish tradition from which it emerged. Unfortunately, part of the reason why Christians have related so poorly to our mother faith is because we often simply don't understand it—many Christians over the ages have used Judaism as a kind of foil, seeing it as embodying a legalistic and rigid religion Jesus "freed" us from. This regrettable idea is based on a poor understanding of Judaism, a poor understanding of Jesus, and a misinterpretation of how Christianity differs from its mother faith.

In this brief space, we cannot go into too much detail,[2] but let's just say that if Christians could learn to see Judaism with open eyes and an open mind, they could see it not as a religion of burdensome rules and regulations and rituals, but as a profoundly spiritual community and tradition formed around the question of how human beings can respond to the ineffable mystery that, for lack of a better word, we call "God"—which means that Judaism has its own beautiful mystical and contemplative heritage that formed the backdrop of Jesus's teachings, and continued to shape the earliest Christian community for generations.

In our time, the concept of Jewish mysticism evokes the esoteric tradition known as Kabbalah, which emerged in the Middle Ages, long after the acrimonious split that separated Christianity and Judaism. The Kabbalah has its own marvelous and distinctive body of wisdom, and some scholars have traced how some Christian mystics, for example Teresa of Ávila and Luis de Leon, were likely influenced by Kabbalistic teaching. In the twentieth century, the idiosyncratic Christian mystic Valentin Tomberg was very much influenced by Kabbalah. The word *Kabbalah* means *tradition*, which in turn implies something handed down from generation to generation. Every lasting expression of spirituality and mysticism around the world has this sense of wisdom being accumulated, preserved, and passed on from generation to generation. Living as we do in a culture that tends be obsessed with the latest and greatest, ancient spiritual traditions like the Jewish Kabbalah or Christian mysticism can help us remember that sometimes we find the greatest value, meaning, and purpose in life not by chasing after the new, but by allowing something venerable and old to form and nurture us.

To understand the Jewish contribution to Christian mysticism, we have to go back further than even the earliest Kabbalistic writings—and turn to the Tanakh, the Hebrew Scriptures—or what is identified as the Old Testament in most Christian Bibles (a better word for this collection of writings might be "First Testament," but many Christian Bible scholars nowadays simply call it the Hebrew Scriptures, so we'll go with that).

The roots of Jewish mysticism—and, therefore, of mystical Christianity—can be found in the prophetic and wisdom writings of the Hebrew Scriptures. Consider this verse from 1 Samuel: "Then the spirit of the Lord will possess you, and you will be in a prophetic frenzy along with them and be turned into a different person."[3] The verse is part of a mandate spoken over the future king of Israel, Saul, by the prophet Samuel. In this single verse we find so much that points to the spiritual origins of both Jewish and Christian mysticism. "The Spirit of the Lord" (literally, "the breath of Yahweh") could be understood by Christians to mean the Holy Spirit; this Spirit is promised to come upon Saul and "possess" him—in other words, to enter into union with Saul, thereby directing his actions, inspiring him into a "prophetic frenzy" (we might say "ecstasy") and leading to a transformation, making him "a different person."

This is not some dried up, desiccated religion of rules and regulations. It is profoundly charismatic, deeply ecstatic, embodied and experiential, and points toward interior transformation.

And while it might be tempting to dismiss this passage as "just for the king, not for anyone else," there are plenty of passages in both the Hebrew and Christian Scriptures that point to the transforming grace of the Spirit being meant for everyone, not just for those who were elite or otherwise deemed especially worthy.

This interaction between Samuel and Saul illustrates the mystical strand within Judaism—a spirituality that is grounded in the encounter with what has been called the "elusive presence" of God. Epiphanies or theophanies—extraordinary and visionary moments when mere mortals find themselves interacting with the God of the universe—can be found throughout the Tanakh:

- Moses's encounter with God in the burning bush
- Elijah's discovery of God in "a sound of sheer silence" on the mountain
- Isaiah's vision of God's majesty and glory filling the temple
- Ezekiel's dramatic vision of God being carried to heaven in a chariot of fire[4]

Indeed, Ezekiel's vision in particular became a central image for Jewish mystics, leading to a school of mystical thought known as Merkavah mysticism (from the Hebrew word for chariot). Jewish mystics in the centuries surrounding the time of Jesus created a body of writings known as the Hekhalot literature, which recounted visionary experiences of mystics being taken into the palaces of God in heaven (Hekhalot means "palaces"). Echoes of this kind of mysticism can be found in the early Christian writings, from the idea that Jesus ascended into heaven at the end of his earthly life, to the mystical ascent recorded by the apostle Paul in his second letter to the Corinthians, when he writes of a person (perhaps himself) who was "caught up to the third heaven."[5]

The mystical strand of Judaism gave Christianity more than just a literary canon of visionary writings. Aryeh Kaplan, a twentieth-century Kabbalist and Orthodox rabbi, wrote a profound book that belongs in the library of every Christian mystic: *Meditation and the Bible* (of course, this means "Bible" in the Jewish sense, consisting only of the Tanakh or Hebrew Scriptures). Rabbi Kaplan offers a rich interpretive understanding of how the visionary stories in the First Testament can inspire us today. For example, he looks at how both the visions of Elijah and Ezekiel, mentioned above, represent a similar elemental movement—Ezekiel moves through the wind, the cloud, and the fire, while Elijah likewise endures wind, earthquake, and fire before encountering God in a sound of sheer silence.[6] Kaplan points out that these parallel experiences represent "the natural agitations of the mind" (the wind), in other words, distracting and undisciplined thoughts and feelings; followed by "an opaqueness of the mind, where nothing can be seen or experienced"—this is the cloud (reminiscent of the Christian mystical teachings on "the Cloud of Unknowing" from the late 1300s)—so, the meditator must face down the chaos of their unruly thoughts, but also the mysteriousness of the silence that lies beyond those thoughts. Those who persevere through the cloud will encounter the fire: the experience of deep "awe, shame, and dread" when faced with the majesty and holiness of the divine mystery.[7]

Both Elijah and Ezekiel represent the universal call to spiritual depth—a call to move into meditation, through distracting thoughts, radical unknowing, and the "fire" of awe, dread, or a sense of deep unworthiness, in order to reach "the sound of sheer silence"[8]—the Divine Presence that has been hidden yet available all along.

Rabbi Kaplan also suggests that biblical texts sometimes lose their mystical meaning when translated out of Hebrew into other languages, like English. Take, for example, Psalm 119:15: the New Revised Standard Version translates this verse as "I will meditate on your precepts, and fix my eyes on your ways." Kaplan translates this verse as "In Your mysteries I will meditate, and I will gaze at Your paths." A subtle but radically different rendering of this verse! He goes on to make the case that the Hebrew word normally translated as "precepts" (implying a legalistic body of rules or regulations) actually carries a sense of deep, hidden spiritual truth, that can only be unveiled through meditation. In other words, *mysteries*.[9]

The Psalms also provided inspiration for generations of Jewish, and later Christian, mystics. Some of the Psalms are luminous with their depictions of divine glory, beauty, love, and tenderness. A recurring theme in the Psalms is the need to wait for God, and in at least a few psalms, such waiting occurs in silence. "Be still, and know I am God," as the much-loved verse Psalm 46:10 states. Psalm 62:1 picks up this theme: "For God alone my soul in silence waits," while Psalm 65 offers another verse that often gets mistranslated, but the original Hebrew says "To you, God, silence is praise."

The prophet Habakkuk proclaimed that God is in God's temple, so let all the earth keep silent.[10] For Christians, this verse offers a unique perspective, since Christianity teaches that, following the destruction of the temple in Jerusalem, our human hearts and bodies have become God's "temple"—so a Christian interpretation of Habakkuk might sound like this: "God is present in our bodies and hearts, therefore let us respond to that divine presence with contemplative silence."

The mystical wisdom in the Jewish Bible offers more than just invitations into the silence of meditation. Consider this verse from the prophet Daniel. "Those who are wise shall shine like the brightness of the sky, and those who lead many to righteousness, like the stars forever and ever."[11] According to Rabbi Jay Michaelson, who writes about nondual Judaism,[12] the word translated as "wise" could also be rendered *"enlightened."* For Michaelson, the Kabbalah suggests that those who contemplate the fullness of wisdom will be enlightened, and thus will shine with a celestial radiance (which calls to mind Jesus's transfiguration or Merton's street corner epiphany).

These are just a few hints of the mystical treasures that are found in the Hebrew Scriptures. Suffice to say, a full understanding and appreciation of Christian mysticism needs to include the mystical wisdom of these ancient writings. By doing so, we follow in the footsteps of Christian mystics since the time of the earliest Christians. For example, the Egyptian mystic Origen of Alexandria suggested that three of the Wisdom writings in the Hebrew Bible: the books of Proverbs, Ecclesiastes, and the Song of Songs, when taken together, represent three broad stages of mystical development, what he and subsequent mystics described as purification, illumination, and union (deification). Proverbs, with its emphasis on virtue and ethical integrity, represents the challenge for mystics to become purified of anything within them that stands in the way of their love for God. Ecclesiastes, with its rich philosophical musings, represents the illumination or enlightenment that God pours into the minds and hearts of those who truly do surrender all other attachments. And the Song of Songs, a deeply sensual, even erotic love poem, represents the intimacy of nondual union with God—an intimacy greater even than that enjoyed in the physical love of the marriage bed.

The primary message of the Tanakh, contrary to Christian misunderstandings, is not about rules and regulations, but about God's great and lasting love for God's people. It's also the story of how human beings have responded to that love, sometimes skillfully, sometimes not so much.

Over the course of the ages, the Scriptures (both Hebrew and Christian) depict God as calling human beings out of slavery or bondage and into freedom. On a big picture level, that's freedom from oppression or injustice, symbolized by the liberation of God's people from the tyranny of ancient Egypt, or Babylon, or Rome. But there's also a personal, "little picture" dimension of the Bible's message. As individuals, we are all called to move into greater freedom as well: freedom from anything within us that holds us back from the liberating power of love, love that comes straight from the heart of God.

THE GREEK CONTRIBUTION:
CONTEMPLATING DIVINE UNION

Mysticism is a modern word: it only dates back to around the year 1700, and only appears in English in 1736. So it isn't found in the Bible or in the writings of ancient Christian writers or Greek philosophers. But the root word of mysticism has an ancient Greek source, so that's a good place to begin our appreciation of the Greek contribution.

Mysticism comes from the Greek word *mueo*, which means "to close" or "to shut." In "Mysticism: An Essay on the History of the Word," French scholar Louis Bouyer says it refers to closing the eyes, while other sources suggest it refers to keeping your mouth shut. In fact, both of these meanings make sense. Yet another source suggests the word means "to initiate into the mysteries," hence "to instruct." Mysticism thus involves shutting, closing, and hiddenness, but also initiation, learning a secret, and keeping your mouth shut long enough to listen for what's really going on.

This spirituality of initiation into hidden secrets (ineffable mysteries) first emerged in the great pagan mystery religions of the ancient world. These religions encompassed a variety of independent communities that were organized around the veneration of a particular deity linked to a mythological story. For example, the Orphic mysteries venerated Orpheus, whose myth recounts how he went into the underworld in a vain attempt to rescue his beloved Eurydice. Likewise, the Eleusinian mysteries are devoted to the goddesses Demeter and Persephone, another tale with a strong underworld theme. Incidentally, this underworld theme is an important clue to understanding mysticism—even after it became Christianized.

Only initiates could participate in the ceremonies associated with the mystery religions. Initiation, as best we can tell, involved participation in one or more rituals in which the secrets of the god or goddess were revealed. Since initiates vowed never to reveal the secrets of the tradition, we know little of these ancient rites.

At least two qualities we associate with mysticism appear to be present in the mystery religions. The mysteries involved a specific *experience*—the ritual of initiation—as well as the suggestion of a particular change in *consciousness* that initiates enjoyed by virtue of having been enlightened by the secrets that were imparted to them. The secrets were, in all likelihood, meant to transform the faithful with a particular feeling or sense of connection with the gods, giving access to divine power.

Louis Bouyer suggests that "what the initiated must forbear from revealing . . . is not a doctrine, nor is it esoteric knowledge, but simply and solely the details of a ritual."[13] The rituals were secret because they included, in a symbolic or encoded way, doctrines or esoteric knowledge designed to foster embodied spiritual (mystical) experiences or heightened states of consciousness. Mysticism thus emerged through rituals oriented toward mythological goddesses and gods, designed to foster spiritual experiences that led to a transformation in consciousness.

But how did this impact the emerging spirituality of the early Christian movement?

Bouyer goes to great lengths in his essay to argue that Christianity did not borrow any secret *teachings* from the pagan religions; it did, however, borrow the *language* of the mysteries. While it is unclear just how the Greek concept of mystery influenced early Christianity, the concept of mystery as "hiddenness" appears in the writings of the apostle Paul and other early Christian mystics—even as it has an entirely different flavor from the pagan contexts out of which the language of mystery emerged. The earliest Christian mystics don't talk about ritual secrets that only initiates can access; rather they talk about *secrets that are revealed*—through Christ, through the Bible, through the Christian sacraments, and eventually, through personal experiences of the presence of God.

Christian mysticism is therefore not a static concept. Rather, it suggests something dynamic—a process, energy, or movement. It involves a continual tension between what is hidden and what is revealed. The development of this nuanced sense of the mystical was a long (and ongoing) process within Christianity.

THE FIRST CHRISTIANS: FROM THE ROAD
TO EMMAUS TO THE THIRD HEAVEN

The Greek word *mueo* appears only once in the Christian Scriptures, when Paul notes that he has "learned the secret" of what it is like to be both hungry and well fed.[14] This mundane use of the word clearly does not give us a lot of insight into the concept of mysticism as we know it. Of more direct interest to our inquiry is the Greek word *musterion*, meaning "mystery." Various forms of this Greek word appear in twenty-seven passages scattered throughout the New Testament. Here are some of the key concepts given in those passages:

- The secrets of the kingdom of heaven. (Matthew 13:11)
- The proclamation of Jesus is "according to the revelation of the mystery that was kept secret for long ages." (Romans 16:25)
- God's wisdom is described as "secret and hidden." (1 Corinthians 2:7)
- Followers of Jesus are "stewards of God's mysteries." (1 Corinthians 4:1)
- In 1 Corinthians 13 (the famous "love" chapter), Saint Paul notes that, even if he could "understand all mysteries and all knowledge," if he lacked love, he would be "nothing."
- Belief in life after death is described as a mystery. (1 Corinthians 15:51)
- In Ephesians 1:9, the "mystery of [God's] will" has, according to God's good pleasure, been "set forth in Christ."
- In Colossians 1:26–27, the mystery of God is described as hidden throughout the ages, but now revealed; the mystery is "Christ in you, the hope of glory." In Colossians 2:2, "God's mystery" is described as "Christ himself."

- In the first letter to Timothy, there are references to the "mystery of the faith" (3:9) and the "mystery of our religion" (3:16), which is explained in terms of events from the life of Jesus.[15]

WHAT DOES ALL THIS MEAN?

Certainly, the concept of mystery as it appears in the Christian Scriptures mirrors, in some ways, the spirituality of the mystery religions. But there's far more to the biblical concept of mystery than just a subtle echo of Greek paganism. Instead of focusing on the spiritual secrets of a polytheistic god or goddess, the New Testament naturally focuses entirely on Christ. The emphasis in much of the New Testament is not on secrets *kept*, but on secrets *revealed*. That's the crucial difference between Christianity and the mystery religions. Jesus himself is the ultimate secret that is revealed. Or perhaps it is more accurate to say that it is through Christ that the ultimate secret is revealed—the secret of the nature of God, the reality of God's unconditional love for us, and our invitation to partake of God's divine nature.

In Jesus, not only is God revealed, but also God's attributes and actions are made manifest—divine mercy, grace and love, and God's plan for spreading glory and hope throughout the world. It's important to keep in mind that "Christ" is not just some abstract concept that is found in a book or a religious ritual. Christ means "anointed one"—so therefore, the mystery of God is Christ (the divine anointing) in us. Not only is God revealed through Christ, but that divine presence known intimately to those who love Jesus, because they abide in Christ and Christ abides in them.[16]

Like the Tanakh, there are plenty of passages in the Christian Scriptures with mystical overtones. We've already considered one of the most powerful: the transfiguration. Another fascinating story is the tale of the two disciples who were traveling from Jerusalem to Emmaus on the first Easter. Jesus accompanies them, but at first they do not recognize him. They have an in-depth spiritual conversation, and the disciples encourage this "stranger" to stay with them at nightfall. But when Jesus breaks and blesses the bread, finally they recognize him—only to have him suddenly disappear.

"Were not our hearts burning within us," they said to each other, "while he was talking to us on the road, while he was opening the scriptures to us?"[17]

Through this story, we learn that Jesus can be present to us, even though we may not recognize that presence; yet we are invited to recognize the divine presence in the wisdom of Scripture, the "breaking of the bread" (an allusion to Holy Communion), and, perhaps most important of all, in each other.

Then there is the mysterious passage where Paul writes of being caught up in the third heaven, which some interpret as an echo of Jewish Hekhalot mysticism:

> I know a person in Christ who fourteen years ago was caught up to the third heaven—whether in the body or out of the body I do not know; God knows. And I know that such a person—whether in the body or out of the body I do not know; God knows—was caught up into Paradise and heard things that are not to be told, that no mortal is permitted to repeat.[18]

Many commentators speculate that Paul is recounting his own mystical experience here, but because of his humility he tries to do so anonymously. But no matter who this person may have been, their experience of being caught up into paradise helps to set the stage for centuries of mystical encounters to come. Paul cannot determine if this is an embodied experience or an ecstatic experience (the word ecstasy carries the sense of being "outside the body"). His uncertainty is a blessing for mystical Christianity, for it creates the space for both kinds of encounter. But he also makes clear that the wisdom of this mystical encounter is *ineffable*, which is to say, it cannot be put into words. This provides the foundation for a long tradition within Christianity of associating mystical encounters with God with a sense of mystery, of darkness or unknowing, of a "knowledge" that paradoxically is only defined by what is not known.

Paul's can't-put-it-into-words experience contrasts with the eloquence and otherworldly mystery of the transfiguration. Christian mysticism, it seems, cannot be reduced to a single type of experience. Mystics may enjoy radiant light, or be humbled by a sense that words only fail. The encounter can happen here on earth, in the body, or "caught up into the third heaven," in a rush of ecstatic wonder. But perhaps most important of all, these mystical moments have to be approached in the light of Jesus's teachings and wisdom. And while Jesus could wax poetic about the love of God and the essential quality of abiding in the spirit, his teachings also remained earthy, practical, and simple.

Love one another.
Forgive one another.
Heal one another.
Care even for your adversaries.
Practice nonviolence.
Let go of the temptation to judge.
Be merciful.

So the elements that form the heart of Christian mysticism—glowing light, contemplative darkness, nondual consciousness, and unspeakable ecstasies—ultimately prove meaningful only to the extent that they help us to embody the radical teachings of the one who gave us the Spirit in our hearts.

The Jewish, Greek, and early Christian contributions all danced together to generate the spirituality we now think of as Christian mysticism. But mysticism is not a static spirituality; it has continued to grow over the centuries. So just as important as the origins of mystical Christianity is the ongoing story of how this adventure of responding to divine love has continued to deepen and blossom with the passing of time.

CHAPTER FIVE

Hermits, Nuns, and Poets: The Evolution of Christian Mysticism

So we have known and believe the love that God has for us.
God is love, and those who abide in love abide in God, and
God abides in them.
—Apostle John (1 John 4:16)

I have found heaven on earth, since heaven is God, and
God is in my soul. The day I understood this, everything
became luminous in me, and I wish to tell this secret to
those I love, discretely.
—Elizabeth of the Trinity

In Jesus, the mystery and hidden secrets of God have been made known. Every generation following the time of Jesus's earthly life has taken the story —of who Jesus was, what he said and did, and how he lived, died, rose again, and ascended into heaven—and embedded it into the spiritual yearning and practices of their time. Thus, mystical Christianity has evolved over the centuries, from the earliest recognition that in Jesus the hidden things of God are made visible, to its current expression as the deeply contemplative heart of Christian spirituality.

For believers, Jesus was not merely a teacher or faith healer, or just a gifted prophet. Jesus is the embodiment of God with a capital *G*—a God who, unlike mythological deities, embodies infinite power and vast, ever-flowing love. And as Jesus is the incarnation of the fullness of God, Christians (which means "Little Christs") become partakers of the body of Christ, which means we become embodiments of the divine as well.

In the earliest expressions of Christian spirituality, this mystery—of the secrets of God, formerly hidden, now revealed—referred not only to Jesus as the revealer of God, but also to the sacred writings of the Jewish people. The Bible itself tells the story of the divine mystery. Some of the earliest Christian mystics—including Clement of Alexandria (ca. 150–216); Origen, also from Alexandria (ca. 185–254); and Gregory of Nyssa (fourth century)—all made names for themselves by their ability to discern the hidden secrets of God in the Hebrew Scriptures.

What did they find hidden in those sacred writings? Beyond the plain meaning of the text, they found symbolic and allegorical clues to the hidden activity of God.

For the early Christian mystics, the First Testament was encoded with hints that pointed to the coming of Christ. Some of these hints were explicit, as when the prophet Isaiah foretells the coming of the Messiah. But others were more subtle, as those in the Song of Songs, with a love poem interpreted as mystically symbolic of Christ's love for the community of faith.

From our vantage point today, this early Christian approach to Scripture—examining ancient writings to find evidence of God's activity by discerning prophetic hints about Christ—can seem quaint and naive. To the early Christians, who did not enjoy the same scholarly understanding of the Hebrew writings that we know today, it made sense. If God's presence were perfectly revealed in Jesus, wouldn't divine secrets be hidden, like Easter eggs, in the sacred writings, just waiting to be discovered? This is the line of thinking that inspired the early Christian mystics to read the Bible in order to find God's hidden purpose.

Out of this foundation of Scripture interpretation emerged the quest to comprehend the mystery of God. In the early centuries of the church, Christians struggled to make sense of their experience of Christ as both fully human and fully divine—as one with God.[1] From Jesus's promise to send the Holy Spirit of God,[2] the earliest Christians recognized "God," "Christ," and the "Holy Spirit" as three different "faces" of the divine. This, in turn, had to be reconciled with the profound belief that God is one.[3] Christians squared the oneness of God with the apparent "threeness" of the Creator, Christ, and Spirit in the doctrine of the Holy Trinity, which celebrates one God in three persons. This complex concept was acknowledged by Christians as early as Cyril of Alexandria (ca. 378–444) as "supremely ineffable and mystical." In other words, it's a concept so mysterious, a truth so hidden, that it is beyond the capacity of human language to contain it. Cyril was right: it is truly *mystical*.

ENACTING THE (CHRISTIAN) MYSTERIES

Christianity involves more than just words, ideas, thoughts, teachings, and concepts, just as there's more to mysticism than abstract ideas. Mystical Christianity invites us beyond merely thinking and talking about Christ. Rather, it's all about relating to Christ, and making that relationship real in our lives. It's about encountering Christ, enjoying the divine presence, and allowing the Spirit to heal and transform us. It's no surprise, therefore, that, in the early centuries of the church, Christianity developed not only mystical doctrines, but also mystical rites—liturgical (ceremonial) acts of worship, in which believers anchored their mystical faith in down-to-earth ceremonies and actions, using material objects to signify and convey spiritual realities. Among the two most important rites are baptism and the Eucharist.

The Eucharist, or Holy Communion, consists of a ritual meal hosted by Jesus the night before he died. It was at this "Last Supper" that Christ said of bread, "This is my body," and of wine, "This is my blood." Over time, Christians developed a rich and poetic language to describe this simple act. Unfortunately, this rite also became the subject of divisions and disagreements that separated Christians from one another. What remains important for our purposes here is noting that the earliest Christian teachers saw Communion as a mystery—where that which is hidden or secret (in this case, the true presence of Christ) became revealed. The Eucharist thus became an essential practice within the mystical expression of Christianity.

Nilus of Sinai (early fifth century) called Communion the "mystical bread," but also the "mystical body"—a term that eventually came to be used to describe the entire Christian people. Around the same time, John Chrysostom referred to Communion as "mystical food" and a "mystical banquet."

While Holy Communion, with its emphasis on the presence of Christ, became the central ritual of the ancient Christians, it was by no means the only mystical rite. Eventually, other liturgical acts—the initiation of newcomers to the faith through the ceremonial washing of holy baptism, the marking of believers with chrism (blessed oil) to signify the indwelling of the Holy Spirit, and pastoral rituals like marriage, confirmation, and the anointing of the sick—were recognized as conduits by which the grace and presence of God was realized in the lives of Christians. These rituals, all of which are intended to make the hidden reality of God manifest, became known in the West as sacraments—a word that means "consecrated act." Among the orthodox Christians of the East, however, the sacraments are called by a different name: mysteries.

When ancient Christians spoke of the mystical dimension of their faith, they not only acknowledged that the *secrets* of God had been revealed (through Jesus, through the Bible, through baptism and the Eucharist), but also proclaimed that the *presence* of God was made known through these things. This led to the fullest flowering of the Christian theology of mysticism—that it involves a conscious experience of the presence of God. Not just a nice, cozy feeling that God exists and therefore all is right with the world, but a feel-it-in-your-bones, more-real-than-real encounter with God's here-and-now presence. These sacramental encounters, paradoxically, point to something more profound than mere human experience.

The sacraments invite us into conscious recognition and embodied knowing (even though it's bigger than human awareness), which means that the "knowing" of a mystic may actually be a kind of luminous unknowing: some mystics might only be aware of God by their awareness of just how hidden God seems to them. But even this experience of God's hiddenness or transcendence can foster a relationship with God, only one that grows deep in the heart, beneath the threshold of ordinary human consciousness.

This matrix of spirituality, immersed in discovering Christ (and indeed, the triune God) hidden in the word and the sacraments, led in the early centuries of Christianity to the emergence of a contemplative movement, where believers abandoned their comfortable lives to seek God in remote settings such as the deserts of Egypt and Palestine or the wilderness of

Ireland. Some of these figures lived as hermits; others formed communities, which became the earliest Christian monasteries and convents. Known as the desert mothers and fathers (in the Middle East) and the Celtic saints (in Ireland, Scotland, and other Celtic-language regions), these seekers of the divine presence were inspired by Jesus's forty-day fast in the wilderness, which culminated in his facing down a variety of temptations from the spirit of evil. Likewise, the desert and Celtic Christians believed that their wilderness sojourns would lead them to do battle with their own demons, causing them to rely fully on divine grace for their own salvation (healing/wholeness) and deification (being made one with God in Christ). From these early mystics we have a treasury of spiritual wisdom, including the first explicit instructions in what we now call Christian meditation or contemplative prayer.

NARRATING THE MYSTERIES

By the Middle Ages, Christians who experienced the presence of God, and even the sense of union with God, were committing their stories to writing. Some were visionaries, like Julian of Norwich (1342–ca. 1416), who received detailed and highly symbolic revelations of the life of Christ and the heavenly banquet. Others, like Francis of Assisi (ca. 1182–1226), received the stigmata, wounds in the hands and feet that echoed the trauma Christ suffered at the crucifixion. Still others were gifted teachers who, like Meister Eckhart (ca. 1260–1328), revealed a profound sense of God's presence through their sermons and writings. In the Orthodox East, Symeon the New Theologian (949–1022) underwent profound changes of consciousness through the indwelling of the Spirit, which he experienced as a presence marked by fire and light, while Gregory Palamas (1296–1359) advocated *hesychasm*, a spiritual practice that seeks the conscious presence of God through continual prayer. By the sixteenth century, as the Middle Ages gave way to the Renaissance and the birth of the modern world, Teresa of Ávila (1515–1582) and John of the Cross (1542–1591) wrote at length about their contemplative experiences and about how the mystical life entailed an uncompromising commitment to prayer, meditation, mindfulness, and ethical behavior.

John and Teresa lived in the tumultuous age of the Protestant Reformation, which forever changed the landscape of Western Christianity. A culture of suspicion developed among both Catholics and Protestants against the idea of personal experience of God. In the Catholic world, obedience to the church became the standard by which faithfulness was measured; in the Protestant world, obedience to the Bible played a similar role. In other words, both sides of the Reformation began to promote a behavioral rather than experiential approach to spirituality. Instead of fostering a spirituality based on encountering the presence of God, Christianity (at least, in the West) became increasingly focused on behavioral markers like submission to authority and moral rectitude as the benchmarks of a "good" Christian life.

Ironically, it is in this context that the word *mysticism* finally emerges (the earliest English use of the word documented in the *Oxford English Dictionary* is from 1736).

At first, however, the word *mysticism* carried largely negative connotations. The Oxford English Dictionary notes that "mysticism implies self-delusion or dreamy confusion of thought; hence the term is often applied loosely to any religious belief to which these evil qualities are imputed." Within the rise of modern science this hostility to mysticism grew, and with it a rejection of what was perceived as religious "superstition."

THE REHABILITATION OF MYSTICISM

By the end of the Middle Ages, the spirituality of divine mystery found its voice in the beautiful writings of mystics who recounted their personal encounters with the presence of God, the love of God, and even union with God.

Between the Reformation and the rise of modern science, however, mysticism became disreputable. Within the established churches, the spirituality of personal experience was ignored as religion became more focused on morality and obedience to authority. Then modern science, with its comprehensive rejection of religious thinking as irrational, seemed to seal mysticism's fate.

Why, then, has mysticism refused to die?

Even though the spirituality of the inner life fell out of favor among Christians in the centuries following the Reformation, people didn't stop having profound experiences of the presence of God, or even of union with God. Every generation has continued to produce mystics and contemplatives.

Over the past few centuries, some of these figures were denounced as heretics—for instance, the Catholic Jeanne Guyon and the Protestant Jakob Böhme—while others, like Thérèse of Lisieux and Jonathan Edwards, expressed their mystical intimacy with God in the context of their conscientious religious observance. In the Eastern Orthodox churches, which were relatively uninfluenced by either the Reformation or the scientific revolution's critique of spirituality, mysticism continued to thrive, fueled by the publication of a profound multivolume anthology of mystical texts, the *Philokalia*, as well as the success of a popular nineteenth-century Russian spiritual book, *The Way of a Pilgrim*.

Meanwhile, new and alternative movements within Christianity kept the mystical flame lit, such as the Society of Friends (the Quakers), who advocated a kind of democratic mysticism wherein God's "inner light" shone within all people. When Christians sat together in silence, they claimed, there was a gathered openness to God, who could present and deliver a message through anyone.

In the twentieth century, experiential spirituality got a boost with the emergence of Pentecostalism, also known as the Charismatic Renewal. In worship marked by ecstatic singing and dancing, Pentecostals joyfully seek communion with God through the Holy Spirit, who in turn blesses believers with spiritual gifts such as speaking in tongues. A generation later, increasing numbers of Christians throughout the West began to explore the wisdom of Eastern spirituality, from the Sufi mysticism of Islam to yoga, Vedanta, Taoism, and Zen Buddhism. This brought a new level of legitimacy to the idea that Christianity itself could return to and explore its own core mystical spirituality.

Ultimately, scholars and thinkers began to take mysticism seriously as a field of study. In the nineteenth and early twentieth centuries, mysticism caught the interest of theologians like William Ralph Inge and Friedrich von Hügel, and of psychologists like William James and popular religious writers like Evelyn Underhill. This revival eventually filtered into the Christian mainstream, where it united with the interest in Eastern spirituality that had emerged in the mid-twentieth century.

During the twentieth century, more scholars began translating the writings of the great mystics into English—many texts translated for the first time—thereby making this wisdom available to everyone in the English-speaking world. The Vatican II Council in the 1960s launched a new effort to encourage Catholic laypeople to embrace the fullness of Christian spirituality—an effort that also influenced Protestants and Anglicans. Finally, the arrival of the internet and the world wide web made a wide range of resources available to Christian spiritual seekers, from access to the texts of great mystical writings, to websites explaining practices like lectio divina and contemplative prayer, to retreats scheduled by monasteries and convents. All of these converging streams made the widespread exploration of experiential Christianity ever more available to ordinary Christians.

Many of the earliest Christian mystics were hermits, solitary seekers who lived in the desert or wilderness. The medieval period was marked by many mystics who were monks and nuns in the great monastic and religious orders. Now, the modern and postmodern eras are becoming the age of the "ordinary" mystics, people who are not necessarily celibate, cloistered, or consecrated. While monastic mystics certainly have never gone away (Ruth Burrows and Thomas Keating being two examples of beloved twentieth-century monastic contemplatives), recent centuries have seen the rise of mystics outside monastery walls. Evelyn Underhill, Simone Weil, Howard Thurman, Cynthia Bourgeault, Caryll Houselander and Anthony deMello are just a few examples of the uncloistered contemplatives of our time.

If there is one unifying image for the contemporary mystic, it would have to be "poet." Many mystics throughout the ages have been poets, and some (like John of the Cross) are as renowned for literary genius as they are for their spirituality. Many mystics of recent times have also been recognized for their poetry—Gerard Manley Hopkins, Evelyn Underhill, Abhishiktananda, and Caryll Houselander among them. Some poets known primarily for their writing also clearly demonstrate at least some sort of mystical sensibility—Denise Levertov, Maya Angelou, and Nikki Grimes are a few examples of such literary mystics.

Not all mystics of recent times are poets, in the narrow sense of the word. But even those who only write prose often use richly descriptive and evocative language as they attempt to capture their essentially ineffable experience. Prosaic writing tends to be linear and logical, while poetry often is more consciously artistic, right-brained, imaginative, and allusive. Poetry, as a literary form, simply has more capacity for describing the mystery of mysticism than prose. So even the most prosaic of mystical writers often have something of a poet's voice within them.

As poets, mystics seek to tell the story of their unspeakable encounter with the divine. They will never fully succeed in this effort, yet they recognize that a poetic failure is better than no attempt at all to speak of the mysteries found within the silence. So the mystics continue to write their poetry (and their poetic prose), and we are all the richer for their efforts.

MYSTERY, REVELATION, EXPERIENCE: A SUMMARY OF THE MYSTICAL CHRISTIAN STORY

We can trace the evolution of mysticism through the many shades of meaning that the words associated with it—*mystery*, *mystic*, and *mystical*—have taken on over the centuries. Mystery, as a spiritual concept, originally concerned religious rituals or ceremonies designed to impart secret spiritual teachings. Within Christian usage, the concept of spiritual mystery kept its notion of "secrets taught," but took on a slightly more democratic notion—that of "the hidden things of God revealed." This is the predominant meaning of mystery found in the Bible, and the "root concept" of a Christian understanding of mysticism.

From the earliest days of the Christian era, Jesus has been acclaimed and affirmed as the incarnation of the Word of God—the revelation of the ultimate mystery. Christ is the manifestation of God in human form, the Word of God made flesh, the secret of divine love made freely available to all. Thus, from the beginning, Christianity proclaimed a message that is completely mystical, which is to say, beyond the ability of language to describe or the human mind to understand fully. This mystical message became codified in teachings such as the doctrine of the Holy Trinity and of the real presence of Christ in the Eucharist.

From the earliest times, Christians performed ceremonies with a mystical dimension, embodying and revealing the hidden things of God. The most important of such ceremonies is the Eucharist, or Holy Communion, which invites partakers to a mystical experience in which Christ becomes present in the bread and wine, and then is mystically united with those who commune.

By the Middle Ages and into the modern era, increasing numbers of individual Christians began to write and teach others about their own unique and remarkable experiences of visions, ecstasies, miracles, and raptures, all pointing back to the heart of mysticism: the experience of the divine presence and of union with God. The fourteenth, fifteenth, and sixteenth centuries have been called the golden age of mysticism, thanks to the witness of many great mystical writers from that era. In the wake of the fracturing of Western Christianity by the Protestant Reformation and the rise of modern science, however, mysticism became an object of suspicion or ridicule—a problem that remains to this day, even though, by the end of the twentieth century, mysticism has become more widely accepted within Christianity than it had been for centuries.

THE FUTURE OF CHRISTIAN MYSTICISM

When Karl Rahner said "the Christian of the future will be a mystic or will not exist," he envisioned how the ongoing evolution of both Christianity and Christian mysticism will depend on each other.[4] To bring this chapter to a close, let's consider what the Christian mystic of the future might be like. Where is the Spirit leading those who have answered the contemplative call?

No one can answer that question definitively; all I can do is offer a few brief thoughts of conjecture. My speculations are based on the trajectory of mystical writings of renowned twentieth- and twenty-first-century contemplatives, whose insights will likely shape the evolution of mysticism in the near future.

The mysticism of the future will continue to emphasize experience, especially the transformation of consciousness. In *Soundings in the Christian Mystical Tradition*, Jesuit author Harvey D. Egan offers interesting insight into how mystical writings (and the study of mysticism) in the twentieth century increasingly began to focus more on *consciousness* than on experience as the central factor in mystical spirituality. Experience, according to Egan, "lends itself to a misunderstanding of mysticism as particular feeling or sensible perception that is too easily separated from understanding, judging, deciding, and loving" whereas consciousness "engenders a view of mysticism as more than unusual sensations. It helps to under-score that mysticism brings about new ways of knowing and loving that involve a transformative decision about how one lives."[5] Although Egan sees this as a novel development in the study of mysticism, this distinction has ancient roots, recognizable in the writings of medieval or early modern mystics like St. John of the Cross or the author of *The Cloud of Unknowing.*

To appreciate this, it's helpful to visualize experience and consciousness as two dimensions of a unified spectrum: mystical experience concerns a passive receptivity to thoughts, feelings, intuitions, visions, locutions, or other phenomena that concern the sense of the presence of God, whereas mystical consciousness entails an individual's capacity to recognize, know, and be aware of that divine presence. You could see it this way: experience consists of whatever happens to a person while consciousness refers to the person's capacity to know, understand and be aware of what's happening. If your consciousness is constrained, all the extraordinary experiences of the world will mean nothing to you, as you are not capable of recognizing or understanding those experiences when they arrive.

And unlike some of the mystical writings of the past that tend to be abstract and highly philosophical, I predict that future mystics will increasingly write about the experience of, and consciousness of, the presence of God as a practical, down-to-earth mystical reality.

The mysticism of the future will be increasingly unconcerned about its relationship to institutional religion. We live in a time when increasing numbers of people choose to reject older models of religious organization, such as the neighborhood congregation/parish model, which emphasizes each "flock" owning or operating its own building and paying a salary to one or more professional ministers, all functioning within regional and larger church and denominational structures.

For some people, rejecting institutional religion is the same as rejecting religion altogether, and they choose to identify as spiritually independent or spiritual but not religious. Others, however, view the old institutional models of religion as obsolete, but they are not ready to give up on the wisdom teachings of Jesus or the great Christian writers (including the mystics). I expect this trend to continue, and while I don't expect the neighborhood congregational church to disappear altogether, it will likely have a much smaller role to play in the Christianity of the future. Christianity will become less professionalized, less hierarchical, and less centralized, as more people seek to learn the ways of Christ through online communities, spiritual direction, monastic oblate groups, emerging church or new monastic communities, or other alternative forms of community.

Because mysticism is ultimately about relationship rather than religiosity, it will find a home in the hearts of all types of Christians—Protestant or Catholic, monastic or secular, lay or ordained, and across the spectrum of ethnic, sexual, and gender identities. Increasingly, the mark of a Christian mystic will be less about their affiliation with the institution (or lack thereof), and more about their willingness to embrace the transforming union of the Spirit in their lives, regardless of where they go to meet that Spirit or to find community with others.

The mysticism of the future will continue to emphasize the importance of social and communal expressions of spirituality, including the spirituality of seeking justice for all people. Many twentieth-century mystics were marked by and remarkable for their emphasis on the relationship between mysticism and social justice. Although this pairing has roots from far earlier in Christian history—Quakers, for example, have long recognized an essential connection between mystical spirituality and efforts to make the world a better place—the twentieth century represented a blossoming of what Richard Rohr calls "action and contemplation"—the recognition that interior spirituality and external work to foster greater mercy and justice intimately depend on each other.

Mystics, scholars of mysticism, and other spiritual leaders like Howard Thurman, Simone Weil, Desmond Tutu, Dorothee Soelle, Pedro Arrupe, Mother Teresa, Kenneth Leech, and many others have expressed a firm understanding of the intimate bond between inner transformation and the outer work for peace, justice, the dismantling of oppression, and the commitment to create a more truly beloved community.

Given the larger trend among many Christians to make social justice a central element of their religious identity as Christians, it's reasonable to assume that mystical and contemplative Christians, likewise, will continue to express their intimacy with God not only in terms of prayer, meditation and contemplation, but also in terms of building community, supporting those in need, and advocating for needed reforms in the church and in the world at large.

The mysticism of the future will increasingly be open to the cross-pollination of wisdom and practices across the lines separating religious and faith traditions. Such ecumenical and interfaith openness began with earnest in the twentieth century. Mystics and contemplatives like Evelyn Underhill, Simone Weil, Valentin Tomberg, Bede Griffiths, Sara Grant, Abhishiktananda, Tilden Edwards, Anthony deMello, Beatrice Bruteau, Beverly Lanzetta, Valerie Brown, and many others have recognized the blessings that ensue when contemplative Christians interact in positive and constructive ways with the teachings and practices of other faith traditions. Not all contemplative Christians sense a call to this kind of interspiritual or interreligious exploration—indeed, plenty of Christians choose not to blend Christian and non-Christian spiritualities. And among those who do sense a need to integrate Christian mysticism with non-Christian spirituality, there are differing perspectives to what extent such spiritualities and practices can in fact be integrated or "mixed," as well as concerning the ethics of appropriation of others' traditions. We are in the midst of a period of tremendous cultural encounter and exchange, no doubt brought about by the emergence of global transportation (like jet planes) and global forms of communication (the internet), not to mention the increasing flow of immigrants and refugees around the world, bringing religious and cultural diversity into just about every major city, at least here in North America (but this kind of diversity is happening globally as well). As more and more Christians encounter other faith traditions and spiritualities, it only stands to reason that such encounters will shape how Christian spirituality in general (and mysticism in particular) will continue to evolve. This is such an enormous topic with wide implications for mysticism, culture, and Christianity as a whole, that we'll take a closer look at it in the next chapter.

Will these trends continue to shape the evolution of Christian mysticism? And what other trends might emerge in addition to these? The answers to these questions remain shrouded in the mystery of the future. In the meantime, we can only live a mystical life here and now, in the present moment. If you are drawn to explore mystical spirituality for yourself, I encourage you to see the past as the source of great wisdom, the future as an invitation into hope, and the present moment as the sacred center where you are called into ever-deepening intimacy with Love-with-a-capital-*L*: right here and right now. If we continue to cultivate our response to divine love in the present, we can trust that mysticism will continue to evolve as it should: under the guidance of the Spirit who is that Love.

CHAPTER SIX

Prays Well with Others: Mystical Christianity and Interspirituality

Anyone who loves God is known by God.
—Apostle Paul (1 Corinthians 8:3, adapted)

Christians need to think "Nothing" when they call God "Love."
Buddhists need to think "Love" when they say "Emptiness." This
will at least wake us up to the fact that words must always fall
short of the ineffable.
—David Steindl-Rast, OSB

In the last chapter we speculated about how Christian mysticism may evolve in the future, including becoming increasingly open to the contemplative and mystical wisdom that can be found in other faith traditions. Numerous Christian mystical and contemplative writers have already undertaken this kind of interspiritual exploration. And it's nothing new, either. Christianity itself emerged by incorporating the culture, language, and philosophies of its time. In the earliest centuries of the Christian era, Clement of Alexandria and his student Origen wrote about Christian spirituality using the language and philosophy of the Greek mystery religions to illustrate their points. Christian spirituality in the Celtic lands of Ireland and Scotland shows clear evidence of being influenced by the Druids. Later mystics like

Augustine of Hippo (late fourth/early fifth centuries) and Pseudo-Dionysius the Areopagite (ca. 500) relied on pagan Greek philosophy, particularly Neoplatonism, to help them articulate the Christian mysteries. Subsequent mystics like Ramon Lull (thirteenth century) and Luis de Leon (sixteenth century) explored wisdom from Sufism and the Kabbalah, respectively, in order to explain their Christian spirituality. Granted, most of these writers were not interspiritual in the way we would understand it—they often would write about non-Christian spirituality primarily to attack or refute it. But they do represent a recognition among Christian mystics that the way of Jesus Christ does not exist in a vacuum.

Meanwhile, some scholars have even speculated that two of the greatest mystics, Teresa of Ávila and John of the Cross, were influenced by the Kabbalah.[1]

Finally, the twentieth century emerged as the great age for the encounter between Christianity and other spiritual traditions. Ours is an age that has approached interfaith spirituality with a more open and generous spirit, hoping simply to encounter those with a different perspective in a genuine desire to deepen wisdom and understanding, and foster a better world.

In the 1960s the Vatican II Council held by the Catholic Church issued a statement encouraging Catholics to respect what is good, true, and beautiful in other faiths. But individual Christians, many of whom embrace a mystical approach to their faith, had already been fostering dialogue and even shared practices across religious lines. Thomas Merton had been interested in eastern spirituality since his days as a student at Columbia University, and continued to write about Zen Buddhism and other non-Christian spiritualities until his untimely death in 1968. Others answered the call of interfaith dialogue and traveled from the Christian lands of their birth to other parts of the world. Bede Griffiths, Jules Monchanin, Henri LeSaux (who took the name Abhishiktananda), and Sara Grant are just four examples of European Christians who relocated to India and began to explore ways to integrate Christian spirituality with Hinduism. William Johnstone, an Irish Jesuit, admits in his autobiography that he went to Japan as young Jesuit to convert the Buddhists, only to find that *he* was the one to change, thanks to his encounter with Zen. Other Christians who have found insight if not enlightenment from their encounter with Buddhism include Tilden Edwards, Hugo Enomiya-Lassalle, Elaine MacInnes, Mary

Jo Meadow, Rueben L. F. Habito, Susan J. Stabile, Bieke Vandekerckhove, and Paul Knitter.

There are so many other examples of contemplative and mystical Christians who explore how other religions, spiritualities, and wisdom traditions can "meet" the mysteries of Christianity in a heart-centered, expansive way. Raimon Panikkar devoted much of his career as a theologian to plumbing the points of affinity between Christianity, Hinduism, and other faiths. Barbara A. Holmes has written about the connections between African religion and Christianity; Valentin Tomberg has explored the affinity between Christian mysticism and Western esotericism, Hermeticism and magic; Richard Twiss and Steven Charleston explored ways in which Christianity can be in constructive dialogue with Native American spirituality. The list goes on.

The question that emerges: Why would mystical spirituality that is anchored in one particular tradition (in this case, Christianity) be so congenial for cross-fertilization with the wisdom, teachings and practices of other mystical and spiritual traditions from around the world?

But before we try to answer that question, perhaps we need to ask, What makes Christian mysticism so, well, *Christian?*

What is the difference between it and all the other mysticisms out there—including Kabbalah (Jewish mysticism), Sufism (Islamic mysticism), Vedanta (Hindu mysticism), Zen (Buddhist mysticism), along with countless forms of shamanism and indigenous mysticism?

On the surface, it's an easy enough question to answer: Christian mysticism is the interior wisdom tradition of Christianity, so it has to do with Jesus, and Jesus's followers down through the ages.

But while that is certainly true historically speaking, how does the Christian expression of mysticism maintain its unique identity today, in the world of global travel, the internet, and an increasing recognition that we are all one family? Today we live in an era where different faiths and traditions coexist in close cultural proximity. More and more Christians, and not just those who identify as mystics or contemplatives, are practicing yoga or studying Zen or learning the Kabbalah, blurring the line that separates Christian mysticism from mysticism in general. Christians who are more theologically and politically conservative are not always happy about this multicultural world we live in. In fact, many Christians fear or reject mysticism—even Christian mysticism—precisely because they see it as a point of vulnerability through which foreign ideas and spiritual practices are infiltrating what they see as "the one true faith." Another ethical issue, that perhaps does not get enough attention, is the matter of cultural appropriation. Especially when people with privilege (like educated whites) mine other religious, spiritual, or cultural traditions for their own enjoyment, without regard for the concerns or challenges faced by the communities whose wisdom they are "borrowing," what seems to emerge is a kind of spiritual consumerism—which may be entertaining for those doing the consuming, but leaves significant ethical and justice-related questions unanswered. Spirituality, like any other cultural treasure, is not simply there for our plunder. If we want to engage with other traditions, we have a moral obligation to do so with humility, respect, and care for those cultures and communities whose wisdom we are seeking.

MYSTICISM IN THE GLOBAL VILLAGE

In our postmodern, multicultural age, people have unprecedented access to many different religious and spiritual traditions. While some may ignore this and choose to express their faith by adhering strictly to one religious path, many others experience an understandable desire to find common ground and shared values with those who come from other parts of the world. Many Christians today, while retaining a sense of themselves as followers of Jesus and practicing members of the faith that bears his name, nevertheless choose to explore the wisdom of other traditions, from Sufism to Tibetan Buddhism, Hasidic Judaism to Wicca, Shinto to Taoism. For what it's worth, I believe this interspiritual trend can be a good and beautiful thing. The more we see ourselves as members of a single global community, the more hope we have for peace and shared prosperity—especially when we approach this encounter with humility, respect, and genuine care for others.

Indeed, mysticism has become a code word for whatever it is that unites all religions, despite their cultural differences. As my dear friend and author Darrell Grizzle put it succinctly, "Mysticism is that which enabled the Dalai Lama and Thomas Merton to meet in the 1960s and to recognize each other as brothers."[2] Such sentiments suggest that mysticism may be the best hope for cultivating a true spirit of peace and goodwill among religions.

Some enthusiastic mysticism boosters insist that, despite the cultural trappings that separate one religion from another, all mysticism is essentially the same. Consider this quotation from S. Abhayananda, the author of *History of Mysticism: The Unchanging Testament*:

> Scholars may imagine that a Buddhist experiences one thing, a Vedantist another, and so forth; but one who has experienced It, whether a Sufi, Christian, or Hindu, knows that It is the final Truth, the only One. There are not different Unitys, one for each sect or denomination; there is only one One, and it is That which is experienced by Christians, Buddhists, Hindus, and Sufis alike. It should be obvious that, if there is such a thing as Unity, and if It can be experienced, then the experience must be the same for all; since Unity, by its very definition, by its very nature, is one.[3]

Not everyone agrees with Swami Abhayananda's assessment. Some Christians might argue that Christianity presents a distinct and unique understanding of truth that is "higher" than the Unity of which he speaks. Others, both Christian and non-Christian, agree with him, and may even go so far as to declare that religion itself is the real culprit since it creates division between people and cultures, unlike spirituality and mysticism, which unites us. Still others might decide that, while it is a nice idea to assume that all mystical experiences have the same unifying center, we really have no way of knowing that this is true. For all we know, what Swami Abhayananda calls "Unity" may be nothing like the unitive encounters Christian mystics like Teresa of Ávila or Meister Eckhart experienced. Can one person ever really know what another person experiences? And even though the descriptions of mystical experience may seem to have many overlapping or common themes or language, when we factor in that different cultures have different languages, different syntax, different worldviews, and different ways of understanding categories like truth or goodness or beauty, it's easy to see just how impossible it is to truly judge just how similar (or different) the many wisdom traditions of the world really are.

A helpful principle to bear in mind when considering the similarities or differences between mystical Christianity and other wisdom traditions comes from Jesus's instruction in the Gospel of Matthew to his followers not to judge (7:1). If you prefer to think of all types of mysticism as pointing to a single source of spiritual unity, beware of the temptation to judge others who seem more conscious of the differences between cultures and religions. If you prefer to focus on what is distinctive and unique about Christian spirituality (or, for that matter, any other religious or spiritual tradition), resist the urge to dismiss those who are eager to see an underlying mystical unity. Perhaps both views are important. Perhaps we need both a commitment to preserve what is unique and beautiful in each particular path, along with visionaries who seek to create bridges of understanding and harmony that reach across the lines that separate belief systems.

I personally love the idea that way deep down, all spiritualities are one, even though it's dangerous to simply gloss over real religious differences and pretend they don't exist. That kind of thinking can pave the way for one group or position to dominate the others, whether intentionally or not.

No matter how much we want to celebrate the unity of all positive spiritual paths, it's important to resist the temptation to gloss over the real differences that distinguish mystical Christianity from all the other types of mysticism—Buddhist, Jewish, Hindu, and so on. For example, we can make this statement: "Mysticism is the path to union with God." For contemplative Christians this seems self-evident, and perhaps it would also be affirmed by other mystical seekers such as Sufis and Kabbalists. But in some traditions this language tends to carry subtly different meanings: "union with God" is understood as being identical with God, rather than being a partaker of God's divine nature or in nondual communion with God. In other words, no matter how deeply the sense of union may be experienced, the Christian tradition maintains that a distinction always remains between creator and creature. Without that distinction, love is impossible: for love requires both a lover and a beloved. To Christian mystics, it is a joyful thing not to be identical with God, whereas other mystics from other paths might see the Christian perspective as a form of illusion or error.

Who's right, and who's wrong? Is this just a paradox beyond the limits of language and comprehension, or is it a meaningful distinction that we need to honor, in order to be honest and authentic about our real cultural differences?

C. S. Lewis, even though he himself declaimed that he wasn't a mystic, recognizes the challenges that arise when we try on a superficial level to insist that all mysticism is the same:

I do not at all regard mystical experience as an illusion. I think it shows that there is a way to go, before death, out of what may be called "this world"—out of the stage set. Out of this; but into what? That's like asking an Englishman, "Where does the sea lead to?" He will reply "To everywhere on earth, including Davy Jones's locker, except England." The lawfulness, safety, and utility of the mystical voyage depends not at all on its being mystical—that is, on its being a departure—but on the motives, skill, and constancy of the voyager, and on the grace of God. The true religion gives value to its own mysticism; mysticism does not validate the religion in which it happens to occur.

I shouldn't be at all disturbed if it could be shown that a diabolical mysticism, or drugs, produced experiences indistinguishable (by introspection) from those of the great Christian mystics. Departures are all alike; it is the landfall that crowns the voyage. The saint, by being a saint, proves that his mysticism (if he was a mystic; not all saints are) led him aright; the fact that he has practised mysticism could never prove his sanctity.[4]

Deeply conservative theologically, C. S. Lewis believed in Christian exceptionalism—that Christianity is the one true faith, and all others are to a greater or lesser extent erroneous. Whether or not you agree with his point of view, there's value and logic behind his argument about mysticism. So what if all mystical experiences are the same? If one is induced by drugs, another by the grace of God, yet another by the self-delusional capacity of the mind, and perhaps even another by a deceptive spirit who is the enemy of love, then we must wrestle with the idea that, even if they "feel" the same, not all forms of mysticism are necessarily equal.

To explore this challenging question further, I want to offer what I suspect is the most whimsical metaphor you'll ever come across in regard to mysticism, a metaphor that might help us to sort all this out.

MYSTICISM IS LIKE TOFU

Since I believe mysticism can be an important doorway to interreligious understanding, I'd like to suggest a new way of thinking about it—or at least a different way of thinking about Christian mysticism. Bear with me and see if this metaphor makes sense for you.

Mysticism is a lot like tofu.

Seriously.

When you cook with tofu, it has a fascinating tendency to adopt the flavor of whatever you cook with it. Scrambled tofu, tofu curry, even barbecue tofu (yes, I'm from the South) all taste more like scrambled eggs or curry or barbecue than like tofu. Likewise, mysticism thoroughly and completely adopts the flavor and identity of whatever wisdom tradition it inhabits. Thus, Christian mysticism has an entirely different cultural and religious identity from, say, Vedanta or Zen.

Granted, tofu is tofu, regardless of the recipe you use it in. Mysticism is mysticism, regardless of the religious or cultural context (that is, all mysticism seeks unity with the ground of all being). In that sense, there is an essential unity of mystical experience that crosses religious boundaries. But if you've ever eaten plain, uncooked tofu, you know just how bland it is. If tofu's strength lies in its ability to adapt to whatever dish it's cooked in, its weakness lies in its lack of defining taste or texture of its own. Likewise, a "pure" mysticism might sound nice in theory—an experience of unity or ecstasy, unencumbered by religious dogma—but in practice, the beauty of mysticism rests in how it manifests unity in a distinct, particular way.

Christian mysticism, after all, is a compound noun—but the proper noun *Christian* also functions as an adjective that modifies *mysticism*. Other forms of mysticism can be understood in a parallel way. The adjective that modifies *mysticism* often reveals what a mystic experiences union with, in that particular tradition. Nature mysticism is a kind of spirituality that seeks or fosters the experience of nondual oneness with nature. Buddhist mysticism seeks oneness with the Buddha—although Buddhists would probably say the point is oneness with one's inner Buddha. So it is with Christian mysticism: the goal here is union with Christ, Christ whom we believe can be found within, but the Christ within is the same as "the" Christ—the second person of the triune God.

Therefore, Christian mysticism is more than just a kind of "pure" mysticism with a little bit of Jesus mixed in. For Christians, this is actually a unique, distinctive, and beautiful expression of God's love and truth. Conservative Christians are likely to believe it is the only expression of such truth, and even more liberal Christians might think it is the best possible way to God. But even if you regard Christianity as no better (or worse) than any other wisdom tradition, I hope you'll recognize that Christian mysticism cannot just be reduced to other kinds of mysticism. There are important ways in which the Christian mystery is unique among world religions—and world mystical traditions.

This is why any serious exploration of Christian mysticism has to look at the nuts and bolts of Christianity as a faith in order to do justice to our topic. Immersing yourself in the world of mystical Christianity means something far beyond just learning to meditate: Christian mysticism incorporates meditation (and contemplation, and prayer) specifically as ways to foster a relationship with the Holy Trinity. This doesn't mean that it is just about thinking pious Christian thoughts. Rather, it means exploring an embodied way of life that is shaped by the love and wisdom of Jesus's teachings—a love that finds expression within the spiritual community that mystical Christianity recognizes as one with Christ—literally, Christ's body.

To truly explore the splendor of Christian mysticism requires a willingness to dive into the great Christian mysteries, like the Trinity and the incarnation—central elements of the Christian story that remain mysteries, which means they transcend and defy logical comprehension. There's no way to avoid it. The mystery of a God who became flesh, or of a God whose very nature consists of loving relationships, forms the heart of what is distinctive about the Christian path. And while these mysteries—as teachings, or part of the story—are not the same thing as the experience of the presence of God, or union with God, they shape and form how that experience is understood and integrated into our lives.

I've occasionally interacted with people who seem to think that Christian mysticism refers to some sort of diluted or heretical form of Christianity. In other words, they might say that adding mysticism to Christianity somehow diminishes it. This line of thinking distorts both mysticism and Christianity. It's important to keep in mind that Christian mysticism existed before the word *mysticism* came along as a way of describing this type of spirituality. The great mystics throughout history have thought of themselves as Christians rather than as mystics—for Christian mystics, mysticism is not a substitute for, or deviation from, "orthodox" Christianity, but rather simply a way of embodying the fullness of the Christian story—not as an abstract set of teachings, but as a living expression of who Jesus was and what he taught. In the mystics, Jesus lives on, and his message lives on as well.

CHRISTIANITY AND THE MYSTICAL TRADITION

Here are three essential elements that distinguish Christian mysticism from other types of mystical spirituality. I hope that by being candid about the unique ways Christian mysticism is different from other mystical traditions, this can contribute to meaningful understanding.

My purpose in writing this is not to judge other spiritual paths, but simply to explain what is unique about this particular flavor of tofu.

Mystical Christianity, like Christianity in general, begins with a unique understanding of God—not only that God is a Trinity (a single deity who mysteriously consists of three distinct persons), but also that God took on human form in the person of Jesus of Nazareth, the Christ, the anointed one. The incarnation and the Trinity form the core of Christian mysticism, because they are the core of Christianity, and they provide the foundation for the mystical sense that God is Love, and we are called into union with that love.

The wisdom of Christian mystics, their teachings and practices, all point to the beauty of divine love and the destiny of the contemplative path as leading to union with God—but it is a union anchored in love, which means the creature and the creator always enjoy the capacity to love and be loved in their ever-blossoming bond. The mystical life, whether here or in eternity, culminates in a loving communion, where mystical unity with God manifests as an eternal loving embrace.

Mystical Christianity embraces the story of faith found in Scripture and tradition. I've made the case that mysticism is a story, and the story of Christian mysticism begins with the Bible, and continues with the lives and teachings of the great mystics and contemplatives down through the centuries. Within Christianity there are many different ideas about how to interpret the Bible, but as a whole the Christian community recognizes the

Bible as the foundational story of the faith. Christian mystics, therefore, do not seek to rewrite the Bible, although they may understand and interpret it in ways that differ from other Christians. Nor does mysticism imply that we must be fundamentalists, or that we cannot read scripture with a critical eye, challenging problems in the Bible such as sexism, homophobia, or the acceptance of slavery. Christian mysticism makes room for an honest and critical way of understanding the Bible. That being said, the basic message is simply this: we live in a universe created out of love by a loving God, and this loving God continues to seek engagement with us even when we resist or reject love; Jesus represents the mystery of divine love in human form, and offers the supreme expression of that love through his death and resurrection, and upon leaving earthly life sent us his Spirit to guide and love us from now until the end of time. Christian mystics anchor their experience of God within, and not in opposition to, this overflowing fountain of wisdom.

Mystical Christianity emphasizes communion and relationship. Some of the world's great mystical traditions seem to be oriented toward what the third-century philosopher Plotinus called "the flight of the alone to the Alone," implying that mysticism involves a solitary quest for individual enlightenment. While Christian forms of mysticism often endorse this kind of personal effort, a far more dominant quality in the Christian tradition emphasizes community, derived from a central teaching of Jesus: "Love your neighbor as yourself." Like Christianity in general, Christian mysticism is not a do-it-yourself project, but rather like an invitation to a dance, where God is the gracious host and everyone finds joy in dancing together.

ANCHORED IN CHRIST, AND OPEN TO ALL

We began this chapter looking at how, throughout the history of Christianity, the contemplatives and mystics have displayed an unusual openness to the wisdom of non-Christian philosophy and religion. From its beginning Christian mysticism had an intuitive recognition of the way in which mysticism is a form of unity that transcends religious difference. It's important to keep in mind that, at some point, Christian mysticism can evolve into something different if it embraces values or beliefs that are at odds with the Christian story. That's not to say that mystics and contemplatives should not be engaged in interreligious exploration or even interspiritual practices. On the contrary, I believe this movement toward deepening our own faith by learning the wisdom of others is one of the great movements of the Holy Spirit in our time.

Speaking strictly of mysticism in the broad sense of the word, no absolutely clear distinction can be drawn between Christian and non-Christian ways of exploring the mysteries. As long as we acknowledge that mysticism is, at its heart, about deep and profound mysteries that cannot be put into words, we can (and, perhaps, should) acknowledge that it is precisely in mystical silence where people of different faiths and different wisdom traditions can relate to each other—not in a spirit of competition or hostility, but in a genuinely open, compassionate, and respectful manner.

In the early 1950s, Howard Thurman, himself one of the great mystics of the twentieth century, preached a series of sermons on the mystics whom he described as "men who have walked with God" (I trust if Thurman were alive today, he would speak more inclusively, saying, "*people* who have walked with God"); among the mystics he celebrated were famous Christians like Meister Eckhart and Saints Augustine and Francis—but he also considered figures like Mahatma Gandhi (Hindu), Plotinus (Pagan), Lao-Tse (Taoist) and the Buddha. Thurman understood that wisdom has no copyright and cannot be limited to just one culture or story or religion. We who seek to drink deep from the wells of mystical spirituality today can learn from Thurman's example. We can learn from all the great mystics of the world, and we can even explore ways to integrate spiritual practices from other faith traditions in ways that are not appropriative, are respectful of the traditions, and are gifts the tradition offers to others. This is the heart of the word *interspirituality*, which invites us beyond merely learning about different traditions, to engaging in practices from other traditions as part of our own faith journey.

Not all Christians feel called to interfaith exploration and interspirituality, which is perfectly fine. But some Christians are. This is not a book about interfaith dialogue or interspirituality, so the focus will remain on mysticism within the context of the Christian story. But for those who seek ways of wisdom offered in other traditions and or grounded in your own, I want to encourage you, as a seeker, to trust your own heart on the call and direction. As Bede Griffiths and Howard Thurman and so many other great mystics of our time have shown, interspiritual exploration does not dilute our relationship with Christ—it can deepen it even as it honors the wisdom of other traditions.

CHAPTER SEVEN

To the Least of These: The Social Dimension of Christian Mysticism

For where two or three are gathered in my name,
I am there among them.
—Jesus (Matthew 18:20)

All mystic charisms are worthless compared to the love of God.
They are as a string of pearls adorning a hungry infant who does
not heed the pearls but only wants his mother's breast.
—Macarius the Egyptian

It is the nature of the human mind to express thought; and in a similar vein, it is the nature of the human heart to express love (and other emotions or passions). Some might even suggest that the thoughts that make up our mental consciousness, and the love that expresses our emotional awareness, originate in the human spirit, and the physical body—including the brain and the heart—does not so much *generate* our thoughts and emotions as *transmit* them from their origin within our soul. However, this way of seeing poses dangers—because it could imply that the body and soul are somehow essentially different, like a driver is essentially different from the car they operate. But if we can avoid the temptation to see the mind and the spirit as a duality, then recognizing that the spirit is the fount from which our being flows, and the body is the material expression of that being, can be a nuanced way of understanding what it means to be human, at least spiritually speaking.

But if we consist of a thinking mind and a loving heart, then what is the appropriate relationship between them? Does the mind serve the heart, or vice versa? Do we think in order to love more fully, or do we love in order to enjoy more sublime thought? Or is any suggestion of a hierarchy in itself a flawed way of understanding the mystery of being human?

While this may come across as an abstract problem, it points to another principle even more relevant to our exploration of mystical Christianity. Love is the key to *relationship*—whether a relationship with God, or with other creatures, or even with one's own self. Thought, by contrast, is a key to *understanding*—our capacity to make sense of life and our place in it.

This seems to relate very much to a story in the Bible, where Jesus and his disciples are visiting the home of two sisters, Mary and Martha. As was the custom of the time, Martha immediately busied herself with the tasks necessary to serve her guests, such as preparing a meal. Mary, meanwhile, flouts the gendered expectations of that culture and sits down with Jesus, clearly wanting to learn from him just as his disciples were attending to his every word.

This annoys Martha, but rather than confronting her sister, she asks Jesus if it bothered him that Mary wasn't helping her. His answer was probably not what she was looking for. "Martha, Martha, you are worried and distracted by many things; there is need of only one thing. Mary has chosen the better part, which will not be taken away from her."[1]

Many commentators have tried to unravel Jesus's cryptic words in this passage. Is he suggesting to Martha that she, too, should give up the limiting roles assigned to her by her gender? Or is he merely suggesting that spiritual learning takes precedence over the mundane cares of the body? (More than one scholar has wondered how Jesus would have responded if Martha simply sat down next to her sister, leaving the dinner uncooked and unserved!)

When I reflect on this passage, I'm reminded of the mind and the heart. Martha seems to be all heart here, motivated not by a need to understand but by a generous desire to serve her guests. Mary, on the other hand, seems to be more motivated by her mental desire to know than her emotional desire to relate.

Is Jesus saying that understanding is more important than love? If so, it seems to contradict his overall message, which is very much about love. "Love the Lord your God with all your heart, and with all your soul, and with all your mind." "Love your neighbor as yourself." And even the most challenging message of all: "Love your enemies."[2]

The mystics in history have also offered different ways of understanding Mary and Martha. The fourteenth-century manual of contemplation *The Cloud of Unknowing* suggests that Mary represents the contemplative life while Martha symbolizes the active life. In other words, Mary stands for those who live in cloistered communities of monks or nuns, devoting their lives to prayer and meditation, while Martha represents those who live "in the world," with families and households and the ordinary responsibilities of secular life.

The Cloud of Unknowing was probably written by a monk, so it's no surprise that he clearly prefers Mary, and echoes the words of Jesus, that she has chosen "the better" part.

On the other hand, Teresa of Ávila in her mystical masterpiece *The Interior Castle* refuses to see one sister as somehow more exalted than the other. "Believe me, Martha and Mary must work together when they offer the Lord lodging. . . . How can Mary give Him anything, seated as she is at His feet, unless her sister helps her?"[3] For Teresa, whether Mary and Martha represent action and contemplation, or love and service, or whatever, the point is not who's right and who's wrong, but how much they need each other. Then again, Teresa also suggested that spiritual progress comes more from love than from understanding: "Remember: if you want to make progress on the path . . . the important thing is not to think much but to love much, and so to do whatever best awakens you to love."[4]

ALONE TO THE ALONE?

The pagan philosopher Plotinus described mysticism as "the flight of the alone to the Alone." This has a kind of romantic ring to it, but at least from a Christian perspective it is a deficient definition. A more truly Christian way of describing mysticism might be "the flight of the community to the Trinity." Both in terms of creature and Creator, the heart of the mystical life is not the insights of solitude, but the relationships formed by and through love.

This is not to suggest that there is no place for solitude in Christian mysticism. On the contrary, Jesus himself called those who wish to pray to enter "the inner room"—which has been traditionally interpreted to mean not so much a physical room (like a prayer closet) but an "interior" room within our bodies, in other words, the solitude of the heart.[5] There, perhaps, love and understanding can come together to form a singular bond with the God who first loves us.

There's more to mystical Christianity than just loving God more and better. "The second commandment is like the first," notes Jesus, implying that the mandate to love our neighbors is integrally related to the mandate to love God. Put it this way: when God loves us (which God does, unconditionally), we are asked not only to return the love to God, but also to "pay it forward" by loving others—other human beings, indeed other beings in general, angels and animals and plants as well as those who share our human nature.

When some of the earliest mystics in the Christian tradition—the desert mothers and fathers—retreated into wilderness places to live as hermits, alone for God, one of the leading bishops of the church, Basil of Caesarea (now known as St. Basil the Great), had one question for them: "If you live all alone, whose feet shall you wash?" His reference, of course, is to the Last Supper as described in the Gospel of John, where Jesus humbly washed the feet of all his friends, and then commanded them to go do the same—footwashing serving as a metaphor and symbol for care and service.[6]

Yes, Jesus instructed us to enter our inner room to pray in secrecy and solitude, but he also told a parable about the end of time, when those who are welcome into heaven will be praised for how they fed the hungry, offered hospitality to strangers, cared for the sick and ministered to those in prison. Meanwhile, others were *not* invited to the heavenly banquet, because they failed to do these caring things! As Jesus summarizes the work of service led by love, he says, "Whatever you did for one of the least of these brothers and sisters of mine, you did for me."[7]

The more we reflect on the teachings of Jesus, the clearer it becomes: the spirituality he endorses is not an "alone-to-Alone" mysticism, but rather a mystical embrace of one another as held together by the love of God.

In the Gospel of Luke (17:21) Jesus is quoted as making a comment about the reign of God, but it gets translated in two rather different ways. Consider this same verse as translated by the King James Version, and the more contemporary New Revised Standard Version:

KJV: "For, behold, the kingdom of God is within you."

NRSV: "For, in fact, the kingdom of God is among you."

What's going on here? Is the kingdom of God found inside us (like the inner room of Matthew 6:6), or among us (like the compassionate caring found in Matthew 25)? The Greek word at play here is ἐντὸς (*entos*), which can be translated either way. In Matthew 23:26, this same word is used to describe the inside of a cup, but here in Luke 17 scholars recognize that Jesus is talking about more than just the interior of a single person: it's our *collective* interior where the reign (presence) of God is to be found.

As the particle and wave are both elements of light, Christ is both within us and among us. Mary finds Christ within, Martha finds Christ without (among). And even if we allow Jesus to say that Mary has chosen "the better" part, it's not meant to dismiss Martha's choice, but merely to suggest that if we want to find (and serve) Christ among people, we had better be paying attention to how we find and love Christ within us as well.

Mystics have recognized throughout history that the most sublime joys of union with God exist hand in hand with a more humble (but no less exalted) life of service and care for others. Most mystics have recognized that, following the teaching of Matthew 25, when we care for others, we care for Christ. Within monastic tradition this is made explicit in the Rule of Saint Benedict, which observes the monastic practice of offering hospitality to travelers and visitors: "All guests who present themselves are to be welcomed as Christ."[8] Benedict appeals to Matthew 25 to drive home his point.

From ancient times to today, mystics have been on the forefront of movements to care for their fellow human beings, often by leading social reform movements or other works of service and care. In her book *Mysticism*, Evelyn Underhill describes mystics as often embodying practical roles in society, as artists, teachers, social reformers, and even political leaders, providing examples, including the fifteenth-century mystic St. Catherine of Genoa, who, "side by side with [her] ecstatic life, fulfilled the innumerable duties of her active vocation as hospital matron and spiritual mother of a large group of disciples."[9]

More recently, the twentieth-century philosopher-mystic Simone Weil combined her love for Christ (surprising because of her background as a Jewish agnostic) with an uncompromising commitment to political activism, supporting workers and trade unionists as they fought for better conditions in the years leading up to World War II. A generation later, Mother Teresa of Calcutta devoted her life to caring for some of the poorest people on earth, while holding on to a deeply apophatic spirituality that only become obvious to people upon the publication of her personal writings after her death. In America, perhaps the greatest mystic/activist of recent times was Howard Thurman, the grandson of an American slave whose distinguished career as a Baptist minister and college chaplain was built on a rich and deeply contemplative inner life. In his masterpiece *Jesus and the Disinherited*, Thurman's meditation on the clear parallels between Jesus's experience living in a land occupied by Roman legions and the experience of Blacks in racist America, he makes this elegantly simple declaration: "Sincerity in human relations is equal to, and the same as, sincerity to God."[10] Perhaps we can interpret "sincerity" as *authenticity* or *meaning/purpose* or even simply love. His words suggest our responsibility to God and our responsibility to each other is in fact the same responsibility.

The list can go on of mystics and contemplatives who have understood how a commitment to intimacy with God both inspires and requires an equal commitment to healthy relationships with our fellow humans. Jesuit activist Gregory Boyle's book *Tattoos on the Heart* tells of his years serving current and former gang members in some of the most impoverished neighborhoods of Los Angeles—and he repeatedly quotes the mystics of the Christian tradition to underscore the spirituality that impels his activism. Dorothee Soelle, a noted German theologian and activist, wrote a book of mystical theology called *The Silent Cry: Mysticism and Resistance*—where the title illustrates the unity between spirituality and activism. And the popular spiritual author Richard Rohr created a ministry called the Center for Action and Contemplation, saying that the most important word in the title of his organization is *and*—pointing to his understanding that mystical spiritual requires an engagement with caring for others (and vice versa).

To fully appreciate the relationship between mysticism and social concerns, it's important to have a broad understanding of mysticism: not all socially engaged mystics will look like the visionary writers associated with classical mysticism, most of whom lived cloistered lives in convents or monasteries. The mystics who truly can inspire us with their contemplative activism often may be what I would call "anonymous mystics," following Karl Rahner's idea of anonymous Christians, meaning those who live meaningful Christian lives without necessarily being actively involved in the institutional church.

Examples of such anonymous mystics might include Harriet Tubman, who devoted her life to liberating slaves and then fighting for the rights of Black Americans after the Civil War; Sojourner Truth, another abolitionist who also was an activist on behalf of the rights of women; and Pauli Murray, who devoted a lifetime as a lawyer to fighting both racism and sexism before becoming the first woman of color to be ordained an Episcopal priest. These individuals are all best known as activists, yet each one was informed by a deep intimacy with God that guided and inspired their work on behalf of others. While they might not have described "mystical experiences" similar to what Julian of Norwich or Teresa of Ávila reported, I suspect that is due to their humble reticence to make a show of their relationship with God—humility, of course, being long recognized as a mark of Christian spiritual maturity.

Two English spiritual theologians of recent times have beautifully articulated the essential unity of mysticism and community: Kenneth Leech and Rowan Williams, both priests and respected writers. Each had a keen understanding of contemplation and mysticism as essential to Christian spirituality, and both clearly saw that spirituality and activism were integral to each other.

Leech, in an essay called "Contemplation as a Subversive Activity" had this to say:

> Contemplation has a context: it does not occur in a vacuum. Today's context is that of the multinational corporations, the arms race, the strong state, the economic crisis, urban decay, the growing racism, and human loneliness. It is within this highly deranged culture that contemplatives explore the wastes of their own being. It is in the midst of chaos and crisis that they pursue the vision of God and experience the conflict which is at the core of the contemplative search. They become part of that conflict and begin to see into the heart of things.

The contemplative shares in the passion of Christ which is both an identification with the pain of the world and also the despoiling of the principalities and powers of the fallen world-order.[11]

Rowan Williams, Leech's contemporary, who served as the archbishop of Canterbury from 2002 to 2012, delivered a talk to a synod of Catholic bishops in Rome in 2008—the first time an Anglican archbishop had ever been invited to address such a body of Catholic leaders. Archbishop Williams chose to speak on contemplation:

> Contemplation is very far from being just one kind of thing that Christians do: it is the key to prayer, liturgy, art and ethics, the key to the essence of a renewed humanity that is capable of seeing the world and other subjects in the world with freedom—freedom from self-oriented, acquisitive habits and the distorted understanding that comes from them. To put it boldly, contemplation is the only ultimate answer to the unreal and insane world that our financial systems and our advertising culture and our chaotic and unexamined emotions encourage us to inhabit. To learn contemplative practice is to learn what we need so as to live truthfully and honestly and lovingly. It is a deeply revolutionary matter."[12]

Leech and Williams proclaim that contemplative prayer and spirituality involves more than just an ever-deepening relationship with God (although that is certainly central to the contemplative life). Contemplation has an essential quality of impelling us not only deep within where we encounter the God who lives in our hearts, but simultaneously it calls us outside of ourselves, where we meet the chaotic and conflicted world we live in, a world marked by racism, sexism, homophobia, transphobia, economic and political inequality, environment degradation, and numerous other problems, with the serene heart of a silent contemplative and the keen mind of a committed activist, dedicated to dismantling systems of injustice and oppression and serving all those who are in need. For each of them, contemplation and community are not two separate dimensions of the life of faith, but two essential qualities of true spirituality: as intimately connected as breathing in is connected to breathing out.

"Love God with all your heart . . . " and "Love your neighbor as yourself"—we begin to understand these are not two separate but equal mandates for the spiritual life: they are, in fact, the same command-ment. Pure contemplation may be breathing in, while service to others is the breathing out.

Some contemplatives and mystics, like Howard Thurman, Pauli Murray, Kenneth Leech, and Rowan Williams, demonstrate their love for neighbors as political activists, explicitly working for justice and reform. Others, like Gregory Boyle, Mother Teresa, and Catherine of Genoa embody the social dimension of mysticism through compassionate care for those in need. All of these "outbreaths" reveal ways to embed mysticism in human relationships—nor is it limited to service in just these ways. The spirituality of communal love can also be expressed in humble family life, in ethical work or business dealings, in volunteer efforts at church or in your neigh-borhood, and in creative expression for the greater good. Just as there is no one right way to pray, or one right way to embody intimacy with God, so too there are a variety of ways to embed a deep encounter with the divine in our life as human beings in relationship. What matters is not *how* you express the social dimension of your spirituality, simply that you respond in love and service.

One of the most consistent ways that mystics have expressed the social dimension of their spirituality is by writing about their journey into the love and intimacy of God. Let's close this chapter with a deeper look at the ways their words have been in service to others on the journey of contemplation.

SILENCE AND THE WORD

Many mystics have also been writers. While you don't have to be a writer to be a mystic, the mystics who shared their journeys are those likely to be remembered. Mystics come in many shapes and sizes and through meeting some of them through their writing, we get to read their words, centuries or even millennia later. There is a rich and vibrant diversity to the litera-ture of mysticism: poetry, prophecy, philosophy, prayers, autobiography, sermons, devotional writings, theological treatises, visionary and ecstatic utterances, and down-to-earth instructional writings. Again and again, the mystics write about what it means to be in relationship with God, and what it means to be a human being (both individually, and in relationship with one another).

Mystics write about prayer. They write about ecstasy and vision, about discipline and humility, about the nature of God and the divinity in nature. They write about finding God in the ordinary and finding the ordinary in the divine presence. They write about love in both human and divine terms and ways. And, as we'll see in chapter 10, the mystics often write about paradox, about ambiguities and discontinuities that lead us not to the logical certainty of the understanding mind, but to the hidden wisdom of the loving heart.

Why do they write? Surely some of the mystics write for themselves, their own impulse to more fully understand the mysteries that surround their encounter with the divine. But I suspect most mystics recognized that their writing would be read by others. Sometimes this is explicit (Teresa of Ávila was famous for complaining about having to write, as most of her writing was done either to satisfy the sisters of her order or the priests who were trying to make sense of her mystical experiences). Some mystical writings have a clear mission to teach others (*The Cloud of Unknowing* was written by an older monk for a younger brother he was mentoring; Walter Hilton's *The Scale of Perfection* was likewise written by a priest for a nun who had turned to him for spiritual guidance). Others may have less of an obvious purpose, but nevertheless composed with a reading audience in mind. In other words, the mystics wrote not to explore "the flight of the alone to the Alone," but as a way of supporting the community of those who sought intimacy with the Trinity.

And in the writings we meet surprising and even playful qualities. One recurring theme in much mystical writing is a compelling urge to *silence*—as if the words of the mystics are actually designed to undermine themselves, pointing beyond language to the wordless wisdom of deep contemplative stillness. Mystical literature therefore functions as a kind of ongoing dialogue between words and silence, language and meditation, symbolic speech and the emptiness that lies between and beyond all thought and emotion.

You do not need to be a writer to be a mystic, just as you do not need to be a social activist, a monk or a nun, or a theologian. But what all these roles have in common is that their deeply personal spirituality is expressed in a way that brings them back into relationship with others, through their shared words. To fall deeper in love with God means to fall ever more fully into the heart of love that always is giving itself away—back to God, and onward to our neighbors, our family and friends, and even our enemies. For it is in the flow of love that mystical and contemplative spirituality have their being.

CHAPTER EIGHT

Singing the Song of Songs: The Erotic Character of Mystical Christianity

Come, my beloved,
let us go forth into the fields,
and lodge in the villages;
let us go out early to the vineyards,
and see whether the vines have budded,
whether the grape blossoms have opened
and the pomegranates are in bloom.
There I will give you my love.
—The Song of Songs 7:11–12

Those who eat of me will hunger for more, and those who drink
of me will thirst for more.
—Sirach 24:21

Almost from the beginning of the Christian era, mystics, saints, theologians
and spiritual teachers have reflected on one of the most beautiful and poetic
writings of biblical Wisdom literature—the Song of Songs —to explore the
mystery of the love of God and how that love seeks intimacy with us, God's
human creatures. The Song of Songs, also known as the Song of Solomon
or the Canticle of Canticles, although called a "book," more accurately

might be called a poem or extended lyric; it's short—only eight chapters and barely over one hundred verses long. It makes up less than one-half of 1 percent of the entire Christian Bible and is one of two books in the Bible that never directly mentions God at all.

Taken at face value, the Song of Songs is a love poem—a deeply sensual, subtly erotic love poem. It describes, in beautiful and lyrical language, the dance of longing and joy as two young people seek the fulfillment of their deepest longing: union with each other.

So why, of all the spiritual and philosophical riches in Scripture, would the Song of Songs be the book that the mystics and many other God seekers turn to, again and again?

The answer may be simply this: since our relationship with God is ultimately bigger and deeper than human language and indeed the entire human mind can contain, we have to rely on metaphors and poetic imagery if we have any hope of putting the mystical life into words. The many mystics who turn to the Song of Songs to illustrate their relationship with God seem to be saying we need to rely on the abundance and fullness of human love—including the passion and physical intimacy of romantic love—if we have any hope to truly express the mysteries of union with divine love.

God's love is bigger than all earthly love, like the entire spectrum of light extends beyond the rainbow of human vision. But if we want to appreciate the splendor and mystery of light, we ought to begin, at least, by embracing all the light that we mortals can comprehend, and then from there extend our understanding of light into the "hidden" regions of light, including infrared and ultraviolet rays and beyond.

I say hidden because such light remains inaccessible to our eyes, but not beyond the mind and heart of God. Likewise in terms of mystical love, the "ultraviolet" and "infrared" dimensions remain hidden to us—or at least to our conscious awareness and understanding—even as they are fully known to God.

Infrared and ultraviolet light are truly *mystical* in the root meaning of the word: such light exists beyond our normal comprehension, and only becomes known to us through special technologies that make them "visible" in a way. When I was a child, blacklights were popular, at least among hippies and flower children: they emit ultraviolet light, invisible to the naked human eye, which make fluorescent items (like petroleum jelly, tonic water, and oddly enough, urine), emit an eerie luminescence visible to the human eye.

Maybe mysticism is not merely like tofu, but like *fluorescent* tofu. Mystical love is like ultraviolet light—hidden from ordinary human perception but capable of leaving telltale signs when viewed in a certain way or by using the right "technology." For mystics, the technology for this enhanced capacity to see is contemplative silence. A Wisdom poem like the Song of Songs overflows with "fluorescent love" that reveals its secrets when exposed to the attentive eye of silent contemplative adoration.

LOVE'S OVERWHELMING POWER

Divine love is powerful, infinitely so; and even mere human love, when expressed through the physical desire of sexuality and erotic yearning, is truly a dynamic force. Sexuality can overwhelm us like a tsunami: it unleashes the capacity for all-consuming ecstasy, obsession, jealousy, and anxiety, and can be as addictive as the most powerful of narcotics. For this reason, early seekers of the love of God—not only in Christianity, but in other traditions as well—began to regard human eroticism as a problem: a compelling distraction that could seduce a person away from the spiritual quest, trading away their yearning for God for the heady pleasures of physical intimacy.

Unfortunately, in Christianity, this morphed into an unhealthy duality: in which too many spiritual seekers regarded eros not merely as a distraction, but as a mistake; and when that combined with ideas circulating in the ancient world that the human body was inferior to the purity of the spirit, some drew the unfortunate conclusion that sexuality, even at its best, was sinful.

Thus you have Saint Augustine, a mystic himself who prior to becoming a Christian kept a mistress, apparently oblivious to how this kind of arrangement was demeaning to women. Then when he embraced the spiritual life, he confused the injustice of his privileged mistreatment of his partner with an erroneous idea that sexuality itself was at fault. He went on to argue that human sexuality was so stained that even married couples committed a venial (minor) sin when they made love. Unfortunately, Augustine, a spiritual genius in many other ways, foisted his unfounded and toxic misunderstanding on the Christian West, fostering a lasting legacy of shame around sexuality that, tragically, became widely embraced in Christendom.

Monks and nuns adopted a celibate life, eschewing sexual and romantic love because they wished to give themselves wholly to God. While in itself, there's nothing wrong with this choice, celibacy—tinged by the thought of St. Augustine—became interpreted through a dualistic lens that rejected sexuality not because it was potentially distracting, but because it was seen as inferior or even sinful to a "chaste" or sexless life given fully to God. This misunderstanding has bedeviled Christianity ever since, and influenced even those outside the cloister. Over the centuries, countless Christian people found their ability to enjoy the pleasures of physical intimacy compromised by the lie that sex—even in the context of committed lifelong love—is somehow contrary to God.

As for the mystics, even though so many of them were themselves celibate, they recognized something else about sexual and spiritual desire: in part thanks to the Song of Songs, mystics viewed romantic and erotic love through the lens of their own contemplative experience. Earthly, physical love—which we could say is represented by the red threshold of the spectrum—matters just as much to the fullness of light as the violet of ethereal or spiritual love. Take away the red, and the rainbow is incomplete. Without red, light itself is incomplete. Likewise, take away to rich and delicious joy of eros, and our capacity to understand the fullness of love—including spiritual or mystical love—becomes diminished.

God does not have a material body as we know it. Although Christians regard Jesus as fully human as well as divine, we only encounter Christ today in spiritual ways. We do not find unity with God in any kind of physical way, but when we envision divine union through the lens of romantic intimacy and sexual union, we are more fully able to appreciate and understand the scope and beauty of oneness with God's love. For those who are asexual or celibate by choice or circumstance, this understanding of mystical unity may be simply a metaphor or an imagined encounter. For those who are blessed with a loving bond with another, our understanding of union with God can be deepened in the light of when we make love. Through eros, we learn something about that "red" part of the spectrum of the mystery of love, which sheds light (pardon the pun) on the fullness of divine union—a love that transcends beyond the limits of what is "visible" to the human heart.

Erotic love alone cannot reveal to us the fullness of divine love, but neither can spiritual love alone. We need the entire spectrum. This is why celibate mystics from Origen to Bernard of Clairvaux to Teresa of Ávila and many others continually returned to meditate upon the wisdom of the Song of Songs. What they themselves may not have experienced physically, they meditated on. They celebrated romantic and erotic love because it spoke to a fully apprehended, complete "spectrum" of divine love.

Those of us who are *not* celibate can also find insight into mystical love by celebrating the beauty, power, and life-affirming joy of healthy erotic love. We know how powerful eros is, and hopefully if we are in healthy relationships, we also understand that the fullness of love requires more than just the pleasures of physical intimacy. But just because romantic love requires more than just sex does not make physical expressions of love inferior or incomplete or somehow wrong.

THE VITAMINS OF LOVE

We can think of sexuality as like an essential vitamin for healthy romantic love. It is not the only vitamin that a healthy marriage requires; in addition to vitamin "E" (eros), a sustainable human partnership requires vitamin "I" (intimacy), vitamin "A" (affection), vitamins "C1" and "C2" (caring and compassion), vitamins "F1" and F2" (friendship and fidelity), vitamin "V" (vulnerability), and vitamin "H" (honesty). Perhaps you can think of several others.

So how does this relate to the mystical life? While mystics and contemplatives seek unity with God, naturally that doesn't mean a physical or sexual bond—but it does imply an experience of yearning for God in our hearts and even our bodies, a longing that could be as passionate and consuming as beautiful erotic desire. We long for God, and we want to give ourselves fully to God. We want to be in relationship with God in joy and even ecstasy. Are we capable of giving God pleasure? That may be up for debate, but God is clearly capable of giving us pleasure. Because mysticism involves a yearning for relationship and unity, it is necessarily a coming together of human and divine, where on our part we certainly want the pleasure of God to fill *our* hearts, souls and bodies.

All of this encompasses the "erotic" dimension of the spiritual life. Notice that it touches not so much on the *physicality* of erotic love (although we may experience a sense of oneness even in our bodies), but it does very much touch on the *inner experience* of eros: of desire, yearning, passion, pleasure, excitement, intensity, and ecstasy available in the mystical relationship between human and divine.

And even though we do not physically make love with God, we do bring our entire selves into our intimacy with God—including our bodies, from head to toe and everything in between. When God promises divine love for us, it is a gift for our entire being; inner and outer, spirit and body, mind, and heart—all of us.

IMAGINING THE FULLNESS OF MYSTICAL LOVE

Hadewijch, a thirteenth-century poet and mystic, often described her experience of intimacy with God in deeply romantic and erotic language.

> So for the soul things go marvellously,
> While desire pours out and pleasure drinks,
> The soul consumes what belongs to it in love
> And sinks with frenzy into Love's fruition.
> So in love the loving soul has full success,
> When Love with love fully gives her love,
> Thus is the loving soul well fed by love alone,
> Where it enjoys sweet love.[1]

Three centuries later, St. Teresa of Ávila used even more explicitly sensual language to describe her mystical encounter with an angel, who penetrated her with divine love as if it were an arrow:

> It pleased the Lord that I should see this angel in the following way. He was not tall, but short, and very beautiful, his face so aflame that he appeared to be one of the highest types of angel who seem to be all afire. . . . In his hands I saw a long golden spear and at the end of the

iron tip I seemed to see a point of fire. With this he seemed to pierce my heart several times so that it penetrated to my entrails. When he drew it out, I thought he was drawing them out with it and he left me completely afire with a great love for God. The pain was so sharp that it made me utter several moans; and so excessive was the sweetness caused me by this intense pain that one can never wish to lose it, nor will one's soul be content with anything less than God. It is not bodily pain, but spiritual, though the body has a share in it—indeed, a great share. So sweet are the colloquies of love which pass between the soul and God that if anyone thinks I am lying I beseech God, in His goodness, to give him the same experience.[2]

The penetration, the heart on fire, the moaning, the excessive sweetness, the intense pain, the bodily nature of this experience—Teresa uses the same words lovers use when they describe the passion and power of their physical union, even though Teresa is speaking not of a sexual encounter but a deeply mystical one. For anyone who is invested in seeing spirituality and sexuality as necessarily at odds with each other, this passage might seem disturbing; such persons will insist that it must not be interpreted as "erotic" in any way. Yet anyone who is open minded and honest can see that there is clearly an erotic quality to Teresa's angelic encounter.

So many mystics down the ages have relied on the language of love, intimacy, and sometimes marriage to describe the boundless union of their encounter with God, that the term *bridal* mysticism is used—where the God-human relationship is likened to the love flowing between a groom and a bride. Because of traditional gender stereotypes, God, the divine lover, is given the role of the groom and so the human beloved is understood to be the bride, regardless of the mystic's gender identity. Along with Hadewijch and Teresa, other female bridal mystics include St. Gertrude the Great, Mechthild of Magdeburg, St. Catherine of Siena, St. Lutgard, St. Bridget of Sweden, and numerous others. Male contemplatives who also embodied this bridal mysticism include St. Bernard of Clairvaux, St. John of the Cross, John Ruusbroec, and others. What all these mystics, regardless of gender, have in common is the use of romantic and marital language and symbolism to describe the power and beauty of their relationship with God. Not all bridal mystics necessarily identify themselves as "brides" but some do, among them Catherine of Siena and Teresa of Ávila, both of whom were explicit in describing their relationship with God as a mystical marriage.

St. Bernard does not go quite so far, but he does rely on language of tender intimacy, speaking explicitly about kissing Christ on the lips as a metaphor for the sublime heights of mystical union.

Some mystics played with traditional gender roles as they plumbed the depths of divine union. In her book *Power, Gender and Christian Mysticism*, theologian Grace M. Jantzen points out at least one instance in the poetry of Hadewijch where she is "spectacularly reversing the usual gender stereotypes: God is Lady Love, while the soul, which as has been noted is always feminine in medieval writing, is the male knight."[3] In this instance, the female mystic explores gender fluidity both for God and for her own soul.

What are we to make of this erotic dimension of Christian mysticism? Is the Song of Songs still relevant as a key to understanding the promise and possibility of intimacy with God, even to the point of union with God? Living in the global West as we do at a time when Christianity has suffered the long heritage of its own dualistic discomfort with sexuality, many people have abandoned the Christian faith because they view it as neurotically hostile to sexuality in any form, outside of the traditional understanding of patriarchal marriage, wherein sex is acceptable only as a means for reproduction. For those who have left the church, conservative Christianity's opposition to queer sexuality, to ethical nonmonogamy, and to sexual activities that do not include the potential for reproduction (such as oral or anal sex) seems to offer little spiritual wisdom—but plenty of dogma, patriarchal control, and neurosis.

This, of course, begs the question: is there a place for a positive appreciation of human sexuality within mystical Christianity? While the mystics of centuries past typically functioned within a religious culture that only affirmed human sexuality in terms of reproduction, some scholars have speculated that a number of mystics may have been what we would today describe as queer. In his book *The Essential Gay Mystics*, Andrew Harvey identifies figures like Dag Hammarskjöld, Emily Dickinson, Gerard Manley Hopkins, and Juana Inés de la Cruz as mystics whose writing could be interpreted as indicating they were gay. Other figures in history whom scholars have speculated could have been gay or gender-nonconforming include Aelred of Rievaulx, Bernard of Clairvaux, Hildegard of Bingen, Joan of Arc and John of the Cross. Pauli Murray, a twentieth-century Black Episcopal priest and Christian activist who likely was nonbinary, did not identify herself as a mystic but clearly had a meaningful and vibrant spirituality, centered on the experience of a loving God. While it's important to bear in mind that persons in the past would not have understood sexuality and gender diversity the way we do today, it's also helpful to consider that the mystics, with their powerful spirituality grounded in an erotic intimacy with God, sometimes represented sexuality and gender in ways that placed them outside their cultural mainstream.[4] The takeaway, for contemplative Christians and other mystical seekers who stand outside the cisgender and heterosexual mainstream, is to remember that more than anything else, mysticism is about love—and the fullest expression of love naturally includes erotic and embodied sexuality and gender expression. For Christians who want their faith in Jesus to be consistent with the best human knowledge and understanding about sexuality and gender, at least some Christian mystics can be seen as inspiring exemplars of a spirituality where love always matters most of all.

Whether you identify as a Christian, a former Christian, or non-Christian, the mysticism of the Song of Songs offers hope both for Christianity as a whole and for mystical spirituality. Unfortunately, Christianity is not the only religion that has been affected by the tendency to see eros and spirituality as somehow opposed to each other. Since the joyful eroticism of the Song of Songs can help us make sense of the sublime beauty of mystical love, the Christian mystics have offered us a new way not only to think about contemplative spirituality, but also to think about sexuality and romantic love.

When we celebrate sexuality as an expression of love, then we recognize that eros is inherently good and beautiful. Religion and spirituality do not need to be opposed to sexuality. And Christians who embrace mysticism's commitment to love might be able to lead the way in helping Christianity as a faith tradition heal itself of its sad heritage of hostility toward eros.

Likewise, mysticism can suffer from its own dualism, and some critics of mystical spirituality decry the tendency among some mystics to retreat from the important social, political, and ethical conflicts of their time. In our day, one of the most important questions facing Christians (and all people) involves rethinking how we understand sexuality and gender. If mysticism is simply an escapist way of avoiding the issues of our day, then mysticism is limited in what it has to offer the human family as a whole. But by recognizing that many mystics utilized romantic and erotic imagery to deepen their appreciation of the love and presence of God, this opens the door for mystical Christians to lead the way in allowing mystical spirituality to inspire them to be more engaged and involved in the pressing issues of our time (including, for just one example, the important questions of how Christian communities can be affirming of LGBTQ persons).

The wisdom of the mystics creates room for us to affirm that love is good, and romantic and erotic love have their appropriate place. This position empowers us (mystic and otherwise) to proactively engage in bringing spiritual wisdom to bear on how to foster a more truly enlightened, welcoming, affirming, and eros-positive world—not just for mystics, not just for Christians, but for all people.

If you are interested in applying the wisdom of the mystics to your life, I encourage you to read the Song of Songs, and allow its frankly sensual and beautiful descriptions of earthly and erotic love wash over you. Enjoy it, exult in it, find delicious pleasure and delight in it. And take it into your prayer.

What can human love, even at its most erotic and physical, teach us about God's love for us, and our longing to respond to that divine love? Such a question, which cannot be answered easily or quickly, leads to a deep and vibrant area for spiritual exploration. Such exploration of love may take a lifetime (and beyond). Take your time and enjoy the pleasures of the search—a search that ultimately takes us to where we've been all along: in union with God.

CHAPTER NINE

The Mystery's Promise: Why Christian Mysticism Matters

You have already been cleansed by the word that
I have spoken to you.
—Jesus (John 15:3)

Mysticism is the antidote to fundamentalism.
—Rick Doblin

For people who are drawn to spirituality or religion, or who seek (or enjoy) a sense of God's presence in their lives, or who simply take pleasure in the history of ideas, mysticism can be a fascinating subject to explore—and a framework for contemplative practice and meaning. Others, who may not feel naturally drawn to this topic, may ask what all the fuss is about. If, having read this far, you find yourself wondering, "What's the point? Does mysticism really make a difference? How can it make life better?" I hope this chapter might offer you some insight.

At its best, Christianity is a religion that proclaims good news (the literal meaning of "gospel"). Any truly Christian mysticism must, likewise, be a conduit for good news, which is to say for hope and encouragement. And such a mystical gospel is not just for those who like to meditate or ponder the inscrutable mysteries of God. It's also (and maybe even especially) for those who suffer, for those who have difficulty believing in God, for those who have difficult or even toxic images of God—for example, the idea that God is just some sort of angry bully in the sky, eager to punish humans for the tiniest infraction. The good news of mystical Christianity offers a new way of thinking about God, and especially of experiencing God. It's good news for everyone, especially for anyone who is seeking a spirituality that is anchored in love, compassion, community, justice, and higher consciousness.

Like the Christian gospel in general, the "gospel of mysticism" can take different forms for different people. For some it may simply be a kind voice of reassurance; but for others it could be a voice that challenges and even confronts. Regardless of the various tones it may take, however, it always points to a promise that life can be abundant and full of joy; it's an invitation to open our hearts to love. At its best, mysticism empowers us to manifest lives transformed by love—and therefore lives empowered to make a real difference in the world, as we explored in chapter 7.

THE PROMISE OF MYSTICISM

Based on the wisdom and teachings of the great mystics over the past two thousand years, here's how I would summarize the message of mystical Christianity:

> *God is love. God loves all of us and wants us to enjoy a meaningful and abundant life. This means abiding in love—love of God, and love of neighbors as ourselves. Through prayer and worship, meditation and silence, we can commune with God, experience the divine presence, find our hearts and minds transformed by the Spirit, so that we may participate in God's loving nature, and be healed and renewed in that love—even to the point of being one with divine love.*
>
> *This new life (what the Christian Scriptures calls "the mind of Christ" and "the body of Christ") will not only bring us joy and happiness, and a sense of meaning (even when we suffer), but also will empower us to be conduits for divine love, that we may bring God's love and joy and happiness to others.*

There is much work to be done, and the task is overwhelming, Even our own need is very great, for we tend to resist God's love, even as we hunger for it. Yet God continually calls us back to the mystery of love and continually empowers us to take on the challenge of bringing hope to our broken world. Because we are one with God, anything is possible, and our hope has no limit.

This message is nothing new. In fact, much of it comes straight from the Bible.[1] Mysticism's promise—the promise of lives transformed by divine love—seems to some, however, to be simply too good to be true. Can we really believe that God is love—infinite, vast, unconditional love? Can we really trust the love of God to make our lives better? Is the premise, and promise, of mystical Christianity really something we can believe in?

For so many of us, it's hard to accept that this ultimate mystery we call God—the infinite source/intelligence responsible for the ongoing creation and evolution of the entire cosmos—is intimately, passionately, and personally in love with each and every one of us here on this tiny planet whirling away at the edge of a relatively small galaxy. But the mystics proclaim that there's more to this than some sort of abstract love affair. God's love is more than just love from afar. Divine love flows out from God, to us and through us; it is poured lavishly on the creation, ready to flow into the heart of any creature willing to receive it.

For mystics, divine love is not just an energy (like the Force of *Star Wars*), but it is alive, conscious, sentient. Love, Love-with-a-capital-*L*, has a face, and seeks to gaze lovingly into *our* faces. Not only does this transcendent being, this supreme consciousness and fountain of love, long to give divine beauty and grace to each individual creature, but we are actually invited, in and through our creatureliness, to participate in the fullness of that infinite love.

This is the message of mysticism.

To participate in God's love means to receive that love, to live in and within it, and, in a true and real way, to *be* love. Christian mysticism spirals out from a profound wisdom found in and through the story of Jesus of Nazareth, a wisdom tradition proclaiming that the source of infinite love and power and consciousness is not just some impersonal energy, but rather an impossible-to-understand confluence of consciousness, unity and community embodied in the Holy Trinity. In the faltering limitation of language, we say "one God, three persons." In this mystery, we find God the Creator (the ground of being, the fount of creation, the source of sources), God the Redeemer (Jesus, who lived and died among us, then rose from death and ascended into heaven), and God the Holy Spirit (the spirit of love and comfort and advocacy that strengthens the community of God's lovers and knits us all together into the one body of Christ). This triune deity pours love into us in an infinite variety of ways: as a parent loves the child, as a friend loves a friend, as a spouse loves a spouse, and as artists love their masterpieces.

The love that God gives you (and invites you to embody) is meant to be expressed in three ways, as Jesus himself pointed out: to love God with all your heart and all your soul, to love your neighbor as yourself, and therefore, to love yourself (Mark 12:30–31). Just as each person of the Holy Trinity is an essential part (or dimension) of God, so each aspect of this triune love forms an essential way to be the person you are created to be. It is the nature of love to give itself away, and so God pours divine love into you so that you may more truly, fully, and wholly return that love to God, both directly and indirectly as you love your neighbor as lavishly as you love yourself. And who is your neighbor? Anyone in need, anyone who suffers, even those you might see as your enemies.

The amazing promise of Christian mysticism is that, when God loves you, the Spirit transforms you into love; when God loves you, God gives the fullness of divinity to you and, through you, to all creation. In being called to partake of the divine nature, you are called to be loved, to love, and to be love. You thereby join in the most amazing of cosmic dances, a dance of joy and fullness, of healing and restoration, of light and rest and delight, that will give you the entire cosmos forever and ever.

MYSTICISM AND CYNICISM

Ours is a cynical world, shaped by pessimism, skepticism, and disdain. It's a world where if your mother says she loves you, you ought to verify that independently. So many of us suffer, and have been traumatized by the endless ways that human beings are cruel to one another, that we have all but given up the hope that God really wants to bless us with joy and abundance.

Because of cultural cynicism, many people may suspect that mysticism is actually foolish or self-defeating—a retreat from reality into fantasy, a thumb-sucking, navel-gazing way of compensating for how much life hurts. We've become too sophisticated to buy into all this "God is love" nonsense. Those who eschew Christianity can be particularly pessimistic about the message of the mystics. It's so easy to look at the many flaws of Christianity—the sexism, the homophobia, the historical toleration of slavery, the ongoing scandals in the church usually involving money or abuse—and assume that the Christian religion is unsalvageably corrupt, and therefore any mysticism bearing its name must also be suspect. How can a judgmental and exclusionary religion be a conduit for divine love?

And so, driven by this cynical suspicion (and an understandable fear of putting our faith in something that has let so many people down), we turn away from what Christian mysticism offers us. We turn our gaze away from heaven and back to earth. Ours is a world that busily (some would say frantically) offers a variety of lesser destinies. Thanks to the dominance of a strictly empirical/scientific worldview, Western society sees life strictly in terms of the verifiable—only what can be scientifically proven is "real." In other words, we live a finite mortal existence in an environment with limited resources, where we participate in biological processes for eighty or ninety years, and then we die. Such a life is clearly limited, so we need to make the most of what little we've got. This worldview dismisses all spiritual beliefs (including mysticism) as merely wishful thinking. In other words, the mystical vision of an eternal dance of loving communion is simply too good to be true.

Such a pessimistic view of the world may seem intellectually coherent to atheists and cynics, but does it really cultivate hope, or joy, or a sense of purpose and meaning? Perhaps we need to be skeptical of skepticism itself. I am persuaded that the cynicism of our age is a philosophical dead end—ultimately, a closed loop and miserable way to view the world. It's also a viewpoint that caters to people with economic or social privilege—it really only makes sense for the small percentage of human beings who live a life of material comfort and leisure, who can emphasize only what is materi-ally real because they have the privilege to enjoy the comforts of earthly existence. But even those who enjoy the best pleasures that the earth has to offer sooner or later discover that the limitations of that life eventually win. Eventually, every one of us will lose our health, our relationships, our very lives. As Buddha said, "Life is suffering." Ignoring that suffering neither makes it go away nor makes it easier to bear.

Human beings simply don't like limits, whether these are the physical limits of a life that inevitably includes suffering and death, or the ideological limits of a worldview that tells us "this is all there is." Consequently, various spiritual theories have emerged over the ages and around the world that seek to answer the question of life's greater meaning. Many of these spiritual narratives are beautiful and inspiring, although some contain their own hidden limits.

For example, one type of spiritual philosophy holds that all material existence is an illusion, and that the only thing that truly exists is one, single, solitary being. You and I and everyone else are only projections or masks that this one being wears in order to create the illusion of separate entities. On the surface, this is a beguiling idea, because it basically offers an easy way to believe that you are one with God (just like everyone else). This theory begins to lose its appeal, however, when you carry it to its logical conclusion. If I am God, and everything else is an illusion, then I am all alone. What's the point of being God if you have no one to share your deity—no one to love, no community of love? What a lonely existence.

By contrast, the bold claim of Christian mysticism offers a much more nuanced and compelling way of understanding the relationship between being human and being divine. Yes, mystical Christianity promises that we are all one with God, but it is more than just some pantheistic identity. Beyond merely saying that we "are" God, Christian mystical wisdom proclaims that we *participate* in God—a subtle but crucial distinction. God remains God, I remain me, you remain you, God is one with us like the ocean is one with every drop of water, and we all are called to love each other. We exist in each other, through each other, in union and communion, here in the beauty of the present moment—and for all of the ever-expansiveness of eternity. This, Christian mysticism dares to assert, is the ultimate promise of life.

It promises the same ecstasy and joy that the all-things-are-god theory claims, but its promised bliss is grounded in relational love—a love that ultimately has no limits, either in space or in time. Eternity, the word Christians use to describe the limitless presence of God, transcends the material boundaries of space and time.

Christian mysticism makes this bold claim: what appears to be naive folly in purely human terms is bracingly and joyfully possible in terms of God. God as the source of infinite possibility is a theme that appears numerous times in the Bible, with lines like these: "For nothing will be impossible with God" (Luke 1:37), and put more positively, "For God all things are possible" (Matthew 19:26). Nothing is impossible: not even the amazing destiny of love-in-divine-communion that Christian mysticism promises.

Traditionally, this has been called the "beatific vision." A Trappist monk I know dismisses that term because it implies stasis. "Heaven is not a spectator sport," he insists. He suggests that a better way to describe our ultimate destiny in God is as a "beatifying communion." I describe it as "consciously living in heaven"—beginning here and now and extending into eternity. It's not just a mind trip, either: this is an *embodied* consciousness, an awareness we carry in our bones as much as in our nerve cells.

This does not negate or eliminate the suffering of human life, the pain of earthly existence. It doesn't magically make sin, injustice, or oppression disappear. But it gives us meaning and a framework of hope and purpose that can inspire us to work for the lessening or ending of suffering, not only our own but the suffering of others as well.

The amazing promise of Christian mysticism is that this vision, this communion, this conscious way of life is available to all of us—right here, right now. You can begin consciously to live in heaven today.

Any cynic who reads this may wonder, "So what's the catch?" And yes, there is a cost. Although you don't have to surrender your earthly life to embrace the beatifying communion, you do have to "die" in at least a figurative sense. Christianity has traditionally called this spiritual death a "dying to self." Some describe it as the death of the ego—that small, selfabsorbed tendency each of us has, a tendency to prefer control or comfort over love.

When you offer God all the parts of yourself that prefer narcissism or pride or anger to love, you begin the process of dying to self. It's not something that happens in an instant, and it's not always painless. But it's a core teaching of the Christian faith that this death leads to a resurrection. When

I die to myself, I rise to Christ—which is another way of saying that I rise to new life, in love—the love of God, in me, uniting me in love, making me one with God, and with all.

Is all this too good to be true? This is not just a rhetorical question. It is the question on which everything hangs. If you decide that the promise of Christian mysticism is too good to be true, then, at a fundamental level, you are deciding that life is not, ultimately, about love. But if the essence of life is not love, then what is it?

One response to this question is that life is all about power ("the person who dies with the most toys wins"). Another is that life is all about knowledge and/or awareness ("the secret of life is to know all the secrets"). Granted, awareness and ability are important keys to a life well lived, but if you organize your life around either of these principles, then you risk missing out on love—or, at best, you experience only a limited, finite love.

On the other hand, if you dare to believe that the ultimate meaning, destiny, and purpose of life is to love and be loved in expanding, eternal divine/human communion—if you dare to believe this is true, this is real, this is the map of how things really are or really can be—then everything changes, literally, immediately, and everlastingly. Despair and cynicism no longer reign. Hatred, prejudice, oppression, and cruelty, even though they exist for a time, lose their final claim over your life; such things are nothing more than transitory problems that sooner or later love (God) will overcome (which is why Christianity at its best mandates that we fight against injustice—it's a fight worth taking up, for good will eventually triumph).

If you give your life to love, you will be asked to die to your small, limited, cynical self. For that matter, you become responsible for cleaning up your own mess. You take on that responsibility not because you are forced to (or in trouble if you don't), but because you believe there is a reason and a purpose for doing so.

This is deeply countercultural, profoundly subversive of our cynical, bitter world. Few people—even those who are supposedly committed to a spiritual or religious life—accept the idea that life is totally and radically about love. We're too dazzled by the competing claims that life is all about power, or all about position or prestige, or all about knowledge, or just about bliss or fun or entertainment. When you orient your life to anything other than love, no matter what you gain, you risk losing out on the fullness of love. When you orient your life to love, however, you discover that you can attain a loving measure of all other good things as well (see Matthew 6:33).

The beautiful promise of Christian mysticism is that, by choosing love over all the other potential blessings that life can give us, we are embracing the best possible life; a life in which all blessings can flow, but always in accordance with love.

LOVE IS THE KEY

Simply put, Christian mysticism is all about love. To explore mystical Christianity means to explore love. It's an invitation to join the noblest of human aspirations. Love has inspired poets and philosophers for as long as human beings have enjoyed telling a good story. Love for the beloved community inspired Martin Luther King Jr., Pauli Murray, and Desmond Tutu. Without love, we would have no Romeo and Juliet, no Tristan and Isolde, no Sappho and Phaon, no Charles Ryder and Sebastian Flyte, no Wandering Aengus and the Glimmering Girl—and, for that matter, no Song of Songs, no Jacob and Rachel, no Ruth and Boaz, no Joseph and Mary. No Jesus giving over a life for Life. Without love, we wouldn't have the passionate work for a better world that informed the spiritual activism of Dorothy Day, Dag Hammarskjöld, Mother Teresa, or Howard Thurman. Whether the topic is love won or lost, love thwarted or misunderstood, comic romance or passionate tragedy, there is nothing so fundamentally human as a good story about love. And Christian mysticism is just that. It calls us to become part of the greatest of love stories. And that's why it matters.

That's why people like you and me are drawn to mysticism. Far from being merely a "head trip," mystical Christianity is the ultimate "heart trip"—a journey into the sacred nature of love.

We are all breathing miracles, living clay with a carefully calibrated capacity to give and receive love. And no matter how that may play out on a human level—for human love, of course, can take many forms and can be joyous or heartbreaking—this thing called mysticism dares to proclaim that you, and I, and everyone else who has ever been given a beating heart and a wondering mind, have all been invited to immerse ourselves in an immediate, experiential, life-transforming relationship with the very source of love in its purest, most original, foundational form. Christians call that source of love "God" and we find God in Jesus, made real and visible and accessible to everyone.

Christian mysticism is grounded in this love. The teachings of the great mystics speculate on the nature of this love, where it came from, and why we believe it is accessible to us all. Mystical wisdom about love is recorded in the autobiographies and memoirs of Christian contemplatives and visionaries who—great and ordinary, ancient and medieval, modern and postmodern, monastic and secular, young and old, educated and not so educated—all tell about how this love surprised them, pursued them, filled their awareness with breathtaking visions and heartrending suffering, demanded almost superhuman sacrifices, and yet overflowed with unspeakable joys.

As we discover not only the stories of the great mystics, but also our own stories, and the stories of our friends and neighbors and others who have heard the whispered call from the ultimate mystery, we sense intuitively that we each have something to say directly and intimately to each other. For Christian mysticism does not belong in a library or a museum. It belongs in beating hearts and contemplative minds, in living bodies and hope-filled souls. And even though there is tremendous diversity among the great mystics of Christianity, at the center of all their lives they are telling the same story. And we each represent, at least in potential, a new chapter in that story, a new verse in the eternal song. The great story of God's love resides in our hearts, just waiting to be given yet another new and unique form of expression.

Christian mysticism encompasses two thousand years of wisdom that shows you how to open your heart to the possibility of receiving this love, to conducting your life in a manner that is both honorable and worthy of it. Through this wisdom, you learn how your mind and heart can perceive and receive the overtures of this love as it comes to you in an infinite and unpredictable variety of ways. In other words, the writings of the great mystics include instructions on how to live a mystical life—a faithful life, a holy life, a life in which we serve communities for justice led by love, a life in which we humbly learn to accept that, ultimately, we have no control over just how mystical or contemplative our experience or our awareness of the divine may be. When you become an acolyte of mystical Christianity, you learn how to pray, to meditate, to contemplate, to read the Bible and other sacred writings in a deeply reflective way, to serve others and to sacrifice for them, to open your heart with hospitality for the world even while you somehow realize that you are, ultimately, the citizen of another country.

That's why mysticism matters.

CHAPTER TEN

The Mystical Paradoxes

You cannot see my face; for no one shall see me and live.
—Exodus 33:20

Blessed are the pure in heart, for they will see God.
—Jesus (Matthew 5:8)

Think without thinking.
—Francisco de Osuna

Christianity has, for centuries now, been locked in a kind of propositional straitjacket, where faith is equated with *assent* to a logical progression of statements and doctrines about God, humanity, sin, redemption, and so forth. The problem is, such statements and doctrines don't always seem to be that "logical" after all, and more and more people in our time have rejected the narrow understanding of religion as a logical map of reality. But what if Christianity isn't logical so much as *paradoxical*? What if the stories of the Christian faith are meant not to present spirituality in a nice tidy box but rather to spring us free from the confines of our own limited rationality, into the breathtaking wisdom of bracing silence? With this in mind, let's consider a series of Christian paradoxes: statements that on the surface appear to be contradictory, but deeper reflection reveals an intuitive truth that takes us beyond the limitation of language and symbol—or of human logic and reason. The mystical paradoxes may very well be the most direct path into a higher or nondual consciousness—not unlike the mind-bending poetry of Rumi or the unsolvable puzzles of Zen koans.

Paradox deconstructs our dualistic concept of truth and falsehood. "Profound truths," according to physicist Neils Bohr, are "recognized by the fact that the opposite is also a profound truth."[1] Paradox opens us to a mysterious place where two or more profound truths pull against each other in a tension that cannot be resolved by the clever machinations of the rational mind.

Mysticism is grounded in paradox, ushering us into the place where God and faith always seem to be pulling us in two directions at once. In the words of the French Orthodox theologian Jean-Yves Leloup, "God has no name and God has every name. God has none of the things that exist and God is everything. One knows God only through not knowing. Every affirmation, like every negation, remains on this side of God's transcendence."[2]

Paradox can be challenging to those who want their faith to be watertight and easy to control. If you have invested your heart and soul in the idea that God makes everything neat and tidy and your job is simply to obey the rules, then you may have no room for paradoxical truth in your spirituality. If the goal of your faith is unassailable certainty, the ambiguity of paradoxical, seemingly contradictory, truths will feel like a threat that must be eliminated.

For mystics—who regard faith as a relationship rather than a belief system—paradox is not nearly so threatening. Faith, when large enough to encompass contemplative wonder and mystical unknowing rather than mere certitude, receives paradox as a source of joy and insight rather than fear or doubt. A spiritual paradox offers evidence that God is bigger than our limited human capacity for reason and logic. Is the kingdom of heaven within or among us . . . or not of this world?[3] Does faith require belief or action? Or is faith without works dead?[4] Such seeming inconsistencies may pose a challenge to some, but can be a source of delight to others—not because they introduce an element of chaos into the landscape of faith, but because they point to an ultimate mystery that is beyond human control, beyond what passes for logic or common sense.

Saint Paul made a commonsense observation when he noted, "When I became an adult, I put an end to childish ways."[5] The spirituality of paradox represents precisely the kind of mature faith to which Paul is alluding. When my faith offers me equivalent truths that beckon me in different directions, I see this as an invitation and a challenge. Rather than pretending that such inconsistencies or seeming contradictions don't exist or don't matter, I feel encouraged to approach the mysteries of God in a spirit of humility, recognizing that no one will ever reduce God to the level of human reason.

To say that mysticism is about paradox is not to suggest that mystical Christianity involves a series of word puzzles or locks to be picked. Mysticism simply requires we take a step back and look at the truths of our faith from a larger, more inclusive perspective. Doing so, in many cases, brings us to the very threshold of mystery. At that place, on the frontier where human reason shades off into divine unknowing, we may find a resolution to the paradox, or at least a sense of acceptance that can help us embrace the apparent contradictions in the spiritual life.

And since God remains inscrutably beyond the farthest reaches of the most brilliant human mind, sooner or later we can expect to stumble across paradoxes that simply cannot be resolved. These insoluble paradoxes invite us into the core of faith. Like Zen koans, such paradoxes call us to surrender the hubris that lurks beneath our apparent understanding and control. A God you cannot comprehend is a God you cannot manipulate. Only such an incomprehensible God is truly worthy of our worship and devotion.

One reason I gravitate to the word *paradox* is that it is a first cousin to that most religious of all words, *orthodox*. The prefix *ortho-* means *right* or *correct*; the prefix *para-* means beside or alongside. These two words are linked by the root word *-dox*, which can mean *opinion* or *teaching* (as in doctrine) or *praise* (as in doxology). Both the praise and teaching sense of *-dox* point us to God—the God whom we praise and from whom we learn.

Thus, a statement is orthodox when it is a settled teaching, generally accepted by the larger Christian community: God is love; we are created in the divine image and likeness; the Holy Spirit is with us always. These are the ground rules by which the Christian faith operates in society and in our hearts. Meanwhile, *paradox*—which doesn't negate orthodoxy, but rather exists "alongside" it—represents the breathing room in which the ongoing guidance of the Holy Spirit occurs. The paradoxes of faith invite you into a deep silent unknowing—that place beyond the reach of human reason, not *pre*rational, but transrational—where God wishes to meet you without the pomp and noise of your finite, gotta-be-in-control mind getting in the way.

THE MYSTICAL PARADOXES

In this chapter we'll survey some of the paradoxes that characterize the wisdom of the Christian mystics. Some of these mystical paradoxes will be familiar to anyone who knows mainstream Christian beliefs, but others are uniquely the province of mystical spirituality. Some are easy to resolve; others are like tenacious vines that simply refuse to yield, even (or especially) when we hack at them with the blade of human reason. To some, these inconsistencies and logical disconnects provide evidence that Christianity is irrational or unworthy of belief. From the perspective of the mystic, however, these open-ended declarations represent the exciting points of departure from which Christian mysticism spirals off into nondual, suprarational, and transrational dimensions.

Mysticism is the quest for God.

You cannot seek God, since God has found you.
Christian mystical wisdom celebrates the passionate love that flows between humanity and God—a love that invites each of us into meaningful intimacy with our maker. Love, after all, requires both a *lover* and a *beloved*.

Looking for true love is a central part of being human. It's the stuff of fairy tales, date movies, and romance novels. Love sustained Jacob day after day when he had to work fourteen long years for Rachel's hand in marriage, and love (with the help of an angel) encouraged Joseph to accept the mystery of Mary's pregnancy. If you're like me, you want every love story to have a happy ending, and you feel the sting when tragic love stories—like Romeo and Juliet—end in unexpected, pain-filled ways.

Christianity teaches that human beings are, by nature, meant to love and be loved by God. This can lead to endless bliss and ever-unfolding joy in a heavenly communion that can begin here and now and will embrace all of eternity. But we are not forced into this relationship against our will. God is a patient, polite, and shy lover, and will only woo us with our consent. If you want divine love, you have to declare to God, and to yourself, that this is truly what you seek.

Such a declaration of love can take many forms. Some Christians seek God simply by following the program laid out for them by their church: they read the Bible, they worship every Sunday, they tithe, they volunteer in programs to care for the needy or otherwise make the world a better place. These are all worthy pursuits, and mysticism is not opposed to any of them. But for some, ordinary religious observance often represents only the beginning of the search. A variety of contemplative practices are available to those who feel called to enter into the deeper mysteries of faith.

For mystics, seeking God is a lifelong pursuit that proceeds even in the midst of down-to-earth activities like working or caring for our families. This quest for divine love is a daily concern and takes place right in the middle of our lives. God, being such a shy and polite lover, doesn't just pop up in your life merely because you say a lot of prayers or meditate every day. God is God, not a formula—not the sum of an equation that will always behave predictably. So the experience of seeking God is always open-ended, uncertain, and mysterious. What will happen if you devote your life to prayer? If you immerse yourself into contemplative silence? Who knows? Pray and see.

Augustine once said that you can seek God only because God has already found you. The point is that, even your seeking—which seems and feels as if you are taking the initiative—is actually already, on a very deep level, a response to God. The seeking may, paradoxically, be evidence of the finding—or, should I say, the having been found.

Mysticism means experiencing God.

Mysticism cannot be limited to experience.
Missouri is called the "Show Me" state, a curious and obscure nickname that, according to legend, originated when Missouri congressional representative Willard Duncan Vandiver declared, "Frothy eloquence neither convinces nor satisfies me. I am from Missouri. You have got to show me." Christian mystics would be at home in Missouri.

It may be only a short jump from "seeing is believing" to "experiencing is believing," but that jump takes us to the heart of mystical spirituality.

Christian mystics may not be as skeptical as Vandiver, but neither are they credulous. Mystics want faith to be born out of inner knowledge, rather than secondhand beliefs. For mystics, a relationship with God must be grounded in conscious and embodied awareness, and not just a by-product of what they have been told. When Karl Rahner mused that the Christian of the future must be a mystic, he was referring to precisely this deeply felt encounter with God that transcends mere ideas or ideology.

Religion without experience is abstract and overly mental—what in popular jargon is known as "being stuck in your head." Not only is such religion based on abstract ideas rather than intuition, it's also built around submission, for, without direct experience, religious authority becomes anchored in some external object (like the Bible, or the pope). Rank and file believers are therefore required not to experience God directly for themselves, but are expected simply to obey (submit to) the external authority. Religion without inner experience is religion without spirituality; it's purpose is little more than the regulation of people's moral lives. This is what Karl Marx rightly derided as the opiate of the people—religion as a set of teachings designed to make people docile and submissive, while keeping them locked in fear-based beliefs in exchange for a promised heavenly afterlife that is only available to those who submit.

The wisdom of the mystics offers a radically different way of understanding Christianity (or any religion), where truth and authenticity are measured by the power of inner knowing and experience. There's a difference between knowing about God and knowing God directly, and this distinction is the key to understanding the difference between stuck-in-your-head religion and truly mystical spirituality. Imagine the difference between knowing that you have grandparents and actually spending time with them, relating to them, interacting with them, and fostering intimacy with them. This is why some Christian theologians who would probably never describe themselves as mystics nevertheless argue that experiencing or directly knowing God forms the heart of what it means to follow Jesus.

But if religion divorced from personal experience is inauthentic, an entirely different set of problems arises if we focus too much on experience—the most obvious being the sheer unreliability of human understanding. We are just as good at deceiving ourselves as we are at hoodwinking one another. Having some sort of remarkable extraordinary experience—whether feeling one with God or seeing a UFO—in and of itself proves nothing. Such experience may be a self-created illusion, the consequence of wishful thinking, or perhaps merely the result of not getting enough sleep. It could be drug induced, or based on inner confusion, or even evidence of mental illness. If we insist that unusual or supernatural phenomena must be instigated by angels, logic demands that we also at least consider that a more down-to-earth explanation of the event is just as possible. A vision of God that comes from a heavenly messenger sounds like a bona fide mystical experience, but such a vision could just as easily come from a less exalted source—it might be little more than an egotistical excuse to feel proud of our own spiritual "advancement."

Not only is our experience subject to a wide variety of interpretations, there is no consistency in what a "mystical experience" looks like. In the annals of Christian history, mystics have had visions, heard angelic voices, been caught up in ecstatic consciousness, and experienced flashes of insight or intricately detailed dreams. No two mystics have walked the same path as they forged their relationship with God. How, then, can we define mysticism only in terms of experience, when it is based on such a wide variety of possibilities? And what about the experience that never happens? Many sincere, dedicated practitioners of meditation and contemplation may never have a sense of "experiencing" God at all, or perhaps have only the subtlest intuition or a vaguely comforting sense that God is present in their lives. Can we really say that such people are not mystics? Is mysticism only for the elite? Do some people receive mystical gifts, but other, "lesser" folks do not?

This flies in the face of the teachings of Jesus, who consistently taught that spirituality is not about who is the greater or more powerful, but rather about who is most willing to love, care for, and serve others. So, while it appears that experience, in some form, is foundational to the mystical life, it is also true that mysticism is bigger than mere experience, and that mystical knowing just might not be "experiential"—or only experiential—at all.

God is immanent.

God is transcendent.

When we ask whether mysticism is fundamentally about experience or points to something beyond experience, this is a question about the God/

human love story from the human point of view. Let's turn this around and try, as best we can, to think about this from God's perspective.

God is greater and more vast than the entire cosmos, but is also present in the smallest of places—intimately involved in the existence of subatomic particles and the tiniest of lifeforms. Paul tells us that, in God, "we live and move and have our being" (Acts 17:28). God is in us, and we are in God. This is called the doctrine of *immanence*, which declares the indwelling or inherence of God. According to Augustine, God is closer to you than you are to yourself.

The twentieth-century Church of England priest J. B. Phillips penned a popular book called *Your God Is Too Small*, warning readers not to pigeon-hole God or box God in, and pointing out the psychological distortion possible when we see the divine only as immanent. The problem with seeing God only as immanent is that, by doing so, we can too easily reduce God to some sort of cosmic butler who exists to serve our needs. As a corrective to the too-small God, Christianity has always insisted that there is a fundamental "otherness" to God. While still immanent, God also is so much greater than all things and so far removed from the cosmos that it's silly to talk about God in human terms at all. God has no limits, God has no duality, God has no imperfection. This is the doctrine of *transcendence*, which confirms that God surpasses the realm of matter, energy, time, space—and the farthest limits of human consciousness.

So which is it? Is God immanent and intimately present, or transcendent and infinitely far away? Can we touch the face of God, or must we remain blinded by a veil that separates us from the ultimate mystery? Is spirituality a way of finding intimacy with the God who is present, or a way standing in awe of the God who is too vast to ever be fully known?

The answer to all these questions is simply yes.

Mystical Christianity involves significant, life-transforming events and changes in consciousness.

The mystical life may seem as "insignificant" as the butterfly effect.
Why are some lovers of God granted truly earth-shattering encounters with the divine presence, while such awe-inspiring experiences seem beyond the reach of so many others? Why do some people seem to be gifted with effortless spiritual intuition, while others struggle even to

imagine God's presence? What are we to make of stories about how some mystics enjoyed truly extraordinary signs and wonders—from Julian of Norwich's visions, to the Teresa of Ávila levitating, or Therese Neumann thriving for extended periods of time eating nothing other than her daily Communion?

I find stories of truly extraordinary mystical experiences both thrilling and inspiring—and just a bit intimidating. And to be perfectly honest, I also find such stories hard to believe—perhaps they represent a little bit of embellishing, the way American folklore includes embellished tales about George Washington or Abraham Lincoln.

Chances are, you and I and most seekers of God will never have visions as vivid as Julian's, or perform charismatic miracles like those attributed to Teresa. Perhaps we can at least find inspiration in these stories and their suggestion that such otherworldly wonders are possible. But is it accurate to equate Christian mysticism only with rare, extraordinary events? Must a spiritual experience be truly supernatural before it can be regarded as mystical?

More than once someone has said to me, "I'll never be a mystic." When I ask the person why they believe this, I usually find that they see mysticism in terms of miraculous or extraordinary events, and assume that they themselves will never have such awe-inspiring experiences. Many people who feel this way are truly humble and down-to-earth people—just the kind of people that Jesus praised as being closest to the reign of heaven. Talk about a paradox—and also a pretty strong criticism of the "signs and wonders" variety of mysticism. If a person has to choose between being spiritually humble and being a signs-and-wonders mystic, I for one certainly hope that humble spirituality wins the day.

To think that mysticism involves only supernatural experiences is as limited as saying that God can only be transcendent. In fact, some of the most renowned mystics are those who have few, if any, extraordinary or supernatural experiences. Take Caryll Houselander for example. This English mystic had several meaningful experiences of the divine presence in her life, but a skeptic could explain most of them away as little more than profound psychological insights. The same can be said about Howard Thurman, or Brother Lawrence, or Thérèse of Lisieux. Each of these renowned mystics were humble in terms of their experience, but truly wise in terms of their insight. The truth is that, sometimes, great mystics are marked, not by the supernatural light that illuminates their minds, but by very simple, almost ordinary, awareness of God's presence in their lives. Such down-to-earth mysticism can inspire a profound and passionate commitment to social justice, to a life devoted to serving the poor, or to some other significant calling that embodies the subtle insights and embodied awareness received from God. In other words, mysticism incorporates humble as well as exalted encounters with the ultimate mystery.

The butterfly effect is a concept related to chaos theory, which holds that seemingly insignificant phenomena can have amazing consequences. The classic way of illustrating this is to suggest that a butterfly in Brazil can, by the disturbance in the atmosphere caused by its wings, set into motion a chain of events that results in a tornado in Texas. We currently lack the ability to measure the relationships between such tiny causes and huge effects. This is also true of mysticism. A single act of compassion or forgiveness can help prevent a terrible crime or a suicide. The decision to say a prayer or spend an hour reading the Bible can lead to an insight that can literally change a person's life.

With this in mind, consider the Holy Spirit as a conscious force for "holy chaos." A subtle, gentle, if-you-blink-you'll-miss-it sensation of God's presence may be all the mystical awareness you need (or can handle). Perhaps most mystical encounters with God operate under the principle that less is more. Perhaps those who have dramatic mystical experiences are simply less well attuned to God's presence to begin with. Unlike those who can quietly discern God's voice in the midst of mundane life, some people need to have their minds blown in order for God to get through. If we can accept that mystical experience comes in all shapes and sizes, then we must also recognize that mystical gifts touch far more people than any of us realize.

Mysticism is a free gift from God, not something we earn by our efforts.

If you remain passive, you may be thwarting the action of the Spirit.
An important, but often misunderstood, element of Christian spirituality is the concept of *grace*. The basic idea is that the experience of, or encounter with, or awareness of God that forms the heart of mysticism is

always freely given, never earned. From a quiet sense of God's presence, to an awe-inspiring shift in consciousness, to a dramatic dream or vision in which Jesus appears to offer guidance or instruction—the traditional teaching is that such mystical moments are always gifts given to us by God, not something we cook up on our own. In other words, they are manifestations of divine grace.

Grace is a free gift. No one can earn grace any more than one can earn God's love. We lack the ability to change God's mind—or heart—concerning us. God's love and forgiveness and favor is always, simply, freely and unconditionally given. We cannot earn grace, or divine love, for such love and grace is always freely given. Choosing to follow Jesus, getting baptized, receiving Communion, reading the Bible, doing good works or refraining from hurtful behavior—none of these can earn God's approval. You enjoy the blessing of God's grace because God loves to lavishly bestow it upon you, not because you deserve it or somehow have proven worthy of it.

Grace is the foundation of the mystical relationship with God. Whether you enjoy a clearly conscious sense of God's presence, or continually search for God as if you were enshrouded by the cloud of unknowing; whether you enjoy amazing moments of blissful union with God, or seem to be forever lost in the dark night of the soul—mystically speaking, it simply doesn't matter. God lovingly and graciously designs every person's unique journey into the divine heart. You cannot manipulate God into giving you some extraordinary mystical experience or insight, any more than you can force God into loving you more than God already does.

Mystically speaking, our experience of God is always shaped by grace. Those who receive extraordinary wonders do so because they need them, on some level. On the other hand, some contemplatives may only experience God through a sense of absence or hiddenness—yet they, too, are receiving from the Spirit exactly what they need. It makes the most sense simply to recognize that God ultimately is in charge, not you. Your job is to sit back and see what God has in store for you. Right?

Well, not exactly.

The apostle James said, "Faith without works is dead." Traditionally, Christians have taken this to mean that no one can grow in their faith if they don't take responsibility for their actions. From a mystical perspective, what keeps faith alive aren't the things we do to try to *earn* God's love and respect (or mystical presence). Rather, what matters are all the things we do *in response to* the grace and love that God has freely given to us. Mystical spirituality is not about making God love you, or cajoling God into giving you divine blessings. God's gift is always freely given. But since that gift has been given freely, it's up to each of us whether or not we accept it, unwrap it, and incorporate it into our lives. Our actions, including our efforts to live a contemplative life help to make the grace of God truly come alive within us.

What kinds of actions matter to the mystical life? Spiritual practices that dispose you to receiving God's presence—which we will explore more fully in the second half of this book. Such spiritual practices are not magical spells that summon or mandate God's presence, but rather expressions of prayer and devotion that foster within us an ever-deepening ability to receive the gift. Contemplative spiritual practices do not change God; but they do change you. Just as it takes exercise and a healthy diet to stay fit, it takes spiritual exercises like lectio divina, daily prayer, meditation, contemplation, participation in a faith community, and serving those who are in need to dispose yourself to the mystical life. If someone doesn't do these things, God can still overwhelm them with the mystery of divine presence—that's how grace works. But when we engage in a spiritual practice, you clear a space within yourself where God can act—in whatever way God sees fit.

Mysticism is the "flight of the alone to the Alone."

God is present "where two or three are gathered" in Christ's name.
The pagan philosopher Plotinus described mysticism as the "flight of the alone to the Alone." Although he wasn't a Christian, Plotinus's philosophy had a strong influence on early Christians. Augustine, renowned not only as a theologian but also considered a mystic, was well versed in his thought.

The philosophy of Plotinus followed the teaching of Plato. His deeply mystical wisdom spoke of the cosmos as an "emanation" from the One, and saw the goal of life to be ultimately in returning to that primal unity. Human existence originated in the One and our destiny, according to Plotinus, lay entirely in returning to that nondual source.

Although his teachings are not found in the New Testament, Plotinus's worldview has loomed large over the history of mystical Christianity.

Following Plotinus, mysticism has often been understood as a spirituality based on renunciation—the renunciation of worldly wealth, bodily pleasure, social standing, and other material benefits, all rejected as inferior to that singular quest for union with God, either in this life or the next. Some of the earliest Christian mystics lived as hermits in the deserts of Egypt and the Middle East. The ideal of the hermit—a person living in solitude, for God alone—is found in Christian writings throughout the ages, and is exemplified by mystics from ancient times to the present day. Julian of Norwich, Richard Rolle, Matthew Kelty, Abhishiktananda, and Matta El Meskeen are just a few of the Christian mystics and contemplatives down the centuries who have embraced solitude or the eremitical (hermit) life as part of their single-minded quest for God. In solitude—in a flight of the alone to the Alone—these contemplatives gave their lives to the search for union with God.

But that's not the only way to be a mystic. An entirely different, and more distinctively Christian, way of looking at mysticism stresses not solitude, but community. This paradox has its roots in the mystery of the Holy Trinity, one God in three persons—God who is both divine unity and divine community. Part of the nature of God is thus the dance of relationships between Father, Son, and Holy Spirit. The Christian understanding of divinity as trinity makes a difference in how many Christians have embodied and understood the mystical life.

In the gospel texts, Jesus says, "For where two or three are gathered in my name, I am there among them" (Matthew 18:20). Although Christ encourages his followers to pray alone (Matthew 6:6), he also promises his presence when Christians gather together. In other words, the Christian life is not just some sort of cozy cocoon where God and the mystic exists in all alone, in holy intimate privacy. Rather, the flow of love between the human and the Spirit is meant to spill over in an essential flow of love among, and between, other humans as well. This is spelled out clearly in the Gospel of John, when Jesus bluntly instructs his disciples, "If you love me, you will keep my commandments. . . . This is my commandment, that you love one another" (John 14:15; 15:12).

Paradoxical as it may seem, for Christian mystics the flight of the alone to the Alone must also be understood as a flight of the community to the Trinity.

God is One.

God is a Holy Trinity.

The paradox of Christian mysticism as both solitary and communal spirituality is mirrored in what is certainly one of the greatest of all Christian mysteries: that God is simultaneously one and three, elegant unity and personal interrelationship.

Like its mother religion, Judaism, Christianity recognizes God as one. Oneness is an essential characteristic of the divine nature. Christianity also recognizes within the one God a unity of three persons—not three natures or three functions, but three persons: the transcendent heavenly Creator, Jesus Christ (the Savior or Redeemer), and the interrelational Spirit of love (also called the Paraclete, our advocate and comforter). The Creator is not the Redeemer, the Redeemer is not the Holy Spirit, and the Spirit is not the Creator. Yet all are God, and God is one.[6]

Critics of Christianity dismiss the Holy Trinity as an expression of the mental wrangling early theologians had to go through as they attempted to preserve Christianity's monotheistic identity while also explaining why their faith encompassed a heavenly Creator, as well as a human incarnation recognized as both one with God and the Son of God, and also an ever-present Holy Spirit sent from God and promised by Christ.

Quite a lot of arguing (not to mention bloodshed) took place in the early centuries of the Christian era over just how to understand this. To this day, the doctrine of the Holy Trinity remains a topic of ongoing theological speculation, even if much of that takes place on an academic level that might seem irrelevant to the average lay Christian.

This criticism can be turned inside out, however. Instead of dismissing the doctrine of the Trinity as a mere compromise required by history, it makes just as much sense to marvel at it as a profoundly novel and beautiful expression of understanding the mystery of God, an expression that arose in response to the life of Jesus and the experience of the first Christians. The Holy Trinity proclaims a spiritual reality greater than the messiness of polytheism and the loneliness of radical monotheism. The trinitarian vision of God transcends the limitations of human intellect and answers the question of how God can be greater than the cosmos and yet still relate to us as a part of his creation.

In the Holy Trinity, the infinite mystery of God the Creator relates eternally and intimately to the physical universe through the embodied life of Jesus Christ and the ever-loving presence within creation of the Holy Spirit. Thus, the Trinity not only embraces the paradox of transcendence and immanence; but also invites us to find our ultimate destiny and fulfilment in our becoming—in the words of Saint Peter—"partakers of the divine nature."

The Trinity reveals the dynamic way in which the loving community of three persons in divine unity expands itself to incorporate the endless flow of love to and from God and God's beloved creation. Christian mysticism, grounded in the trinitarian understanding of God, fosters an openness to receive the gift of divine union that overflows from the loving relationships found within the Trinity. The union of God and God's beloved creation, as understood in the Christian faith, is actually a communion, in which we are invited into the loving unity with the Spirit, with Christ, and, through them, with the infinite mystery of the infinite Creator—the fullness of the one triune God.

Christ is fully human.

Christ is fully divine.

Along with the mystery of the triune God, another most remarkable and controversial Christian teaching is the doctrine of the incarnation, which holds that Jesus of Nazareth is both fully human and fully divine. This is the unique mystery of Christ.

Like the doctrine of the Trinity, this central tenet of the Christian faith took centuries to hammer out. Some early Christians emphasized Christ's humanity, insisting that to call him "Son of God" was merely an honorific that carried no real meaning when it came to explaining his relationship with God. Jesus may have been specially blessed or favored by God, but was no more divine than you or I. Other Christians rejected the humanity of Jesus, insisting that, because he was divine, his holiness could never be enmeshed in the messy reality of human flesh. For them, Christ's humanity was just an illusion, a "form" he took on so that he could relate more easily with us. Eventually, Christian orthodoxy rejected both of these extreme perspectives and accepted the more paradoxical view—that, as a human,

Christ was one of us in every way, except without sin; as God, Christ was as fully divine as the other two persons of the Trinity.

While this has become a central article of faith for all Christians, it is particularly helpful to understand how mystics experienced the relationship between the Trinity, Christ, and ourselves. Mystically speaking, Christ is the great bridge builder. He is one with God the Creator (John 10:30). But he is also "one" with all of us by virtue of his humanity. When Joan Osborne sang her 1995 hit song "What If God Was One of Us?," Christians could reply, "In Jesus, God is already one of us."

Some people might object that Christianity sets up some sort of two-tiered system that distinguishes between Jesus and lesser mortals. This criticism stems from a profound misunderstanding of Christian wisdom, however, and totally ignores the mystical understanding of Christianity as partaking of the divine nature. God poured the fullness of divinity into Mary's womb, and so Jesus was born—who, in turn, pours the fullness of Christ's divinity into each and every Christian, through the power of the Spirit. We are not mere spectators of the presence of God; through the fully human and fully divine paradox of Christ, we partake of that very presence.

The literal meaning of the word *Christian* is "little Christ"—and so, each Christian becomes, in a mysterious (mystical) way, a representation of Christ, a part of Christ. Just as Christ remained fully human even while he was fully divine, Christians never stop being human, even though we are invited to become part of the divine mystical body. Therefore, we share not only Christ's full humanity, but also Christ's full divinity.

Seek the light.

Embrace the dark.

This paradox emerges from two seemingly contradictory Bible verses. In John, Jesus declares, "I am the light of the world." In Matthew, during his Sermon on the Mount, he says, "You are the light of the world."[7] Hidden in this apparent opposition is an important clue to just what the Christian mystical life is all about.

Christianity is not a "two-light" system, as if Jesus were one light and we—the community of Christians, or little Christs—are, collectively, another. Rather, the light that Jesus says shines from him and from us is the same light. When we are united in Christ, we are incandescent with divine spiritual light. Intuitively sensing this truth, Christians have been seeking the light of Christ ever since, both yearning to have it shine on us, and also hoping to be worthy for it to shine through us.

The light of Christ is true light, a spiritual light, something other than a physical energy stream to which our eyes can respond. The apostle Paul explains, "For it is the God who said, 'Let light shine out of darkness,' who has shone in our hearts to give the light of the knowledge of the glory of God in the face of Jesus Christ."[8] Thus, the light of Christ can most properly be understood as a light of knowledge (wisdom), an inner enlightenment that reveals and makes plain what was previously shrouded in darkness.

The Gospel of John also uses imagery of light contrasted with darkness to express the difference between good and evil. For mystics, however, the tension between light and dark can be understood in another way—as the tension between the mystery that is revealed and the mystery that remains hidden. And since the mystery of God is never fully revealed to us, this means that God will come to us, not only as light, but also as a divine darkness.

"If the visible light is intangible, how can the hidden Light be comprehended?" mused the fourth-century mystic Ephrem the Syrian.[9] Another ancient mystic from the Middle East, Pseudo-Dionysius the Areopagite, wrote about the "dazzling darkness," suggesting that what appears to us as the darkness of God's hiddenness is actually a spiritual light so bright that it blinds us.

Mystics throughout the history of Christianity have played with this tension between light and dark. In the lovely poem called "One Dark Night," the Spanish Carmelite mystic John of the Cross compares the soul's yearning for God to a nighttime tryst between lovers. He also wrote a commentary on the spiritual meaning of this poem called *The Dark Night of the Soul*, which is now regarded as one of the greatest Christian mystical writings. His treatise has given its name to the experience of profound, ego-shattering darkness that some mystics experienced as they surrender themselves more and more to God's deep transforming presence.

Taken on another level, the idea that Christ is light while God is enshrouded in darkness can lead to a holistic appreciation of both the light and dark parts of life. Ironically, spiritual seekers can be as susceptible as anyone else to judging their own lives—particularly when things aren't going well. When times are harmonious, pleasant, and joyful, we conclude that God is present. When we are plagued by suffering, doubt, despair, illness, or sorrow, God seems absent. The paradox of light and dark turns that simplistic approach on its head. Perhaps we are more likely to feel the loving presence of God in the "light" times of our lives. But the witness of the mystics assures us that God remains present even when we don't feel that presence, even—and, perhaps, especially—in the profound shadow times. The God of darkness is a hidden God, and may feel like an absent God. On a level deeper than mere human experience or consciousness, however, God remains truly present.

Take delight in God.

Trust even suffering.

"The fullness of joy is to behold God in all," proclaimed Julian of Norwich. That *all* means God is just as present in the painful or difficult times of life as in the more joyful, light times. This is the paradox of finding God both in joy and in suffering. "Take delight in the Lord," says the Psalmist, "and God will give you the desires of your heart."[10] To open yourself up to God's love is not merely a spiritual blessing, but will make a positive difference in every part of your life. Delight in God leads to a delightful life.

That sounds lovely. The only problem is that life doesn't always seem to work that way. Although blessings abound for many people, at least some of the time—the love of family and friends, the joy of a good meal, the excitement of sport, the pleasure of romance, the satisfaction that comes with setting and achieving goals—life's pleasures can often seem to be just out of reach, whether because of illness, poverty, oppression, addiction (in our lives or the lives of those we love), or other challenges. Even in the most joyful and carefree life, pain and suffering are never far away. Everyone will, sooner or later, face illness, injury, loss, and death—and, worse yet, will watch loved ones suffer. Suffering is an unavoidable part of life. In ancient India, Siddhartha Gautama was so stunned by his discovery that life is full of suffering that he embarked on his own spiritual quest, which culminated in his enlightenment as the Buddha.

An immature or selfish spirituality thinks of God as a year-round Santa Claus who exists only to shower divine blessings on those who are deserving;

and prayer, therefore, is merely the means for convincing God to bestow such favor on us. This kind of religion gets pumped up in the good times, but can lead to despair and angst when times are tough. But Jesus calls us to leave behind our childish narcissism and to embrace the fullness of life in all its moments, from times of suffering to those filled with joy. This is one of the lessons encoded in traumatic death of Jesus: through his suffering, we are saved (made spiritually whole). This wholeness is not just some sort of promise for life after death; rather, it offers divine blessings to us right here and now, even when life is difficult or painful. Christ makes no promise to remove your suffering. But he redeems it, by bringing his presence into it and thereby transforming it from pointless pain to a smaller part of a larger, meaningful whole. A woman in the pain of childbirth can bear her suffering because she knows it leads to the joy of giving birth and welcoming her new child into the world. In the mystery of Christ, we see that all suffering has the potential to be a "birth" experience—giving birth to a newfound appreciation of God's presence and of his ability to turn anything, no matter how bad or painful, into a new possibility where divine love and presence can shine forth.

God is all-merciful.

God's justice is uncompromising.
Various Christian mystics throughout history, from Clement of Alexandria in the second century to Faustina Kowalska in the twentieth, emphasize the importance of obeying God's law as a foundational requirement for anyone seeking to explore the path to divine union. Here in the twenty-first century, many people might find this focus on "the rules" difficult to swallow. We want our spirituality to be grounded in love, mercy, compassion and care, in God's unconditional acceptance of us and infinite mercy.

For so many of us, the point of Christian spirituality is to find, establish, and deepen an experience of loving intimacy with God. Just as a truly happy marriage must be built on love rather than a prenuptial agreement, the mystical quest for union with God gives precedence to love and relationship over rules and regulations.

Yet many of Christianity's most renowned mystics insisted that obedience to God's law is the necessary foundation for a relationship with God. This classic mystical hunger to live in submission to divine precepts seems old-fashioned if not obsolete, but it is certainly a part of the tradition of Christian mystical wisdom. Such traditional ways of understanding "God's law" are increasingly questioned by critics of our time, both inside and outside the institutional church. Science, psychology, philosophy, and sociology have all inspired far-ranging debate that has led many to rethink old approaches to morality and ethics and wrestle with profound questions of how we truly become *good*—in both personal and social ways.

For some people, the widespread deconstruction of old religious certainties has led to an acceptance of ethical relativism, where all individuals ultimately must follow the dictates of their conscience. Others react to the uncertainty of our age by adopting one of two apparently opposite but equally rigid responses—either to cynically reject time-honored ideas of divine law altogether, or to retreat into an inflexible, fundamentalistic mentality that defends "traditional values" against all questioning, at all costs.

The Bible teaches that God's law is holy and just, but also that God is all-merciful.[11] So what does it mean to say that God represents pure justice as well as pure mercy? How do these two qualities merge? Are Christian mystics, like all Christians, required to submit to an external moral code, or are we expected to calibrate our lives toward an emphasis on mercy—not just for ourselves, but for everyone?

On a purely human level, justice and mercy seem to subvert each other. Justice demands that wrongs be set right, that we are all held accountable for our actions, that those who are vulnerable or oppressed have their day in court against those who victimize them or exert privilege over them. Meanwhile, mercy promises forgiveness for wrongdoing, and leniency in punishment. I suspect that, deep down inside, we all want God to be just toward all those who have wronged us or offended us. But we also want God to show mercy to us and to those we care for. This is not surprising, and is human nature to want to care especially for our own.

Mysticism, on the other hand, suggests turning this human impulse inside out. The mystics enjoin us to police *our* behaviors—our own thoughts, behaviors, spending habits, and other actions—with an eye to observing God's law, while trusting in God's mercy to shower forth love and forgiveness on everyone —even on those who may have hurt us, or who oppose us politically, or whose moral values are at odds with our own. Jesus, after all, asked God to forgive those who crucified him—even though we have no reason to believe that they repented of their violence toward Jesus, or asked for God's forgiveness.

If Christian spirituality is about following Jesus, then shouldn't we ask God's forgiveness for all those whose behavior doesn't meet with our approval—whether or not they ever express sorrow for their actions?

I don't know how to resolve this paradox. But I do believe that much of what is dynamic and beautiful about the Christian mystical and contemplative life is propelled by this creative tension between seeking to live a life of uncompromising justice, and seeking to be an ambassador for God's lavish and abundant mercy.

Seek to be holy.

Practice hospitality.

This is an extension of the justice/mercy paradox we just considered. To the extent that God stands for uncompromising justice, God calls us to live conscientious and pure lives. To the extent that God stands for all-embracing mercy, God calls us to live by the dictates of hospitality. Holiness is exemplified in the biblical letter to the Hebrews, where a holy priest is described as "blameless, undefiled, separated from sinners, and exalted above the heavens." By contrast, hospitality is characterized by the parable of the great banquet, where a rich person invites everyone to a feast—even those who are impure or unclean.[12]

Holiness is about purity: the pure absence of anything contrary to God's love and glory. Hospitality, on the other hand, can be messy and chaotic. Holiness implies rigorous self-control and unwavering commitment to standards of righteousness. Hospitality, by contrast, works only when flexibility and a willingness to meet people where they are come first. Holiness and hospitality seem to pull us in opposite directions. Yet mystical Christianity operates under the assumption that God calls us to both: to a life of luminous holiness and all-embracing hospitality.

No one could deny that holiness is a central quality promoted in the Christian faith. Even a cursory reading of the Christian Scriptures reveals that a core characteristic of life in Christ involves refraining from behaviors regarded as "impure"—the worship of false Gods, lying, theft, sexual misconduct, drunkenness. And while we may not worry anymore about some of the concerns expressed in the Bible—for example, I have never been tempted to eat meat that has been offered to idols—other spiritual principles remain as relevant as ever (for example, abusive rage and selfish ambition simply do not mix well with a life committed to spiritual growth and responding to divine love).

Holiness is not passive: it requires more from us than just the quality of a life surrendered to God's grace. Choosing to foster a more holy life is the first and essential requirement for all who wish to see God. Jesus tells us that it is the "pure of heart" who "will see God."[13] Yet no one gets it right all the time, which is why Christians always have the opportunity to own up to their failings and do what it takes to set things right (in religious jargon, this process involves repentance, confession, contrition, and making amends). From the Catholic sacrament of reconciliation to a Southern Baptist altar call, various Christian communities have ways to help those who seek to make amends for their mistakes and to recalibrate their lives to the beauty of divine grace. The key seems to be in striving for a more holy life. We may never achieve the purity of holiness, but Jesus calls Christians to be faithful, not successful.

Regarding holiness and purity, the mystics have tended to be even more uncompromising than Christians as a whole. The desert fathers and mothers expected faultless moral behavior from themselves and their disciples, and purity of thought as well. Indeed, it was out of this quest for mental sanctity that the earliest practices of Christian meditation and contemplation emerged.

Yet here is another paradox: the quest for purity can result in its own form of impurity, as those who desire to be holy before God can all too easily succumb to spiritual pride. Meanwhile, there is a danger that overemphasizing holiness and purity can exacerbate emotional or mental health challenges such as scrupulosity and obsessive/compulsive behaviors. Holiness and purity may be lofty goals, goals that may run a risk of spiritual or psychological danger when pursued excessively.

Perhaps a contemplative approach to holiness involves not just the quest for moral purity, but also an acceptance of gracious, joyous, and messily imperfect hospitality. When Christ enjoined his followers to "be perfect,"[14] he wasn't advocating moral rectitude so much as a limitless love that flows to good and evil persons alike. This includes, paradoxically, loving the very people who offend you by their very lack of ethical integrity. And I don't just mean "loving" people in the abstract. Hospitality goes beyond merely writing a check to your favorite charity or voting for the politician whose values you most admire.

Jesus wants more from us. He wants us to reach out to the homeless person who lives on the street corner near the office; he wants us to learn to engage in positive and charitable dialogue with those whose political values are opposed to our own; he even wants us to shower ourselves with forgiveness when we fail to meet your own internalized standards of "purity." For while Jesus promised that the pure of heart will see God, he also insisted that we will find him among those who are hungry, poor, homeless, or naked. Showing hospitality to those who are truly in need— no matter how pure or "worthy" they might or might not be—may, ulti- mately, be a far shorter route to mystical union with God than a lifetime of contemplation.

Embrace the depth of Christian wisdom.

Explore all positive mystical paths.
One practical way that the purity/hospitality paradox plays out is in the question of how Christians ought to relate to other wisdom and spiritual traditions. For example, I have two friends who are both devout Christians who love Jesus and seek to do his will in their lives. But they are like night and day when it comes to how they express their faith, especially in relation to other religions.

One sees her faithfulness in terms of keeping herself pure before God. To her this means rejecting any kind of spiritual activity, practice, or idea that has a non-Christian origin. She is uncomfortable with some forms of Christian meditation, for example, because they are too similar to tran- scendental meditation, which has Hindu roots. For her, there is so much splendor and beauty in the gospel and the tradition of the Christian saints and mystics that she sees no point in muddying the waters by blending Christian spirituality with elements from other religions.

The other friend, however, sees things differently. Not only is he a faithful and active member of a large Christian church, he is also a leader of the Atlanta Sufi community. He loves to read the Gnostic Gospels, the poetry of Rumi, and the writings of various Eastern teachers like the Dalai Lama and Thich Nhat Hanh. His faith in Christ is deepened by the delight he takes in learning about other faiths and their spiritual practices.

Think about my two friends in terms of the purity/hospitality paradox. One embodies the quest for spiritual purity untainted by any "foreign" elements. The other embodies the quest for a spirituality of hospitality, in which devotion to Christ leads to an openness toward the wisdom and insights of other faiths. Both are sincere in their faith and genuinely want their relationship with Christ to transform their entire lives into holiness and beauty. Their different perspectives represent the two dimensions of this paradox. Christian mystics are called to plumb deeply the seemingly endless riches of the Christian tradition. Paradoxically, however, the contemplative life can inspire a genuine and heartfelt desire to find ways to share, and even integrate, Christian and non-Christian perspectives on spirituality.

It would be very easy, at this point, to get distracted by a debate over which of my friends is "right"—which is to say which one is being more faithful to the gospel. Instead, we can follow the advice of Matthew 7:1: "Judge not." This paradox asks us to consider how each perspective can be a powerful expression of devotion. Each approach has its limitations or "blind spots." The person who embraces various traditions can wind up adhering to a kind of blended spirituality that lacks any real identity and appears to be rooted in nothing deeper than individual preferences. Meanwhile, the person who eschews any spiritual tradition that isn't Christianity out of a desire to maintain a kind of spiritual purity runs the risk of falling into a fundamentalist mentality that considers itself the only valid or virtuous approach, and judges other traditions as harmful or fears them, rather than simply trying to love all people as Christ demands.

Put another way, perhaps both the "embracers" and the "purity seekers" are called to remain open to a continual process of conversion. Those who embrace other faiths indiscriminately may need conversion to the virtue of stability, by which they can learn to trust the deep roots of the Christian tradition to nurture them spiritually. Those who insist on a "Christian only" purity may need conversion to a deeper charity, by which they can learn to relate to those who are different from themselves with a gracious openness rather than a defensive resistance and an unwillingness to learn or understand.

Love God's creation.

Do not love the world.

Christianity holds a tension between the "earth" and the "world." The earth is God's creation, and—especially in the Hebrew Scriptures—it is celebrated as a good thing, a gift from God. "I brought you into a plentiful land to eat its fruits and its good things," says the prophet Jeremiah, speaking for God. "But when you entered you defiled my land, and made my heritage an abomination."[15] Herein lies the crux of the paradox. What God has created—the earth, the land, nature and her bounty—is good. "God called the dry land Earth, and the waters that were gathered together God called Seas. And God saw that it was good."[16] What we do with it and to it, however, is another story. "Do not love the world or the things in the world. The love of the Father is not in those who love the world."[17]

It's tempting to read the language of "not loving the world" as mandating some sort of split between humanity and the rest of nature. It can also be seen as enforcing a split between the human mind and the human body. The mind, or consciousness, is more akin to spirit, while the body is obviously part of nature. This kind of thinking leads to dualism—a distorted way of seeing the universe in which only spirit is good, while matter is rejected as fallen or evil. Dualism originated in Greek philosophy and in ancient religions like Zoroastrianism and Manichaeism, not in the original teachings of Jesus or in the Jewish culture in which he lived.

At its best, Christian wisdom understands a distinction between *the world* as an abstract symbol representing the human capacity for error, and *the earth* as the beautiful creation God has given us, including nature, the land, and our bodies. This is not to say that the physical universe is entirely benign. Indeed, the capacity to act in ways contrary to the love of God—what in traditional language is called sin—has personal, social, and even cosmic dimensions.

In light of the perceived conflict between spirit and matter, we are faced with two contrary temptations. One is simply to accept uncritically the urgings of worldly nature without careful discernment: "If it feels good, do it." While an appropriate enjoyment of pleasure is not sinful, unrestrained hedonism can lead to selfishness and the exploitation of others—where human beings and indeed all of nature are treated not as miraculous gifts from God, but as instruments to be used for personal pleasure or material gain.

The other temptation, which is more common in Christian circles, takes us in the opposite direction—away from the undiscerning embrace of material pleasure, to the rejection of even that which is good, including rejecting the body and nature as fallen or evil. Not only is this the error of dualism, but it ironically plays into the first temptation. If something is evil or fallen, why not treat it merely as an exploitable resource rather than as a gift from God?

Once again, this paradox is an expression of the purity/hospitality issue. Rejecting the errors, addictions, abuses, and injustices of the fallen world is a function of the quest for purity, while embracing and celebrating God's good creation (even in its messy imperfection) is a form of spiritual hospitality. Both are essential to the mystical quest. To resolve this paradox requires a willingness to affirm the material world as created good, but to regard it with thoughtful and careful discernment, so that the potential for misusing creation is always subject to mindful ethical and spiritual conscience.

Humanity is sinful (we resist love and justice).

All of humanity is invited to participate in union with God.

This paradox, like the one before it, involves one of the most unpopular and misunderstood Christian concepts: sin. Generally speaking, sin refers to the condition of being alienated from God, and making choices in life that either actively or passively result in resisting love and justice as the principles by which we live our lives.

When you fall in love with someone, really fall in love, you can become almost painfully conscious of all the ways you fail to live up to your beloved's expectation of who you are (or your own expectation of who you want to be). That is a fairly apt analogy for a useful understanding of the Christian understanding of sin as well as repentance (which means "adopt a new consciousness" although it also implies turning away from sin). A person might lead a carefree life, cheerfully ignoring all the many ways they resist or reject the demands of love in their life. But if they consciously choose to draw closer to God, they are much more likely to become keenly aware of their own imperfections—just as shining a bright light on an object makes its imperfections more readily visible. Repentance emerges out of love, out of the loving desire to respond to love, and it is oriented toward self-transformation for the sake of love. This is a far cry from the common misperception that repentance is merely something we mortals do to make God stop being angry with us.

Some Christians focus their faith more on an emphasis on how "bad" or sinful we mortals can be, rather than appreciating how good God is. Such sin-focused Christians forget that the word *sin* means simply "mistake," and does not necessarily involve "evil."

Here's one way to understand sin: whenever you make a choice that entails unloving or hurtful behavior, you have made a mistake, and sooner or later you will need to clean up the mess you've made.

This makes you just like every other human being who has ever lived. We all make mistakes, and we all have that something inside us that can make us act selfishly, where we willfully choose the self over love. But it's important to keep this in proportion, rather than succumbing to the ominous conclusion that "humankind is evil." Some people reject Christianity because they see it as a negative, pessimistic religion. But the problem of sin (and how to deal with it) is only one part of Jesus's overall message.

Christianity also promises that those who choose intimacy with God through Jesus will—in a process that begins now and lasts into eternity—actually become, in the words of Saint Peter, "partakers of the divine nature." You don't just get to meet God in the afterlife, as if heaven were some sort of cosmic reward for a job well done. Nor is your destiny limited to just an externalized dynamic of loving and being loved by God (but always remaining separate). The ultimate destiny for Christians, as understood by the great mystics throughout history, is *deification*—a word that basically means to become one with God. Becoming immersed in God, you become part of God. This doesn't mean becoming identical with God (as a friend of mine quips, you won't be responsible for supernovas), but the mystical union between creature and Creator represents the closest love and intimacy that any two beings can enjoy—or as a priest I once knew used to say during Mass, "God is closer to you than you are to yourself." That is the beginning of deification, of participating in the divine nature, of finding union—communion—with the Trinity.

Can a sinful—which is to say, broken and wounded and often narcissistic—humanity actually be destined to *participate* in God, the fount of ever-expansive love and delight? It's a paradox.

"The fear of the Lord is the beginning of wisdom."

Perfect love casts out fear.

Jesus consistently encouraged his disciples not to fear. Sometimes he says this to express reassurance; other times he seems to be scolding them for their timidity. Meanwhile, even Jesus's critics acknowledged that he himself was afraid of no one.[18] Nevertheless, Jesus does draw a distinction between not fearing those who merely can hurt the body while still fearing God, who alone has power over the soul. The fearlessness Jesus advocates in relating to other human beings is, paradoxically, related to a deep humility and awe that we should direct only toward God.

When the book of Proverbs in the Bible says "the fear of the Lord is the beginning of wisdom,"[19] perhaps the most important word in that verse is "beginning." Fear, dread, or existential angst, are emotions that can initiate a truly transformational spiritual journey. But if wisdom is born out of fear, it reaches its full maturity only through love. Love casts out the kind of fear that undermines our integrity and self-esteem; it purges us of seeing God as a force for punishment or condemnation. Love does not lead us to some sort of flippant place where we blithely ignore God's call to ethical integrity. The casting out of fear does not mean we can disregard the demands of the love that has been so freely given to us. Fearlessness is not the same as mindlessness. The love of God is not a sweet, sentimental emotion that ignores or denies such things as sin and suffering. We find fearless freedom in divine love precisely because we have known fear, and therefore know how to treat love with the respect it deserves.

Hope for the future when we are promised conscious union with God

Live now; we will only ever find God in the present moment

Not everyone gets to experience a jaw-dropping, eye-popping, mind-twisting encounter with the presence of God—what we colloquially call a "mystical experience." But pretty much everybody has peak experiences of some kind—what the twentieth-century mystic Evelyn Underhill calls "unitive experiences," or experience of oneness with God and/or the cosmos. In the words of psychologist Gerald G. May, "unitive experiences occur far more commonly and frequently . . . it appears, in fact, that they may well be virtually universal."[20] Such unitive experiences do not necessarily require a specifically religious or Christian setting; they may occur as a consequence of falling in love or feeling awe and joy when holding a newborn baby. They may manifest as a sense of getting caught up in a majestic mountain vista, where suddenly you and the mountains become one. Or they may be grounded in a similar feeling of joyous littleness when standing beneath the Milky Way on a dark, cloudless night, far enough away from the insidious glare of urban neon that the soft luminescence of the galaxy can be seen.

Peak experiences happen. Such unitive moments feel beautiful, joyous, even ecstatic. Even a humble experience of the beauty of nature can have a lifelong impact that changes how we understand real happiness or joy or simply feeling truly alive. Peak experiences offer us glimpses of how the future evolution of human consciousness can unfold and what humankind may experience in the centuries and millennia to come. Ken Wilber, whose work explores the evolution of consciousness, suggests that peak experiences are the harbingers of how human consciousness will evolve.

For Christians, peak or unitive experiences may not only represent hints of future evolution, they may also signify a present reality—the possibility of real, deep, lasting joy to be found in the presence of God. After all, if a work of art can evoke a sense of wonder, how much more remarkable it would be to intimately know the artist who created it. So peak experiences, even when triggered by nothing more than the grandeur of nature, are hints at the beauty that lies hidden in the mystery of God.

Remembering a wonderful peak experience can be a source of consolation, and hoping for a future mind-expanding encounter with God can be a means of inspiration that can keep us focused on the disciplines of the spiritual life. But life is not lived in the past or the future, no matter how glorious it was or how lovely it promises to be. Life is lived right here and right now, in the present moment. Which means that this is where mysticism happens as well.

Live by faith.

Live the truth.

Since mysticism concerns experience—such as the experience of loving God, of feeling loved by God, or taking responsibility to do the kinds of things that open you up to the sacred presence—then it seems counterintuitive to say that mysticism actually concerns faith. In fact, wouldn't faith even be a hindrance to mysticism, since faith, as described in the Bible, is "the assurance of things hoped for, the conviction of things not seen"?[21]

In posing this question, I'm reminded of Yoda, who, when teaching young Luke Skywalker, sternly admonished his apprentice to do the task given to him—not merely to "try." Wouldn't Christian mysticism work the same way? We are called to experience God's presence and love, not merely hope for it or believe in it.

Well, yes and no.

Mysticism encompasses more than just experience. It concerns *mystery*, and the mystery of God cannot be controlled, predicted, engineered, or manipulated. While God may compassionately grant some sort of unitive awareness to all sincere seekers, it may not be the kind of experience you hoped for or secretly think is necessary for a "real" mysticism. In fact, if you're not careful, your encounter with God's hidden and mysterious presence may be so subtle that you miss it altogether.

Just as there is no such thing as a perfect human being, so too there is no such thing as a perfect experience of God. Even mystics need faith, because the human knowledge and experience and awareness of God will never be perfect, at least not on this side of eternity. Faith is the lifeline that pulls us through the darkness—the darkness of our limited knowledge and awareness, the darkness we create for ourselves through our sin and our fear, the darkness of the pain and suffering that characterizes so much of life, and even the darkness of the mystery of God. We experience all of these shadow times, and sometimes even catch glimmers of God's presence in the dark. But there are other times when we may have only a dull sense of the darkness as, well, dark. And that's where faith proves essential.

Religious faith and spiritual experience are not at odds with one another. Experience is not a higher doorway to God that is opened for the deserving few, while faith is the breadcrumbs left on the table for those who fail to make the mystical grade. Rather, faith and experience work together just as the mind and the body work together. Those who listen to their hearts but not their heads (and vice versa) can quickly do foolish things. For example, romantic love without common sense can lead you to the wrong person, whereas common sense without love can lead to a life of joyless drudgery. "Use your head" and "follow your heart" are both great words of advice—especially when they are offered in tandem. Meanwhile, trusting your embodied intuition is very much akin to following your heart (perhaps they're the exact same thing).

Faith in God, and spiritual experience, relate together in much the same way. On the surface, merely assenting to the ideas or teachings of the Christian tradition can be a dry intellectual exercise. But faith is more than just choosing to agree to a set of propositions. In terms of following Jesus, faith is primarily about making a commitment to a relationship. It means giving one's entire self—heart as well as mind, body as well as soul—to the One who calls us into new life. That self-giving is, in itself, an experiential act. So you can't truly have faith without it having some sort of experiential foundation. And it works the other way as well. Take Paul's conversion on the road to Damascus. By itself, it was just an extraordinary experience. But since Paul was able to respond with faith to what was asked of him in that supernatural encounter with Christ, his experience became far more than just some sort of psychic anomaly. It became one of the most famous mystical encounters in Christian history. Like Paul's, all encounters with the mystery require this creative marriage of experience and faith. Without that melding, instead of being true mystical experiences, they would just be interesting spiritual phenomena. It's faith in the mystery that puts the mystery into mysticism.

Christian mysticism conforms to biblical wisdom and church teaching.

Mysticism means following spiritual vision to greater freedom.

What makes a person a Christian? Some will simply say "loving or following Jesus." Others may add that it also means worshipping Jesus, acknowledging him as the Son of God, as the Christ, and trying to live your life in a Christlike way. Still others may say it depends on whether you accept the authority of the Bible, which denomination (type of church) you belong to, or whether or not you believe in specific doctrines or teachings, such as the doctrine that God is a Trinity or that Christ is truly present in the Eucharist.

Christian mysticism, likewise, is not always easy to define, and different people will understand it in different ways. Some define it loosely as an undiscriminating tendency toward "out there" experiences. Others take a much more limited approach, insisting that you must be a good Christian in a religious sense in order to truly be a Christian mystic. What is at issue here is the role that Christian doctrine plays in the mystical life. Those with a more casual understanding of Christian mysticism may not particularly worry about Christian doctrine; while those with a narrower definition of what it means to be a Christian mystic probably have a stronger commitment to dogmatic teachings.

Although our larger society tends to value personal freedom above group identity, for most Christians the shared values of the community really do matter. A spirituality that is all about "doing your own thing" is ultimately centered not on Jesus but on the individual's personal freedom, which is given higher value than the wisdom of the community. Someone with that viewpoint might be a mystic, and might even respect Jesus, but perhaps they are not, ultimately, a *Christian* mystic.

But once again, here is a paradox. Christian mysticism conforms with the essential teachings of the Christian faith—but it also acknowledges, and even celebrates, the fact that the individual's subjective experience forms an essential part of the mystical life. To be a Christian mystic means taking Christian teachings seriously, but it also means trusting the truth of your own experience.

This can be tricky. Consider Galileo, who ran afoul of the church because he dared to promote scientific theories that contradicted what Christian authorities taught in their interpretation of the Bible. History has shown Galileo to be the wiser, an innocent victim of religious leaders who placed more faith in their own limited dogma than in an open-minded appreciation that biblical wisdom does not undermine scientific truth. Mysticism is not the same thing as science, but the tension is similar: whenever a mystic has a vision or receives some sort of insight into spiritual wisdom, there can be a genuine disagreement between the mystical experience and accepted religious teaching.

Consider these two Bible verses:

- *Where there is no prophecy, the people cast off restraint, but happy are those who keep the law (Proverbs 29:18).*
- *Do not let anyone disqualify you, insisting on self-abasement and worship of angels, dwelling on visions, puffed up without cause by a human way of thinking, and not holding fast to the head, from whom the whole body, nourished and held together by its ligaments and sinews, grows with a growth that is from God (Colossians 2:18–19).*

The verse from Proverbs suggests that "prophecy" (some translations render this as "vision" or "revelation") is actually connected to religious law. Without vision, people lose restraint. The function of vision is thus not so much to set you free in some sort of anti authoritarian sense, but rather to help you find a deep freedom in God in order to live in harmony with divine law—and, by extension, with human law as well, insofar as it is consistent with God's law. On the other hand, the passage from Colossians warns that visionaries, when "puffed up without cause" by a "human way of thinking," can lead us astray, simply because their pride gets in the way of the radical freedom that comes from the Spirit.

This paradox—that Christian mysticism conforms to Christian teachings, but also involves the potentially liberating experience of direct encounter with Christ—can be resolved only through discernment and a willing relationship with a wise and loving spiritual guide. This is not about control; it is about identity. Part of what gives Christian mysticism its identity is the recognition that not all spiritual ideas or insights are necessarily consistent with the Christian worldview or message. History shows that the greatest Christian mystics are those humble enough to work with a spiritual guide who can help them discern when their experiences are (or are not) consistent with the overall meaning of faith in a loving God. Letting go of visions or other mystical experiences that appear to undermine such faith may be a painful experience, but it serves a greater good—the glory of God and the health of the entire body of Christ.

Become like little children.

Love God with all your heart, soul, and mind.

This paradox emerges out of two teachings of Christ that appear, on the surface, to be contradictory. In Matthew 18:3, Christ says, "Unless you change and become like children, you will never enter the kingdom of heaven," while in Matthew 22:37, he says, "Love the Lord your God with all your heart, and with all your soul, and with all your mind," requiring a fully developed, adult capability for reasoning, knowing, loving, and willing. Comparing these two verses, you may wonder which is more important—to have a simple, childlike faith, or a more mature, intentionally comprehensive love for God?

Children often seem much more likely to take things on faith. They need no convincing to dream, to wonder, to play with possibilities. But there is a shadow side to this childlike openness: gullibility or naïveté, which can result in an uncritical acceptance of ideas or values that may not be good, beautiful, or true. Loving God with all your mind suggests making the effort to balance a childlike faith with a keen adult willingness to ask questions, to weigh evidence, and to seek the truth that may not always be explainable in a way that a small child can understand.

So what is Jesus asking of us? To be faithful but gullible, or to be discerning but skeptical?

Perhaps the resolution of this paradox emerges from another comment Christ made to his followers: "Be wise as serpents and innocent as doves" (Matthew 10:16). Jesus appears to suggest that his disciples hold different levels of consciousness within themselves simultaneously. The serpent represents the "adult" consciousness: shrewd, discerning, wise. The dove represents the "child" consciousness: innocent, simple, in the present moment. The key seems to be a matter of adopting the uncomplicated clarity of a child's mind, while simultaneously considering all the nuances that only an adult mind in its full maturity can attain. Christ appears to be calling us to have adult minds that remain childlike: to be both master and amateur, expert and humble beginner.

I suspect few of us have mastered this state of adult/child consciousness—
if we've ever achieved it at all. Perhaps some of the political wrangling in
the church (if not in society as a whole) seems to be driven by a rift between
those who are more faithful to their childlike minds and those who are
more faithful to their adult minds. We need both—both a pure and simple
childlike faith, and the discerning and wise mind that can come only out
of maturity. If we can't find them within ourselves, let us at least learn how
to respect and honor them in one another.

God is Father.

God is Mother.

God is nonbinary (God transcends gender).

Here is a triple paradox. The Nicene Creed—which for many people is the
single most succinct statement of just what it means to be a Christian—
begins with the words "I believe in God the Father Almighty," linking
God with male language. Likewise, most images of God in the Bible are
masculine, and Jesus explicitly calls God his father. Add to this all sorts of
historical imagery associated with God that is embedded in our cultural
understanding of maleness—God as king, warrior, mighty in battle, a
lover wooing a wayward bride—and many people seem convinced that
God is male.

But, like grass sneaking through the cracks in an urban sidewalk, some
images found in the Scripture paradoxically point to a more feminine image
of God. Both biological and cultural depiction of God as a mother occur in
the Bible. Isaiah describes God as a mother in labor and Moses compares
God to a mother nursing her children. In the story of Adam and Eve, God
adopts the role of a seamstress, tenderly making clothes for her disobedient
children. Jesus, meanwhile, compares God to an old widow seeking a lost
coin, and even presents himself as a mother hen who seeks to gather her
chicks under her wings.[22]

Meanwhile, the Holy Spirit is even more explicitly associated with feminine imagery. Not only is the Hebrew word for "spirit" feminine, but the
Spirit is linked with the feminine personification of wisdom, Sophia, and
with womanly traits like giving birth. Indeed, for several centuries after the
time of Christ, some Christian communities viewed the Spirit as feminine,

and some theologians today, like Robert Hughes, are calling us to reclaim this ancient, feminine tradition.

Many Christian mystics throughout history have celebrated the feminine face of God. Medieval mystics like Bernard of Clairvaux, Aelred of Rievaulx, and William of St. Thierry used feminine or maternal imagery when speaking of Jesus. Julian of Norwich, whom I would call the patron saint of the divine feminine, bluntly said, "As truly as God is our Father, just as truly is God our Mother."[23] In our own day, many Christians of all genders have embraced the idea of the Motherhood of God, presenting it as a healthy corrective to centuries of overly masculine imagery for the Ultimate Mystery.

So which is it? Is God our father, or our mother? Or does this paradox point to an even deeper truth?

The third part of our paradox comes from Saint Paul's declaration that in Christ "there is no longer male nor female" (Galatians 3:28). As best we know, the Jesus of history was a cisgender male, but Paul's surprising insight points to a way of understanding God that includes all genders, and/or transcends gender. To assign either masculinity or femininity to God is to diminish the essential divine unknowability. To assign gender to God is to limit God, and runs the risk of suggesting that one gender is "closer" to God, and also marginalizes not only the "other" gender but indeed all those whose gender identity or expression falls outside of the male/female binary.

Gender is so hard-wired into our culture, our languages, and our ways of organizing society and families, that for many people even merely questioning the traditional "God the father" formula feels deeply threatening. On the other hand, many people find the idea of assigning God a gender to be absurd or even a way of enforcing oppression against women and transgender persons. What, then, is a contemplative seeker to make of this?

From a mystical perspective, perhaps the best way to approach the question of God and gender is with a light touch, a willingness to be nonattached, and the humility that comes from unknowing. Yes, the tradition calls God the Father, but some voices also name God Mother—and at least one significant Bible verse makes room for moving even beyond the gender binary when relating to God.

The mystics remind us that restricting God to just one gender is a way of projecting our human biases on to God. Because human beings are embodied (and gendered) creatures, historically we have relied on masculine or feminine language to try to make God somehow more approachable. Seeing God as a father figure (or as a nurturing mother) makes God more relatable, at least for many people, than does the purely abstract language of a disembodied deity who cannot be captured by any image or category of human thought.

Mystery insists we remain fluid and flexible in the images we hold of God, including the question of gender. Mysticism, with its keen understanding of God as the ultimate mystery, makes room for us to do just that.

Mysticism is an intellectual pursuit.

Mystical union occurs in the heart.
Mystics like Meister Eckhart, Augustine, John of the Cross, and Thomas Aquinas possessed towering intellects, and certainly exercised their minds in their efforts to connect with God through knowledge. Their writing is deeply philosophical, often abstract and reliant on technical language to depict the intricacy of their understanding of the divine mystery.

Other renowned contemplatives, like Francis of Assisi, Jean-Pierre de Caussade, Thérèse of Lisieux, and Angelus Silesius, are known not for their mental prowess, but for the simplicity and beauty of their heartfelt devotion to God. And many mystics, even those of a more intellectual bent, have insisted that when it comes to embracing the mystery of God, the heart matters more than the mind. In the words of *The Cloud of Unknowing*, "we can't think our way to God. That's why I'm willing to abandon everything I know, to love the one thing I cannot think. [God] can be loved, but not thought. By love, God can be embraced and held, but not by thinking."[24]

So is mysticism a matter of keen intellectual insight into the Christian mysteries, or a simpler, emotional approach to loving God?

Perhaps this is a variation of a paradox we already considered: how we are called to love God with all the strength of our minds, and yet we are enjoined to become as simple as little children. How can we love God with our whole mind if the mind is ultimately cast into darkness by God's divine brilliance—meaning that we can know God only through unknowing?

It is human nature to seek God through intellectual means, following an innate desire to know, to understand, to comprehend. However, just as the quest for knowing requires a balance of the humility of unknowing, the intellectual quest for understanding requires being tempered by the affective, or emotional, dimension of mysticism. Challenge your mind as deeply as you can when you seek God; just make sure that you're also opening your heart. Intimacy, after all, requires loving more deeply than it does understanding, even as important as understanding is.

This same argument can be made in reverse, however. Reducing spirituality to merely sentimental feelings about God seems to be a way of avoiding the challenge of fostering true inner knowledge of the divine. The unknowable mystery is more than just a feel-good experience. It's one thing to enjoy a feeling of love for God, or a sense of release upon sensing God's mercy and forgiveness. But if we aren't discerning and mindful about the object of that love, perhaps all we are experiencing is an emotional projection of our own egos. That may feel like bliss, but is it really mysticism? Some spiritual writers, like Maggie Ross and Denys Turner, worry that our contemporary preoccupation with experience leaves us at risk of misunderstanding the wisdom of the great mystics—or, worse, of reducing mysticism to merely a type of spiritual narcissism. They have a point.

We resolve this paradox by saying yes. Is mystical wisdom mostly about the mind? Yes. Is contemplative spirituality mostly about the heart? Yes. The limitations or shadow side of each can be addressed by the gifts of the other.

Mysticism encompasses both abstract intellectual theory and feel-it-in-your-gut passion. Mysticism is visionary, and mysticism is erotic (in the best and highest sense of the word). Some mystics are more naturally "head" philosophers; others are more naturally "heart" lovers. For the fullness of the splendor of mystical Christianity, we need both.

Practically speaking, this means balance. Mystical seekers do well to immerse ourselves in the great stream of Christian wisdom and thought, from the teachings of the Bible to the visionary philosopher of the great mystics themselves. Yet we also need to put down all the books and retreat into silence and solitude to encounter the God who calls all of us more deeply to love. Then, the mystical life is about returning from solitude to engage in real-world life and relating to other people in love and joy, in conflict and challenge, in suffering and trials. What you think, what you feel, and how you love all matter to the mystical journey.

The mystical life is like climbing a mountain—it's a lifelong journey to reach the place God is calling you.

There's nothing separating you from the love of God—right here, right now. Here we face the question of degrees in the spiritual life. Does the path of the mystic involve a developmental process, moving from beginner, to intermediate, to adept, to advanced student or even master of the God-filled life? Or, is mysticism really just a matter of discovering that you already—always, completely, without qualification—exist right here and right now in the eternal and infinite love and presence of God?

The answer to both questions is simply yes. Many great mystics and contemplatives in the Christian tradition taught that the spiritual life is a process that unfolds through stages. The most common "map" of this process was first developed by the third-century mystic Origen of Alexandria, who felt that three of the Wisdom books of the Hebrew Scriptures (Proverbs, Ecclesiastes, and the Song of Songs) symbolize three stages of spiritual growth: purification, illumination, and union. The anonymous author of *The Cloud of Unknowing* suggested that contemplatives go through a four-stage process, while Evelyn Underhill, expanding on Origen's idea, outlined five stages. Other mystics, like Beatrice of Nazareth or Marguerite Porete, saw the mystical life as a journey with as many as seven stages. One of the most renowned of Christian mystics, Teresa of Ávila, also came up with a system of seven "mansions" that the soul traveled through in its journey toward Christ in what Teresa called *The Interior Castle*.

The number of stages on the path is not important, and it's helpful to remember that "the map is not the territory"; thus any system of trying to understand the lifespan of the mystic in stages is just that: a map, that may not always be helpful in all situations. Nevertheless, it's clear that many mystics envision the spiritual life as a journey that, like any process, requires time, effort, and the passing of recognizable landmarks along the way.

But what about mystics who suddenly encountered or embodied the unmediated presence of God, without going through all these stages first? There's the apostle Paul, who heard the voice of Jesus even while he was still in the business of persecuting Christians; and Julian of Norwich, who had a life-altering vision after apparently doing little more than praying for blessings from God. Jesus told a parable in which a man hired workers to work on his land, and he paid the same wage to those who worked there all day long and those who arrived at the last hour. Did Jesus intend to imply by this that the fullness of union with God is available to anyone, at any time, not just those who work the "long hours"?

Just as we saw earlier that no spiritual method or technique of prayer is necessary to achieve intimacy with God, no linear beginner-to-advanced process is required either. To say something is not essential, however, is not the same as saying it is never useful. After all, love at first sight may exist, but most people in happily-ever-after relationships go through a slow and steady process of becoming acquainted before making a lifelong commitment.

And so it is with the spiritual life. When John of the Cross compared the mystical life to the ascent of Mount Carmel, he was not declaring that anyone with any hope of experiencing God's presence must climb the mountain in the very same manner. He was making the important point that, for many lovers of God, the journey can be quite long—and arduous. When we think of the mystical life in this way, we can approach the wisdom of great mystics like John of the Cross as signposts along the path that help seekers to find their way. And one of those signposts says, "Not everyone has to follow this route; some of you can get there in the twinkling of an eye."

In his book *Beloved Dust: Tides of the Spirit in the Christian Life*, theologian Robert Davis Hughes recasts the traditional purgation/illumination/union sequence in different language—as conversion, transfiguration, and glory. But as his "tides" metaphor suggests, Hughes argues that these "waves" of spiritual experience can wash up on the shore of the soul in any order, in any sequence, in any way. Perhaps we can truly say that the mystical life will, sooner or later, call us to conversion, to transfiguration, and to glory. But as for how these experiences will manifest in any one person's life—only the Spirit knows for sure.

God meets us in silence.

Mystics seek to express the ineffable through words.

The mystical life is grounded in silence. Most forms of meditative prayer (or prayer that prepares us for contemplation, like Centering Prayer) are steeped in silence. Monasteries are silent places. Traditionally, even neighborhood churches have been places for quiet reflection, and the desert or the wilderness (locations traditionally linked to the lives of many mystics and contemplatives) are places that invite deep solitude.

Silence is an essential vitamin for the spiritual life in general, and the mystical life especially. This may seem odd to our generation, whose lives are filled with electronic gadgets that continually generate sound and noise. But, when you stop to consider it, all the sonic clutter in your life functions as little more than a distraction that can keep you from attending to the unobtrusive (and profoundly silent) presence of God.

A mystery is something that cannot be explained; in spiritual terms, the ultimate mystery, the mystery of God, cannot even be put into words. We cannot fully and finally capture the fullness of the divine ineffability in mere human language.

Perhaps our words can give us a vague sense of what we believe about God, or what our faith tells us that God has revealed to us. But, even then, words leave us with more questions than answers, and often lead us straight into paradox. Since God is so ultimately unknowable—the divine light is so dazzling that it blinds us—perhaps it's reasonable to say that the word of God is so overpowering that we can experience it only as (and through) silence.

As soon as I say that, however, another paradox emerges, for I am using words to testify to God's "meta-wordness." This paradox has been part of the mystical tradition since the days of the biblical writers (if not before). We cannot put God into words. And, it appears, we cannot stop trying to do just that. In the Gospel of John, one of the names of Christ himself is "the Word of God." Yet the word of God—Scripture—teaches us again and again to be silent as a way of praying to, praising, and knowing God.[25]

G. K. Chesterton famously said, "If a thing is worth doing, it is worth doing badly."[26] And this seems to be the motivation behind mystics who talk about, write about, or teach others about their experience, their visions, their insight, their speculations and ruminations about God. Of course, all their words fail—some more spectacularly than others. Some are even rejected for how their words are interpreted (or misinterpreted). Mystics from Origen to Meister Eckhart to Pierre Teilhard de Chardin are admired for their contemplative genius, even though their teachings—their words—have been questioned by some Christians as being just a little too "out there." Then there was Thomas Aquinas who, after his mystical vision on the Feast of Saint Nicholas, stopped writing because he realized that all his words were worth little more than straw.

Well, compared to the silent splendor of the divine mystery, he's right. But I, for one, am glad that Aquinas at least tried to give expression to his encounter with the mystery. And I'm glad that Teresa of Ávila and John of the Cross and Julian of Norwich and John Ruusbroec and Howard Thurman, Thomas Merton, and Evelyn Underhill and countless others tried as well. Surely, all of them knew in their own way just how impoverished and error-prone and limited their words were as they tried to describe the mystery of God. And they were right. Before the great silence of the unknowable splendor of God, all words fail. But even the words that fail need to be spoken, for that can guide us back into the mystery.

Only God can satisfy the longing in our heart.

The more we have of God, the greater our longing becomes.
The book of Sirach (found in Catholic and Orthodox Bibles, but considered Apocrypha by Protestants) records God as saying,

> Come to me, you who desire me,
>   and eat your fill of my fruits.
> For the memory of me is sweeter than honey,
>   and the possession of me sweeter than the honeycomb.
> Those who eat of me will hunger for more,
>   and those who drink of me will thirst for more.[27]

On a purely physical level, if we are hungry or thirsty, we become satisfied when we have something to eat or drink, and we can stop consuming, at least for a while until the hunger or thirst returns.

Meanwhile, it is a truism among mystics that only God can ultimately satisfy our longings. In the words of Augustine, "Our hearts are restless until they rest in You, God." Perhaps this is one of the reasons why so many human beings suffer from addictions, or hoarding behaviors, compulsive spending, and so forth: we are seeking to satisfy a spiritual hunger within us that can only be satisfied by God.

But, as Sirach points out, the attainment of God paradoxically *increases* our desire rather than satisfying it. C. S. Lewis suggested that this longing "is distinguished from other longings by two things . . . though the sense of want is acute and even painful, yet the mere wanting is felt to be somehow a delight. . . . This hunger is better than any other fullness; this poverty better than all other wealth."[28] Mystical spirituality is based on what a former spiritual director of mine called "the God-shaped hole" found in each of our hearts (see the quote from Augustine). Even though Christians believe as a matter faith that God is already present in our hearts (see Romans 5:5, and consider the idea that God is *omnipresent*, present everywhere), so many people experience God as absent—some of the time, or even most or all of the time. So our experience of God is sometimes an experience of longing for God, hungering for God, desiring God. And even if or when we are blessed with a sense of God's presence, even of union with God, this blessing has the paradoxical quality of *increasing* our sense of longing, rather than satiating it. Or both together. And following Lewis, mystics wouldn't trade away that longing-for-God for the world.

This is one of those paradoxes that cannot be resolved, at least not on this side of eternity. It is part of the human condition to long for God (even agnostics and atheists long for God under other names: names like meaning, or purpose, or love, or insight or the ground of all being). Only God can satisfy this longing-for-God, and yet the experience of God, no matter how fulfilling or complete it may feel, always serves to *increase* this longing. Mystics wouldn't have it any other way.

Mysticism is the way of power.

Mysticism is the way of powerlessness.

In his book *The Power of His Resurrection: The Mystical Life of Christians,* Episcopal bishop Arthur A. Vogel suggests that religion in general, and mysticism in particular, are meaningful because they give us access to the power of God. "Religion and God are means by which people discover ultimate meaning," he writes. "But if belief in God is worth anything it must make a difference in our lives. We must be able to experience the power of God. . . . Mysticism is the experience of the 'more'—God—in one's life. It is the tasting of God's power as one's daily bread."[29] These are wise words, and they address the crisis of many Christian churches today, where people are abandoning institutional religion precisely because it does not seem to make much of a difference in many people's lives.

Still, when I read Bishop Vogel's words, I felt resistance, because of this paradox: *mysticism is also about powerlessness.* Christians are called to be *empty* like Christ became empty when taking on human form.[30] Jesus consistently taught a spirituality of nonresistance—"Turn the other cheek"— and of humility—"the last shall be first . . . those who lose their life for my sake will find it".[31] How can a spirituality based on principles like "Blessed are the meek" be about *power*?

This paradox requires us to understanding the difference between earthly and heavenly power. Jesus's teachings are clear that when human beings engage in power games with one another, we can only expect never-ending conflict to ensue (if you have any doubts about this, just spend some time on social media, making sure to read posts across the political spectrum). As great visionaries like Mahatma Gandhi, Howard Thurman, and Martin Luther King Jr. understood, sometimes the best political move is a move where power is expressed not in terms of force or violence, but only in terms of love and compassion. Back to Bishop Vogel: the power of mysticism is not the power of force, but the power of love. And sometimes we can only make ourselves available to the power of love by, paradoxically, surrendering the power of force. This is exemplified in Psalm 46: "Be still and know that I am God"—the meaning of this verse in the original Hebrew carries a sense of "become undefended, lay down your arms, and in that quiet place you will know the living God."[32] For a mystic, knowing the living God is the greatest power imaginable. But to receive that power might just involve surrendering power in many lesser forms.

TAKING THE PARADOXES (NOT SO) SERIOUSLY

One way to look at all these paradoxes, and all the ideas and words that go into explaining them or making sense of them, is to approach them all as a form of play. We tend to take our relationship with God very seriously—which is understandable, since a major theme of at least the Western religions is to order our behavior in a way that makes it pleasing to God. But Psalm 37:4 invites us to *take delight in God*—so perhaps a little bit of joy and even playfulness can be woven in with our seriousness.

This is not to suggest the mystical life is frivolous, merely that there is more room in it for smiling than we (who sometimes tend to take ourselves too seriously) may do. And this, I believe, is what paradox ultimately teaches us. We do not have it all figured out, under control, managed, and packaged. God is slippery and keeps wriggling out from our feeble efforts to pin God down. To the extent that we want (consciously or subconsciously) to be in control of our lives, we are likely to find this idea of God delighting in playful paradox rather hard to take.

Yet that's precisely how God appears to want it.

God tries to keep us on our toes—not because God has a twisted sense of humor and wants us to feel uncomfortable, but because God knows that the best antidote for taking ourselves (and our spirituality or religion) too seriously is to fill our faith with all sorts of apparent contradictions. Sooner or later, you just have to throw up your hands and say, "Okay, God, I give up. There's no figuring you out." At that point, God comes to you "as a little child," laughs in your face, and says, "That's great, because all that really matters is how much I love you! Let's go play!"

PARADOXICAL CONSCIOUSNESS

God is paradoxical, not only because God transcends human logic, and not only because God wants us to learn to have a more childlike, playful trust in divine love and mercy, but also because paradox can be a springboard to mystical consciousness.

Given that mysticism is all about mystery, it follows that the hardest paradoxes to crack are, in essence, profound mysteries. These mysteries/paradoxes function within the Christian tradition in a manner similar to how koans function in Zen Buddhism. Practitioners of Zen receive a koan from their roshi (teacher), often in the form of a question that seems rationally impossible to answer. One famous koan, for example, is "What is the sound of one hand clapping?" As part of their meditation practice, these students of Zen wrestle with the koan, not simply to find the correct or appropriate response, but—more to the point—to reach the limits of rationality and then move beyond those limits into the expansive place of pure presence where a new or heightened state of consciousness may arise.

A significant, but often ignored, declaration of the apostle Paul is that "we have the mind of Christ" (1 Corinthians 2:16). But what exactly *is* the mind of Christ? The Greek word *nous* offers a variety of connotations: mind, understanding, wisdom, comprehension. The pagan philosopher Plotinus spoke of the *nous* as an emanation from the divine source. This reminds me of a fascinating statement by the psychologist/contemplative Gerald May, who, in his book *Will and Spirit*, wrote, "It seems quite certain, in fact, that rather than saying, 'I have consciousness,' it would be far more accurate to say, 'Consciousness has me.'"[33] So, perhaps one of the gifts we can receive from the many paradoxes of mystical Christianity is the opportunity to bump up against the limits of our own finite human consciousness, and thereby open ourselves up to let the divine consciousness (the mind of Christ) "have" us. When this happens, all the paradoxes melt away into nonoppositional, nondual awareness—pure love, pure being, pure light and pure joy. God does not resolve paradox. God simply transcends it.

And God invites us along for the ride.

CHAPTER ELEVEN

Christianity's Best-Kept Secret

So you have pain now; but I will see you again, and your hearts
will rejoice, and no one will take your joy from you.
—Jesus (John 16:22)

We have heaven within ourselves since the Lord of
heaven is there.
—Teresa of Ávila

I often get asked some variation of this question: "If Christian mysticism
is so wonderful and important, why don't you hear more about it from the
church?"

I wish I could provide a concise answer. In fact, there are a number of
historical, theological, and institutional reasons that have kept mysticism
hidden on the margins of mainstream Christianity.

Many in the institutional church—ministers, priests, and other church
leaders—either never talk about mysticism at all, or seem to be uncertain
about its role in the Christian life. An Episcopal priest once told me, "I'm
not sure what mysticism means anyway. My focus is on discipleship, and
discipleship involves a direct and personal, as well as social, relationship
with Jesus and with God." His comment suggests that, for many Christians, the language of mysticism, with its emphasis on mystery, darkness,

unknowing, and paradox, can be intimidating or even threatening—or, at the very least, seems irrelevant to those who may not be naturally drawn to mystical language and concepts.

For many Christians, there is a distinction between a "direct and personal" relationship with God and the profound but ineffable union that forms the heart of mysticism.

This is nothing new. Fifteen hundred years ago, an anonymous mystical theologian who used the pseudonym Dionysius the Areopagite wrote,

> Theological tradition has a dual aspect, the ineffable and the mysterious on the one hand, the open and more evident on the other. The one resorts to symbolism and involves initiation. The other is philosophic and employs the method of demonstration. . . . The one uses persuasion and imposes the truthfulness of what is asserted. The other acts and, by means of a mystery which cannot be taught, it puts souls firmly in the presence of God.[1]

In other words, Christianity for centuries has operated on a kind of dual-track system, where a "mainstream" tradition presents faith as a system of morals, or a set of rituals to mark important life transitions like birth, coming of age, marriage, and death, and a story of God's love preparing us for heaven after we die.

The alternative tradition, often hidden away in monasteries, regards faith as a process of inner transfiguration where the focus is not on going to heaven after we die, but on allowing God to transform us from the inside out, basically getting heaven into us (instead of getting us into heaven). This tradition of inner transfiguration is the mystical tradition. It's available to those who earnestly seek it, but many Christians may not want it, may not seek it, or may not even know about it.

There are historical reasons why mysticism has fallen out of favor in mainstream Western Christianity, largely aftershocks of the Protestant Reformation. But perhaps the most compelling reason has more to do with the nature of mysticism itself. Mysticism simply doesn't "preach" very well because it challenges the comfort and ease by which most of us settle into established religious observances, accepting the relatively modest demands of church membership (to live a quiet, obedient, and moral life) in exchange for an abstract belief that God loves us and will care for us, now and after we die.

Mysticism upsets this status quo, not because it is less demanding that mainstream religion: on the contrary, it is *more* demanding, but it also carries a much more visionary promise.

Mysticism can shake the foundations of everything you believe or think you know about God. At the same time, it subverts our contemporary addiction to entertainment and excitement, for contemplative practice demands a daily commitment to spiritual practices that, sooner or later, can feel boring or stifling. Trappist monks describe their lives as "ordinary, obscure, and laborious." Mysticism promises union with God, but the commitments it requires of us seem pretty daunting: a life of daily discipline, continual growth in humility and self-sacrifice, and letting go of everything in our lives that does not foster love. Moreover, while we are assured that, through spiritual discipline, we will partake of God's loving presence, there's no guarantee that we will experience it consciously—just because we trust the wisdom of the mystics that God is present in our heart does not mean we will feel something "special." All this is to say that Christian mysticism simply may not appeal to those who do not feel impelled to explore it.

NO SILVER PLATTER

A friend of mine recently told me a story that illustrates the ambiguous relationship between mysticism and religion, at least within Christianity. Like many people, he had been a spiritual explorer, exploring yoga and Zen and other practices from around the world before settling into a more prosaic spiritual practice as an Episcopalian. While he liked the Episcopal Church, before long he began to chafe at what he thought was a rather superficial approach to spirituality. Where was the depth that he had encountered in Eastern meditation? Finally, he took his question to his priest. "It's hidden in plain sight," was the minister's response. "The Christian tradition has just as much depth as any other wisdom tradition, but no one's going to hand it to you on a silver platter. You have to go looking for it." The priest went on to recommend a few books—like *The Philokalia* and *The Cloud of Unknowing*—challenging my friend to take responsibility for his own spiritual quest.

Valentin Tomberg, a Russian philosopher and mystical writer, once wrote about the personalities of angels. He suggested that angels are always eager and ready to assist us in whatever way we need, but, because of their evolved sense of ethics, they never interfere in human affairs unless asked to. I believe this is the same dynamic that governs the Holy Spirit's relationship with us as we stand on the threshold of the mystical life. We become mystics or contemplatives only through the grace of God at work in our lives. Any effort we make to do it strictly on our own is likely doomed to failure. Indeed, the author of *The Cloud of Unknowing* has stern words for those who, through pride and the folly of their own imagination, try to become mystics or contemplatives without humbly relying on the guidance of the Spirit. He calls these pseudo-mystics the "devil's contemplatives." Contemplation and mysticism are always gifts from God. But God will never force those gifts on anyone. God is not in the business of spiritual coercion.

It's not easy to scale a mountain. If you want to climb Mount Everest, you need to be in great shape, capable of withstanding harsh weather conditions and high altitudes, and prepared to pay for guides and assorted other expenses. You also need companions; it's not a trip you can take by yourself.

Mystical spirituality (Christian or otherwise) works much the same way. You need to be spiritually fit to withstand the challenges of the mystical life. You must be prepared to withstand the harsh conditions of profound inner doubt, facing the pain and suffering of the world, and releasing your own sinfulness into the cleansing grace of God. You need to "pay" for your experience with a disciplined life grounded in faith. And, as we have seen while there may be an inherent solitude in the contemplative experience, it is a solitude that must be embedded in some form of communal experience. Every mountain climber needs a base camp; every pilot needs a ground crew; every mystic needs a spiritual director or companion, and some sort of spiritual community.

The mountain-climbing metaphor fails, however, at a certain point. It makes mysticism sound too much like some sort of grand hobby, available to anyone willing to pay the spiritual price. This metaphor fails if it gives the impression that mysticism is some sort of spiritual extreme sport that affluent individuals can enjoy at their leisure. The mountain climbing metaphor is intended merely to show how spiritually arduous mysticism can be, to help explain why so few people choose to respond to the contemplative call. Thankfully, not every peak is as inaccessible as Everest, nor does everyone feel a compulsion to climb it.

The mystics who devote their lives to scaling the highest peaks do so because they are called to it. And they will be the first to tell you that every single step of their spiritual lives would be impossible were it not for the grace that blesses them at each point along the way.

For every person who is called to scale the highest spiritual peaks, there are countless others who are called to climb the foothills—to walk their own unique spiritual paths that may seem "lesser" than the highest summits but are demanding in their own way and still promise profound joy and meaning to those who accept the challenge. And even those who are not called to climb mountains can still discern within their hearts an inner stirring to retreat into the wilderness for a day or a weekend for rest and renewal.

Here's yet another paradox of mysticism: there is only one path to follow, yet each of us must find our own way. We are all tellers of a unique tale, and yet all our stories are woven together by the Spirit into one grand narrative. Ultimately, there is only one story, only one tale to tell. Nevertheless, our part in the story is always unique: it's a waste of time trying to climb someone else's mountain, follow someone else's path, tell another person's tale.

Hidden drives to be just like someone else can confound your spiritual life, just as surely as they can complicate your career or your marriage. The path of the contemplative is at times dark and hidden in the cloud of unknowing; it requires tremendous trust and a profound willingness to be led by a Spirit who communicates with you in only the softest of whispers. This includes trusting in the singular beauty of your own path, no matter how unexceptional (or unfulfilling) it may seem, at times, to be.

But mysticism is not just about discipline and drudgery, either. Ultimately it is about falling ever more deeply in love with Love. The mystical dimension of Christianity is founded on the infinite creativity of our divine lover. Every one of us is called to be intimate with God and worship and enjoy God in a way that is unique and personal and can never be repeated by anyone else. What this means, of course, is that no program of mystical development, no game plan for mastering contemplation, no step-by-step process for becoming a mystic, can ever be written or implemented. There can never be a one-size-fits-all approach to the unfolding of the splendors of mystical Christianity in your life. You can read the instructional writings of

Teresa of Ávila or John of the Cross and, hopefully, their words will inspire you, challenge you, beguile you, call you to enter more fully and deeply into the mysteries of God. But no one other than the Holy Spirit can show you the path you must take to become a contemplative. Mystics are like angels; no two are the same.

This may be why, as important as the written word has been to mystics and contemplatives down the ages, the ministry of one-on-one spiritual companionship (known as spiritual accompaniment or spiritual direction) has been such a central part of Christian mysticism. Spiritual directors are not gurus or even mentors, for in the Christian tradition it is understood that the one true director or guide for the inner life must always be the Spirit. Because we are each unique, we each face different challenges and opportunities for our own individual journeys into the heart of God. Rather than making yourself miserable trying to conform your own walk with God to what you think you "ought" to be doing, open your heart (and your mind) and share your inner life with a loving and wise spiritual companion so that the Spirit can more easily guide you on your own personal path (see chapter 13, "The Mystical Body," for more about spiritual accompaniment).

The mountain-climbing metaphor helps to illustrate why Christian mysticism doesn't get proclaimed very often in Sunday morning sermons. It's not that the clergy are necessarily hostile to it. It's just that most churchgoing Christians do not seem to be interested in immersing themselves in the Christian mysteries on such a profound and life-changing level.

Imagine your priest or minister preaching a sermon that challenges the assembly to embrace the mysteries of God, to surrender traditional ideas of faith for the profound paradoxes and ambiguities of a spirituality that cannot be put into words, and to enter deeply into silence and unknowing, all to seek profound inner transformation under the guidance of the Spirit. For those who do not feel called to such a contemplative or mystical spirituality, a sermon like that might seem troubling—or perhaps even threatening. Every Christian is called to a relationship with God, yet many choose to limit their spirituality to something very gentle and simple. I point this out not to criticize people, but to try to explain why mysticism can only be found on the margins. The radical potential of mystical spirituality is born out of silence and solitude, rather than preaching and public announcements.

Some Christians, particularly those from evangelical or fundamentalist backgrounds, may think that mysticism is somehow at odds with the teachings of Jesus. While I am convinced that such a perspective is based on a poor understanding of what mysticism is, and an equally poor understanding of mysticism's place in the history of Christian spirituality, unfortunately it is a fairly widely-held set of misunderstandings. When mysticism is perceived as being more about subjective feelings than objective spiritual truth, some are too quick see it in a negative light. Others may assume that mysticism has more to do with Eastern or occult spirituality than with historic Christianity. Again, this is a misunderstanding, but unfortunately it can dissuade many sincere churchgoers from exploring how mysticism can bring blessings to their faith. As we saw in chapter 6, mystical spirituality and contemplative practice often appeal to Christians who also feel called to learn from the wisdom of other faiths. Such interfaith exploration does not make a person less of a Christian; but to those who feel uncomfortable with any kind of religious belief other than their own, this kind of work can seem dangerous. Unfortunately, in the minds of many of its critics, Christian mysticism appears to be basically equivalent to interfaith spirituality—and equally to be avoided.

While some Christians (both clergy and lay) are hostile to mysticism, many others are either indifferent to the topic, or perhaps are curious about it, even if they have difficulty expressing that curiosity using the language of their church-based spirituality. Meanwhile, nearly all of the people now generally regarded as the great mystics of Christian history have been engaged with the external expression of Christianity as much as they have been dedicated to the pursuit of inner spiritual growth and transformation. With that in mind, it's a mistake to assume that mysticism and the church are somehow fundamentally at odds, or to assume that mysticism is good, and organized religion bad.

MYSTICISM VERSUS SPIRITUALITY

For many Christians, spirituality is simply a word to describe the inner experience of faith—in other words, a word that can be used to describe prayer (public or private), Bible study, efforts to live a good and ethical life, the use of formal or memorized devotions like the Catholic rosary, participation in charismatic prayer groups or evangelical revivals, or simply regular attendance at Sunday worship services.

All of these are valid and much-loved expressions of Christian spirituality, and none of them are necessarily opposed to mysticism. Indeed, all of these can be portals into a deeper appreciation of the Christian mysteries. But what separates the mystical dimension from all the other variations of Christian spirituality is that it explicitly embraces the profound mystery that can be encountered at the heart of religious experience—and that can be apprehended only through the grace of God.

Some forms of so-called spirituality, Christian or otherwise, can subtly reinforce experiences, not of God, but of the ego. Christian mysticism, on the other hand, concerns the more daunting task of surrendering the ego before the cross of Christ. It's about immersing your self-identity into the cloud of unknowing and the dark night of the soul. It is the hidden or "negative" path where, ultimately, all is stripped away before the awesome presence of God.

Many sincere and dedicated churchgoers seem to neither want nor need such a profound encounter with mystery. Perhaps they have not yet been called to go deeper or higher into the darkness of unknowing. Perhaps they are called to keep things simple, more explainable, at least for now. Whatever the reason, for many Christians, their spiritual path simply does not presently entail an encounter with the divine mystery at the heart of mysticism.

If you feel called to mystical spirituality, I encourage you to remember Jesus's teaching to "judge not" and therefore to refrain from judging or criticizing those who seem not to share your hunger for divine mystery. Everyone's path is unique, and the community of faith is large enough to encompass both those who are drawn to contemplation and those who aren't (or aren't yet). Remember Karl Rahner's prophetic words: "The Christian of the future will be a mystic or will not exist at all." Perhaps the Spirit will call more and more people into the splendor of the mysteries, for the purpose of transforming the entire body of Christ into a more truly mystical community. Such a revolution will take place one person at a time.

Christian mysticism remains hidden in plain sight, even in the very Christian churches where Jesus is adored and love is proclaimed. It's encoded in the Bible; it swirls around such universal practices as baptism and communion; it is potentially a part of the inner life of anyone who bothers to pray or who feels a longing to be quiet in the presence of God. It is only by the grace of God that anyone is called to the contemplative life. But no one is going to hand the mysteries to you (or anyone else) on that silver platter. It may not be hard to find, but it requires that you go looking for it.

The noted scholar of Christian mysticism Bernard McGinn wrote these words about a medieval mystic named William of St. Thierry: "Seeing God, then, begins with a vision that is not really a vision but is God's invisible presence working within us by grace and by faith, not yet in an experiential and perceptible way. . . . The development of the ability to see God is one and the same as advancing in the love of God. . . . If seeing God is really loving and knowing God on a new level, it is also nothing more nor less than becoming God."[2]

If you are like me, words like this fill you with wonder and inspire you to imagine the possibilities of ever-deepening intimacy with God. Or, such words might not impact you much one way or the other. Trust your own relationship with the Spirit, and remember, each of us is unique in how we are called to respond. Your journey into the mysteries of contemplative and mystical spirituality is unique. Do not compare yourself to me, or to William of St. Thierry, or to the average person attending church on Sunday morning. Seek *your* relationship with the Holy Spirit, and let the Spirit be your guide.

This brings us to the conclusion of the first part of this book. As we transition into part 2, our journey will be less about trying to discover what mysticism is, and more oriented toward how ordinary people like you and me can begin to apply the wisdom of the mystics to our lives. The journey is just beginning.

PART II

The Contemplative Life

Be still, and know that I am God!
—Psalm 46:10

For it is not what you are, nor what you have been, that God
beholds with merciful eyes, but what you desire to be.
—*The Cloud of Unknowing*

CHAPTER TWELVE

The Embodied Heart

The joy I saw in the words shown to me surpasses all that the
heart may know or the soul may desire.
—Julian of Norwich

God has made everything beautiful in its time,
and has set eternity in the human heart.
—Ecclesiastes 3:11 (my translation)

When I learned how to drive a car, I had to complete two courses. The first
took place in a classroom, where I learned about traffic laws and safety
principles. Once that was done, I moved to what we called the "behind the
wheel" course, where a driving instructor accompanied me in a car and we
put into practice what I had learned in the classroom.

This book is structured in a similar way. Part 1 was the classroom material, in which we explored the basic ideas of mystical Christianity. Now
we move to the behind the wheel course, where we can explore how the
contemplative path might become part of our lives, here and now.

I write these words with a deep and abiding sense of humility, knowing that I have no authority to teach anyone how to become a mystic or
to live a mystical life. Indeed, no one has that authority—it belongs to
the Holy Spirit alone. I write these words not as a teacher or master of

the contemplative life, but simply as a fellow seeker. Think of us—you and me—as two hungry people, desperately searching for food. Thanks only to the grace of God, and the wisdom of my own teachers over the years, I've caught a glimpse of where we might find the nourishment we so desperately need. So now I am saying to you, "Here, let's go this way." That's the extent of my authority here.

You, of course, need to weigh everything I've written throughout this book, in the light of your own intuition and discernment. Spirituality is not a spectator sport; ultimately you can only embrace the mystical life by following the wisdom of your own heart. Anything you might learn from a great mystic like Julian of Norwich, a more recent contemplative teacher like Howard Thurman, or even from a fellow seeker like myself, must ultimately be tested in the crucible of your own heart. For it is in your embodied heart where you, ultimately, are called to encounter and embrace the mystery of divine love.

It's very easy to get stuck in our heads when talking about, thinking about, or even seeking to live out the mystical dimension of Christianity. As we transition out of the purely theoretical and into the more practical exploration of our topic, therefore, our first essential task is to get out of our heads and into our bodies. To do that, let's engage in a series of reflections on the *heart* and its role in biblical and Christian spirituality. According to the Bible, the heart is a treasure house: in it we find the gifts of eternity, of wisdom, of love, and indeed of the Spirit herself. My book *Eternal Heart: The Mystical Path to a Joyful Life* is an extended meditation on a variety of gifts that God has placed in every human being's heart, all of which are documented in the Bible. In other words, you have everything you need to embrace the mystical life, right here, right now, given to you in your heart of hearts. You don't have to earn it or achieve it, you simply need to consent to the gifts you have been given and learn, with God's grace, to calibrate your life according to the wisdom, serenity and joy that those gifts make available to you.

The biblical concept of the heart can be understood a metaphor for the entire human body. In other words, the mystical life—the contemplative practices and spiritual experience that open and direct us to union with God—happens *in the body* and therefore true mystical Christianity is earthy, embodied, and sensual. We are invited to find God in our own hearts, our own bodies, and therefore to find God in all things. In his letter to the Romans, the apostle Paul wrote, "God's love has been poured into our hearts through the Holy Spirit that has been given to us."[1] As gifts of the heart go, that's about as good as it gets. With the Spirit and the love of God already embodied in our hearts, we are now called to live by the wisdom and guidance of such interior treasures. And with the Spirit guiding us from within, we become capable of recognizing divine presence not only in ourselves, but indeed in others and in the world at large. As Julian of Norwich so succinctly put it, "The fullness of joy is to behold God in all."

We may not *feel* the presence of the Holy Spirit or the love of God in our hearts, but if we accept Paul's words, then we may trust that the divine presence is there, whether we consciously experience it or not. This is the foundation of mystical theology and contemplative practice.

When we are willing to trust that God is in our hearts, we can also recognize that we are one with God—and have been so all along. Mysticism is not something we earn or achieve, it is something we recognize and receive. But while it is earthy and humble, paradoxically the sky is the limit: there is no end to the how deeply we can be transfigured by this recognition event, which means there is no limit to the joy we can embrace or the love we can share with others.

The Bible bluntly proclaims that nothing is impossible for God, and with God, all things are possible.[2] The mystical life offers us limitless potential and unbounded possibility. What is possible here? Infinite joy, wonder, delight and reverie, lost in the beauty of the divine presence. But the mystical tradition makes clear that the graces of the interior life are never given to us merely for our own enjoyment—they are always a means to an end, the end being our capacity to love and serve others, to work for making the world a better place by dismantling all forms of injustice, privilege, or oppression, and fostering relationships and communities based in equity, inclusivity, peace, and justice.

So how do we access the presence of the Spirit, not to mention divine love, in our hearts? Perhaps Jesus himself shows us the way in the Sermon on the Mount, when he taught this principle for prayer: "Whenever you pray, go into your room and shut the door and pray to your Father who is in secret; and your Father who sees in secret will reward you."[3]

Christian mystics down the ages have interpreted "your room" as a way of speaking about the heart. After all, many of the common people who heard Jesus speak when he preached in the villages of Galilee would not have had an extra room in their house just for prayer. But the one "room" that everyone has is the inner room of the heart. To "go into your room and shut the door" is to center your awareness in your heart, what Orthodox contemplatives call "letting the mind sink into the heart." We "shut the door" by closing our mouths (settling into silence) and our eyes (resting within, and not just being carried away by external stimuli).

Once we are settled in our inner rooms and we have closed the door on external stimuli, distractions, and the chattering noisiness of our stream of thoughts, then we may begin the practice of learning to pay attention to the quiet activity of the Spirit of Love, at work deep within us. This takes time. Just as someone who is not a trained artist cannot always tell the difference between different shades of the same color, or someone without a musical background cannot always discern the difference between musical notes, sharps and flats, so too when we are beginners in the path of contemplation we are not always capable of discerning the subtle ways that the Spirit of Love is transforming us from the inside out. So we begin our journey not by always feeling aware of everything going on within us, but by gently learning to consent to the action of divine love that we trust is hidden deep within.

Like becoming a great artist or an accomplished musician, mystical Christianity is a lifelong process, something that takes continued perseverance in prayer, meditation, and contemplation to truly manifest in its fullness. In his historical survey *The Foundations of Mysticism*, Bernard McGinn tells of the fourth-century mystic Gregory of Nyssa, who taught that "the goal of the Christian life, both here and in heaven, is the endless pursuit of the inexhaustible divine nature."[4] God's love and being can never be fully embraced by the human heart—that's like trying to hold the ocean in a spoon. It makes more sense to simply allow the spoon to be immersed in the ocean. In a similar way, we seek to embrace the fullness of God in our hearts, only to find that God is calling us to immerse ourselves in the limitless ocean of divine love. It's a process that we begin on earth, will continue in eternity, and will never end. Don't despair if you are just starting out late in life, for there are blessings on the contemplative way even for beginners. This is not a race, there is no finish line, no reward for achievement. It is simply a process of responding ever more deeply to love, love that is already in you.

FOUR WAYS TO APPROACH THE CONTEMPLATIVE LIFE

We can think of mystical Christianity as operating in our lives on several levels. Here are four complementary ways of understanding or approaching mysticism:

1. Mystical Christianity is a tradition of wisdom, a way of knowing who God is, how God is present, and what God accomplishes in our hearts and lives. In this way, mysticism operates in our minds.
2. Mystical Christianity is an embodied experience of God, a present reality that is at work in our hearts whether we recognize it or not, but that truly only makes a lasting difference when we consent to the action of the Spirit within, choosing to cooperate with that action and to calibrate our lives to the guidance and leading of divine love. In this way, mysticism operates in our bodies.
3. Mystical Christianity is a story, a story of God and of humanity, a story that tells us who we are and reminds us of who we are. When we listen to this story and orient our lives to what it has to say, then we become agents of love and expressions of Christ in the world. In this way, mysticism operates in our souls.
4. Finally, all three of these dimensions of mystical Christianity can lead us to share the love God with one another, deconstructing the aggression and power structures of the world and slowly creating systems of relationship that are anchored in compassion, justice, mercy, and care. In this way, mysticism fosters and supports the creation of beloved community.

THREE CONCEPTS TO BEAR IN MIND

You have probably noticed that the words *love*, *silence*, and *wisdom* show up again and again, not only in this chapter but throughout this book as well. We can make the case that the three essential "vitamins" or nutrients of the contemplative life are, indeed, silence, love, and wisdom. Wisdom enlightens our minds, love inspires our bodies, and silence brings rest to our souls. As we pursue the contemplative life, seeking those nutrients that our famished hearts and souls so desperately need, pay attention to how wisdom, silence and love continue to weave together in all of the practices we explore. I encourage you to pray regularly that God may bless your heart, mind and body with wisdom, love and silence. This, as much as anything, can usher you onto the mystical path.

CHAPTER THIRTEEN

The Mystical Body: Christ within Us, Christ among Us

No one has ever seen God; if we love one another, God lives in
us, and his love is perfected in us.
—Apostle John (1 John 4:12)

The Christian is not merely "alone with the Alone" in the
Neoplatonic sense, but he is one with all his "brothers in Christ."
His inner self is, in fact, inseparable from Christ and hence it is in
a mysterious and unique way inseparable from all the other "I's"
who live in Christ, so that they all form one "Mystical Person,"
which is "Christ."
—Thomas Merton

If you stopped some random passersby on a crowded city sidewalk and
asked them what comes to mind when they think of "mystic" or "mysticism," I suspect you will get a wide variety of responses. I imagine a lot of
people might associate mysticism with Eastern religions and spiritualities:
with Zen, Vedanta, yoga, Taoism, and so forth. Others might equate it with
Wicca and witchcraft, or magic, paganism, the occult, Tarot, astrology, and
so forth. Still others might equate it with Western religions, pointing to the
Kabbalah within Judaism, Sufism within Islam, and maybe even Christian

contemplatives like Teilhard de Chardin or Teresa of Ávila. But I suspect that no one—or at least, no one very often—would connect mysticism with your local Catholic, Orthodox, Protestant, or evangelical church.

In fact, based on my own (admittedly limited) experience of neighborhood Christian churches, I suspect it is more likely that some, maybe many, Christians would say that mysticism is not a topic ever discussed in their church—and maybe even would not be a welcome topic. That's because in their mind mysticism is something that new agers or adherents of Eastern religions do, but it's not part of the ordinary Christian life. I still remember a guy in a high school prayer group I attended when I was a teenager confidently telling our group that mysticism is dangerous, tossing off this platitude: "Mysticism begins in mist, ends in schism, and is centered on 'I.'"

I've pointed out that at least one renowned twentieth-century Christian writer, Karl Rahner, predicted that the Christians of the future would be mystics, or would simply not exist. The fact that he felt the need to say something like that reveals how, for many adherents of Christianity-as-religion, mysticism is *not* part of their experience. Christians think of themselves as followers of Jesus, believers in God, disciples, Spirit-filled, or even spiritual. But as contemplatives or mystics? It seems far too few church-going Christians would see themselves that way.

This is a problem, both for Christianity as a whole, but also for anyone who is interested in exploring Christian mysticism, whether or not they think of themselves as Christians.

It's been my experience that many Christians are either indifferent to mysticism or actually hostile to it, mainly because they associate the topic with spiritual beliefs and practices that they consider to be un-Christian or otherwise unacceptable. Many other people who may be very interested in both the study and practice of mystical spirituality may actually reject Christianity, probably because they are conscientiously opposed to many Christian beliefs and practices. Finally, it seems that there is a small subset of both groups that are open to the uniquely Christian expression of mysticism. Some of these people identity as actively engaged with the Christian faith; others do not, but they all share in common a willingness to embrace the teachings and practices of the mystics.

There are a number of reasons why this disconnect between Christian religious observance and Christian mystical spirituality is so pronounced.

For centuries, the serious pursuit of mystical spirituality within Christianity was largely confined to monks and nuns—in other words, to those who gave their lives to living as celibates in an intentional religious community. Even in the Middle Ages, there began to be evidence that at least some Christians outside of the cloister also felt drawn to the contemplative life. But then, with the arrival of the Protestant Reformation in the West, the split between Catholicism and Protestantism created a climate, on both sides, that was incongenial to the mystical pursuit of personal experience of God. Even to this day, devout Catholics and Protestants can be profoundly suspicious of each other; at the risk of oversimplifying, it can be said that each side began to view mysticism as a "problem" that they associated with the other side! Think of it this way: Catholicism views the church, with the pope at its head, as the single recognized authority governing people's spiritual lives. Protestants rejected this emphasis on the church, and instead proclaimed that only the Bible was the source of supreme religious authority. In the middle of this argument, mystics and contemplatives find their spiritual "authority" grounded in their own experience of God's presence in their lives. To Catholics, mysticism seems to be too Protestant, while ironically, for Protestants, mysticism is too Catholic.

This is a radically simplified explanation of how mysticism became suspect in Christianity (a scholarly book that details this unhappy process in greater detail is *Beloved Dust* by Robert Davis Hughes). But Christians today, living more than five hundred years after the Reformation, are the inheritors of a religion that has been stripped of its own mystical birthright because of this centuries-old conflict. The result: for many people, being a Christian is about either being a good church member, or being a good student of the Bible. Mysticism has been dismissed as a dangerous or unstabilizing influence.

Following the rise of the scientific revolution and philosophy that has increasingly been critical of religious ideas, societies where Christianity once was the dominant religion have in recent centuries become increasingly secularized. Many people simply no longer accept the metaphysics of Christianity: the idea that a God directs the affairs of human beings, demands sanctity and righteousness from us, and sent his own Son to teach us and even die for us as a way of saving us from our sins. To them, the Christian worldview is based simply on myth, and not a very compelling myth at that. Institutional Christianity seems to be interested in only two things: mitigating peoples' fear of death by promising a pleasant afterlife (to those who believe), and then demanding adherence to a particular moral code during this earthly life. Sadly, because Christian dogma has included the message that outsiders (either those who never were Christian, or those who rejected or abandoned the practice of Christianity) will be condemned to an eternity of conscious torment in hell, many people conclude that the Christian story is not only obsolete, but is actually toxic, cultivating fear and intolerance in the hearts of its adherents.

Ironically fear and intolerance sound like the opposite of mystical spirituality, with its emphasis on love, joy, and inner spiritual growth. Perhaps the reason why Christian doctrine seems toxic to so many people is because the church has lost its own mystical heart.

Thankfully, many people who remain committed to the Christian message have worked hard to restore its loving heart, emphasizing the teachings of Jesus that stress forgiveness, compassion, mercy, and caring for those who suffer or are in need. Any historian of religion can point out how religious groups evolve and change over the centuries, and Christianity is no exception. Yet, while some Christians endeavor to shape their faith in ways that emphasize inclusive community and social justice rather than fear of hell or a wrathful God, for too many people this is too little too late.

But those who abandon the practice of religious Christianity do not necessarily turn their back on spirituality or the belief in God (granted, some people do choose atheism or skepticism as an alternative to religious observance, but others opt for being spiritually independent or spiritual-but-not-religious). Such spiritual refugees often approach the inner life in a broad and inclusive way, accepting elements of teachings from multiple sources. So we live in a time when many contemplative seekers admire the Dalai Lama (Buddhist), Mother Meera (Hindu), Starhawk (Wiccan), Kabir Helminski (Sufi), and Monica Berg (Kabbalah) as much as they might admire Christian thinkers like Desmond Tutu or Joan Chittister. Likewise, increasing numbers of spiritual teachers either have no formal religious affiliation at all, or else their religious identity is less important than their interspiritual work as teachers for all of humanity. Indeed, for spiritual seekers who find meaning in learning from representatives of multiple wisdom traditions, the idea of limiting oneself to just one path,

Christianity or otherwise, seems unthinkable. For some ex-Christians, their main problem with institutional religion is simply the fact that too many followers of Jesus dismissively reject any teachings or wisdom that comes from non-Christian sources.

Finally, it needs to be noted that many people have walked away from the institutional church because the church has not been safe for them. Christianity as an institution has historically been very socially conservative, which means that far too many expressions of Christianity, even today, remain patriarchal (give men privilege and insist that woman play a subservient role), homophobic and transphobic (assume that heterosexuality and cisgender identity and expression are the only forms of gender and sexuality acceptable to God), and complicit with the status quo of our society, including racism and economic inequality. As if all this weren't bad enough, the institutional church often will protect itself when dealing with the problem of clergy or lay leaders who abuse those in their care. Abuse is never acceptable, but Christian leaders who have victimized others have too often been shielded by their institutions—which only makes the trauma the victims experience that much worse. Many people who have been victimized in this way need for their own healing and safety to stay away from institutional religious communities. Others, who may not have been directly harmed by such abuse, but who are appalled that the institutions have too often chosen to protect the predators rather than support the victims, feel conscientiously bound to disaffiliate from such institutions as an act of solidarity with those who have been harmed.

So, then, how does the practice of Christian mystical spirituality fit in to our world, where so many Christians have no interest in mysticism and so many mystical seekers have no interest in (religious) Christianity?

It is not the purpose of this book to argue for or against the practice of institutional Christianity, whether Catholic, Protestant, or otherwise. At the same time, so much of the foundational practices of the mystical life are embedded in Christian religious observance, that anyone serious about the practice of contemplative Christianity needs to at least be familiar with Christian religious observance, regardless of whether you yourself identify as a Christian.

The relationship between Christian religious practice and Christian spirituality (including mysticism) can be compared to the relationship between the body and the soul. As we have seen, one ancient image for the

Christian community of faith—in other words, the church—is the "body of Christ." Without a soul, the body is a corpse—and many people, both inside and outside the church, might agree that the Christian religion as it currently is practiced by too many Christians has become so soulless that it practically *is* a religious corpse. Karl Rahner's warning comes to mind again. Without a living mystical heart, Christianity is in danger of going extinct—and it's clear that all the various churches are shrinking in terms of how many people are actively participating in the community life of faith. Without mysticism, Christianity is slowly dying. So if you are reading this book as a Christian who is dedicated to your religion but not sure about mysticism, I sincerely hope you will prayerfully consider ways to integrate the wisdom and practices of the mystics into your daily walk with Christ. Not only will it make your personal faith more meaningful and joyful, but it is also a way to help nurture the health of the universal body of Christ.

But what about those who seek mystical wisdom but have no interest in the religious side of Christianity? A body without a soul is dead, but what about a soul that has no body? Can mysticism, specifically Christian mysticism, thrive without being embedded in the "church" in some form?

Just as a body with no soul is dead, I would argue that, at least here on earth, a soul without a body is powerless. The body provides us with the structure we need to make things happen in our lives: a skeleton to hold us together, muscles to work, a brain to think, a heart to feel, internal organs to maintain life and health. By having a body, we can make a difference in the world in which we live. We all will someday lose our bodies to death, and I believe the soul lives on, but we will no longer have the power to make a concrete difference in the world after that day. So just as the body needs a soul, likewise the soul needs a body. If you are reading this book because you are drawn to mysticism, I hope you will seriously engage the question of how you can express your spirituality in communal ways. This does not mean you have to join a church to explore the mystical life. As I've already noted, many people have good and conscientious reasons not to be church members. But just because church no longer works for you is no reason to ignore the powerful message of Jesus and his followers that spirituality requires love, and love requires community.

If you do participate in a church, bear in mind that religious Christianity can bring you many blessings, but in all likelihood your neighborhood church is probably *not* the place where you will go to study and apply the wisdom of the mystics in your life (although I do sense that slowly this is changing; more and more Christians today seem to be open to mystical or contemplative Christianity than they were a generation ago, no doubt thanks to the guidance of the Spirit and the good work of mystical and contemplative teachers of our time, like Richard Rohr, Barbara Holmes, Martin Laird and Mary Margaret Funk).

Life is often about recognizing that the reality of our circumstances often fall short of our hopes and ideals, and so we learn to manage that shortfall. No marriage or parent-child relationship is perfect, and so we all have to find ways to manage our imperfect relationships. Yes, sometimes such relationships are so toxic that the only workable solution is divorce or estrangement. But many other times, we learn to manage the imperfections so that the relationships may continue in some form. The relationship between the "body" of religious Christianity and the "soul" of mystical spirituality will, for most of us, be yet another imperfect relationship.

What I'd like to do for the rest of this chapter is try to describe what an *ideal* bond between Christianity-the-faith and contemplative mystical spirituality could look like. Then we'll explore some practical ways that you can integrate Christianity and mystical spirituality in your life, regardless of your relationship (or lack thereof) with the institutional church. Finally, we'll touch on another meaningful way to find community, whether or not the church is part of your life—by working with a spiritual director.

CHRISTIAN FAITH AND MYSTICAL
SPIRITUALITY: AN IDEAL MAP

Imagine a Christian community that could truly support your hunger for union with God, for contemplative practice, and for deep inner transformation. What would such a community look like?

For starters, a healthy contemplative church would be a community with a deep sense of the abiding presence of God's love—and therefore, *not* a place where fundamentalism or fear of "the other" is promoted. That, in itself, might be the single most important mark of a mystical community. In some ways, contemplative Christians might observe their faith in ways similar to what "non-mystical" Christians do (from public worship to Bible study to investing time and energy toward serving those in need), but hopefully always grounded in an abiding sense of being cared for, and sustained by, the omnipresent Spirit of love.

I once was on a conference call with the Christian writer Brian D. McLaren, and he made an interesting observation. The primary purpose of the church, he suggested, is chiefly to help each generation of Christians pass their faith on to the next generation. This made perfect sense to me. After all, neighborhood congregations place a great emphasis on educating youth, not only in religious matters but also in general (many churches are affiliated with private schools). From baptizing babies, to Sunday school and other faith formation programs, to adolescent rites of passage like first Communion and confirmation, churches invest an incredible amount of time and energy into teaching the Christian faith to youth.

Let's imagine what it would be like if that educational process had a specifically contemplative and mystical quality to it.

I grew up in a blue collar home where education was something only for the kids, but as an adult I've discovered the pleasures of lifelong learning. Adults sometimes pick up a musical instrument, or take up a creative pursuit like writing or painting, or go back to college to finally get that degree. Religion works the same way, and sometimes even adults who received religious education as children will enjoy going back to the basics and learning the principles of their faith, no matter how old they might be.

Education, naturally, is progressive: we have to master simple principles before graduating (pardon the pun) to more complex material. We do not send six year olds to college (the occasional prodigy, of course, is a rare exception). Think in purely physical terms: babies must learn to crawl before they can stand, and must master standing before learning to walk, and must walk before learning to run. Most healthy people master these skills so early in life that by the time we reach adulthood we have forgotten what a challenge each stage of the learning process represented to us.

Likewise, if you want to play a guitar or some other instrument, you have to learn the basics (like playing scales) before you can hope to master the more complex skills required to actually make music. If you don't master the basics, you may never achieve the more advanced skills. Babies who live with a disability that prevents them from crawling may never walk, simply because their bodies cannot master the motor skills necessary for that more advanced task.

So how does all this apply to mysticism? In the ideal church, followers of Christ would grow spiritually the same way babies learn their motor skills: we would begin by learning the spiritual equivalent of crawling, then standing, then walking, then running—think of these as the basics of what it means to reach spiritual maturity through the way of Jesus Christ. And then, God willing, the next step would be to learn to fly: to soar on the wings of the Spirit through the gift of contemplative and mystical practices.

For all its flaws, institutional Christianity—encompassing a vast infrastructure of churches, seminaries, church camps, retreat centers, chautauquas, seminaries, monasteries and convents, and other centers where the Christian faith is passed on—continues to do its best to teach the body of Christ how to crawl, stand, walk, and run. The missing element, the contemplative and mystical element of Christianity, is what we need to learn to fly.

But most of us, whether or not we are engaged with the religious observance of Christianity, can benefit from those crawling/standing/walking/running skills.

Christians learn to "crawl" when we are first exposed to the story of Jesus's wisdom teachings, along with the other spiritual teachings found in the Bible and in the writings of Christian thought leaders down the centuries.

Then we learn to "stand" when we begin to put these teachings into practice in our own lives, by participating in a community of faith, seeking to embody the spiritual principles that Jesus and his followers espouse, and partaking in the ritual observances of Christianity (like getting baptized and receiving Communion).

We learn to "walk" by making the effort to connect with God in our day-to-day lives, through reading the Bible, praying, and seeking to orient our lives toward love and compassion rather than to selfishness and indulgence. Christianity is a demanding religion, expecting its adherents to be people of kindness, mercy, forgiveness, and charity, while also uncompromising in our commitment to peace, justice, and community (yes, yes, I know most Christians fail miserably at this, I certainly do! But remember, we're imagining the ideal here).

And then, Christians learn to "run" as we make the effort to truly embody our faith in daily life in such a way that we can make a real, meaningful difference in our communities. Mature Christians at this level regularly care for others, with a particular heart for those who are poor, bereaved, sick, addicted, imprisoned, elderly, or otherwise in need. They become known for their kindness, their gentleness, their joyfulness and serenity. People at this level of spiritual maturity are spiritually attractive and others may confess that they "want what they've got." In traditional religious language, such people have begun to embody what the Christian faith calls *holiness* (although a better word for this might be "joyful integrity" or "conscious compassion").

Finally, contemplative Christians learn to "fly." Here the analogy may seem to break down, because human beings are not birds, we have no wings and can only fly in our dreams. But to the contemplative or the mystic, this analogy still holds because *the mystical life is always a gift of grace*. We do not "achieve" contemplation so much as we "receive" it. By the grace of the Holy Spirit, we receive the gift of paying attention to the silence deep in our hearts. We receive the gift of beginning to notice how God is always present in our lives—and always has been. We receive the gift of the heady recognition that God is not only present, but indeed in an impossible-to-put-into-words way, that we are one with God—again, not by the fruit of our own efforts, but the beautiful fruit of the Spirit's grace and action in our lives.

Mystical and contemplative spirituality are always gifts, and that plays out in our developmental analogy: the gift of flight can be given at any time, even to the infants that are still trying to crawl, stand, or walk. God, you see, is in charge of how this gift is manifested in people's lives. We cannot engineer or manage our own mystical unfolding. All we can do is consent to God's action in our hearts, trusting that the contemplative and mystical graces we will receive are precisely what *we* need.

One of the problems with the gratuitousness of mystical grace is that we might assume that, since we ultimately have no control over when and how we receive the gift of flight, then it doesn't really matter if we ever bother to master the "lowlier" tasks (crawling, standing, running, walking). Do I really need to be baptized in order to be a Christian mystic? Do I need to study the Bible or learn the ins and outs of Christian doctrine? Is the sacrament of Holy Communion a requirement to receive the grace of communing with God in our hearts? Must I become holy or sanctified before I can hope to be immersed in the joyful encounter with God's presence in my heart? I imagine most honest Christian contemplatives would acknowledge that, in an absolute sense, none of those religious practices are necessary prerequisites. But that's like saying Mozart didn't need to go to conservatory to write his beautiful symphonies. For some reason, God only graces one or two people each generation with the abilities of a Mozart. For every person who receives supreme gifts (not only in terms of mysticism, but of creativity or any other blessing in life) purely by grace, there are thousands or millions more who need to climb the mountain the old-fashioned way—by starting at the bottom and slowly ascending, step by ordinary step.

That's what the ideal faith community does (or could do) for us. It gives us all we need to learn to crawl, stand, walk, and run in our faith. And by learning all those spiritual skills, we prepare ourselves to consent to the gift of flight, a gift only God can bestow.

WHY COMMUNITY MATTERS

The wisdom teachings of Jesus encompass more than just mystical or contemplative messages. The heart of his message is love, love that directs us to union with God. But Jesus's words have social, moral, ethical, and even political ramifications, alongside their more explicitly spiritual or mystical meaning. This is why many people fall in love with Jesus and his teachings without necessarily feeling a call to practice a contemplative or mystical spirituality. Meanwhile, for those of who do approach Jesus primarily seeking mystical guidance, it's important we take his more down-to-earth teachings seriously as well.

People embrace Jesus's message because they desire forgiveness, or healing, or an end to suffering, and he gives them hope. They find in Jesus's teachings the inspiration to work for a better world, a world where justice and freedom, kindness and compassion, mercy and peace matter.

"God leads souls by many paths and ways," notes Teresa of Ávila.[1] For Christians, the contemplative path begins with a serious reckoning with Jesus's message—including his call to be people of love and compassion, which is to say, people of community.

Christianity is an incarnational faith, which means at its best, it proclaims the joyful, healing, and transformational presence of God right here, right now, in the physical world—the world of flesh and bones, of dirt and dust, of family and friends, of ordinary work and rest. Another word for *incarnational* is *enfleshed*. According to the best Christian wisdom, you don't have to escape the world to find God. You don't have to reject your body or your physical nature to embrace spirituality. You don't have to deny the earth to embrace heaven. On the contrary, Christianity makes the bold claim that, since God in Christ became a human being, the nexus in all the universe where humanity meets divinity is right here, right now, in our mundane physical world.

This beautiful message has several practical implications. The earth and the human body are good enough for God to inhabit—whether we're talking about Christ living in a human body two thousand years ago or the Spirit dwelling in our hearts today. If the earth and the body are good enough for God to dwell in, then they are good enough for us to love, honor, cherish, and nurture. If you want to reach out for God, seeking and yearning for divine presence in your life, then you can begin right here and right now, by seeking that presence in your own heart, your own body—and also in others. And this is where the importance of community comes in.

No matter how spiritual or ethereal Christian mysticism might be, it's also embedded in our materialist, earthy world. It is enfleshed in the way we organize our lives and relate to one another. It manifests in the social and institutional tools we have created to support one another spiritually. And when such tools are broken or malfunctioning, mystical wisdom inspires us to work to make things better.

Christianity teaches that we don't have to climb a mountain to find God. We can find God in the open hands of a homeless beggar on the street, or in the haunting eyes of a frail old woman, lonely and ravaged by dementia, at a nursing home just up the street from where you live. And you can even find God in your neighborhood church.

In chapter seven we looked at how Luke 17:21 provides a key to understanding this mystery is the divine presence embedded in community. In this verse, Jesus says one of two things, depending on the translation:

The kingdom of God is within you.

or

The kingdom of God is among you.

From the perspective of mystical or contemplative spirituality, the idea of the reign of God (in other words, heaven) being found *within* us is particularly appealing. This suggests that the key to true spirituality is found chiefly in our hearts—through interior reflection, meditation, and contemplation. And indeed, such practices are essential to the mystical life.

Yet ἐντὸς (*entos*), the Greek word found in Luke 17:21, is deliciously ambiguous. While it does carry the sense of "on the inside," the phrasing of the verse suggests a plural meaning—inside "all of you," or, inside the community of believers. This paradox means that we find heaven and the key to contemplative life by turning both *within ourselves* as individuals, and *to one another* in a community of faith. The richness of Luke's message helps us enter fully and truly into what is most distinctive and beautiful about the Christian contemplative life. As spiritual seekers, we can turn both within ourselves as individuals to cultivate a deep and rich interior life, and also to a community of faith where heaven may be found within and among the family of believers. And indeed, Jesus tells us so: "For where two or three are gathered in my name, I am there among them."[2]

Since the reigning presence of God is within us, any approach to exploring the mystical life will naturally include exercises and practices such as meditation and contemplation, intended to help us become more open to the hidden (mystical) presence of God within. As worthy as such practices are, by themselves they are incomplete. Our journey to divine union also needs to be nourished by participation in some sort of community of fellow seekers who are trying, as best they can, to figure out what loving and following Jesus is all about.

THE GIFTS OF COMMUNITY

Plenty of people find the "two or three" (or more) who gather together in the name of Christ by participating in their local Christian church. Catholic or Protestant, Anglican or Orthodox, evangelical or nondenominational, the neighborhood community of faith can be a meaningful part of people's lives and a beautiful way to find and serve Christ through other people.

A healthy (or healthy enough) church community provides its members with access to the teachings of Jesus and other spiritual guides in the biblical and Christian traditions. It provides a way to cultivate a sense of love for God through communal worship and prayer. Most Christian communities provides meaningful rituals—sacraments—that use ordinary elements like water, oil, bread and wine to help us embody our faith in material ways. Baptism ritually washes us; Holy Communion ritually feeds us. Human beings are creatures of ritual, and so these ancient ceremonial acts speak to us at a level deeper than mere rational cognition.

Finally, at its best, the church offers us opportunities to serve one another and to form friendships with others who share our desire to learn from the wisdom of Jesus. And while many Christians in the church may not be conscious of a desire to grow in a spirit of contemplative or mystical prayer, perhaps those who are learning today how to walk or run may tomorrow find themselves being called to fly.

For those who seek the mystical life while participating in a Christian church, they may struggle to integrate their contemplative practice with the more humble or prosaic dimensions of church life—but if we believe that God can come to us "in all things" (as St. Ignatius and other mystics have proclaimed), then part of the contemplative life is learning to embrace both the earthly and the more spiritual dimensions of Christian wisdom.

What if you are one of the many people who find the traditional neighborhood church to be spiritually toxic rather than nurturing? Then I hope you will seek other meaningful ways to embed your spirituality in community and service. Can contemplative or mystical spirituality flourish without participation in the institutional church? Certainly so, for "with God all things are possible."[3] But to be a "spiritually independent" Christian contemplative will require you to be proactive about finding your own way to balance the interior and communal dimensions of spirituality. You will need to find your own way to cultivate a heart of worshipful adoration of God. You will have to take responsibility for your own education in the wisdom teachings of the Christian tradition, from studying the Bible to reading the writings of the great mystics. You will need to be on the lookout for your own unique opportunities to serve others and cultivate generosity, hospitality, and compassion in your life.

For some people, cultivating a mystical heart might be much easier outside the church than inside. But spiritual independence carries its own danger, including the risk of becoming spiritually complacent or even narcissistic. But given the dangers of the institutional church (from fundamentalism or authoritarianism to the risk of abuse), whatever choice we make in regard to spiritual community will have a downside. We need to be aware of where the pitfalls are.

Some contemplative seekers might find that a small community is more conducive to their spiritual growth. A Centering Prayer group, a monastic oblate or lay associate community, or a group spiritual direction circle can provide meaningful support for spiritual seekers, even when the institutional church is not part of the picture.

THE LIMINAL CONTEMPLATIVE

Throughout history, many great mystics lived on the margins of the church—sometimes literally, sometimes metaphorically. In the third and fourth centuries, the desert mothers and fathers of Egypt, Syria, and Palestine lived on the edge that separated civilization from the wilderness. Many great monastic orders chose remote locations for their homes, settling on the margins between church and society on the one hand, and the untamed forests, mountains, or wetlands on the other. Francis of Assisi rejected a posh life as an affluent merchant's son, choosing instead to live on the fine line that separated respectable religion from a life of poverty.

Julian of Norwich lived on the edge of her society, in a cell where she enjoyed solitude, but attached to a parish church where she participated in communal worship and provided spiritual direction to those who sought her guidance. Simone Weil, a Jewish philosopher who embraced Christian spirituality but refused to be baptized, never even fully entered the church, at least not sacramentally. Pierre Teilhard de Chardin, as a paleontologist, inhabited the frontier between religion and science, while Hugo Enomiya-Lassalle, Sara Grant, Bede Griffiths, and Swami Abhishiktananda were all called to live out their faith in the gray areas between Christianity and the wisdom traditions of Buddhism or Hinduism.

So it is a common theme among mystics to express their faith and devotion to Christ in an in-between sort of place, often between the institutional church and the society in which it is embedded—a place that stands on the margin of the Christian religion, places like the wilderness, poverty, science, or non-Christian traditions. But living on the edge of religion did not lead these great mystics and contemplatives to be careless or narcissistic in their spiritual observance. On the contrary, their lives are marked by a deep love and respect for the core wisdom teachings of the faith, even though they remained open-hearted to people and places that seem profoundly "other" than established Christian thinking and dogma.

The fancy, Latin-based word that describes this place of "in-betweenness" is *liminal*, which means "of the threshold." Many great mystics often lurked on the thresholds between institutional religion and the real (or figurative) wild places of the world. As liminal figures, they were in the best position to drink deeply from the well of Christian tradition, but also to express their relationship with God in a completely authentic way. They respected the sacraments and the graces of the church, but also truly loved and befriended those who, for whatever reason, remained outside the boundaries of organized religion.

It is not easy to live authentically in these liminal spaces. Both the church and the world tug at those who stand on the threshold between them, urging them to move away from the door because "it is dangerous out there" (or "in there"). Like all institutions, churches too often seem overly concerned with their own preservation and expect their members to serve the institution, no matter the cost. Meanwhile, beyond the boundaries of the Christian religion, there are plenty of forces that beckon those on the threshold to abandon spirituality altogether. The only way to remain truly centered in this in-between place is to remain anchored in meaningful relationships, beginning with a relationship with God that is grounded in prayer and contemplation.

Perhaps the in-between places that separate religion and spirituality from the rest of the world are the most natural habitat of contemplatives, who feel impelled to follow God wherever they are called—sometimes in religious settings and sometimes not. Perhaps those who discern in the call to love God and neighbors a mandate to love both "church" and "world" equally and unconditionally are the natural residents of liminal space. Holiness is grounded in the concept of being set apart for God. Contemplatives are those who are doubly set apart—from the world at large by their relationship with God in Christ, and from mainstream religion by their devotion to the

Spirit within through the cultivation of inner silence and the embracing of the mystery of darkness and unknowing.

Being interested in the wisdom of mysticism and the practice of contemplation will not magically make membership in a faith community easier. In fact, it may even be a source of frustration as you try to relate spiritually to those whose religious values seem at odds with your own. Learning to navigate the tension between religion and spirituality, even if only within yourself, can be a crucial element in opening your mind and heart to the splendor of God's grace and presence.

THE COMMUNITY OF TWO

Ever since the apostle Paul provided mentoring to his young assistant Timothy, Christianity has recognized the value of personal guidance as a tool for helping people grow in their faith. This has certainly been true among mystics and contemplatives. Mentoring and guidance were important elements in the spirituality of the desert fathers and mothers; in fact, one of the founders of European monasticism, John Cassian, traveled from Gaul (now France) to the deserts of Egypt to receive mentoring from the desert fathers (even today such a trip is not casually made; in the fifth century it was an arduous and dangerous journey). *The Cloud of Unknowing*, the fourteenth-century manual on contemplation, was written by a spiritual director to help guide a young monastic. Margery Kempe, in the early fifteenth century, described how she received spiritual direction from the reclusive Julian of Norwich. In sixteenth-century Spain, Teresa of Ávila provided spiritual guidance to John of the Cross, both of whom are now recognized as among the greatest of Christian mystics; in twentieth-century England, Evelyn Underhill received mentoring from Friedrich von Hügel (in his day quite renowned for his writings on mysticism, although now she has become more widely known than he is). And although Martin Luther King Jr. is not widely thought of as a mystic, his spiritual mentor was one of the great mystics of the twentieth century: Howard Thurman.

The experience of one-on-one mentoring, guidance, or companionship in the spiritual life is far more intimate than the kind of religious education or faith instruction found in most church congregations, or even in small groups devoted to prayer and spirituality. The ability to turn to an elder or respected mentor for support and guidance has, unfortunately, not always been readily available to ordinary Christians—for many centuries, ongoing spiritual direction was typically available only to clergy, nuns, or monks. But beginning in the mid-twentieth century, interest in spiritual formation among lay Christians has increased, with more and more people seeking spiritual mentoring, guidance, or companionship—not only from clergy, monks, and nuns, but from anyone seasoned in prayer and gifted at listening. This, in turn, has led to increasing numbers of Christians, both clergy and laypersons, taking on the role of spiritual director or spiritual companion, providing guidance and support to those who are interested in a deeper life of prayer. Many churches and educational institutions now offer formation programs to help mature Christians develop the skills necessary to provide such spiritual companionship to others.

One-on-one spiritual accompaniment can happen in the most informal of ways, and some of the best spiritual directors may not necessarily have any official training at all. Whenever two people with a shared interest in the spiritual life come together for mutual support and encouragement, one-on-one spiritual companionship can occur. At its most informal, such personalized spiritual support can even be shared between friends who are willing to listen to one another and respond to each other's spiritual journey with thoughtfulness and care.

In other words, spiritual friendship, regardless of how casual and informal it may be, can be valuable in its own way for contemplative seekers, just like a more formal mentoring or guidance relationship. The Celtic Christians had a lovely word to describe the beauty of this type of peer-to-peer spiritual relationship: *anamchara*, meaning "soul friend."

For anyone interested in the Christian contemplative life, working with a spiritual director or cultivating a close relationship with a soul friend can be an integral part of the journey. As beneficial as reading the writings of the great mystics or participating in a Centering Prayer or monastic oblate group may be, there are clear advantages to regularly meeting with a wise companion who can assist you as you seek to listen the guidance of the Spirit, deep at work in your own heart. It has been said that a spiritual director does not "direct" us in the sense of telling us what to do spiritually, but rather helps us to find our own "direction" by calibrating our lives to our inner compass, under the guidance of the Holy Spirit (who, after all, is the ultimate spiritual director, at least for Christians).

A prayerful spiritual director can be especially helpful in supporting a contemplative practice and assisting you in many other aspects of your spiritual life, including discerning God's will or call in your life. If you're serious about pursuing contemplative spirituality, try to find a trusted spiritual director or soul friend.[4]

CHRISTIAN MYSTICISM'S PRELIMINARY PRACTICE

Tibetan Buddhism includes the concept of *ngöndro*—a word that means "preliminary practices." These are spiritual practices that novice monks need to undertake before formally beginning their study of the dharma (Buddhist wisdom). Such practices include both external acts (like reciting mantras or sutras) and the cultivation of interior dispositions (such as *bodhicitta* or the enlightened mind). Preliminary practices are not seen as "lesser" activities, but they are regarded as foundational for anyone who seeks to truly take refuge in the Buddha, the dharma, and the sangha (the community).

Christian spirituality does not have an equivalent concept to *ngöndro*, but maybe it would be a good idea. Christians who aspire to the contemplative or mystical life could take refuge in Christ, in the gospel (the wisdom teachings of Christ), and in the mystical body of Christ: the community of faith (whether or not this means the institutional church). It seems that even when Christians by choice or circumstance live in solitude, there is always a call to express spirituality in some sort of relational way.

Relationship forms the heart of Christianity, whether we are relating to God or to one another. Christianity undermines the idea, prevalent in today's secularized society, that God is nothing more than a metaphor for the deepest, highest, or best parts of ourselves. While faith in Jesus invites us to seek God within ourselves, we are not seeking just a part of ourselves. Rather, we are seeking to become part of something much bigger than ourselves—the God who is greater than the cosmos. We can seek this because, paradoxically, this transcendent God has been seeking us all along. We love God in response to God's love for us. Likewise, Christianity also offers an alternative to the pervasive narcissism and self-obsession of our time, by calling us to look for God not only inside ourselves, but also through each other. Meister Eckhart once cryptically remarked that "the eye with which I see God is exactly the same eye with which God sees me. My eye and God's eye are one eye, one seeing, one knowing and one love."[5] Since God is in each of us, when we gaze into the eyes of our friends and neighbors and fellow Christians, we are gazing into the temple of the Holy Spirit.

Perhaps the final word on the mystical body should go to the desert mothers and fathers, those Christians who in ancient times moved into deserts and wilderness settings to live as hermits, following the example of Elijah, John the Baptist, and others who have embraced solitude as a way to draw closer to God.

We have seen that Jesus himself spoke of solitude—what he called the inner room—as an important setting for our prayer.[6] As helpful as solitude may be, by itself it is inadequate for a complete expression of the Christian spiritual life. Remember the question that Basil of Caesarea asked of the desert hermits: "If you live alone, then whose feet shall you wash?"

For contemplative Christians, an important preliminary practice is finding feet to wash, which is to say, being in relationship with people we can serve and/or care for. Whether we are caring for family members, friends, neighbors, or those in need—those who are poor, hungry, homeless, sick, elderly or imprisoned—what matters is that we serve. "Whatsoever you do to the least of these, you do to me," taught Jesus. It is in community that we make our home in the heart of Christ.

CHAPTER FOURTEEN

Emptiness and the Dance

Let the same mind be in you that was in Christ Jesus,
who, though he was in the form of God,
did not regard equality with God
as something to be exploited,
but emptied himself,
taking the form of a slave,
being born in human likeness.
—Apostle Paul (Philippians 2:5–7)

God became human, so that we might become God.
—Athanasius

Mystical Christianity, like Christian spirituality in general, invites us into a real, life-transforming relationship with Jesus of Nazareth, the Christ (anointed one) of God. But this mystical bond means more than just thinking about Jesus all the time. A passage in the New Testament attributed to St. Peter speaks of us as "participants of the divine nature"[1]—in other words, we are called to be so intimate with God-in-Christ that we literally are *one* with Christ—and therefore with God. Athanasius, an early Christian teacher, equated the incarnation of Jesus ("God becoming human") with the deification of humanity ("that we might become God").[2] To say "we become God," is not to suggest that we are all gods like members of some sort of polytheistic pantheon. Rather, our deification is a mystical union/communion with the infinite source of all divine love, the one true God. We are drops of water called to become one with the ocean.

The mystical life is not a program for making this happen; rather, it is a process of learning to recognize that this is a gift already given to us by the encircling love of the triune God: our Creator, Redeemer, and Sustainer. As we pursue the practices of contemplative spirituality—practices like contemplation, meditation, prayerful silence, and lectio divina—each of these spiritual exercises is meant to support us in discovering and realizing deep intimacy with Christ, an intimacy already freely offered to all who seek to respond to divine love.

How do we enter into this relationship with Christ, which is in turn a relationship with the trinitarian God?

To begin, let's consider all the ways we can encounter Christ, just in the ordinary stuff of life.

We can encounter the wisdom teachings of Jesus—the foundation of Christian mysticism—in many ways. Jesus speaks through the stories of the faith, beginning with the gospels and other biblical writings. His wisdom is passed down through the teachings of great saints, mystics and theologians from all the centuries of Christian history. Even the culture of Christian art and beauty testify to the divine love at the heart of this tradition—the timeless works of art, church architecture, literature, hymns, and praise music all testify to the divine love at the heart of this tradition.

Anyone may encounter Jesus in liturgies and the sacraments of faithful community, from the cleansing waters of holy baptism to the nourishing bread and wine of Holy Communion, mystically consecrated as the real presence of Christ's body and blood. For that matter, Christ becomes present to us through the lives of other people, particularly those who are vulnerable, poor, in need, or who mirror our own imperfection or brokenness. Jesus continues to teach us through the poetry, visions, and contemplative writings of the saints and mystics—the exemplars of the Christian mysteries, both past and present, who have given their entire lives over to the service of love.

Ultimately, Jesus most surely is present whenever we encounter genuine love, especially love that is freely given without any thought of reward.

THE HISTORICAL JESUS, THE CHRIST OF FAITH, AND THE MYSTICAL BODY

Over the past few generations, many Christians have devoted significant energy to a quest for the "Jesus of history"—an attempt to understand, as fully as possible, who Jesus was when he walked the earth and what can truly be known about him. Often, this quest includes a critical or skeptical tendency to reject the miracles and supernatural stories about Jesus as mere mythology. For many people, this quest is both an expression of faith and an attempt to keep Christianity relevant in the age of scientific thinking. This quest has especially taken place through institutions of higher learning, whether secular universities or theological seminaries. And while it has the laudable goal of speaking about Jesus in honest ways for our time, it has also led many people to question whether a religion stripped of mythology is worth believing in.

Mystical wisdom holds that we can never know God fully through ordinary human reason, but can only approach God through love. Therefore, the focus of contemplative practice differs from the intellectual quest for the historical Jesus. Scholarly Christianity and contemplative spirituality can coexist beautifully, but strictly speaking the quest for the historical Jesus is an academic, rather than spiritual, exercise. Mysticism seeks a *relationship* with Christ that goes beyond merely having an intellectually honest knowledge about Jesus. This contemplative relationship is grounded in two other, equally important, ways of knowing him—by encountering the Christ of faith and by immersion in the mystical body. These are heart-centered approaches to Christ, in contrast (but not in opposition) to the primarily academic approach of the quest for the Jesus of history.

The Christ of faith is, in the words of Saint Paul, a mystery: "Christ in you, the hope of glory."[3] We encounter the Christ of faith from within, where the human heart can discern the mystery of the divine presence in and through our own thoughts, feelings, hopes, imagination, dreams, and love. Of course, part of the human condition is that our inner lives are, to be candid, pretty messy: in addition to love and hope and dreams, we all harbor within ourselves aggression, selfishness, bitterness, and envy, and other ways we ignore or even resist the power of love in our loves. Christianity proclaims that the Christ who loves us seeks intimacy with us in our entirety—affirming our own capacity for love, while inviting us to be healed and transformed so that our resistance to and rejection of love might be transfigured and made whole.

Because God is love, Christ within us represents the coming of love into the totality of our being, but this is not just some sentimental, "feel-good" love. The divine love that is poured into our hearts[4] is a force for renewal, an agent of transformation, and a challenge to *metanoia*—a word often anemically translated as "repentance" or "conversion," but that in the original Greek has a much richer meaning of "changing your mind" or perhaps more accurately "adopting a new consciousness." The Christ of faith is not a harsh task master and does not place unreasonable expectations on us, but does ask us to follow him, and to take responsibility for our own limitations, mistakes, and failings.

Whereas one could learn about the Jesus of history while maintaining a kind of objective distance, thus having no emotional investment in his teachings (just as you might learn about some ancient philosopher or political theorist or any other historical figure), the Christ of faith wants a relationship with us—therefore, seeks a response. Offered the unconditional love of God, what is your response? Do you meet divine love with your own love, however humble or feeble it might be? Are you willing to follow Christ, and calibrate your life to his teachings about love, mercy, forgiveness, compassion, justice, and inner transformation? Do you agree to accept the challenge and the promise of metanoia, opening your mind, heart, and your soul so that Christ's Spirit can slowly transform you into the love you are created to be, thereby making you a fully present as a member of his mystical body? These are the questions that the Christ within—the Christ of faith—asks of you. By saying yes, you respond to divine love in your heart, and you change your life for all eternity—and you embark on the limitless mystical journey.

When you say yes to the Christ of faith, you say yes to the Spirit of Love, who leads you to your place as a member of the mystical body of Christ. It is only by the eyes of faith, given to you by Christ, that you will be empowered to see and encounter the mystical body of Christ—which is to say, the divine presence here on earth, in the hearts of all who love God (whether or not they call themselves "Christian" or participate in the institutional church).

As you nurture your inner relationship with the Christ of faith, you will find that this hidden (mystical) bond with him nurtures your outer connection with the Christ you meet in the heart of others—and vice versa. Human beings are messy, imperfect creatures, and we have a habit of disappointing one another. If we take seriously the promise that the realm of heaven can be found both *within* us and *among* all who follow the mystical path, we need to be fortified against the inevitable disappointments that arise both from our own inner brokenness/woundedness, but also from the all-too-human foibles and limitations that we encounter in one another. We must continually nurture our own inner bond with Christ in order to meet and love Christ in other people, and the nurture, care, and sometimes even challenge that other people give us makes it possible for us to continue to find the Spirit within ourselves.

Incidentally, the mystical body of Christ encompasses more than just all the lovers of God who are alive today. All the saints, martyrs, and mystics of the past continue to be part of the mystical body, and although in earthly terms they have died, they live on in the eternal presence of the Spirit. For that matter, the mystical body even includes all the generations yet to be born. "Jesus Christ is the same yesterday and today and forever."[5]

THE FIRST STEP TOWARD THEOSIS IS KENOSIS

The wisdom of mystical Christianity points to a glorious destiny. The apostle Paul instructs us to let the mind of Christ be in us, which is a parallel teaching to Peter's affirmation that we are partakers of the divine nature. These New Testament teachings are understood to be the foundation of what in Greek is called *theosis*, which in English means "deification" or "divinization": to be one with God, or at least God-like, to be filled with the utter fullness of God. While this sounds like the ultimate prize of the mystical life, it needs to be understood not as a goal, but as a promise. It's not a reward that is offered only to those who earn or achieve it, but rather a manifestation of divine love that is available to all who truly consent to receive it. Mortals do not attain deification like an Olympic athlete wins a gold medal. Rather, our task is to approach Christ in confidence of the promise of divine love, trusting that we all are freely offered the gift of Christ's own divinity.

Like all gifts, you have no control over how the gift is given to you, when you will receive it (or, perhaps more accurately, when you will realize that you've received it), or even what the experience of receiving the gift will be like. But as an aspiring contemplative, what you do have control over is the way in which you open your heart to the love of Christ, a gesture of consent in humble trust and faith for the promise. The mystical key to how we can best accept the promise of deification or theosis lies in another Greek concept: kenosis.

Kenosis literally means "emptying." It's a rich word that carries other shades of meaning, including "futility" and "foolishness." It appears only a couple of times in the New Testament, but the most essential passage comes from the second chapter of Philippians, in which Saint Paul sings the praises of Christ:

> who, though he was in the form of God . . .
> emptied himself . . .
> being born in human likeness.[6]

The apostle tells us that Jesus did not grasp or hoard this divine nature. For Christ, the character of divinity is not power, or glory, or might, but rather emptiness, humility, obedience, and even death. Jesus realized that the splendor of being the Son of God meant being able to empty himself of this very godliness.

Who would have guessed? Divinity is like love: it works best when it is given away.

This has powerful implications for Christian mysticism, and for anyone interested in the contemplative life.

First of all, mystical Christianity is less about attaining unity with God (after all, if we take the New Testament seriously, that unity is a gift already given), and more about creating the inner emptiness where you can offer God hospitality. This has implications in how to read the Bible, how to pray, and ultimately how to relate to the presence of the Holy Spirit in silence, both externally and internally.

Likewise, to the extent that the Spirit does pour Christ's divinity into you, the point is not to hoard the glory of your joyful and felicitous relationship with the ultimate mystery, but rather to immediately give it away, by lavishly loving, caring for, and serving other people. Jesus taught that "all who exalt themselves will be humbled, and all who humble themselves will be exalted."[7] If you yearn for theosis because of your longing for communion with God, you are wise to set your heart on kenosis, emptying yourself—of your fear, your hatred, your pride, your arrogance, your need to be in control or to be adored, and your sense of entitlement or self-importance, choosing instead to give yourself away and to lose yourself in love. This, truly, is the doorway into the Christian mystery.

OPENING OUT TO THE HOLY TRINITY

"Where Jesus is spoken of, the Holy Trinity is always to be understood," said Julian of Norwich.[8] I know a Trappist monk who believes that one of the problems with Christianity is that we tend to over-emphasize Jesus and under-emphasize the Trinity. I believe he's right. As central as Jesus is to Christian mysticism, the mystery of the Trinity is central to the mystery of Jesus.

Mystery really is the operative word here. If you try to just make rational sense of the Trinity, you may well reach the conclusion that it is little more than a fancy piece of artificial dogma—a philosophical way by which early Christian theologians tried to reconcile their stated belief in the oneness of God with the obvious threeness of the Creator, Jesus the savior (healer), and the sustaining Spirit. Perhaps the Trinity makes sense only when approached mystically, rather than logically. Rich in paradox and functioning like a Western koan, the Trinity forces us to accept that God simply cannot be reduced to the level of human reason. Someone once said, "A God small enough to understand wouldn't be big enough to worship." The Trinity is a mystical sign that God is indeed far too big to figure out.

Once we let go of having to make the triune God fit into our minds, we become free to approach the Trinity with our hearts instead. What the mind cannot fathom, the heart gently may embrace. The Trinity "works" as an image of God because it is, first and foremost, about love. The traditional language for the Trinity describes three persons who together comprise the undivided one God: the Father, the Son, and the Holy Spirit. Today many Christians prefer a more gender-inclusive way of speaking about God, and so we can speak of the Trinity as Creator, Christ, and Spirit, or Creator, Redeemer, and Sanctifier (or Deifier). Whether we prefer traditional or more gender-inclusive language, the three persons of the Trinity are united in and through love, and form a community within the perfect unity of God. The communion between the Creator, the Christ, and the Spirit is splendid in that they are personally distinct and simply one, simultaneously and eternally. Julian was right: when we speak of Christ, we truly are speaking of the Trinity, so seamless is their union and integration. And yet, the Creator is not the Christ, for it is only in their distinctness that they have the space to love each other. And the same holds for the Spirit. Perfectly one, and perfectly distinct: their mystical nature embodies the fullness of love itself.

A wonderful Greek word helps to illuminate the splendor of the Trinity: *perichoresis*, which literally means "mutual indwelling," suggesting that each person of the Trinity gracefully abides with and in each other. It comes from the roots *peri-* meaning "around" and *chorein* meaning "to move." On a poetic level, perichoresis evokes a lovely image—of a circle dance (think of similar words like "perimeter" and "choreography"). The Trinity is an eternal, joyful, radiant manifestation of love, loving, and being loved. Three dancers join together in one eternal dance. The love that flows between, and in, and among the Lover, the Beloved, and the Spirit of Love is the very love that creates, sustains, and keeps the universe. It is the love by which you and I and everyone lives—in the words of a pagan poet that the apostle Paul quotes in the Acts of the Apostles, in God—divine love—we "live and move and have our being."[9] And of course, we not only live in this love, but it is the divine presence to which each of us will return when we die. Becoming intimate with God means to participate in the dance, now and for all eternity.

THE DYNAMICS OF THE CIRCLE

The apostle Paul proclaimed God is in us, because we are in Christ.[10] As members of the mystical body, Christians actually partake in the divine nature of the Trinity. We do not merely watch the dance, we dance the dance. We join hands with Christ and the Spirit flows through us and between us and our feet move always in the loving embrace of the Creator. In that we are members of the mystical body of Christ, we see the joyful love of the divine mystery through the eyes of the beloved Christ. And with every breath, we breathe the sustaining Spirit of divine love.

Mystical Christianity proclaims the ineffable truth that God and Christ are one, and that the community of Christ's friends are one with God in the Spirit. And just as the doctrine of the Trinity reminds us that Christ's unity with the Creator does not erase their personal distinctions, so will our unique identities as lovers and followers of Christ always be our birthright, no matter how fully we enter into the dance. When we open our hearts to the Christ of faith, we immerse ourselves into the endless delight of the perichoresis. Through the self-emptying of kenosis we replace pride with humility, fear with love, and self-absorption with self-emptying, thereby creating the space within us where the dance may occur. God pours the divine Spirit into our hearts, dwelling in us because we abide in Christ. It all makes perfect sense, and yet it is beyond the full comprehension of our mortal minds. The dance illuminates our hearts, and to enter into it means to embrace a profound darkness marked by unknowing and paradox.

As we reflect on the promise of joy at the heart of the trinitarian dance, we need to remember how one of the dancers has wounds in his hands. Christ is the victorious incarnation of God, and also the crucified one, who died to remove our sins—understood mystically, this means he died to empty us of everything within us that resists the love of God, anything and everything that we cannot remove by our own efforts. The crucifixion marks the climax of Christ's own kenosis; through this, the dynamics of the circle changed forever. In Christ's emptiness, we find the grace to receive love, but also the call to embrace our own suffering as we give that love away. Although everyone's path is different, eventually everyone comes to a place of loss and suffering. With Christ as our guide, we can enter into whatever pain that comes to us, not in a masochistic way, but with confidence and trust—viewing our own cross as the means by which we will undergo our own resurrection. We cannot do this by ourselves; only by the grace of God is it possible. Because God comes to us as the self-emptied Christ, we need not be afraid of God as we follow Christ's own life-giving example. To be part of the body of Christ means to carry your own cross. But we carry our cross not just to death, but all the way to the resurrection. And the dancers: the Lover, the Beloved, and the Spirit of Love—will accompany us every step of the way.

CHAPTER FIFTEEN

Becoming Who You Already Are

.

So if anyone is in Christ, there is a new creation: everything old
has passed away; see, everything has become new!
—Paul (2 Corinthians 5:17)

Do not think to found holiness upon doing; holiness must be
founded upon being. Works do not make us holy. It is we who
must make works holy. For no matter how holy works may be,
they do not make us holy because we do them, but in so far as we
within ourselves are as we should be, we make holy all that we do,
whether it be eating, or sleeping, or working, or what it may.
—Meister Eckhart

The mystical life proclaims that we are unconditionally loved by God, who
invites us to join in the beautiful, heavenly, ever-expanding circle dance
of love. But the writings of some mystics, especially from centuries past,
often seem to present a very different message. It seems that many of the
mystics emphasize not so much the promise of joy, but the fear of judgment.
Even some of the figures widely recognized as the greatest of the Christian
mystics—figures like John of the Cross, Teresa of Ávila, Francis de Sales,
and Catherine of Siena—seem to proclaim a message that accentuates
the human conditional as sinful and fallen, and God's uncompromising

insistence that the spiritual life requires a resolute conversion *away* from sin before we can begin to trust that God will bring us toward divine joy. Again and again, it seems that the spiritual teachers now widely acclaimed as mystics tend to focus their work not on topics like mystical experience, nondual consciousness, or the happiness that ensues from a felt awareness of divine presence—but rather an emphasis on virtue, on sorrow for sin, on painstaking efforts to deconstruct selfishness or pleasure-seeking with a staunch, relentless fixation with being pure and spotless for God.

To be candid, many of the mystics come across not so much as spiritually mature, but as obsessive and compulsive—neurotic about sin rather than joyful about God.

Is this just another mystical paradox? How do we reconcile the promise of mystical beatitude with writings from the mystics that often seem to be focused more on how bad humans are, rather than how good God is?

I don't think this is necessarily a paradox, but has to do with a traditional understanding of how the mystical journey plays out over the course of our lives. From the earliest centuries of the Christian tradition, the spiritual life has been broadly understood as unfolding over three stages or phases of growth and development. These stages are *purification* (also known as purgation), *illumination*, and *union*. Incidentally, the "union" stage encompasses the *theosis* or deification that we explored in chapter 13. Even if we accept the idea that union with God is a gift freely given (and therefore always available to us), the question remains about how do we *receive* this gift. What do we need to do—either on our own initiative or with the help of God's grace—to make ourselves ready to fully consent, receive, and manifest the wonders of divine union in our lives?

There's where purification and illumination come in. Incidentally, the Greek words for these stages are *katharsis* and *theoria*. Although these words cannot be precisely equated with their English cognates, it's still insightful to use the Greek words to shed light on these spiritual stages of development. The initial stage of purgation, or catharsis, is a stage of radically letting-go of everything in our lives that gets in the way of the intimacy with God we desire. If that sounds like kenosis, the two are certainly related. Out of that self-emptying, we prepare ourselves to receive the truth of God, the "theory" of divine love and wisdom that will enlighten or illuminate us. Put these two together and they combine to create the conditions within our hearts for the consent and acceptance we wish to offer to God: the willingness to receive the fullness of love that emerges out of divine union.

In his perceptive book on the spiritual life, *Beloved Dust*, theologian Robert Davis Hughes suggests that we should think of purification, illumination, and union as "conversion," "transfiguration," and "glory." Hughes also suggests that it may be more helpful to see these stages or dimensions of the spiritual life not as a ladder, implying that we move from one stage to the next in an orderly ascent, but rather like tides in the ocean, waves the crash upon the shore in a circular rhythm of progression and recession. So we never fully "graduate" from purification to illumination, or from illumination to union. Rather, in the ever-circular dance of the divine Spirit's healing presence in our lives, we are led from one to another of these three phases in a cyclical fashion, moving from letting-go to acceptance to consent and back again, always growing even as we sometimes have to repeat even the most basic of spiritual practices and principles in our lives. So it's not like purification is the stage of the apprentice, illumination the stage of the journeyman, and only union the stage of the master: rather, all three stages are equally present in our lives whether we are beginners or advanced in our spiritual practice. In a way, we are always beginners; in a way, we are already "masters" because of the grace of the Spirit who is already present in our hearts. The entire circle is the mystical journey: everyone at every stage is truly a contemplative, truly an initiate into the endless mysteries of divine love.

One ancient mystic, Origen of Alexandria, compared these tides of the spiritual life to three books in the Hebrew Bible: purgation is like the book of Proverbs, with its emphasis on learning virtue and holy conduct; illumination is like the book of Ecclesiastes, with its emphasis on wisdom and insight, and union/deification is like the Song of Songs, which we have already seen is a lovely poetic metaphor for the intimacy of divine love in our hearts.

Another approach to these three dimensions of the spiritual life can be seen by comparing them to the initiatory sacraments of Catholic Christianity. The Catholic tradition recognizes seven sacraments, ceremonial ways in which Christians can experience God's grace in their lives in material, earthy ways. Three of those seven sacraments are known as the sacraments of initiation, but receiving these sacraments is seen as a way to be fully initiated into new life in Christ. The sacraments of initiation are baptism (where the new Christians are immersed in water or have water poured on them in the name of the triune God), confirmation (where their faith is "confirmed" by acknowledging the Holy Spirit present in their lives, marked by anointing of oil), and Holy Communion (where they are fed spiritually with the body and blood of Christ, present in the consecrated bread and wine). Because baptism represents the washing away of sin, it's the sacrament of purification; the confirmation of the presence of the Spirit celebrates the ongoing process of illumination, and the real presence of Christ in Holy Communion is a sign of God's presence in our hearts and lives.

Back to the mystics of old, and their dour emphasis on virtue, turning away from sin, and striving for sanctification. Seen in the light of the three stages of the mystical life, it seems as if the mystics were so focused on the purgative stage that they never got around to talking about illumination or union.

With writings filled with stern language that counsels repentance from sin, austere self-denial, harsh projects of discipline and simplification, it's clear that what they intended was for their readers to create, in our hearts, that place of interior emptiness that *kenosis* represents. For the most part, we can assume that the mystics often saw their writing as meant for beginners in the interior life. The assumption would be that our job is to focus on our purification, and trust the Spirit to guide us on the paths of illumination and union. Furthermore, it's helpful to remember that most of the great mystics lived long before the insights of modern psychology—their spirituality would have been shaped by the limits of the theology and philosophy of their time, which for much of Christian history tended to emphasize penitence rather than grace, God's judgment rather than love.

Even the most sullen of mystics often would leaven their stern writings about the necessity of becoming holy with insights into the splendor of mystical joy and the beatitude of a life given to God in love. When they would get around to the topics of illumination or union, the words of the mystics dance with visionary joy and heavenly excitement. They promise us that the spiritual life calls us into insight and felicity, exaltation and ecstasy, unitive consciousness and nondual knowing—in short, the language of immersion in and identification with divine love. So even the harshest teachings about turning away from sin and toward holiness was always offered with eyes on the prize: the happiness that emerges from intimacy with God.

Like Robert Hughes, Evelyn Underhill is another commentator on the wisdom of the mystics who observed that the itinerary of the mystical life often involves a kind of cyclical back-and-forth between purification and illumination, between emptiness and the dance. We who seek to integrate mystical wisdom and contemplative practices in our lives today are invited to allow both of these dimensions of mystical teaching to shape and form us continually as we consent to divine love and grace in our lives. When we strive for purification, we can do so in the light of the dance, and when we bask in the light of contemplation, we can bear in mind how the emptiness of kenosis is itself a means of grace for us.

With this in mind, let's take a closer look at this intimidating, but ultimately liberating, concept of *holiness*—as a way of being initiated into the mystical life. But first, I want to acknowledge that holiness can be a difficult concept, especially for people who have been hurt by toxic religion. Traditional religious concepts like holiness, humility, obedience, repentance, sanctification, and surrender, have too often been used as language to enforce a division between insiders and outsiders in religious circles, or to shame those whose behavior (especially in terms of gender and sexuality) is deemed unacceptable.

One could argue that the emphasis on holiness has not been particularly useful at inspiring the average person to embody the Christian fruits of the Spirit, including love, joy, peace, kindness, and goodness.[1] While we can't resolve or even fully examine these arguments here, it's important to try to approach holiness from a contemplative perspective, always seen in the light of the promise of God's unconditional love and indwelling presence. In other words, holiness is not some sort of arbitrary set of rules that powerful people use to decide who is acceptable and who isn't. Rather, it is a radical invitation to all people to find the path toward love, which includes letting go of anything that impedes our ability to love and receive love. We'll try to unpack this in the pages to come, but for now, I encourage each of us to consider how holiness might be related to *wholeness*—to what mystics like Thomas Keating have called "the true self." Holiness is not so much about conforming to some external standards, but about becoming who we truly are, who God created us to be from the inside. It's a word we can reclaim from those who have used it to exclude people—a word to describe a life oriented toward ethical integrity, conscious compassion, and joyful care and concern for healthy relationships.

MYSTICISM AND HOLINESS

A Trappist monk whom I admired and studied under had a different understanding of mysticism than I do.

"Not everyone is called to be a mystic," he used to say, "but everyone is called to holiness." For this monk, mysticism was a special and rare calling that involved supernatural experiences of God and extraordinary phenomena that indicated God was present in the mystic's life in a dramatic and singular way.

Indeed, mysticism can result in some profoundly remarkable experiences or manifestations of God's presence. Christian history is filled with stories of charismatic mystics and contemplatives who could levitate, bilocate, prophesy, perform faith healings and other miracles, and who received extraordinary visions or locutions from God, Christ, Mary, or the angels or saints. Many people nowadays might dismiss such stories as folklore or hagiography (embellished legends that surround renowned saints, similar to how George Washington is said to have been able to throw a silver dollar across the river). But even if you accept such stories at face value, it's pretty obvious that mystics who work miracles or have other supernatural experiences are pretty rare in the annals of history. Meanwhile, many of the mystics themselves insisted that supernatural or extraordinary phenomena is not the point of mysticism—but rather, the point is always intimacy with God, which might be manifest in most people's lives in very humble and down to earth ways.

Here's how I see it. Most people love music, and many people take up musical instruments or learn how to sing; but in every generation, there's only a few musicians who we think of as geniuses—people like Paul McCartney or John Coltrane, Ella Fitzgerald or Taylor Swift. Such musicians are legendary for the ability to compose or perform, and countless other musicians aspire to be like them. But can you imagine how sad the world would be if people believed that only geniuses deserve to be thought of as musicians?

How many singers and performers who make music just for love, or who have careers only in their hometown or region, never achieving fame or notoriety—how sad it would be if those musicians were all ignored, or worse, silenced. I marvel at the amazing talents of Joni Mitchell or Jimi Hendrix, but there are so many others whose music has brought joy to themselves and others.

So I disagree with my friend the monk. He limits mysticism to just those who are spiritual geniuses: the Evelyn Underhills and Howard Thurmans and Edith Steins of the world. Yes, they are brilliant and amazing and deserve all the renown that they have accrued. But there are countless others whose spirituality might not be as dramatic or supernatural, and consequently are not as well known, but they deserve to be seen as mystics too.

If mysticism involves only extraordinary, singular, and rare experiences of God's supernatural activity, then any kind of desire to obtain such mystical experiences paradoxically suggests a lack of humility. Jesus made it clear that becoming humble, "like a child," is the path to heaven.[2] Given this mandate to be humble, how can we square that with an ambition (no matter how "spiritual") to have the most extraordinary experiences of God—experiences that most Christians, indeed most people, never will enjoy? "Humility goes before honor," insists the book of Proverbs, which seems to confirm that the honor of enjoying mystical experiences can only truly be given to us after we have chosen the path of humility. This implies that the summit of mystical experience paradoxically will occur only in the lives of those who couldn't care less if they are mystics or not.

But back to the logic of my friend the monk.

While he believed that mysticism, as he understood it, is only for the chosen few, he insisted that holiness is for everyone. Moreover, it is proper, indeed necessary, for all Christians to seek ethical integrity for their lives. But what if holiness and mysticism are more intimately related than this monk seems to think? What if holiness could simply be another word for mysticism (as I understand it)? What if holiness—a life of conscious compassion and ethical integrity—represents a more egalitarian and inclusive way of approaching the mystery of divine love? By this understanding, you don't have to have supernatural experiences in order to be a mystic; therefore, everyone is called, if not to a life of extraordinary phenomena, then at least to the ordinary mysticism of seeking divine love and joyful compassion through a contemplative life.

Now, if someone decided they didn't want to bother with the demands of conscious compassion, but focus their energy just on "being a mystic," they likely would end up like the hapless person in Jesus's parable who built a house on sand.[3] The first storm (i.e., the first challenge to their so-called spirituality that came their way) would cause their spiritual house to topple, simply because it lacked a secure foundation.

If you are like my friend the monk, and you have a "high" view of mysticism and believe it is something supernatural that is given to only a chosen few, it makes sense to focus your efforts on living a holy life. Indeed, the quest for holiness is the best way to offer yourself to God, leaving it entirely up to the Spirit whether you are graced with mystical experience. On the other hand, if your view of mysticism, like mine, is more egalitarian, it nevertheless makes sense to prioritize the quest for conscious compassion: for a slow, undramatic, unspectacular process of joyful transformation into the self-forgetful, God-centered life of holiness may be the one sure way to anchor your contemplative aspirations on a rock-solid foundation. It is the altar on which you humbly offer yourself to God. To seek the mystical life, begin by seeking a holy life.

Whichever way you approach mysticism, it appears that the great mystics of the Christian tradition got it right. All three dimensions of the mystical life—purgation, illumination, and union—are driven by grace. But of the three, it is through purification that we are called to cooperate most actively with God's grace. Purgation is the area of the contemplative life that is the most dependent on our choices and actions. That's why the great teachers of the tradition emphasize it so much in their teaching. As John Ruusbroec said, "You are as holy as you want to be."[4]

LIVING A HOLY MYSTICAL LIFE

Part of the challenge we face as we try to understand holiness today is the fact that so many different approaches to questions of ethics, morality, and goodness and justice have become part of our cultural landscape. While everyone may still agree that murder and theft are bad and helping others and showing deference to the elderly and handicapped are good, in so many other ways our society simply has no unified, consensual understanding of what constitutes holiness—at least in a comprehensive sense of the word. Does "being holy" entail heroic acts of virtue, like the years Mother Teresa spent serving the poorest of the poor in Calcutta? Is it possible to be holy and yet still struggle with serious imperfections, addictive behaviors, and besetting sins—the kinds of mistakes we make over and over no matter how hard we try (and pray) to do better? Is holiness just something that "great" people embody, or is it something that can be found in the homeless person who sits quiet and unnoticed at the back of the church every Sunday?

Even within the Christian community, significant differences of belief can contribute to sometimes radically diverse opinions on what goodness or righteousness entails. I once heard a popular young Christian author asked, when speaking on a college campus, to express his opinion about a controversial moral issue. I was impressed by his carefully considered response. He paused a moment (I suspect he was praying), and then talked about the differences of opinion concerning this particular issue within the church. Without revealing his own stance, he noted, "We Christians have to learn how to disagree well." He then went on to state that he felt it was our job as Christians to love other people, not to judge or convict or "save" them. When he finished speaking, the audience applauded.

Perhaps everyone was happy with this author's response to this hot-button question. Some may have wanted him to speak more definitively about it; perhaps half the audience wanted him to make a declaration on one side of the issue, while the others equally desired to hear a statement in support of the opposing side. But instead of taking sides, the speaker acknowledged the controversy, and then spoke eloquently about how love and compassion and understanding can help transform even our conflicts and disagreements. And there are plenty of conflicts and disagreements over the many divisive questions facing the Christian community today. Here are just a few of the challenging issues faced by the faithful today: questions about social justice, personal morality, the relationship between religion and politics, how best to care for the environment, how Christians ought to relate to persons of other faiths, our responsibilities to those who are economically deprived or politically oppressed. In the Christian understanding of bioethics, medical ethics, and other concerns, moral decision-making must be applied to the ever-evolving and increasingly complex world of science and technology. Unfortunately, it is so easy to become caught up in these contentious issues that Christians can lose sight of the many distinctive and unifying ways that the wisdom of Jesus can inspire all people to grow in holiness (in other words, to grow in love, kindness, compassion, and care for others). A commitment to contemplative spirituality includes a call to spiritual integrity that goes beyond merely finding the "right" side of contemporary conflicts. Rather, it calls us to seek a higher perspective where even bitter disagreements might find resolution by the leading of the Spirit—even if that resolution may take years or even decades or centuries.

In the early centuries of the Christian tradition, there was profound disagreement over how to understand the relationship between Jesus and God the Creator. It literally took centuries for some of those disagreements to be resolved. Some of the moral, ethical, social, and political issues that we find controversial in our day might likewise take several generations for us to work through. If we trust in the Spirit, we will follow our conscience and seek to live holy lives and strive for justice in our societies, even though we may not live to see the fruit of our labors.

Many of the conflicts within Christianity today (including some of the ones I listed in the preceding paragraph) arise out of the evolving and uncertain relationship between Christian ethics and scientific knowledge. I recognize that those who seek the splendors of mysticism may likely disagree with one another on this or that issue. I don't think we have the luxury to just avoid the difficult issues of our day (avoiding conflict is typically only something that privileged people, with social, economic or political power, can do), but neither do we have to allow the conflicts in our lives to overwhelm our desire to find union in the Spirit. Whether we like it or not, ours is an age in which our collective spiritual wisdom must be forged in a great and grand conversation between traditional Christian values and the vast pool of human knowledge and insight that exists in the scientific community and, for that matter, in the wisdom traditions of other faiths and philosophies. In the midst of that grand conversation, we must ask, What does it mean to embrace—and to seek—a holy life?

There is no simple formula for manifesting such a life, other than to seek God's grace as you grapple with the big questions of life and with your own personal process of surrendering sin and cultivating virtue. There are, however, certain steps that anyone can take to help us determine the unique way that holiness will characterize our own contemplative walk.

KEYS TO *QADOSH*

The Hebrew word for holy is קָדוֹשׁ, *qadosh*, which means "set apart" or "consecrated." The Greek counterpart is ἅγιος, *hagios*, which has a connotation of "religious awe." These words reveal the first and most fundamental truth about holiness: only God is truly holy. Only God is fully set apart from the messiness and brokenness and corruption that characterizes human life—the stuff that leads inevitably to suffering, pain, and ultimately death. However, God's holiness is more than just a type of purity. For while God is indeed set apart from the messiness of mortal existence, in the person of Jesus Christ, God chose to become immersed in our decidedly not-very-holy world. Holiness, therefore is paradoxical. It has the quality of being set apart, consecrated, great enough to inspire awe, and yet it continually gives itself away, undermining its own set-apart-ness and immersing itself in the very mess above which it stands (this brings us back to the holiness/hospitality paradox we explored in chapter 10). The set-apart God entered the less-than-holy world in the physical life of Jesus Christ, and continues to do so perpetually through the ongoing loving presence of the Holy Spirit.

It has been said that all people are called to manifest this self-giving love, what twentieth-century theologians called "the universal call to holiness." Aspiring contemplatives can embrace and answer this call, by gently holding on to this paradox between being set apart for God, and following the Spirit's immersion in the world even in its messiness and imperfection.

Jesus echoes this paradox when he emphasized the two great commandments:

> *You shall love the Lord your God with all your heart, and with all your soul, and with all your mind.*
> and
> *You shall love your neighbor as yourself.*

"On these two commandments," he insists, "hang all the law and the prophets."[5]

Love God with all your heart, soul, and mind, he tells us (other versions add "strength"). Here is the call to be set apart, to immerse yourself in the infinite light of divine love, seeking a kind of purity of heart that can come only as a gift from God. By our own efforts, we cannot make ourselves pure, any more than we can, by our own efforts, prevent the inevitable march of old age and death. Whatever purity anyone may have—whether it be selfless humility or an innocent ability to live in love and joy and all the other fruits of the Spirit[6]—it is manifest not by dint of human effort, but through the grace of God. We work to become holy primarily by getting out of our own way, cultivating an interior spirit of willingness, allowing God the freedom within us to transform our hearts and souls through the healing power of divine grace.

Meanwhile, the second commandment is both like and equal to the first: to love your neighbors as yourself. Notice that the standard for loving others is how well you love yourself. Jesus isn't saying, however, that if you hate yourself you have permission to dislike others. Rather, encoded in this commandment about loving others is the call to love yourself as well. The implication is that we ought to love ourselves—and others—with the same vast, infinite, compassionate love that God has for each of us.

Right away, we encounter a humbling thought: never mind the idea that we need to master the work of purification before we can hope to enjoy the blessings of illumination or deification. I suspect that for nearly all of us, it will most likely take our entire lives to learn how to obey just these two commandments. I am convinced that if every Christian, especially every aspiring contemplative, made a rock-solid, serious commitment to live according to these two directives, the world would be transformed. Certainly the Christian community itself would be changed radically for the better. So much of the tension and conflict that exists between Christians of different denominations, or between "traditionalists" and "progressives," would simply disappear. When you stop judging others and start loving them instead, you create space in your heart for the Spirit to enter and lead you into conscious compassion. Likewise, take care to stop judging yourself, thereby creating space in your heart for a healthy self-love—not a narcissistic pleasure-seeking love, but a mature love that is inspired by and seeks to imitate the love God has for you.

I know a monk whose daily prayer is this: "God, teach me how to love the way you do." This, then, is the first step to living a holy life. And for most of us, it is a lifelong assignment.

TEN DECLARATIONS OF FREEDOM

Making a commitment to live a life of love may be the heart and soul of ethical integrity, but this leads to an important question: How do we truly know the love of God? What can we do to cultivate that love in our hearts, both as a response to divine love, and to more perfectly (or less imperfectly) love ourselves and our neighbors?

If holiness is best understood as living a life of love, it is open to so many possible interpretations that it might seem almost meaningless. One person may have a notion of "tough love" that seems at odds with someone else's rather sentimental idea of love as "everybody's happy." And what about the relationship between mercy and justice, or pleasure and self-restraint, or defense and nonviolence? How can we truly discern what it means to both love God and love our neighbors as ourselves?

Traditionally, Christians have turned to the heart of Jewish ethics—the Ten Commandments given to Moses on Mount Sinai—as a blueprint for the life of love. This simple and ancient moral code still inspires us with its clarity and its demands. Sadly, for many today, the Ten Commandments have become a symbol of the conflict between people with different political perspectives on how to maintain the boundaries that separate church and state. For others, they have become so familiar that they have lost their power to challenge and confront. We've heard them so many times that our eyes just kind of glaze over when we encounter them again.

But the Ten Commandments, taken on their own terms, can play an important role in the mystical call to ethical integrity and joyful compassion. To explore this, we need to look at this ancient code of conduct from a new perspective. Perhaps the most powerful interpretation of the commandments I have seen comes from theologian Brian Haggerty. Haggerty suggests that the Ten Commandments are best understood not as a simplistic code of moral behavior, but as a statement of what it means to be truly free. At the time of Moses, when the Hebrews received the commandments, they had just been liberated from centuries of enslavement in Egypt. Haggerty suggests that, to truly understand the full meaning and power of the commandments, we need to understand them as a sort of spiritual Declaration of Independence. The chosen people of God obey these commandments as a sign of their liberation from all human forms of oppression or slavery. Haggerty points out that most English translations of the Bible fail to convey the concept of freedom that lies at the heart of the commandments, and provides his own restatement of the ten principles:

1. *You shall not worship transitory gods but shall serve only the living God.*
2. *You shall not enshrine any notion, ideology, or interest as God and allow yourself to be dominated by it.*
3. *You shall not lay exclusive claim to God's blessing or call upon God to bless your selfish purposes.*
4. *Show reverence for the land; regard those who labor with respect.*
5. *Treat the elderly with respect and deference.*
6. *You shall not threaten the lives of others by your aggressive or irresponsible behavior.*
7. *You shall not threaten another person's marriage or family life.*
8. *You shall not deprive other people of their freedom.*
9. *You shall not cause another person to be treated unjustly.*
10. *You shall not grasp after what belongs to someone else or seek for yourself what belongs to all people.*[7]

The first three commandments expand on what it means to love God; the remaining seven provide a framework for our love for neighbors and ourselves. Let's look at each of these in turn.

The first commandment—to serve only the living God—challenges us to consider what material or spiritual objects in our lives we have chosen to worship (place ultimate value in). We worship a "transitory god" whenever we place our ultimate hope and trust in anything other than the ultimate mystery, the source of love from whom we derive our being, our health, our salvation, and ultimately our deepest happiness. Materially speaking, such ephemeral gods may include money, the stock market, real estate, and other tangible goods. But there are many other transitory "gods." Some people place their trust in human knowledge, or prestige, or power. Others bow before the government, political party, employers, parents, or cultural icons. Sources of pleasure often become our gods, and there is often a fine line between worshipping something and becoming spiritually enslaved by it. Remember, the purpose behind these commandments is not to shame us into being prigs, but to guide us into preserving our freedom which comes only from the limitless living God.

The second commandment expands upon the first, by prohibiting idolatry—the creation and veneration of man-made "gods." Idolatry can extend far beyond the worship of graven images. We can make idols out of political views, or economic systems, philosophies of life, and even our religions. To worship an idol means, sooner or later, to allow ourselves to be dominated by it. Only in the worship of the God who transcends all idols and all ideologies can we truly be free.

The third commandment, which directs us not to take the divine name in vain, has been debased in our culture to mean, "Don't swear." Granted, swearing is impolite and may arise from a heart shaped more by anger than love, but it is only the tip of the problem that this commandment addresses. To "not lay exclusive claim to God's blessing or call upon God to bless our selfish purposes" reminds us that we love to feel like we are in control. We try again and again to shape God in our own image, usually by insisting that God behave in the way we expect (often in accord with our own favored and biased way of interpreting the Bible). Christians have a long and sorry history of trying to use God to justify our own selfish aims, with just one glaring example being how privileged people as recently as the nineteenth century insisted that the Bible justifies slavery. This commandment reminds us that, whenever we try to use the name of God to promote hatred, oppression, injustice, exclusion, scapegoating, or social privilege, we are using God's name in vain—and trading away both our honor and our collective freedom by doing so.

The fourth commandment, traditionally "Remember the Sabbath," challenges us to balance work with rest, labor with leisure, and—perhaps most important for aspiring mystics—activity with contemplation. There is a social and political dimension to this mandate which links respect for laborers with respect for the land. Rather than taking a legalistic view of "keeping Sabbath" (Jesus himself tended to approach the Sabbath pragmatically rather than legalistically, even though it meant he was continually being criticized for this by his opponents), we can honor the spiritual dimension of this commandment: respect the gifts of nature and human toil to create wealth, and preserve the freedom of those who labor by safeguarding their right for rest and rejuvenation. In our day, many of us tend to hide behind the idea that Jesus broke the Sabbath rules to give ourselves permission to be workaholics—so while a pragmatic approach to this commandment makes sense, some of us need to remember that ignoring it can lead to bondage, even in our own lives.

Haggerty gives the fifth commandment, "Honor your father and mother," a broader sense of treating all the elderly with kindness and respect. I would add to this a moral imperative to care for those who are handicapped or disadvantaged. Striving to honor the most vulnerable members of society is an important component of working to respect the dignity and worth of all people; and only a society that cares for its most vulnerable members can truly be said to be free.

The mandate not to kill is perhaps the commandment that most obviously safeguards freedom. But Jesus added another dimension to it by teaching that "killing" someone in the anger of one's heart is, morally speaking, as great a violation as actual violence. Haggerty expands on this by suggesting that threatening others, through either vicious or negligent actions, also qualifies as violence that is therefore forbidden under this commandment.

The prohibition against adultery has become strongly associated, at least for many Christians with all sexual acts outside of marriage. While integrity in sexuality is certainly an important aspect of any meaningful spiritual life, Haggerty reframes this commandment by taking the focus off of a narrow rejection of sexual misconduct, and expanding it to forbid any action that can harm marriage or family bonds, including emotional infidelity, breach of trust, or the poisoning of another's relationship, for whatever reason.

Likewise, Haggerty turns the self-explanatory "Do not steal" into a more sweeping prohibition against anything that threatens another's freedom. To deprive people of their rightful property undermines their freedom to use or enjoy what belongs to them. His perspective on this commandment suggests that, anytime we impinge on other people's individual sovereignty, we steal from them, depriving them of dignity, identity, and freedom. Such theft is contrary to the will of God.

The ninth commandment prohibits lying, which Haggerty describes as "causing another person to be treated unjustly." Lying is a fundamentally unjust act that destroys relationships, trust, and possibly even entire communities. Whether it is a stated untruth or a passive deception, lying undermines the bonds of honor and goodwill that hold relationships and communities together.

The last commandment against coveting another person's belongings extends not only to other individuals, but also to society as a whole. This has powerful environmental as well as social implications. Like the prohibition against stealing or dishonesty, however, this commandment challenges us to let go of any action by which we secretly place our own interests above those of others.

The Ten Commandments are not meant to function as a rule book that provides concrete, relevant guidance for every possible moral dilemma we face. As concise ethical statements that challenge the human family to surrender dysfunctional self-interest in favor of a more expansive and generous commitment to family and community, however, they make a powerful statement about love. True spiritual love elevates us out of egocentric, "me-first" morality, demanding instead that relationships and bonds of trust and goodwill define our understanding of right and wrong.

If you are like me, and I suspect like most people, even these simple ethical guidelines may leave you feeling humbled (if not ashamed) at how far you fall short from living a truly holy life. It's tempting, when faced with our own stubborn sinfulness, to decide that the quest for holiness is for others, that we lack what it takes to achieve holiness. The truth is, we *do* lack what it takes—all of us, even those who manage to project the appearance of being holy. And this is where grace comes in. No one can earn God's love and favor—not by being holy, or morally upright, superreligious or pious, or, for that matter, even by being a contemplative or a mystic. We are all faced with the paradox of being called to live according to uncompromising ethical standards while, at the same time, being loved and accepted just as we imperfectly are—through God's grace. The quest for holiness is not something we do in order to make ourselves perfect; it is something we do in response to the fact that God already loves us so perfectly.

THE FRUIT OF THE SPIRIT

Together, the two great commandments of Jesus and the Ten Commandments of Moses provide brilliant general principles for ethical conduct. If we accept these two sets of commandments as the summation of what it takes to be holy, however, we run the risk of seeing ethical integrity as merely a function of human effort.

But holiness is not primarily about our initiative; it's primarily about God's grace. Your efforts to become holy can be offered only in response to that grace.

To help underline this spiritual truth, let's consider a third set of standards from the New Testament, given in Galatians 5:22–23. I've already alluded to the fruit of the Spirit; here is the complete list as detailed by Paul:

> *The fruit of the Spirit is love, joy, peace, patience, kindness, generosity, faithfulness, gentleness, and self-control.*

With this list, the apostle describes the contours of a holy life, not in terms of what holiness *does*, but in a more existential sense of what holiness *is*. This is not a list of what is forbidden, but a descriptive list of how holiness positively manifests itself in peoples' lives.

These qualities of holiness are not achieved by following rules. We can cooperate with the fruit of the Spirit being cultivated in our lives through spiritual practices including observance of the commandments, commitment to prayer, and striving for emotional maturity and integrity. But most important of all is reliance on grace, the recognition that it is God who ultimately brings these fruits to bear in our hearts.

Notice that love, the mandate of the two greatest commandments, takes its place as the first fruit of the Spirit. All the other fruits describe what a loving spirit looks like; indeed, I would suggest that the remaining eight fruits of the Spirit are like refracted colors, a rainbow of qualities and characteristics that together shape what a loving character is like. A corollary to this is the famous "love chapter" in Corinthians often read at weddings, but useful far beyond its popular association with matrimony. It says, in part,

> *Love is patient; love is kind; love is not envious or boastful or arrogant or rude. It does not insist on its own way; it is not irritable or resentful; it does not rejoice in wrongdoing, but rejoices in the truth. It bears all things, believes all things, hopes all things, endures all things.*[8]

To reflect on the promise of the fruit of the Spirit in a life dedicated to holiness, we can ask ourselves questions for discernment: Am I living a truly loving life? A truly joyful life? Am I marked by peace, by patience and goodness and kindness? Am I shaping my quest for holiness with faith and gentleness? Is self-control (moderation) a factor in my spiritual life?

Of course, no one can truthfully say they perfectly embody the characteristics of love. The purpose behind these questions is not to shame us into discouragement or despair, but rather to remind us that, ultimately, holiness can come only through God's grace—grace that we receive in part through our humble willingness to ask for and receive the Spirit's action in our lives. In a very real way, holiness is not something you *do* so much as it is something you *allow*, by getting your ego and your small-minded self-interest out of the way long enough to let God's love and joy and grace flow gently through you. Holiness is a gift we receive, not a quality we achieve.

THE GIFT OF GRACE

Each of these biblical teachings concerning holiness—from Jesus, Moses, and Paul—functions as both a challenge and an inspiration. God loves us enough to not settle for second best in either our behavior or our character. While the commandments provide useful general guidelines to the qualities of holy behavior, ultimately we are called to a holy character, as Paul describes. Christians understand that all good things are gifts from God; therefore, the fruit of the Spirit comes to us always through divine grace. Like all gifts from God, such grace is given to us, not for our pleasure or self-satisfaction, but always for our well-being which in turn supports our ability to love and serve others.

It seems that these gifts are rarely if ever given to us in an easy or instant way. The characteristics of holiness are slowly shaped and formed in us over time, just as all the characteristics associated with mystical spirituality—a contemplative outlook, the ability to meditate, an ongoing desire for God and the things of God, and a humble acceptance of our limitations tinged with sadness over our sinfulness—are all shaped and formed in us over time.

It is a mistake to assume that one must "master" the purgative way before hoping to enter into the splendor of illumination or union with God. Each of the three ways—*katharsis*, *theoria*, and *theosis*—represents a lifelong process. Purification is never finished while you live and breathe on this earth. Like all aspects of mystical spirituality, holiness emerges gradually, over time.

I know this has been a long detour into fairly foundational spiritual teaching, but given how central the topic of holiness is to the writings of many of the great mystics, it seems important that we take the time to at least begin to emphasize how important holiness is to the overall mystical life. To end this chapter, I'd like to share an insight that came from a person who attended a retreat I led at the Monastery of the Holy Spirit in Conyers, Georgia, several years ago. We were talking about the three mystical stages of purification, illumination, and union. The retreatant offered this observation: "It seems to me that the first stage is about learning the rules, while in the second stage you move from the rules to wisdom, and in the final stage you move into love." I marveled at how succinctly she described these three tides of the Spirit. Keeping our cyclical theme in mind, we can acknowledge that one never fully graduates from "following the rules"—but hopefully as we mature in the life in the Spirit, we make room in our hearts not only for law, but also for wisdom, and ultimately for love. This is the promise that holiness—and mysticism—points us to.

CHAPTER SIXTEEN

A Pathless Path of Light

Draw near to God, who then will draw near to you.
—Apostle James (James 4:8, adapted)

All the way to heaven is heaven.
—Catherine of Siena

To embrace a contemplative or mystical life, we do not need to master *katharsis* before we begin to discover the beauty of *theoria*. But if we are committed to the spiritual practices associated with the mystical life, we can trust that, sooner or later, God will call us into the path of illumination, the path of *theoria*.

We prepare ourselves for the illuminative way by learning the basics of the spiritual life (which, for Christians, includes finding a meaningful spiritual community), and opening our hearts so that the Spirit can cultivate within us the character of holiness (or, at least, of a life calibrated to love and freedom in the spirit). Along with these foundational practices, aspiring contemplatives also engage in exercises geared to the consenting to God's presence and action in our lives—exercises such as prayer, meditation, contemplation, and *lectio divina*, which we will be examining more closely over the next few chapters. All these practices of spiritual living function as necessary prerequisites for the *theoria* stage of the mystical life, that we may realize in our hearts and minds these illuminating mystical truths: God is present, God is love, and God is one with us in our hearts.

The Greek word *theoria* translates into English as "theory" but also as "contemplation." In common English parlance, we equate theory with ideas, ideas that explain a system, process, or principle. We also associate theory with a hypothesis, for example Darwin's theory of evolution: in this sense, a theory needs to be investigated to determine whether or not it is true. But the Greek word *theoria* that points to our spiritual principles of illumination or contemplation carries a much richer meaning than simply concepts or premises. Mystical illumination is "theory" in the sense of something that needs to be examined, explored, *seen* in order to be understood and realized. In this sense, "God loves you" is a theory—not theory in the hypothetical sense of "it may or may not be true," but rather in the sense of "you won't truly believe it until you see it for yourself." Likewise, "God is love" and "God is present in your heart" are further dimensions of mystical theory: statements of faith that mystics down the ages have given their lives to, so certain are they of their truth; and yet each new generation must once again experience these truths for ourselves. It's one thing to say, "Yes I believe that God is unconditional love and that this love resides in my heart"—but words are cheap, and we can easily roll these words off our tongue without truly embodying the conviction that they are true. Such conviction can only come from our own inner experience, experience that only emerges from a sustained contemplative practice.

When we do recognize that this enlightening mystical theory is indeed true—that yes, God really *is* love in divine form, and God really *does* love each of us unconditionally, and God really *is* one with us in our hearts, and therefore we really *are* holy and called to share that love unconditionally in the world—this realization floods us with uncreated light. This, then, illustrates the meaning of *illumination* as the second stage of the contemplative journey.

Jesus said "I am the light of the world" and he also proclaimed "You are the light of the world"—we've already looked more than once at the mystical meaning made evident when we pair these verses.[1] At the surface, this could be just two Gospel writers remembering Jesus's teaching in different ways. But on a deeper, more contemplative level, here is the crux of the contemplative life as it encompasses both practice and theory: in other words, as it encompasses both the path of purification and of illumination. We are the light of the world in that we embody the theory of God's love in our lives, in our bodies. When we say we are the light of the world, we say we are one with Christ, who has already proclaimed his divine status as the Φῶς τοῦ κόσμου, *phōs tou kosmou*—the *lux mundi,* the light of the world. Christ is the *lux mundi,* and we are the *phōs tou kosmou,* since we are one with Christ, and that oneness inspires our imagination as a spiritual light.

Thomas Merton proclaimed, "There is no way of telling people that they are all walking around shining like the sun."[2] There is no way to tell people this because everyone needs to experience it for themselves. The way to practice this theory is through the contemplative exercises of prayer, meditation, contemplation, and lectio divina, all woven together with the long slow work of consenting to the Spirit restoring our true, holy self within us, the self who loves God, neighbors, and even enemies, the self who embodies the radical freedom enshrined in the Ten Commandments, the self who is shaped and formed and characterized by the fruit of the Spirit.

The illumined life of mystical spirituality is not just a tidy process that we can manage by learning all the right methods or techniques of prayer, meditation, contemplation, moral living, or community involvement. Rather, the illuminating life is an invitation into an ever-expanding process of growth in grace and in response to love. There's an interesting Greek word that an early mystic, Gregory of Nyssa, emphasizes in his writings: ἐπέκτασις, *epektasis,* which only appears once in the New Testament, and carries the sense of continual striving toward a goal or desired object. Here's how the word is used in Philippians:

> Brothers and sisters, I do not consider that I have laid hold of it, but one thing I have laid hold of: forgetting what lies behind and **straining forward** to what lies ahead, I press on toward the goal, toward the prize of the heavenly call of God in Christ Jesus.[3]

You can see echoes of the contemplative journey in this passage. The path of purification is the process of "forgetting what lies behind"—especially everything that gets in the way of our free response to divine love. Paired with that is the *epektasis,* the unending effort to grow into the ever-expanding gifts of love God offers us. So the illumination of contemplation is not a goal, some end-point toward which we gear our spiritual practice. Rather, it is an ongoing process: an ongoing journey, an ongoing participation in the dance. It has a beginning—when we choose to consent to the gifts God eagerly seeks to give us. But it has no ending, for it invites us into the never-ending felicities of union with God in eternity.

If community life and the quest for holiness constitute a type of contemplative boot camp, the "preliminary practices" of the mystical life, then *epektasis* refers to the unending joys that are promised to us in the practices of contemplative spirituality: from consenting to God's action in our lives through prayer, meditation and contemplation, to all the ways we seek to share that divine action by loving our neighbors as ourselves, whether that means being kind to people as individuals or striving for justice for all.

In other words, having committed ourselves to the path of purification, we make ourselves available to receive the gifts of illumination. In all of this, we are saying yes to the contemplative life as a journey of mystical awakening.

THE JOURNEY THAT ISN'T A JOURNEY

Since the mystical life is a dance, we dance in a circle: we go everywhere and remain centered in place.

I have been describing the contemplative life in terms of a journey, of following a path. In doing so, I am using one of the most common metaphors for mystical spirituality—a way of speaking about the inner life that has been passed down for centuries. Early mystics like Origen of Alexandria and Gregory of Nyssa found inspiration in biblical tales of journey and pilgrimage—such as the stories of Moses and the exodus of the freed Hebrew slaves who journeyed from Egypt to the promised land. In the Middle Ages, Dante explored mystical spirituality in his sprawling poem-epic *The Divine Comedy*, which describes a journey through hell, purgatory, and heaven. One of the most well-known examples of the spiritual life described as a journey is found in John Bunyan's *The Pilgrim's Progress*, a deeply symbolic and allegorical tale of a person called only "Christian" who journeys through the trials and tribulations of life as he perseveres toward the final goal: the Celestial City.

This allegorical spiritual journey is often understood in terms of climbing or ascending a ladder, a staircase, or a mountain, as seen in the titles of several major mystical writings: *The Ladder of Divine Ascent* by John Climacus, *The Stairway of Perfection* by Walter Hilton, and *The Ascent of Mount Carmel* by John of the Cross.

But not all contemplatives use the metaphor of a journey, nor do all consider it particularly useful. Instructive here is the Irish poet, philosopher, and mystic John O'Donohue, who said, "There is no spiritual program." In other words, we ought to be wary of linear models of mystical development that present the contemplative life as a nice tidy progression from point A to B to C. As O'Donohue notes, "When time is reduced to linear progress, it is emptied of presence."[4] In other words, if you are so hypnotized by the notion of a journey, you can too easily dismiss your past as worthless and regard the present as merely an instrumental moment useful only for launching you into the future, which in turn is valuable only insofar as it beckons you to the next "stage." This model reflects the human insistence of being in control, which is at odds with the deep contemplative mandate to surrender our controlling into the love of God.

We've seen how Robert Davis Hughes suggests that, as an alternative to a linear understanding of the three-stage journey, the metaphor of waves crashing on the beach can be used to describe the various dimensions of spiritual growth and development. Water flows, dances, and cascades. Waves do not move in straight lines; they advance and recede according to the overall thrust of the tides. Hughes suggests that we think in terms of "tides of the Spirit" when talking about the journey of faith. This metaphor can provide a useful alternative to the tendency to think of the mystical life as a hierarchy involving prerequisites and an orderly, predictable sequence of development.

Once again mysticism invites us into the realm of paradox. The mystical life is a journey—and it's not a journey. It's a climb up the mountain; and it's a transformation that happens right here, right now—no movement necessary. Since paradox is at the heart of mystical experience, the journey/not-journey becomes yet another key to unlocking the depth of the Christian mysteries.

Rather than try to pin down the various stages of the mystical journey, it's probably more helpful to think of the contemplative life more like GPS system, bearing in mind that a GPS is simply a high-tech map—and "the map is not the territory." Like any adventurous spiritual travelers, sometimes we might even turn the GPS off and explore terrain that has not yet been mapped out. We may even find that the map/GPS is not always the best guide to getting where we want to go, since ultimately our desire is not to reach some mystical end-point, but to foster divine intimacy, which may begin here and now—no journeying required.

The inner life is organic, and simply cannot be reduced to a universal model or outline. The manner in which you, or me, or anyone else interested in the contemplative life, may actually explore or experience the mysteries of Christian spirituality may be nothing like anything anyone has experienced before.

As we continue our exploration of this pathless path, we'll begin to take a closer look at the kinds of prayer, meditation, and contemplative exercises traditionally associated with mystical and contemplative spirituality. We'll begin with a medieval practice with roots in the spirituality of contemplative monks: *lectio divina*. Lectio is an excellent exercise for both beginning and seasoned contemplative practitioners, because it weaves together four essential spiritual practices—Bible reading, prayer, meditation, and contemplation—into a single method of spiritual exploration. The journey-less journey does not require that we know where our destination might be, for ultimately that knowledge is God's alone. All that is asked of us is that we be willing to move forward in faith, one step at a time—or to trust the dance, even if means we keep moving in circles.

CHAPTER SEVENTEEN

The Word Is Very Near You

Finally, beloved, whatever is true, whatever is honorable,
whatever is just, whatever is pure, whatever is pleasing, whatever
is commendable, if there is any excellence and if there is anything
worthy of praise, think about these things.
—Paul (Philippians 4:8)

Let all my world be silent in your presence, Lord, so that I may
hear what the Lord God may say in my heart. Your words are so
softly spoken that no one can hear them except in a deep silence. But
to hear them lifts him who sits alone and in silence completely above
his natural powers, because he who humbles himself will be lifted
up. He who sits alone and listens will be raised above himself.
—Guigo II

Words are powerful. Words enable us to think and to communicate; they
are the foundation of human knowledge, intellect, and understanding. With
words we can bless—or curse; we can express love or other dimensions of
how we feel or how we relate to one another.

Words, of course, are the basic building block of the stories that shape
our lives and give them meaning.

Stories give life meaning and purpose, they reveal possibilities and the solution to problems, and they help us to know, and to remember, who we are.

We have already reflected on how mysticism is, in essence, a story: a love story of the mutual desire and intimacy that brings the God who is love into our lives and enables us to bask in that divine love and also find inspiration in it to create the best possible life for ourselves and our loved ones.

For Christians, Jesus—the incarnate second person of the Trinity—is the Word, the Word of God in human form. "In the beginning was the Word," proclaims the Gospel of John. Jesus is the way God expresses divine love and presence to the human family. But Christians also see the Bible—the collection of sacred writings that tell the foundational story of Christian faith and spiritual practice—as another expression of the word of God.

For Christian mystics and contemplatives, the Bible records the origin stories of our faith; it in turn is explained and unpacked by the writings of the great mystics down the ages. Thus, an essential part of any contemplative practice is daily immersion in the word. Such immersion can happen in several ways. Many churches and faith communities have a tradition of daily prayer called the liturgy or the divine office; such prayers are typically drawn from the Psalms and other parts of the Bible, and provide a daily structure for anyone who seeks to be immersed in a prayerful practice of seeking closer intimacy with God. In monasteries and convents, the daily liturgy is a communal practice where monks, nuns, and their guests gather to pray together, often chanting the prayers in a service of deep beauty (Gregorian chant comes from this ancient practice of singing the daily Psalms and prayers in a monastic church). Many people who do not live in monasteries still incorporate liturgical prayer in their personal spiritual practice, using breviaries (daily prayer books) to give a shape and form to their daily immersion into the words of their faith.

Just as important, yet perhaps more accessible for those who do not live in monasteries or convents, is the ancient practice of praying with the Bible or other sacred writings known as lectio divina (Latin for "sacred reading"). Emerging from the monasteries of ancient and medieval times, sacred reading combines prayer, meditation, contemplation, and reading of Scripture (or some other worthy text) into an integral practice where the word of God meets the silence of the soul.

WHAT MYSTICS DO

If you are a teacher, you teach. If you are a physician, you heal. If you are an artist, you create. And if you are a mystic or a contemplative, then you pray.

For mystics and contemplatives, prayer is the essence of the spiritual life. Anything else we might associate with mystical or contemplative Christianity—from religious observance, to acts of self-discipline or denial, immersion in silence, and so forth—all makes sense only to the extent that it is an expression of prayer.

Simply put, prayer is communication with God. We associate prayer with "saying prayers," and that's certainly important: a way of speaking to God, to open our hearts and minds to God's presence in our lives, often as a way of expressing our gratitude, need, sorrow for sin, or some other dimension of how we want to express ourselves in the face of the divine mystery.

But just as communication between two human beings requires both speaking and listening, so prayer requires more than just words we express to God. There is also a listening component to prayer as well. In prayer we listen to our hearts (trusting that God is present there), but we also listen to the words themselves that we pray, often finding that the very words we are offering to God also bring God to us, or help us to find a deeper and richer understanding of God. Finally, we also listen to God in the most mystical way of all—by placing ourselves gently into the presence of silence.

This chapter and the ones that follow it are all different approaches to prayer as the fundamental contemplative and mystical practice. The two essential elements in prayer are language and silence. As we begin our journey into prayer, let's start with language, reflecting on the idea that we meet Christ (and therefore God) in words—for Christ *is* the Word. We'll begin with the words that have been given to us through the millennia of Christian spiritual tradition: the words of the Bible and of the liturgy, words that generations of seekers have immersed themselves into in order to foster a deeper connection with God. In subsequent chapters we'll also consider the spontaneous words that emerge from our own minds and hearts and finally we'll consider the heart of mystical practice: the invitation to dive deep into the very silence of God.

PRAYING THE SACRED WORD

Visit a traditional Christian monastery or convent and you will notice that the monks or nuns who are resident there will gather several times a day to pray together. Collectively, these communal prayer times are called the liturgy of the hours—hours meaning the hours of the day, and liturgy coming from a Greek word that means "the people's work"—*lit-* is related to *lay* as in a layperson, and *-urgy* is related to energy, meaning the power that makes something happen. In liturgy, people gather to make prayer happen. It's an ancient practice of prayer and worship that has been part of the monastic tradition ever since the first monks and nuns gathered together in the ancient deserts of the Middle East, and it's a practice that lives on today not only in cloisters but also in the homes of anyone who wishes to pray in a more structured way.

The liturgy of the hours is inspired by Psalm 119:164: "Seven times a day I praise you." The earliest monastic Christians interpreted this to mean that an ideal life of prayer will include as many as seven "prayer times"—morning, mid-morning, noon, mid-afternoon, evening, before going to bed, and even in the middle of the night. Not every monastery continues to observe this sevenfold liturgy, although many do; others have adapted it to anywhere from twice a day (morning and evening prayer), four times a day (morning, noon, evening and night) or some other recurring schedule. Individuals who pray the liturgy by themselves in their own homes can be even more flexible, and might pray all or only part of the daily liturgy, as their schedule permits.

What does the liturgy consist of? There are different liturgies, from different traditions (Catholic, Orthodox, Anglican, Protestant) or based on the unique practices of specific monasteries or faith communities. What they all have in common is an outline of prayer that is grounded in the Psalms and other passages from Scripture, often paired with intercessions or general expressions of thanksgiving, confession of sin, or praise for God. The liturgy is always an expression of prayer to God directly ("We praise you, O God, we acknowledge you to be our lord")—but also the language of the liturgy is for *our* ears, too; the words of these prayers teach us who God is, and how people have been relating to God over the centuries.

When we pray, we open up the mind and the heart to the presence of God. What matters in prayer is that we consciously choose to be aware that God is present in our lives, that we seek to honor, worship and grow in intimacy with God—but that we also want to foster a deeper sense of union with God, which includes getting to know God better. The words of the liturgy (and, for that matter, of the Bible and the wisdom of the mystics in general) are all ways we can allow our hearts and minds to be more fully formed in response to God's love in our lives. Even when the prayers in the liturgy are addressed *to* God, such prayers always convey insights and information *about* God, that can stimulate the human imagination to more fully recognize and appreciate God's silent but real presence in our hearts.

For people who live in monasteries or otherwise have close ties to monastic communities, the liturgy becomes the soundtrack of their spiritual lives. Not everyone has such access to monasteries, and may find the daily practice of reciting prayers from a book in solitude to be difficult to maintain. Fortunately, there's no requirement to pray the liturgy in order to draw closer to God. For many people, simply fostering a daily practice of spontaneous prayer, or contemplative practices like Centering Prayer or the Jesus Prayer, serve as meaningful alternatives to the ancient practice of reciting prayers from a book. This leads to the practice of lectio, which has roots as ancient as the liturgy, but combines feasting on the word of God (the Bible) with essential spiritual practices, including meditation, prayer, and contemplation.

READING THE SACRED WORD

Lectio divina (which means "sacred reading") is an ancient monastic practice that employs a mindful, heart-centered approach to reading the Bible or some other worthy text, like the spiritual writings of a saint or mystic. Lectio divina is easy to learn, yet functions as a powerful tool for opening up to the presence of God, mysteriously hidden in your life, and especially in your interaction with sacred Scripture or other contemplative writings.

Lectio is a nexus where the wisdom of the word encounters, and is immersed in, the complementary wisdom of silence—the portal to the mystery. For those who do not live in monasteries or can participate in communal liturgy, it is the single most foundational spiritual exercise that supports the Christian mystical life. If you decide to engage in only one practice from this book, I hope it will be lectio. Anyone who wishes to engage in Christian meditation or in contemplative prayer is wise to begin with it.

Lectio opens us up to allow God to lead us where God so chooses. Prayer, meditation, and contemplation are powerful disciplines of the mystical life precisely because they are outgrowths of this practice. As disciplines of silence, meditation and contemplation function like a house in which you will live out your journey into the mystery of Christ. Lectio, by contrast, is the foundation upon which that house is built.

What makes lectio such a helpful practice is that, like the liturgy, it combines face-to-face engagement with God with the opportunity to learn more about God (and about the contemplative life).

Let me illustrate this with an example. When I was just three years old, I watched the Beatles perform on the *Ed Sullivan Show*, which initiated a lifelong love for rock-and-roll music. As I grew older, my interest in music grew with me, and I wanted to learn everything I could about it—who the best artists and bands were, how rock and roll evolved from earlier musical forms like folk and the blues, and how technology was influencing the evolution of rock sound. It seemed that a natural extension of my love for the music was a desire to learn as much as I could about it. Eventually, that interest even extended to reading biographies of my favorite musicians, learning to play the guitar and bass (not very well, I'm afraid), and keeping an eye on what my favorite critics were saying, while being careful not to let their opinions sway my own perspective on which bands made the best music.

This natural hunger to learn more about our favorite things also holds true for the spiritual life. Part of the mystical life is taking the opportunity to learn more about the history and philosophy of the Christian tradition. This may come to you through the actual study of Christian doctrine or biblical theology, or in more down-to-earth ways—through absorbing the ideas and values of the faith, by participating in Christian worship, or by getting to know the great stories of the life of Christ or the heroism of the saints: stories that help to define what it means to be a follower of Jesus. The joy you take in worship and in prayer, the choices you make to cultivate a willingness to be holy, and the actions you take to build fellowship and community with other Christians all come alive for you when you make the effort to learn about your faith.

However, as valuable as this knowledge is, it's also important not to reduce the Christian mysteries to mere topics for intellectual exploration. Seekers can become so caught up in trying to understand the Trinity or some other exercise in theological hair-splitting that they can lose sight of the profound invitation to love that lies in and beneath all the words. As joyful as it is to learn about God and Christ and the faith that bears Christ's name, we need to take care that these mental gymnastics don't become an obstacle to actually becoming intimate with this God we are so busy studying.

This tension between studying God and intimately encountering God forms the backstory to lectio divina, which is a way of reading the Bible and other sacred texts that is significantly different from traditional methods of study. This essential difference is the key to relating to the words of wisdom at the heart of the tradition as containers in which the silence of God can be discerned.

We are very fortunate to have access to the Bible, which, for most of Christian history, was simply not available to the ordinary person. Before the advent of the printing press, few people had access to, let alone owned, a copy of the Bible. And before the coming of modern ideas of scholarship, research, historical criticism, and other aspects of the academic pursuit of knowledge, nearly all those who wrestled with the words of Scripture did so to acquire a spiritual, rather than an intellectual, understanding of the text. In other words, for most of Christian history, reading the Bible was not an exercise in intellectually understanding religious doctrine, but rather a practice for encountering God through the medium of the written word. But with the arrival of mass-produced, easily available Bibles, along with the rise of modern scholarship, for many Christians "Bible study" became more of an intellectual exercise, rather than a spiritual practice. It was all about the head rather than the heart.

I'm sure that many people who engage in serious Bible study will insist that, for them, a critical, scholarly approach to sacred scripture is very much an exercise in drawing closer to God. Far be it from me to dispute that. Nevertheless, the ancient spiritual practice of lectio divina suggests that, in terms of fostering intimacy with God, there are approaches far more valuable than mere study and analysis.

A strictly academic reading of the Bible may stimulate the intellect, but doesn't necessarily transform the heart. When it comes to the divine mystery that is at the heart of Christian mysticism, more is required of us than just a cognitive understanding. Knowing about God does not necessarily lead to the powerful transformation that lies at the core of Christian mysticism.

THE KEY TO THE MYSTERIES

What is the key to true mystical intimacy with God? The wisdom of the Christian mystics suggests that the doorway into the divine mystery is entered not by filling our minds with words, no matter how holy or edifying they may be, but rather in bathing our minds and hearts, our awareness, our consciousness in silence.

Mystery lies at the heart of all our thoughts, images, experiences, notions, ideas, and speculations about God. Nothing reveals God perfectly; indeed, everything that reveals God also conceals God. Our experiences of God's closeness conceal the divine transcendence. Our sense of God's judgment can blind us to divine mercy. If we accept the gendered idea that God is our father, we risk cutting ourselves off from the rich gifts of God's motherhood (or even God as our nonbinary lover, whose care for us transcends and includes all gender). The paradox at the heart of mysticism emerges from the paradox of being human. That which is infinite cannot be squeezed into a finite container, no matter how grand and noble and beautiful that container may be.

If we talk about how God is present in our hearts (and such talk begins with the Bible[1]), we proclaim ourselves as containers of God. But we are finite, whereas God is infinite. We can ponder God's presence throughout the cosmos, but even the entire expanding universe remains finite when compared to the infinity of God. We trust traditional ways in which God is revealed to us—the Bible, the church, the wisdom of the great saints and mystics of the past. Yet we need to remember that even these voices of wisdom are, in the end, finite containers holding—or attempting to hold—an infinite God. All conceal even as they reveal.

Without denying the insight and information that may be gleaned from studying the Bible, the contemplative tradition offers an entry into

Scripture that, spiritually speaking, invites us deeper into the Christian mysteries.

For those eager to encounter the divine mystery, the Bible—and indeed, all worthy spiritual writing, not just that which has been canonized as sacred Scripture—is best engaged in a spirit of silence, of meditation and reflection, and, most important of all, in the context of prayer in order to realize its power to transform us. And this is precisely the function of lectio divina.

A NEW WAY OF READING

The actual process of lectio divina is deceptively simple—so simple, in fact, that the medieval monk who wrote the classic instructions for it, Guigo II, did so in an essay that is barely twenty pages long. The key to lectio is not just in learning a simple method, but also in rethinking your entire approach to the meaning and purpose of written words and how we use them. Lectio does not change the Bible, but it does change how we approach it. Therein lies the secret of its power.

Humanly speaking, the written word is a tool and, like all tools, it serves as a means to an end. When we read a book, a magazine, or a website, we usually do it to learn something new, to gather information, to get entertained, to stay in touch with friends. The ability to read is such a profound blessing that we consider literacy to be the primary indicator that separates those who are educated from those who are not. The power to read is essentially a means by which we maintain (or seek to expand) control over our lives. We read to attain something we may not otherwise have—more knowledge, more pleasure, more mastery, more skill, more data, more fun, more love and social contact. All of this is very good; clearly, the ability to read is a true blessing.

However, everything that reveals God also conceals God. One of the challenges we face when we read a sacred or mystical text is the very hiddenness of God.[2] When we read a spiritual text in the ordinary way of reading for personal mastery or control, it sometimes can have the unintended consequence of seeming to push God farther into hiding. For every question that is answered, three more emerge.

The mystical practice of lectio divina turns the normal goal of reading—for attaining mastery and control—on its head. When we practice lectio, we do not seek to control, but rather to yield. Lectio does not offer us mastery over the words, but rather an invitation to serve the Word. Whereas we typically read to discover new ideas or enjoy entertaining stories, in sacred reading we are invited to turn ourselves over to the divine mystery and let God be the master, the one in control, the one wielding the power. Whereas we usually read with the subconscious intention of helping ourselves, lectio leads us to ask the question, "How may I be of service (to God)?"

It is a practice for formation, rather than a means of gathering information. As a spiritual exercise, lectio divina involves opening one's heart and soul in order to be formed (and transformed) by the Spirit of God.

The process of lectio divina is a simple, four-step exercise. It involves reading a passage from the Bible or some other sacred text—as an act of slow, deliberate prayer. This in turn leads to three distinct but interrelated ways of prayerfully interacting with the words that you've read.

Lectio: prayerful, slow, heart-centered reading of a short passage from the Bible or some other spiritually nurturing text;
Meditatio: deliberate pondering of the message in the text, with an eye to what it means;
Oratio: responding to God's message with honest, sincere prayer;
Contemplatio: allowing the prayer to dissolve into wordless, silent contemplation, while simply resting in the divine presence, beyond the limitations of human thought.

Lectio divina is a subversive activity (indeed, I would suggest that all mystical practices have a subversive quality about them). Lectio is subversive because it challenges us to surrender our willfulness and control to the leadings and promptings of the Spirit. Thus, it runs counter to the mainstream values of our "can do," type-A, gotta-stay-on-top-of-things culture. In the intentional slowness of lectio, we are reminded that mystical spirituality emphasizes God's action and our response—not the other way around. Thus, lectio is a practice in which you slow yourself down, creating space in which you can gently learn to seek, and discern, God's presence hidden in the sacred text and in the subtle stirrings of your heart and mind.

By opening up to the divine presence through the written word, you simultaneously open yourself up to the deeply relational nature of the Christian contemplative life, which is indeed the heart of the mystical path. The Christian mystery is not merely a process for finding the God within, although that is a crucial element of Christian spirituality and mystics throughout the ages have encouraged us to recognize how the reign of heaven is within. Even more important than that inner gaze, however, is the ultimately paradoxical nature of the divine encounter within lectio divina. It's a paradox to read and seek an encounter with God who meets us in the words that come, not from within, but as a gift from outside us (in this case, mediated through the writings of authors who lived many years ago). Finding God in the word given to us does not mean God is not to be found within. But that works the other way around as well. When we encounter God within us, mystic wisdom reminds us that God comes to us through the gift of other people (including the prophets, contemplatives and mystics from ages past). Lectio gives each of us the opportunity to celebrate the mystery of encountering the God who is both intimately one with us in an interior way, and simultaneously, paradoxically, wholly transcendent and "other"—the one who is found *among* us as well as *within* us.

To finish out this chapter, we'll take a closer look at the first two steps in the lectio process: lectio (reading) and meditation (reflecting). We'll save the final two steps for subsequent chapters.

Lectio

To engage in the practice of lectio divina you need something worth reading. Traditionally, lectio was a practice for pondering sacred Scripture, and in terms of mystical Christianity, naturally this means applying lectio to the writings of the Bible, especially the four Gospels. But there's nothing that says you can use *only* the Bible when practicing lectio. The writings of the great mystics can richly reward anyone who approaches them in the slow, meditative style of lectio. If your schedule permits, try practicing lectio divina twice a day: Scripture reading in the morning, and the writings of one of the great mystics in the evening (I would especially recommend the writings of Evelyn Underhill, Julian of Norwich, Teresa of Ávila, or Howard Thurman for anyone new to lectio divina).

Once you've selected your text (or texts), set aside enough time to read a short passage slowly and deliberately—ideally, in a quiet place where you feel comfortable reading and praying, and are not likely to be interrupted. Set aside at least twenty minutes to allow not only for lectio, but also for the subsequent steps of meditatio, oratio, and contemplatio (half an hour to an hour is ideal). Resist our culturally conditioned tendency to rush. This is about quality, not quantity. You can read a short passage and go very deep with it. Lectio can be a powerful and transformational practice even if you read only a sentence or two. Remember, the goal is not to amass knowledge or information. You can always supplement your lectio practice with other time spent in more informational spiritual reading. Lectio is time given to God in prayer, so the intention of this exercise is simply to create a space where the divine mystery may encounter you via the medium of the sacred word.

To begin, read a sentence, or a few—but no more than a paragraph or two. Then stop. Go back and slowly reread the passage, and perhaps even a third or fourth time, at as unhurried a pace as possible. When you notice yourself analyzing the text, gently let it go. Let go of any urge you may feel to figure out the text; just keep an open mind. Let the text read you. Be open to discerning a particular word or phrase that speaks to you with particular meaning or relevance.

When you encounter such a word or phrase, stop reading. That is your signal to move on to the reflective, meditatio, stage of the practice.

It's simple—deceptively so, especially for Westerners who are used to processing an endless stream of information. Setting aside the mind's tendency to analyze and dissect all that you read is not an easy task. Indeed, lectio divina can help us cultivate a sense of humility as we come face to face with how we tend to resist the gentle invitation to silence and unknowing—an unwillingness that may appear again and again in the quest to become more deeply contemplative. As you seek to engage in the deep silence and openness of lectio, you will inevitably catch yourself getting lost in your mind's analytical chatter. When that happens, simply return to reading silently and attentively, focusing on the words in front of you rather than the words that arise in your mind.

One way to let go of the analytical mind during lectio is to make time for more traditional forms of Bible study in addition to your lectio time. It can be very fruitful to read the Bible or other sacred texts in both a contemplative and a scholarly way. Just set aside different times for each approach; do not try to blend contemplative and scholarly reading. Commit to one approach or the other when you sit down with your Bible. When you make time to explore both a mystical and a scholarly approach to the Bible (or other spiritual texts), you can discover profound and multilayered wisdom within the writing.

Meditatio

The second stage in the lectio process is meditatio, or meditation. This may be perhaps the single most misunderstood element of this spiritual exercise.

In the popular mind, the heart of mysticism is meditation. This comes from the influence of several generations of Eastern spirituality on Western culture. Eastern spirituality—from the yogi reciting a mantra to the Zen Buddhist's relaxed attention on breath—has become the cultural standard by which many Westerners understand meditation.

In traditional Christian spirituality, however, meditation is not viewed as an exercise in moving beyond thought. It is, rather, a gentle process of pondering and reflecting on a holy text or a point of doctrine (like the incarnation or the Trinity). This process of meditation (which, in the exercise of lectio divina, comes after reading and before prayer) occurs during the pause in which, having read the sacred text, you stop to mull over its meaning and its relevance in your life. This type of meditation, far from seeking to move beyond the cognitive mind, actually involves calm thinking—a meditative thought that moves best when it moves slowly. Just as sacred reading requires you to slow down and lay aside your illusions of being in control, sacred meditation asks you to slow down the normal high-speed chase in which one thought seeks to overcome another in the chattering, endlessly frenetic arena of the mind.

This frenzied inner babble is what Buddhists call "the monkey mind." Christian contemplative author Martin Laird calls it the inner "cocktail party." One time I was teaching a class on prayer, and a participant said her mind was like a cocktail party with a monkey running amok through it!

Some meditation practices encourage us to learn how to quiet, or at least ignore, the chattering monkey mind. In the Christian tradition, however, meditation is not so much about silencing the mind as it is about seeking a middle ground between the extremes of letting the mind chatter away and attempting to get it to shut up. In this middle ground, seek to find a serene freedom within, with the understanding that you wish to keep your attention prayerfully focused on a point of faith or an insight of wisdom consistent in tone with the gentle, unrushed, God-focused activity of lectio.

Meditation thus serves as a bridge between the word that is read—or prayed—and the final resting point of silent contemplation. It is a fulcrum point between the word quietly received and our still response, gently offered to God in prayer (oratio). As such, this moment of reflection does not need to be a long or involved process. After a few minutes of lectio, you may spend only a minute or two in meditation, pondering the text that you've read and reflecting on how its message can inform your prayer—your gesture of opening your mind and heart to God. Prayer, in turn, leads to contemplation (contemplatio), which is the point at which you really do seek to gently turn your attention away from your monkey mind and simply rest in God's presence.

To summarize: in lectio, we encounter words of wisdom and life in a calm and unhurried way; in meditatio, we ponder thoughtfully what a particular word or phrase means to us, and how God may be using it to communicate with us, individually. Eventually, we may feel inspired to engage in your own verbal, prayerful response to God's word. This, then, is the oratio stage—a time to pray honestly, simply, sincerely. We pray not to make a good impression, but simply to be intimate with the One who loves us unconditionally. Eventually, the words will drop away and the wordless silence will embrace us as we simply sit still in contemplatio—the contemplation of God's presence.

CHAPTER EIGHTEEN

The Heavenly Conversation

What should I do then? I will pray with the spirit, but I will pray
with the mind also; I will sing praise with the spirit, but I will sing
praise with the mind also.
—Paul (1 Corinthians 14:15)

Just as no one comes to wisdom except through grace, justice
and knowledge, so no one comes to contemplation except by penetrating meditation, a holy life and devout prayer.
—Bonaventure

The mystical life is a life shaped by prayer, immersed in prayer, devoted to
prayer, inspired and energized by prayer. For mystics, prayer is to the soul
what oxygen is to the body: an essential element for life itself.

The exercise of lectio divina is a fourfold process of prayer. Beginning
with feasting on words that form and shape our spirituality, meditating
on those words to allow them to truly nourish us, then responding with
our own words of prayerful expression, leading ultimately to the deepest form of human-divine communication, resting in silence—all the
movements of this foundational contemplative practice are dimensions
of prayer. Nevertheless, most people equate prayer with, to put it simply,
talking to God. We've seen how monks and nuns and other contemplatives over the ages have developed liturgies, structured and scripted

prayers that may be offered multiple times a day to express our human longing for, and desire to worship, God. Related to this is an entire literary tradition of written prayers, from universally known prayers like the Lord's Prayer/Our Father, to eloquent expressions of spiritual yearning like these three prayers:

Lord, make me an instrument of your peace: where there is hatred, let me sow love; where there is injury, pardon; where there is doubt, faith; where there is despair, hope; where there is darkness, light; where there is sadness, joy.

O divine Master, grant that I may not so much seek to be consoled as to console, to be understood as to understand, to be loved as to love. For it is in giving that we receive, it is in pardoning that we are pardoned, and it is in dying that we are born to eternal life. Amen.

—Attributed to Saint Francis of Assisi

Take, Lord, and receive all my liberty, my memory, my understanding, and my entire will. All that I have and possess, you have given to me. To you, Lord, I return it. All is yours; dispose of it entirely according to your will. Give me your love and your grace— that will be enough for me.

—Saint Ignatius of Loyola

God, of your goodness, give me yourself, for you are enough for me. I may ask nothing less that is fully to your worship, and if I do ask anything less, ever shall I be in want. Only in you I have all."

—Julian of Norwich

Countless books have been published that gather together prayers like these, prayers that can be used in any occasion, from morning to night, before meals or while traveling, to bless a home or to comfort those who are sick or dying. Prayers like these appeal to people not because they are formulaic, but because they help us express the yearnings of our heart and soul that often we do not know to put into words.

Nevertheless, meaningful prayer involves more than just a formulaic recitation of rote words. Great mystics like Teresa of Ávila have written entire books on how to pray (in her case, *The Way of Perfection*). And even when they do endorse the use of written prayers—Teresa argued that the Lord's Prayer was the only prayer anyone ever needed to pray—the understanding is that we need to bring a mindful awareness and a heart-felt authenticity to the words. In other words, prayer is diminished when the words are just rattled off, almost like an actor reciting memorized lines from a script. To pray most fully, the words on our lips must be calibrated to the awareness of our minds and the intentions of our hearts—whether or not the words are read from a book, recited from memory, or expressed spontaneously.

We do not have to send our prayers "up there," as if God were only to be found in the farthest reaches of heaven. Mystical spirituality rests on the encounter with God in our hearts. But just because we know and trust God is there, this does not mean we always consciously feel or experience that divine indwelling. Sometimes God remains shrouded in mystery, and can seem distant, absent, or cloaked in the darkness of unknowing. We yearn for complete and total union with God, but we recognize that we may not fully or daily experience that joyful presence, at least on this side of eternity. So we have to make do with the joys of a relationship in which God is both revealed and concealed. Part of this making do involves the imperfect, but nevertheless joyful, process of prayer.

When you communicate with someone over a telephone line, you cannot touch, caress, or embrace the person with whom you speak. Indeed, even hearing that person can sometimes be difficult because of static or interference on the call. Sometimes when the phone rings, you are irritated at the interruption; at other times, you wait impatiently for the call. Sometimes, a ringing phone can be a cause for joy; at other times, it can be an ominous harbinger of bad news.

The same can be said of prayer. Sometimes prayer is easy—you're eager to open your heart and mind to heaven, effortlessly making time and happily entering into the silence where you hope to taste the good presence of God. At such times, it's easy to make a commitment to pray regularly, perhaps once or twice a day. But then will come times when prayer seems dry as dust, when you may feel duty bound to set aside time for prayer but it feels more like a bother than a joy. Sometimes prayer can inspire you to cry; sometimes it makes you writhe in shame. Prayer can evoke feelings of wonder, of delight, of felicity, of quiet love, of embarrassment, of self-consciousness, of humility. The silence at the heart of prayer can feel like a delicious moment of respite in an otherwise frantic life, or it can feel cold and impersonal, an unforgiving barrier that separates you from the love and acceptance you crave so deeply. Prayer can feel like the most important thing you could ever do, or it may leave you wondering at just how point-less or empty it seems.

Christian mystics are people who have given their lives to prayer. To be a contemplative is to be a person of prayer. Even if you have only a passing interest in Christian mysticism and contemplation, this could be evidence that God is inviting you to find transformation and healing in the practice of prayer. At the heart of the Christian mystery is the call to intimacy with God, and prayer is the tool by which we respond to that call.

THE CENTRALITY OF PRAYER

The practice of prayer is common to all people of faith, including those who have little or no interest in mystical or contemplative spirituality. Given the tremendous diversity that has come to characterize the various denomina-tions and branches of Christianity, prayer may well be the only common spiritual practice that unites Christians from across the spectrum of the faith. Those who are illiterate or learning disabled may not be able to read the Bible, but they can still lift their hands and eyes in prayer.

Conversational prayer—a spontaneous sharing of your thoughts and feelings with God—is the third step in the practice of lectio divina. But conversational prayer is not the only way to pray. Teresa of Ávila, throughout her mystical writings, identified nine different forms of prayer, of which vocal (conversational or formal) prayer is only the first step. She goes on to describe other forms of prayer, using language that now seems archaic or arcane: mental prayer, recollection, the prayer of quiet, the prayer of transforming union. For our purposes, it is simplest to categorize prayer using the four steps of lectio: prayer includes engaging with words, images, or ideas that convey wisdom to us; meditating on such sources of wis-dom; communicating with God using our thoughts, words, or deeds; and contemplating the love of God as most directly encountered in silence. Thus, meditation and contemplation both fall under the umbrella of prayer, at least in a Christian context; so too does anything we do to receive the presence or wisdom of God, whether it comes to us in words, images, art, music, or even in the hearts and faces of other people—a smile from a baby can make a powerful statement about the love of God.

Ultimately, anything you do to foster an experience of communication with God—disclosing your own thoughts and feelings to God, or listening for God's word for you—is a form of prayer.

Christians don't need to be mystics in order to pray; but they do need to pray in order to seek a mystical life.

UNHURRIED, UNANXIOUS, UNCEASING

The nineteenth-century philosopher Friedrich Nietzsche wrote, "The essential thing 'in heaven and earth' is . . . that there should be long obedience in the same direction; there thereby results, and has always resulted in the long run, something which has made life worth living." These words inspired a contemplative Christian author, Eugene H. Peterson, to name one of his books *A Long Obedience in the Same Direction: Discipleship in an Instant Society*. Obedience is a word that at its root means "listening"—compare it to the word *audience*. To obey God means, more than anything else, a willingness to listen deeply and mindfully to God's words of love and truth and beauty and goodness in our hearts—and then act in accordance with those words. With all due respect to Nietzsche and Peterson, I'd like to suggest that prayer, therefore, is a *long listening in the same direction* (the direction being toward God, located simultaneously beyond the universe and in our hearts). But it is also a *long self-disclosure in the same direction* as well.

Prayer is communication, and communication requires both give and take. We listen for God, and we make ourselves vulnerably present to God. And the "long . . . same direction" bit implies that we do this over time, persevering and proceeding with commitment and clarity.

The apostle Paul instructed his readers to "pray without ceasing" (1 Thessalonians 5:17). These words can be interpreted in a number of different ways. For example, the desert fathers and mothers, who lived solitary lives, understood their commitment to prayer in a very specific way. Their routine entailed reciting all 150 Psalms, every day. It takes more than four hours to read or recite the Psalms out loud. While four or more hours of recited prayer every single day may not literally be praying "without ceasing," it's still quite a commitment.

Eventually, the solitaries of the desert founded the first Christian monasteries, a more communal (and sustainable) arrangement for those who seek a deeply contemplative way of life. Monks and nuns live in communities, but in such a way as to preserve, as much as possible, the emphasis on silence and solitude that characterized the spirituality of the desert. One of the benefits of communal living is the opportunity for shared, corporate prayer—the chance to pray with one another, using the liturgy of the hours. And so, from the beginning of their history, monasteries have structured their communal lives around this idea of praying without ceasing.

Another means of praying without ceasing was developed among Greek Orthodox monks and mystics. Known as the Jesus Prayer (or the Prayer of the Heart), this practice involves a simple prayer—"Lord Jesus Christ, Son of God, have mercy on me" or some similar variation—that may be synchronized with the rhythm of breathing, so that disciplined practitioners can rhythmically recite it as continuously as they breathe. Another Western spiritual practice developed by the Carmelite friar Brother Lawrence, "the practice of the presence of God," may sound a lot like our contemporary idea of mindfulness—an intentional practice of cultivating a God-focused state of mind that anyone can enjoy, even while doing mundane chores like washing the dishes. While these forms of prayer begin to push the boundary that separates word-based praying from silence-centered contemplation, they do signify some of the many ways that Christians throughout history have sought to follow Paul's instruction and make intimacy with God an unceasing aspect of their lives.

The mystics invite us to approach this invitation to ceaseless prayer in a variety of ways. Certainly it can (and should) include some sort of daily practice. Like going to gym or washing the dishes, prayer works best when it is a regular, ideally daily, part of life. This is true whether our preferred way of praying involves spontaneous conversational prayer, recited prayers like the Daily Office, repetitive prayers like the Jesus Prayer or the rosary, or a daily practice of God-centered silence. A balanced diet of sacred reading, formal and conversational prayer, and informal/wordless prayer can be a deeply satisfying anchor for a contemplative life.

In addition to Saint Paul's invitation to pray unceasingly, I'd like to offer two other ways to approach prayer: to be *unhurried* and *unanxious*. Even as I write these words, I recognize that they might be difficult for some people. We live in a busy, fast-paced, stressful culture that frankly seems to reward anxiety—and indeed, many of us suffer from chronic anxiety that can impact the quality of our lives. If you experience anxiety regularly, the last thing you need is something like me telling you that your prayer needs to be "unanxious"! So please know that I am offering these approaches as a gentle invitation, something to aspire to, not something to turn into another obligation or a way to feel bad because we aren't doing it right.

Whether anxiety and hurry is something you struggle with or not, I hope you can imagine prayer as a way of creating some time in your life, even if only five or ten minutes a day, when you can slow down, breathe deeply, be still, and simply accept God's love for you. Mystical prayer is not about earning God's love, proving ourselves worthy, or making the grade. It's always meant as a gesture of relaxed response, responding to love and compassion that God freely gives to us, no matter how good or pious or spiritual we are (or aren't). We can take a deep breathe, exhale gently, and allow prayer to be a time of respite from the hustle and stress of life today. When we give ourselves the gift of an unhurried, unanxious commitment to daily or at least regular prayer, we create the space in our hearts to be vulnerable before God, to consent to the action of God's love in our lives, and to slowly be transformed by that divine union for which we hunger.

TWO WAYS WE SELF-SABOTAGE OUR PRAYER

I've been leading retreats, teaching people about prayer, and presenting introductory workshops on Centering Prayer and other types of contemplative practice for a number of years now. I've met many people who are beginners to a life of committed, discipline prayer, and others who have been praying intentionally since before I was born.

What I have discovered is that almost everyone secretly thinks they are lousy at prayer. And the people who are willing to share this secret with me usually express one or both of these basic, self-defeating thoughts:

- I don't pray very well.
- I don't pray often enough.

By "I don't pray very well," people usually mean that their mind wanders too much when they pray; they experience an endless assault of distracting thoughts, feelings, daydreams, and so forth (that monkey in the cocktail party again). Even though people who teach prayer will emphasize that it's normal to have lots of distracting thoughts, it seems that many people who explore a commitment to prayer will assume that their minds are *too* distracted, *too* unruly, *too* monkey-ish.

Over four hundred years ago, long before the distractions of TV, mass media, and the internet that keeps feeding our mind-monkeys, Teresa of Ávila complained that her consciousness was like a group of wild horses. So apparently, distractions during prayer is not a new problem.

But then there's that other little self-defeating thought: I don't do it often enough. I know people who reliably pray twice a day—and worry that they should be doing it three times a day! Or who pray once a day, almost never missing a day, but they think they ought to be praying twice daily. Or who only pray a few times a week, and feel bad because they aren't managing to pray every day.

Notice a pattern here? It seems to me that both of these ideas: I'm not good enough, and I'm not doing enough of it—are simply types of spiritual self-sabotage. I encourage you to give yourself permission to be an imperfect person of prayer. Remember G. K. Chesterton: "If a thing is worth doing, it is worth doing badly." In other words, it's important to accept that we may want our prayer to be "better" than what we experience. We want to be more attentive; we want to be more disciplined. Those are beautiful desires, and they might help us to grow in our prayer. But not if we use them as excuses to beat ourselves up over how poorly we're performing, or worse yet, to convince ourselves that we are failures and may as well give it up.

Some other kinds of thoughts that people have shared with me, that seem to arise as they explore prayer:

- I just never can find the time to pray.
- Prayer discourages me. I feel as if I'm just talking to myself.
- When I pray, strong feelings, whether positive or negative, emerge and I'm not sure what to do with them. Frankly, I find prayer to be rather unsettling.
- I feel ashamed of my sins. I don't think I'm worthy to pray.
- I don't know what to say to God. After all, God already knows everything I need!

These objections are all variations on a single theme: As much as we want to be closer to God, we also resist it. In the words of Marianne Williamson, made famous by Nelson Mandela, "Our deepest fear is not that we are inadequate. Our deepest fear is that we are powerful beyond measure."[1] I believe we can make a similar statement about spiritual seekers: "Our deepest fear is not that there is no God. Our deepest fear is that God does exist and wants to become an intimate part of our lives, changing us forever." When two people fall in love, often their relationship can be troubled by one or both of two fears: the fear of loneliness or abandonment ("Please don't leave me") and the fear of engulfment ("I need my space"). When it comes to relating to God, for many people it seems that fear of engulfment is the greater of the two. It manifests in our "not having enough time" to pray, or getting lost in our distractions, and in other ways that we seem to avoid a regular practice of seeking intimacy with God.

Prayer, therefore, is like physical training or learning any new skill. It challenges us to make enough effort to move through resistance, and it requires profound courage to pass through the scary places it can take us. Thankfully, God promises grace to those who believe; indeed, without such grace, a disciplined prayer life might prove to be ultimately unattainable. Without the grace of God who loves you, your resistance will overwhelm your desire. Without the grace of God beckoning you and calling you into relationship with him, prayer too quickly gets lost in the hectic pace of life. But let's reframe those sentences to accentuate the positive (thank you, Johnny Mercer). Thanks to the grace of God, we know that our desire to pray can overcome even the strongest resistance. Thanks to the grace of God, even the most hectic life can find the space for unhurried, unanxious, *unceasing* prayer. Grace is the secret ingredient that can, finally, lead anyone to overcome their resistance.

TIPS FOR ESTABLISHING (OR STRENGTHENING) A REGULAR PRACTICE OF PRAYER

Here are a few points to consider as you explore the possibility of starting or deepening your commitment to prayer without ceasing.

Don't go it alone. We are all social beings, and we are far more likely to embrace a new discipline and stick with it if we don't try to do it all by ourselves. This is one of the reasons why participation in a community of faith is so helpful. For years I struggled with my daily prayer practice, but after I started participating in a weekly Centering Prayer group, I discovered that knowing I had other friends with a similar commitment to the inner life, and that I would see them each week, inspired me to embrace my prayer practice more fully. Having others to turn to for advice, encouragement, accountability, and instruction can make all the difference in following through on your commitment, particularly when the novelty wears off and the practice feels dry. Likewise, a spiritual director can be an invaluable help in dealing with some of the difficult feelings that can emerge in prayer—like doubts that God doesn't exist or doesn't care, or overwhelming feelings of sadness, guilt, or anger that can emerge.

Start small. If you're out of shape and want to do something about it, you don't begin by running twenty miles each morning. Physical training has to be tailored to your current abilities; as your strength develops, your workout can gradually become more challenging. A prayer "workout" functions the same way. If you have difficulty finding time to pray, consider making a commitment to pray for just one minute a day. Allow that to become a regular part of your daily life before you stretch out to five minutes, or ten minutes, or beyond. Even for seasoned contemplatives, twenty to thirty minutes twice a day devoted to prayer is usually enough. And not everyone needs to, or can, devote that much time to prayer. If you are retired, you probably have more time on your hands than a working mom with three small kids to care for. A trusted friend or spiritual director can be of great help in discerning just how much daily prayer time is right for you. Even if your heart longs to give an hour every day to God, take it slowly at first. It's better to establish a daily practice that becomes as anchored in your life as brushing your teeth. Once your everyday pattern is established, you can start to stretch out the amount of time you give to prayer.

Establish a routine. Any kind of discipline can thrive when it's part of a settled, workable routine. Ideally, your prayer routine will fit in with your overall commitments: for example, if you need to leave for work every morning at 7 a.m., work out how much time you need for breakfast, showering, and so on, then get up fifteen minutes earlier than that to devote those first few minutes to your spiritual practice. Make that a regular part of your morning (which also implies getting to bed early enough the night before). In addition to finding a set time for prayer, select a specific place—ideally a quiet corner in your home where your family or roommates will not disturb you and you can avoid distractions like the computer, TV, or telephone. Put a Bible or cross or crucifix in your prayer space so that it is clearly a center for fostering intimacy with God.

Experiment. Remember St. Teresa's nine different types of prayer (and there are other ways of praying beyond what she described). No one has to master all the many different methods of prayer that have evolved over the centuries. You may find that your devotion to God is nurtured more by the rosary than by the liturgy of the hours (or vice versa); likewise, you might be more at home with the Jesus Prayer than with Centering Prayer. Some of us are naturally more comfortable with recited prayers; others chafe at anything that doesn't come spontaneously from the heart. Try to pray with different approaches, and over time you will get to know how your prayer life shines.

Pray as you can, not as you can't. This advice, from the English monk John Chapman, is so helpful. Because prayer is all about fostering intimacy with God, every person's prayer life will be unique. The way God communicates with you and the way you respond to God will be yours alone. Let go of any worries you might have about finding the "right" way to pray. If all your friends love the rosary, but you have a clearer sense of God's presence when you take a long walk in the forest gently sharing with God whatever's on your mind, give thanks for your uniqueness. When others are pulling out their beads, head for the woods.

Remember, it's all about God, and it's all about love. A disciplined prayer life is a commitment that requires a certain maturity to get through the dry periods. During those dry spells, it may feel like anything you do to pray goes wrong. It's important, therefore, to remember that most of what's "wrong" with your prayer life is a reflection of your own human limitations, if not your inner poverty and brokenness. But don't be a masochist about it. Prayer is about God, and God is love. Remember the fruit of the Spirit: love, joy, peace, patience, kindness, generosity, faithfulness, gentleness, and temperance. Pay attention to how qualities like these are (or aren't) part of your prayer life. If your prayer feels joyless, burdensome, and feels like continual drudgery, talk it over with a trusted friend or spiritual director. Sometimes an arid prayer life is a sign of being called more deeply into contemplation, but it can also be a signal that something else is out of joint. Don't give up on your walk with God or grow cynical; don't lose faith in the mystery of love. Keep your eyes on the prize. Focus on the God who is love, even when prayer becomes difficult. With your heart set on love and the caring support of a prayer partner, even the longest dry spell can be a time for growth.

Don't dream it, be it. Reading a book on prayer is never a substitute for actually praying. Ultimately, all you can bring to your prayer—your time offered to God—is yourself. Far more important than your thoughts or your eloquence is, simply, your heart and your soul. Simply be willing to offer yourself to God, and to dispose yourself to the possibilities that lie just beyond the reach of your senses or your rational mind. Even faith is optional in prayer! Some of the best prayers emerge out of profound doubt and questioning. But a certain flexibility of mind and heart certainly helps. If you are arrogant, either in your unbelief or in your conviction that you have a rock-solid knowledge of God, your prayer may fall flat. Humility and an open-hearted vulnerability, coupled with a willingness to let God take the lead, is probably the most helpful attitude to embrace. Prayer is not about impressing God (as if we could do that); it's about getting real with God.

Accessorize (this is optional). Some people love to fill their prayer space with sensual aids—candles, incense, icons, or recordings of Gregorian chants playing softly in the background. None of this is necessary, however, and sometimes these things can be more distracting than reinforcing. If you like those sorts of things, great. If not, think no more about it. They are neither necessary nor always helpful for prayer.

RECITED AND SPONTANEOUS PRAYER

Back in the 1970s, the theologian Matthew Fox insisted, "Prayer is not saying prayers."[2] I think he was on to something, but a more accurate statement would be, "Prayer is more than just saying prayers." If praying could be compared to riding a bicycle, then prayers that we recite—the Lord's Prayer, grace before meals, devotional supplications found in inspirational books—function like the training wheels of the mystical life. In other words, they teach us the language and the rhythm of intimacy with God. Prayers that we read and recite can set us free to enter, eventually, into unscripted intimacy with our divine lover.

This is not to suggest that formulaic prayers are unnecessary or inferior. On the contrary, just as great musicians practice their scales throughout their careers, mystics and contemplatives rely on the most childlike forms of prayer even as they move deeper and deeper into the splendors of wordless adoration. Beautifully written but formulaic prayers, from a child's bedtime prayer to the liturgy of the hours, can be a continual source of spiritual nourishment and can inspire us to eventually embrace spontaneous ways to seek intimacy with God.

At its best, prayer—even a simple, memorized prayer like the Our Father—is like healthy digestion. It works best when, unhurried and unanxious, we take our time to "chew" the words and "digest" the thought. On the other hand, when we rush through our prayers, we may set ourselves up for spiritual indigestion. To recite even a rote prayer in a contemplative way, slow the process down enough so that each word can be fully "chewed," broken apart and savored both consciously and subconsciously as you make your way through the prayer. No one experience of praying will ever be perfect. But, to the extent that you slow down your engagement with the prayers you say, you will be prepared for deeper and more intimate forms of prayer. In learning to recite formal prayers mindfully, you will be preparing yourself to share with God the truest and most hidden thoughts and feelings that emerge from deep within you, offered up spontaneously, in your own words—or even in sounds and gestures that, inspired by the Spirit, are "too deep for words" (Romans 8:26). Just as recited prayers eventually lead to conversational or spontaneous prayer, prayer from the heart eventually shades off into the postverbal experience of wordless prayer, which takes us to the spiritual frontiers of silent contemplation.

TRADITIONAL PRAYERS

Let's take a closer look at some of these training-wheel prayers, including those that come from the Bible or other traditional writings.

Basic prayers. Every Christian sooner or later will know the Lord's Prayer—not only is it found in the Bible (part of Jesus's Sermon on the Mount),[3] but it is recited at every Catholic Mass, many Protestant church services, and during many liturgical (daily) prayers as well. Various other Bible passages, hymns, traditional prayers, and nuggets of wisdom from great saints or mystics, can all be memorized and recited from the heart. One of the earliest Christian monks, John Cassian, recommended regular prayer of this verse from the Psalms: "O God, come to my assistance; O Lord, make haste to help me."[4] My wife and I love to recite the prayer from Julian of Norwich found earlier in this chapter, or Thomas Merton's famous prayer "Lord, I have no idea where I am going" found in his book *Thoughts in Solitude*. These simple prayers are easily memorized and can be recited at any time throughout the day. Such recitations can also be used to begin or end periods of time set aside for lectio divina, meditation, or contemplation.

The rosary. This popular Catholic devotion combines recitation of memorized prayers (particularly the Lord's Prayer and the Hail Mary) with reflection on various key events in the lives of Jesus and Mary. Part meditation and part prayer, the rosary can be a powerful tool for slowing down the monkey mind and discerning God's silent presence.

The Jesus Prayer (Prayer of the Heart). Entire books have been written about this simple prayer and its power to transform your life. *The Way of a Pilgrim*, written by an anonymous Russian Orthodox monk concerning this prayer, is a classic of mystical literature. Several variations of the prayer exist, the most common being: "Lord Jesus Christ, Son of God, have mercy on me" (you'll also see it with the ending "have mercy on me, a sinner"—although since Western Christians historically have overemphasized their sinfulness and underemphasized God's mercy, I find it spiritually helpful to leave those last two words off). When you entrain the prayer to your breathing—inhale as you pray "Lord Jesus Christ, son of God"; pause; exhale as you recite the rest of the prayer—and repeat it slowly and gently as you breathe, this prayer is arguably the best tool for meeting Paul's challenge to pray without ceasing. The Eastern Orthodox spiritual tradition of *hesychasm*—from the Greek word for contemplative silence—is anchored in the use of the Jesus Prayer, and its repetitive nature is clearly reminiscent of the mantras found in Eastern forms of meditation. Like the rosary or Centering Prayer, this practice can help foster an experience of acquired contemplation.

The liturgy of the hours. Also called the Divine Office or the Daily Office, the liturgy is a form of communal prayer used in monasteries and in Catholic, Orthodox, Anglican, and some Protestant churches. Different churches and monasteries have their own forms of the liturgy, which usually consists of between four and seven "offices" or services of prayer to be prayed at appointed times throughout the day. Each office includes Scripture readings, Psalms and other canticles, hymns, antiphons, and prayers. Because it is designed as a communal form of prayer, even if you recite it in solitude, you are on some level participating in the larger praying community of the church. We know from the Gospels that Jesus prayed the Psalms. So, by joining in the Divine Office, you are joining in a tradition of prayer that extends all the way back Jesus's own spiritual practice. The liturgy of the hours is a complex form of prayer; different readings, Psalms, and canticles are assigned to each day, and the days themselves are influenced by the season of the church year (Advent, Lent, etc.), as well as the days on which the lives of saints are commemorated. While it can be daunting to learn to pray the Office, once you become familiar with it, it's a lovely tool for anchoring a daily practice of prayer.

CONVERSATIONAL (SPONTANEOUS) PRAYER

Many people find that, over time, recited prayers may begin to feel stiff and overly formal. This is not necessarily a sign to abandon them, but rather to stretch out and begin to pray without a script, offering to God your uncensored thoughts and feelings, along with the silent spaces between your thoughts and feelings.

Conversational prayer is prayer that comes from the heart, in your own words. Ultimately, it works best when it's extemporaneous and unrehearsed. Even so, it's helpful to consider categories of prayer that are traditionally associated with this kind of extemporaneous reaching out to God.

Adoration. God is love, and therefore infinitely lovable. So what better way to express yourself to God than by offering words of love? This is easier said than done, however, if you have images of God that are less than loving: God as angry father, God as implacable judge, or God as indifferent Creator. Of course, God is beyond all our images (whatever reveals God conceals God—even our ways of thinking about God), so if you become aware of ways in which you imagine God as unloving, you will find tremendous healing in choosing a more kind and compassionate understanding. Learning to trust God and to pray words of love can be an important part of coming to know God as love.

Confession. No one is perfect. Everyone makes mistakes. And everyone is capable of making unloving choices, even with full knowledge and consent. Facing the God of infinite love means facing our own unloving choices, behaviors, and dispositions as well. While coming face to face with our own sinfulness may seem to encourage shame or guilt, the Christian tradition is less interested in you feeling sorry for yourself and more interested in finding healing for our unloving actions by honestly confessing our faults to God as a key step toward embracing a new (or renewed) life of love, and when necessary, fostering reconciliation when we've harmed or broken relationships through our unloving actions.

Thanksgiving. The Benedictine monk David Steindl-Rast calls gratefulness "the heart of prayer." Meister Eckhart suggested that if a person had nothing else to do with God than to be thankful, that would be enough.[5] Counting our blessings and acknowledging God as the ultimate source of all that is good in your life is essential, not only for our spiritual health, but also for our mental health. Gratitude creates the space in our hearts for love, peace, joy, and hope; praying our thankfulness can be a powerful tool for learning to live in gratitude.

Petition and intercession. Petitions are prayers made on your own behalf; intercessions are prayers in which you appeal to God on behalf of someone else. Some people think that prayer is primarily about petitions and intercessions—about asking God for blessings, for healing, for favors, whether for yourself or for others. For contemplatives, however, prayer is about far more than just begging for blessings—prayer is primarily about establishing, or strengthening, a relationship with God based on trust, love, and intimacy. Although petition and intercession remain important ways to communicate with God, even for contemplatives, those who truly seek to embrace the divine mystery will understand such "asking prayer" to be only one part of an overall prayer discipline. Even when we do offer petitions and intercede for others, such requests extend far beyond just seeking material benefits. Mystics pray for healing, for strength, for confidence and faith, for comfort, for spiritual blessings (as well as material needs), and for a sense of God's presence and guidance in their lives. It's important to remember that such asking prayers is not about trying to change God's mind, or to get God to do something God would not otherwise do. We pray out of the trust that God knows what is best, and that the answer to our prayer may come in ways we don't necessarily expect or want. Whether or not prayer changes external circumstances (like a cancerous growth), it always changes the internal circumstances of the heart, the soul, and our capacity to trust in the goodness and love of God. In all these ways, intercessory and petitionary prayer remains invaluable—even for those whose faith may be unsure.

Lament and complaint. Things don't always go well in life. Bad things happen. Disease strikes; divorce breaks up families; crimes occur; jobs are lost; loved ones die. It's a mistake to assume that prayer should always be positive—as if we have to reassure God that we have everything under control and there's nothing to worry about down here. On the contrary, prayer can be its most effective when we are broken, hurting, angry, scared, lost, or confused. The key is to bring these feelings to God, dark and shadowy though they may be, without censorship or self-editing. When we lament, we share with God just how bad things are for us; we express our frustration, particularly for God's perceived absence or inaction. God is big enough to take on our sorrow and our anger, and if we truly believe in God, then we believe that prayer changes things—even if the primary "thing" being changed is our own heart. Perhaps prayers of lament create the space in our hearts for God's healing action to occur—and for God to inspire us to work for making things better, whether just in our lives or in the world at large. But if we do not honestly and vulnerably offer these parts of our lives to God, our spiritual life may remain impoverished.

OTHER DIMENSIONS OF PRAYER

Under the umbrella of "the heavenly conversation," three other dimensions of Christian prayer are worth nothing: Ignatian prayer (a method of praying using the imagination inspired by the wisdom of St. Ignatius of Loyola), charismatic or Spirit-filled prayer, and prayer offered to angels, saints and Mary. All of these ways of praying have their own mystical dimension.

Ignatian prayer. Saint Ignatius of Loyola, who lived in sixteenth-century Spain, is famous for creating a thirty-day retreat experience known as the Spiritual Exercises. The Spiritual Exercises leads the person making the retreat through an in-depth experience of praying to Jesus, following the story of his life as recounted in the New Testament. It is a rich and moving spiritual experience, and people who make this retreat often will report a deepened sense of Christ as present and real in their spiritual lives. Central to the Spiritual Exercises is a particular way of praying that has come to be known as Ignatian prayer. It involves using the imagination to visualize yourself encountering Jesus and interacting with him, often based on a scene from his life story as recounted in the Gospels. This way of praying, like lectio divina, begins with taking a passage from one of the Gospels, reading it, but then meditating on it by imagining yourself actually present with Jesus when the events being described originally occurred. So, for example, you might imagine Jesus walking on the water—using your mind's power of visualization, you visualize yourself as one of the persons in the boat alongside the disciples, frightened at the storm, and then stunned by the sudden appearance of Jesus walking on the water. Using your power of imagination, you place yourself in the story. Then allow your imagination to play—imagine yourself talking to Jesus (or the disciples); what would Jesus say to you? How would you respond? What question would you ask Jesus? What question might he ask of you? What would you say in return? This way of praying may seem like "make believe," but it rests on a sound spiritual principle: if the Holy Spirit is in our hearts, as Christian scripture proclaims, then it only makes sense that this in-dwelling Spirit can use even our imagination to foster intimacy and communication with us. Although our imagination is imperfect like anything else, this can still be a powerful way to foster a sense of friendship and closeness to Jesus—and therefore, to God.

Angels, saints, and Mary. Orthodox, Catholic, and Anglican Christians are more familiar with the idea of praying to saints, angels and Mary, while many Protestant and evangelical Christians may consider this way of praying controversial. The idea is simple: prayer, which can be described as opening our hearts and minds to God, can also be directed toward spiritual beings who are intimately connected with God, including saints—people Christians believe are in heaven, including Mary, Jesus's mother—and angels, supernatural beings that are traditionally seen as God's messengers. We do not pray to saints or angels expecting them to work miracles in our lives like God does; rather, we pray to them the same way we interact with other human beings: we seek their friendship, inspiration, guidance, and support. We also ask them to pray for us. Angels, in particular, have long been seen as guardians and guides for human beings, so the idea of asking for their blessings and help as we navigate our human life can be comforting—and maybe even a source for blessings to flow to us and those we love. For seekers of contemplative and mystical spirituality, prayer to saints and angels often is related to the rosary, which can be a deeply meditative/contemplative practice; Mary is regarded as the "mother of contemplatives," so asking for her guidance and blessing might be especially meaningful. Likewise, angelic blessings might be seen as particularly helpful for those who seek to more fully embrace the blessings of silence (one of my favorite icons is the icon of "Blessed Silence," which sometimes depicts Jesus but also depicts a silent angel). No one is required to pray to angels, saints, or Mary, but those who find this practice meaningful feel that these heavenly beings really are messengers of God—bringing God's grace and love to us just as they bring our prayers to God.

Charismatic prayer. Charismatic prayer literally means "gifted prayer," and refers to prayer inspired directly by the Holy Spirit. According to the Christian scriptures, charismatic prayer is given "in the spirit" and expressed in the "language of angels."[6] The fancy word for this is *glossolalia*, or speaking in tongues, a lovely but unintelligible "prayer language" that characterizes this way of praying. The apostle Paul identifies the miraculous ability to speak or pray in an unknown language as one of the gifts associated with the presence of the Spirit. While at least one story in the Bible suggests that speaking in tongues includes the miraculous ability to speak a human language unknown to the speaker,[7] the concept of the "language of angels" implies that at least some forms of glossolalia involve utterance that is not related to any earthly vocabulary, grammar, or syntax. Critics of glossolalia insist that these unintelligible words and sounds have no rational or logical meaning; in other words, they're little more than devotional nonsense, a kind of prayerful vocalise. But adherents of charismatic prayer insist that such worship in the spirit has a deeper or higher meaning that is hidden (dare we say mystical?) from ordinary human knowing. Whichever you choose to believe, it is clear that for those who pray in tongues, this method of prayer is deeply liberating—it frees the mind from having to be in charge of the prayer. By allowing the syllables to flow forth, often in a beautifully melodic song, the person who prays in tongues is free to let the experience be driven by love in the heart rather than the thought in the mind. Praying in the spirit is a way to offer God love and joy, at a level beyond what mere words can hope to express.

Not everyone has or wants the gift of tongues, and Paul discourages believers from going out of their way to seek it. If you don't have a natural ability to pray in tongues, follow the Bible's advice and seek the "higher" gifts of growth in wisdom and love. If praying in tongues and singing in the spirit is a part of your spiritual experience, reflect on how there is a profoundly mystical dimension to this form of prayer. Because charismatic prayer functions at a level beyond normal human reason, it can serve as a doorway to the deepest and highest form of prayer: contemplation.

BEYOND THE LANGUAGE OF PRAYER

The four-step process of lectio divina leads from sacred reading to meditation to prayer to contemplation. Eventually, your thoughts fall away before the deep and profound silence that characterizes the presence of God. Sooner or later, you discover that your words, no matter how eloquent and meaningful they may be, are like distracting noises in an otherwise restfully quiet cathedral. You cannot hear even your own words, let alone any word from God, if there is too much noise interfering with your prayer. Words need to be expressed in at least a relative degree of silence in order to be heard and understood. Eventually, your interest and focus in prayer will turn from your words—even if they're offered spontaneously—to the silence that lies behind and beneath and before them.

Although prayer, in its many forms, ultimately leads to the serene silence of contemplation, it would be a mistake to think of the heavenly conversation as merely an opening act—the hors d'oeuvre before the meal. Whether formal or conversational, liturgical or spontaneous, prayer that involves words and thoughts is not only a necessary prelude to contemplation, but also a necessary companion to an ongoing contemplative practice. When you fall deeply in love with someone, you can enjoy many quiet hours together. But that does not mean that you no longer need to talk or listen to what each other has to say. On the contrary, a deeply contemplative spirituality needs prayer as surely as a beautiful diamond needs a golden setting in order to be fully appreciated.

Prayer is not just a means to some mystical end. Saying the rosary or the Jesus Prayer often enough will not somehow qualify us for supernatural experiences or extraordinary levels of consciousness. Prayer is an end to itself, and functions as its own reward. But it's also a way for God to prepare us for the blessings of deep silence and to foster within us the fruit of the Spirit, from love and joy to kindness and gentleness. Through the discipline of prayer, everyone is invited to an ever-unfolding adventure in loving God.

Learning to pray is a lifelong process that no one will never complete, no matter how many years we devote to prayer or how deeply intimate our relationship with God becomes. Everyone who prays will encounter dry spells, unsettling feelings, fear or angst, and even doubt or uncertainty that can threaten to overwhelm our feeble efforts to connect to God through words and thoughts. To keep it meaningful, it's wise to integrate prayer into all areas of our lives—our work, our relationships, our creative endeavors—and to explore communal as well as solitary ways to pray. By embedding our prayer in the reality of human relationships, it becomes easier to love God and neighbor simultaneously.

CHAPTER NINETEEN

Eternity Within

God is in the holy temple;
let all the earth keep silence before God!
—Habakkuk 2:20 (my translation)

If you wish to know yourself, to possess yourself, do not seek
yourself without, but go within. You are one thing, what is yours
is another, what surrounds you yet another. What surrounds you
is the world; what is yours is the body; within, you are made to the
image and likeness of God. . . . On the outside you are an animal
in the image of the world, so that a human being is called a micro-
cosm; within, you are a human according to the image of God, so
that you are able to be deified.
—Isaac of Stella, medieval Cistercian monk

In her book *The Interior Castle*, Teresa of Ávila describes the human soul
using the luminous image of a castle made of a diamond. In this castle are
seven "mansions" or dwelling places, with the innermost mansion being
the throne room where Christ resides. We live our lives, seeking always to
enter more deeply into the castle, with each of the dwelling places representing a different stage on the mystical journey, or a different approach to
faith, spirituality and prayer. The first three mansions invite us into foundational practices for the spiritual life: cultivating a character of humility

and holiness, learning to persevere in our practice of prayer, and gradually discovering our capacity to recognize the divine presence, not only in the center of the castle (the soul), but indeed in all things.

Beginning with the fourth mansion, however, Teresa begins to describe a new dynamic at play in the spiritual life. From here on out, the activity of the mystical life is less about our efforts, and increasingly shaped by the Spirit's action in our soul. We never become *passive*—as the old saying goes, Ginger Rogers did everything Fred Astaire did, only backward and in heels. The Spirit leads the dance, and we are called to consent, to cooperate, to actively receive divine guidance with a spirit of trust and generous service.

As our prayer moves out beyond the limitation of language and verbal communication into the depths where only silence can shape our communion with God, we are increasingly invited into this posture of active acceptance and conscious consent. This, truly, marks a kind of informal but no less real initiation into the mystical life: a life shaped by contemplative willingness and silent prayer.

Interior silence rests at the threshold of consciousness, the ground of human awareness, the screen on which all thought and imagination is projected, the abyss between every heartbeat. It is also, so the mystics proclaim, the language of God, indeed the very face of God as found within ourselves. In her book *Practical Mysticism*, Evelyn Underhill described contemplation in terms of discernment, recognition, and acknowledgement. Martin Laird uses the beautiful image of *an ocean of light* to chart the slow blossoming of human consciousness from reactivity, to receptivity, to luminous union with God—all grace, all gift given by the Spirit, a gift we cannot engineer or control, but for which we are always invited to open our hands and hearts to receive. In this way the prayer of contemplation marks the summit of traditional mystical practice: the prayer that is no prayer, the language that has no words, the union with God where light is suffused with darkness and vision refracts into the cloud of unknowing.

PRAYER BEYOND WORDS

"Meditation is the mother of love, but contemplation is its daughter," said Saint Francis de Sales.[1] We have seen how Christian meditation represents a way to relax and open up the praying mind, to ponder gently and expansively the wisdom and teachings of Jesus and the mystics. Such a practice forms an important bridge between the word of God as we encounter it externally (through a book, a sermon, or some other source), and the interior word of prayer that we may offer to the God we encounter in our hearts.

What, then, is contemplation? A source as prosaic as the *Catechism of the Catholic Church* offers a beautiful and succinct definition. According to the catechism's glossary, contemplation is "a form of wordless prayer in which mind and heart focus on God's greatness and goodness in affective, loving adoration; to look on Jesus and the mysteries of his life with faith and love."[2]

The spiritual practice of contemplation is anchored in two key qualities: silence and love. It emerges at the point in prayer were thought is laid gently aside; the point at which the present moment becomes the moment of presence. Time given to contemplation is time dedicated exclusively to God and love and emptiness and unknowing. This is the spiritual practice where we come most fully to that place where we brush up against the mystery of God—the frontier within us where our thoughts and opinions and beliefs suddenly become tiny in relation to the vast, awe-inspiring silence of the dazzling divine presence. In this awesome place deep within us, we are invited to think little and love much.

Another succinct definition of the prayer of contemplation comes from the nineteenth-century saint John Vianney, who describes prayer in the simplest of ways: "I look at God and God looks at me." This is the heart of contemplation.

SILLY PRAYER

Contemplation is, in fact, a silly way to pray. *Silly* is a rich word that comes from the old German *selig*, meaning "blessed," and also "foolish." To be silly is to be foolishly blessed. The apostle Paul said we are called to be "fools for Christ's sake."[3] It has also been said that this way of praying is "wasting time with God." I have mixed feelings about that understanding, since *waste* implies something ruined or stripped of its goodness, but as a metaphor, it has its use. Contemplative prayer is time wasted foolishly for God and for God's love, the way we might eagerly waste time when we have the chance to spend an hour or a weekend with someone we dearly love. When we are immersed in love, our time does not need to be productive—the love itself is its own justification and its own reward.

Contemplative prayer is silly and foolish and even "wasteful" because you can't control it, master it, program it, or figure it out. All you can do is enter into it, be present to it, and offer yourself to the mystery. Sometimes, once in a while, contemplation even offers us a potential portal into an ecstatic experience of mystical union, although that's hardly the point. The deepest heart of mysticism is not ecstasy, but love. So for most us, this silly way of prayer offers us rewards—read: blessings—that are gentle, humble, and even ordinary. And while saying this is time wasted for God is a way of saying that rewards or benefits are not the point (love is the point), even a fretful and distraction-laden half-hour of silent prayer is never truly wasted, for God is present always, even in our fidgety distractions, even in the monkeyest of monkey-minds, the noisiest of inner cocktail parties. For that matter, God is present always in our suffering, our doubts, our restlessness, and our boredom. Just like it is never a waste of time to share love with someone you truly care for, so time given to contemplation is always time for love shared with the Spirit who created you, loves you, and keeps you.

To be a contemplative, mystically speaking, is to be a person who integrates wonder and openheartedness into your commitment to prayer. I know I keep circling back to this basic point, but it truly is a central tenet of mystical Christianity. Unless we recognize the unity of prayer, contemplation, and silence, the mysterious blessings of this spiritual practice can remain lost to us—the time we spend in contemplation will seem to be time squandered rather than time set on fire with a love that cannot be measured or mapped.

In the practice of lectio divina, contemplation is the final act: the summit of the process of prayer that begins with words of wisdom, is deepened with meditation and verbal prayer, and then blossoms into this silly symphony of inner silence. It's important to remember, however, that contemplation does not make other ways of praying obsolete or superfluous. If we abandon the more word-centric ways of praying, we are acting like sailors who launch a boat into the open sea without bothering to bring a compass or a GPS. Contemplative prayer needs to be anchored in an overall spiritual practice just as a successful journey needs to be guided by useful and effective navigational tools.

THE SILENT TEMPLE WITHIN

Contemplation is a word with a murky history. It comes from the Latin verb *contemplare*, which means "to observe" or "to notice." It also is linked to the word *temple*, so contemplation has a rooted relationship to sacred space, a place set aside for spiritual matters. In its pagan usage, *contemplare* involved the reading of auguries—a divination technique in which people sought guidance from the gods or other spirits. Once Christianized, contemplation lost its association with prognostication, and came to signify a present-moment practice of attending to the silent Spirit within. While this link to the concept of temple might suggest that contemplation has a communal quality to it—"where two or three are gathered, I am there among them" as Jesus put it—it also can be seen as pointing to the inner temple, the solitude of the human heart.[4] Mystically speaking, contemplative spirituality consists of the effort to spend time in the hidden (mystical) temple where we go within to be silent with God. In contemplative prayer, therefore, you listen in receptive silence, and hold yourself open for the purpose of fostering an encounter with God's presence within you—a presence promised by Scripture.[5]

In addition to this idea of the human heart as a temple for encountering the silence of God, we can also consider nature as another kind of "temple." The process of moving from praying-with-words into the silence of contemplation can be compared to moving from time spent in a lush, verdant garden into a more austere landscape where life is sparse and marked by at least some measure of suffering. It's easy to fall in love with the garden—and, by extension, with prayer that anchors itself in the sweetness of experiencing (or even merely imagining) divine love and heavenly bliss. But, just as not all landscapes are lush with vegetation, not all prayer is automatically suffused with an experience of joyful connection with God. It's instructive to remember that the roots of mystical Christianity are found in the desert, the landscape of austerity and emptiness that inspired the desert mothers and fathers. In the Celtic lands of northwest Europe, other early contemplatives found inspiration in wilderness settings or on remote windswept islands, where their ancient stone dwellings still stand today.

Some of the earliest Christian mystics, those who abandoned a comfortable life to seek God in the deserts of Syria and Egypt, entered into deep silence to pray—a practice written about by spiritual teachers like Evagrius Ponticus. Such wordless prayer is not just a relic from the ancient desert, however. Monasteries—settings devoted to austere living and the renunciation of personal wealth or family life—became the "deserts" for later generations of contemplatives and spiritual seekers. The practice of silent adoration as a central Christian spiritual activity marked the spirituality of monastic and cloistered mystics in the Middle Ages (such as the author of *The Cloud of Unknowing*), after the Renaissance (Teresa of Ávila, John of the Cross), and into the modern and postmodern eras (Howard Thurman, Cynthia Bourgeault).

To become a contemplative, then, implies leaving the "garden" of spirituality shaped by language and discursive thought, to enter into the desert/wilderness of silent attentiveness. Sooner or later, mystical seekers need to leave the garden and move into the wilderness. Like the desert mothers and fathers of old, we who seek the contemplative path need to take several deep breaths and face the wilderness within—the untamed chatter of your mind, your murky passions and the self-serving desires of your deep subconscious, and the shadow dimensions of the multilayered human psyche.

Some of these wilderness places may be dry and arid, like a desert; others may be thick with nearly impenetrable vegetation, like a rainforest; still others may be stark and uncaring, like the endless gray of the postmodern urban landscape. But, just as Jesus retreated into the desert to fight the demons and ultimately experience the loving care of the angels, so all contemplative and mystical seekers must travel their own path into the barren unknown when embarking upon the spiritual life. We must walk this path because others have walked it before us, because Jesus walked it, because the wisdom of the mystics tell us that to learn to discern the presence of God, we must learn to find the Spirit in all things—not just in joy and happiness and abundance, but also in emptiness, in unknowing, in the shadow places, and even in the midst of the roiling frenzy of your own soul.

ENTERING THE TEMPLE

Strictly speaking, there is no program for becoming a contemplative, just as there is no program for becoming a mystic. In the famous words of Thomas Merton, "I have no program for this seeing. It is only given. But the gate of heaven is everywhere."[6] To see like a mystic or a contemplative does not depend on mastering any particular method or technique of prayer. Over the centuries, various spiritual teachers have in fact developed methods or exercises for fostering inner silence. But contemplation itself can never be reduced to a mere procedure. Contemplative prayer is not so much about mastering silence or achieving a desired state of consciousness as it is a gentle, unforced opening-up of your mind and heart—a simple process of allowing yourself to sit in the uncreated presence of God. In other words, contemplation is not something you achieve; it is something you allow. It is a gesture of consent. You open yourself to spend time with God, just as you allow yourself to spend time with anyone you deeply love.

To enter into contemplative prayer requires nothing more than a commitment to spend time in silence, with the specific intent to offering the time to God. Time spent in contemplation is time spent listening gently for God's soft whisper. This is more easily said than done.

We live in a particularly noisy world, increasingly defined and dominated by technology, and therefore by the noise and stress that technology brings into our lives. From machinery to music, from telephones to traffic, from broadcast media to mental chatter—our world is filled with persistent, ever-present, and often simply frantic noise. As a result, silence feels foreign and awkward, if not anxiety-provoking, for so many people. Even the best-intentioned Christians face many obstacles to contemplative prayer: a busy life, an active mind, a nervous body. These can all contribute to forces both external and internal that conspire to prevent us from simply sinking into the silence where God's presence may be discerned as a "sound of sheer silence."[7]

For this reason, contemplation is not something that we can do just once or twice—or even just once in a while. Like any meaningful relationship, mystical spirituality does not thrive when only practiced on occasion. Like any other endeavor designed to foster genuine intimacy with another person (or, in this case, with God), time spent together needs to be a frequent and regular part of the relationship. For contemplatives, this means time spent in the inner temple of silence.

The communion with God we seek through contemplation can be found only within the context of a recurring—ideally, daily—practice. Since contemplation is the final step in the exercise of lectio divina, the most direct way to foster a daily discipline of contemplative prayer is to establish a daily commitment to lectio. Even if you rest in contemplative silence for only a few minutes at a time, this regular practice can foster a deepening sense of intimacy with, and transformation in, Christ.

When you give our attention to silence—whether for half an hour or just for half a minute—the temptation arises to fill this time with "stuff," with words, ideas, images, and thoughts. It's normal to want to tell God all about our needs, and the needs of others. Silence often can inspire us to sing God's praises and express in creative ways just how much we love and adore the Spirit. This is one reason why it is so important to pair silent prayer with other, more verbally based ways of praying. Take the time to tell God all that you wish to say, and then allow the words to open up into the silence that exists before, beneath and beyond all human cognition.

The all-too-human urge to clutter up silent prayer with endless mental static is simply a way of trying to control the agenda. Thankfully, God is loving and kind. The Spirit of unconditional love waits patiently for us to let go of our need to control, whether that takes us five minutes, five months, or fifty years. God waits for those times when we gently allow ourselves to breathe through our distractions and simply let them go, allowing the silence to wash throughout our consciousness like a cleansing wave of crystal water.

Part of what can be challenging about the prayer of wordless adoration is that we do not always sense—or even intuitively feel—the divine presence during the time we give to God as a contemplative offering. The prophet Isaiah wryly remarked that God is a God who hides,[8] and sometimes it feels like God delights in playing hide-and-seek when we enter the inner temple.

Even when we give up trying to think our way into managing or controlling our prayer experience, the mental monkey is never far away. We often find ourselves continually distracted by the endless kaleidoscope of stream-of-conscious thoughts, ideas, spontaneous mental imagery, or the endless capacity to daydream ourselves away from the unclenched awareness of the present moment. However, despite all the ways we can fail to place our attention on the silence within us, grace still arises in surprising and unexpected ways, leading us into occasional moments of unplanned wonder. Sometimes, we may notice the uncreated presence within and beyond the silence that rests quietly beneath our mental chatter. Sometimes, our time spent in contemplation opens up into a quiet sense of resplendent joy and profound encounters with heavenly love. For most who walk the path of contemplation, these times are unpredictable, and less common than we hope—and appropriately so. God comes to us to be in relationship, not just to make us feel good. So the unthought prayer of silent love ultimately promises to nurture us at a level far deeper than emotions or conscious awareness.

Silence is not only the single most essential element of mystical spirituality; it is also the Rosetta Stone that unlocks and clarifies the meaning of all other spiritual exercises. By choosing to make ourselves available for contemplation, we are brought to the threshold of the mysteries, and then ushered in deeper, and then deeper still. Seeking deeper intimacy with us, the Spirit takes us beyond any place the heart can control, the mind can understand and the tongue can recount. And we will never outgrow the invitation to go deeper, and deeper still.

THREE FORMS OF CONTEMPLATION

In *Practical Mysticism*, Evelyn Underhill articulates a threefold way of understanding contemplative prayer. Her model is quite useful and well worth summarizing here.

Discernment. The first form of contemplation invites us to recognize how God can be found in all things. This is a recurring theme in the writings of the mystics, and the theological term for God's presence in creation is *immanence* (which is paired with *transcendence*, the principle that God cannot be contained by any created thing, not even by the universe as a whole). Discernment, in the sense Underhill uses the term, refers to our capacity for awareness of the immanent presence of God in and through nature—including the nature within us, which is to say our own hearts. Contemplative discernment means learning to sense the presence of the artist by gazing upon and appreciating the beauty and wonder of the artwork.

Recognition. The artistry of creation introduces us to the Spirit who dwells in us and in all things, but it can never capture the fullness of that divine presence—an immanence that is also paradoxically transcendent. Knowing that the God who is not elsewhere also transcends all created things, we are invited to enter the "cloud of unknowing" where we seek God, not in any created object, but in silence and darkness, in the mysteries of our own being and consciousness, knowing that even the human soul, vast as it is, can never fully embrace and reveal the limitless splendor of our divine lover.

Acknowledgment. As we discern God's presence in all things, and recognize God's mysterious unknowability, we are moved to accept the limits of even our own consciousness and spirit; we humbly acknowledge that no created thing, not even the diamond-fashioned interior castle, can ever fully reveal God to us, and so we consent to wait in the silence and darkness, trusting that, even beyond all human experience, God can, will, and does come to us without any effort on our part. This marks the transition from "active" to "infused" contemplation—in other words, the transition from contemplation as our intentional practice, moving instead to the humble acknowledgment that contemplation is *God's* practice, which we receive as a free gift of grace. Acknowledgment transforms our prayer from an exercise in seeking spiritual fulfilment to a fully God-centered act of loving response to the infinite, ultimate, ineffable mystery.

While Underhill's three forms of contemplation are certainly not the only way, or even perhaps the best way, of understanding the process by which we enter into the wordless wonder of silent adoration, they do illustrate that contemplative prayer is not something anyone can master; it is not some technique to work at until you get it right. Contemplation is a lifelong (and beyond) process of ever-unfolding possibilities that move us deeper and deeper into encounter and intimacy with God—an encounter that occurs beyond the limits of all our thoughts, ideas, mental images, and ability to know the ways of the Spirit.

To climb halfway up the mountain is not to reach the summit, even though the view from that mid-point of your journey may be spectacular. The mystical life calls us to the summit. When we embrace a spirituality that calls us into silence and beckons us to let go of the comforting but constraining cocoon of spiritual ideas and religious thoughts, ultimately we are being called into a process that will never end—not even in the silence of eternity. We will have no choice but to see this journey through to the very heart of the mystery—not only here and now, but everywhere and forever.

CENTERING PRAYER

While it is important to bear in mind that contemplation, being relational in nature, can never be reduced to a mere method of praying, it is also human nature to develop rituals, patterns of behavior, and methods for just about any aspect of life. Prayer is no different. As we seek to foster a truly contemplative heart in our lives, it's helpful to consider several methods of prayer or meditation that have been developed by mystics and contemplatives over the years. One such method, that I myself practice, is Centering Prayer—I've alluded to it numerous times throughout this book. Now I'd take to briefly introduce readers to this method of praying, commending it to anyone who seeks to prepare themselves for the grace of contemplation.

The monks who developed Centering Prayer, based on ancient Christian wisdom teachings from sources like the desert mothers and fathers and *The Cloud of Unknowing*, note that this is not ultimately a technique of contemplative prayer, but rather a way of praying that helps to prepare us for the grace of contemplation, which is always a gift from God. This is a subtle but meaningful distinction.

Centering Prayer, as a method, was developed by several Trappist monks in the late 1960s and 1970s, inspired by the wisdom of Thomas Merton, who spoke of contemplation as prayer "centered entirely on the presence of God." This also echoes the *Interior Castle* with its lovely image of Jesus reigning in our hearts at the very center of our souls.

As a method of prayer, Centering Prayer invites us to relax into the natural silence that persists beneath the thoughts and images of normal consciousness. The guidelines for how to practice this way of praying are very simple:

The Four Basic Guidelines of Centering Prayer

1. *Choose a sacred word or a sacred breath as the symbol of your intention to consent to God's presence and action within.*
2. *Sitting comfortably and with eyes closed, settle briefly and silently introduce the sacred word as the symbol of your consent to God's presence and action within.*
3. *When engaged with your thoughts, return ever so gently to the sacred word. Thoughts include body sensations, feelings, images, and reflections.*
4. *At the end of the prayer period, remain in silence with eyes closed for a couple of minutes.[9]*

The foundational purpose behind Centering Prayer is repeated twice in the guidelines: to consent to God's presence and action within. We consent by getting out of our own way—through gently setting aside our impulse to control and manage our lives by our ego-driven thoughts and ideas and agendas, the thoughts that flow down the stream of consciousness like so many boats on a river. But it can be so difficult to simply rest in the silence between and beneath our thoughts. Therefore, following instructions found in *The Cloud of Unknowing*, the guidelines for Centering Prayer ask us to choose a single word—our "sacred word"—that we can return to any time we noticed our awareness getting lost in extraneous thoughts or distractions. When we begin our Centering Prayer, we silently introduce the sacred word into our awareness, simply as a symbol of our intention to consent.

We can pray this way for as short or long a period of time as is practical. Many teachers of Centering Prayer recommend allowing twenty to thirty minutes, twice a day, to fully allow for the stream of inner thoughts to slow down enough where we can begin to appreciate the beautiful silence that is always within us—but usually "masked" by the chattering of the ego.

Notice that the sacred word is not the same thing as a mantra. In a mantra meditation, a particular word is silently repeated over and over again during the meditation. But in Centering Prayer, the sacred word is repeatedly only when we notice ourselves distracted by thoughts. If it so happens that a spacious moment of silence arises, and even the sacred word itself should fall away, leaving you objectlessly aware of the silence at the center of your soul—then simply rest in that beauty.[10] Soon enough, another thought will come down the stream of consciousness, and it will time to silently recite the sacred word again.

Of course, if the thoughts are coming thick and fast, you may find that you are repeating the sacred word pretty much nonstop. That's okay too. There's no one right or wrong way to pray in this way. Simply follow the guidelines and seek to rest in the silence that is always there, between your thoughts. For this reason, I would say the fourth point of the guidelines is especially important—when the time for your prayer comes to a close, allow for a couple of minutes when you can gently rest. Often this is the sweetest part of the Centering Prayer experience—like a little bit of Sabbath rest after your prayer.

Many people will end their time of Centering Prayer, after the couple of minutes of gentle rest, by slowly reciting a short prayer they find meaningful, like the Lord's Prayer or the prayer of Julian of Norwich (see chapter 17).

Centering Prayer can seem maddening to people whose lives are geared toward our bottom-line-driven, goal-oriented, pragmatic, and utilitarian society. This is because it feels as if you're doing nothing—back to that "wasting time" notion again. Although the attention you give to the silence is profoundly relaxing and can lead to feelings of well-being, serenity, and even euphoria, it can also lead to feelings of restlessness, or to an emotional release that taps into hidden wells of anger, grief, or sadness. Because of its profound orientation toward silence and toward the places in your consciousness that take you beyond rational or cognitive thought, it can leave you feeling empty rather than spiritual, meaningless rather than God-infused. You might also find that some days seem more "prayerful" than others.

It's helpful to balance your experience of Centering Prayer (or any other method of silent prayer) with the collective wisdom of the larger Christian contemplative community. Christian saints, monks, nuns and mystics have had much to say about feeling discouraged in prayer, struggling with a sense of God's absence, dealing with feelings of meaninglessness or shame or discouragement, or questioning their commitment to God and to the spiritual life. The wise teachers of the past encourage us to persevere through those times when prayer and contemplation seem frustrating rather than edifying. Silence invites you to a place of mystery—a place beyond the safe zone where you can rationally interpret what is going on inside you. If you choose to enter this place of mystery, you open yourself up to the frontier of wonder and hiddenness that many mystics have explored before you. To enter that place requires surrendering all the objections of your practical, rational, used-to-being-in-control, egoic consciousness.

When we seek to embrace God even beyond the limits of our thinking minds, we need to make peace with the fact that the mind will scoff at this and see it as a silly, stupid, impractical endeavor (there's that word *silly* again). Only by clinging to the wisdom of those who have gone before can we gently and confidently turn aside the protests of the ego and faithfully enter into the cloud of unknowing, where the opportunity to respond to the love of the hidden God matters more than the limited human mental images that too easily get in the way of our spiritual growth.

RESISTANCE TO CONTEMPLATION

Because silence takes us to a place where our talkative ego is asked to surrender its control to the leading of the Spirit, it may not be surprising to consider that some people—including people who follow Jesus—find this practice threatening. Since mysticism remains Christianity's best kept secret, many Christians today are unfamiliar with contemplative spirituality and practices like lectio divina or Centering Prayer. Unfortunately, there are also a small minority of Christians who have decided that contemplation is either bad or unchristian, and are outspoken in their objection to it. Their objections usually take one of two forms:

1. Contemplative spirituality is "unbiblical."
2. Contemplative spirituality seems to be too much like the practices of Eastern non-Christian religions like Hinduism or Zen.

It is true that the word *contemplation* does not appear in the Bible. But the Bible contains numerous passages that encourage us to seek the presence and love of God through silence, solitude, and stillness. Nowhere does the Bible forbid seeking God in silence and stillness. If we assume that Christians can lawfully use only tools and practices that are mentioned in Scripture, then modern medicine, computers, and automobiles must all be forbidden.

Even if they accept that there is no scriptural basis to prohibit contemplative practices, however, many Christians continue to be uncomfortable with it because they believe it blends Eastern practices with the Christian faith. But as I have already noted, practices like Centering Prayer are based on Christian teachings that go back to ancient or medieval times. The real issue is not that Centering Prayer is based on Eastern spirituality, but simply that is *resembles* Eastern forms of meditation (for example, in Zen Buddhism there is a meditation practice called *shikantanza*, from a Japanese word that literally means "doing nothing but sitting"). To me, the fact that Eastern and Western spiritual practices are so similar is not a cause for alarm, but a cause for celebration, indicating that these universal spiritual practices can help us grow spiritually and cultivate well-being, regardless of our cultural or religious identity.

The real problem here is not the infiltration of "foreign spirituality" into Christianity, but rather the judgmental attitude of those who are too quick to jump to conclusions about spiritual practices with which they are unfamiliar.

Anyone who is nervous about practices like Centering Prayer ought to read the ancient writers who have inspired the modern Centering Prayer movement, writers like Evagrius Ponticus in the fourth century or the anonymous author who wrote *The Cloud of Unknowing* in the fourteenth. These ancient and medieval Christians were uncompromising in their love and devotion to Christ and to the teachings of the Christian faith. Centering Prayer keeps their wisdom alive for new seekers of the contemplative path today.

The purpose of contemplative and mystical spirituality is to foster greater intimacy with and devotion to God, which in itself is a universal goal of all religious and spiritual traditions that are God-centered (Buddhism does not require belief in God, so in that sense it's a philosophy). Mystical, contemplative spirituality invites us deep into the wisdom of a path without insisting that it is the *only* path. This is true for contemplative Christians as well as for contemplatives of other traditions.

Contemplative spirituality truly is the path of mystery, for it calls us to sit still and silent in the center of the mystery that can never be put into words, but we use the word *God* since it's a traditional way of naming the unnameable. Mystically speaking, the contemplative life invites us to a spirituality where God is a question more than an answer, where God responds to all our questions by asking deeper questions still.

I do not mean to suggest that contemplative practices lead only to confusion or doubt. Far from it! In my experience, most people who commit to an ongoing practice of contemplative ways of praying find it to be meaningful, joyful, and transformational. Many who cultivate a sustained, daily practice of contemplation discover not only a deeper sense of well-being and serenity in their lives, but also a heightened awareness of God's continual presence, and of divine love flowing to and through them—particularly in their dealings with others who may suffer, or who are wounded or in some manner of need. Such subtle blessings cannot be reduced to a simple formula, however. ("Sit in silence an hour a day for a year and you will suddenly feel God's presence all the time.") God cannot be reduced to an equation. Contemplative prayer is a spiritual practice, not a magical spell.

To engage in mystical Christian spirituality means to join in solidarity with the long tradition of contemplatives who have gone before us—and no doubt who will also come after us. It means to pray along with Francis of Assisi, Howard Thurman, Evelyn Underhill, Julian of Norwich, Teresa of Ávila, John of the Cross, Meister Eckhart, Desmond Tutu, Thérèse of Lisieux, Abhishiktananda, Dag Hammarsköld, Simone Weil, and countless others. These renowned mystics who are known to us because they were great writers or teachers represent only a tiny fraction of the great contemplatives in Christian history, most of whom were lovers of God in obscurity and are now known by name to God alone. When you embrace the prayer of deep silence, you join in their communion—a communion that transcends the normal limitations of time and space. For all the contemplatives throughout Christian history (and extending into the future), silence is praise and stillness is a song of love. When we surrender the tight control of the thinking "monkey" mind to enter into the dazzling darkness of the unknowing of

God, we embrace the promise to realize that we already are "partakers of the divine nature."

IS CONTEMPLATION FOR YOU?

The author of *The Cloud of Unknowing* insisted that not everyone is necessarily called into the kind of deep, objectless silent prayer that is associated with the path of contemplation. It occurs to me that the Christians who loudly object to contemplative spirituality may be motivated, in part, by a deep sense that this type of spiritual practice is not for them—or at least, not for them now. The advice of John Chapman, "Pray as you can, not as you can't"—seem to apply here. So it's a question worth asking: How do we know for sure that we are called to this particular kind of spiritual practice?

The Cloud of Unknowing offers some guidance here. The author suggests that if you are interested in contemplation, there are two signs to look for to help you recognize that you are truly ready to engage in this type of spirituality. First, you will notice that you feel a growing, daily desire for this kind of prayer, a desire so strong that it impinges on your daily prayer. If you aren't already praying daily, it's possible you are not ready for contemplation. Christian contemplation emerges from a mature prayer life. Toddlers crawl before they walk; likewise, aspiring mystics may find they need to be immersed in practices like verbal prayer or meditating on scripture before moving to the more demanding practice of sustained silent prayer.

The second sign, just as important as this inner longing, involves feeling a sense of joy or enthusiasm concerning your relationship with God, not just during prayer, but also when you are merely thinking about your spiritual practice.

Everyone who desires intimacy with God is called to pray, but not everyone needs to, or necessarily should, engage in contemplative practices (at least, not now). If the thought of entering into sustained periods of silence on a daily basis strikes you as daunting or overwhelming, then you don't need to do it. At the very least, limit your time spent in silence and focus instead on more foundational practices such as lectio divina or the liturgy of the hours. There's no need to force contemplation. Trust your heart and focus on other spiritual disciplines that you find more appealing. Share the dynamics of your inner life with a trusted spiritual friend or director, and be mindful of the subtle ways the Spirit may call you in the future—including, perhaps, a call to enter silence more fully when the time is right.

Mystical prayer emerges naturally out of a mature spirituality. If you do not feel a sense of longing or joy related to contemplation, take the time to understand what spiritual exercises or prayer practices do appeal to you. Lectio, meditation, conversational prayer, and the Daily Office can all, in themselves, foster a more intimate sense of relationship with God—which is to say that they are all means by which you can enter into a mystical dimension of your faith. You might also find that you feel drawn to express your faith in activist ways: such as working to dismantle systems of privilege or injustice in your community, or providing services to those who are in need. Do not dismiss such practices as unspiritual—remember Evelyn Underhill's first form of contemplation: we seek to find God in all things, which can include finding God in a homeless shelter, a political rally, or a nursing home. Anywhere we can find God (in other words, anywhere at all) is a place where we can be invited into the mysteries of divine love.

Whatever you do to nurture your soul, make it a regular part of your life. A sustained, disciplined practice of prayer (in any form) can till the soil of your inner garden, thereby preparing you for an eventual transition into a deeper experience of contemplation.

Anyone who lacks the longing and the enthusiasm for contemplative spirituality today, may simply not be ready for it. It is possible to have a cursory interest in mysticism and contemplation and yet not be spiritually ready to immerse yourself in it. Many people may feel uncomfortable, or not prepared, to engage in a robust daily practice of sustained prayer, meditation, and wordless adoration. Silence may appear to some not as an intriguing mystery waiting to be explored, but rather as a source of fear and uncertainty. Such unease might be a sign that a person is better off pursuing some other form of prayer, at least for now.

Another important point to consider, however, is that feeling "not ready" for silent prayer could be a mark of humility rather than a sign of warning. Humility is by its nature paradoxical—authentic humility can signify a readiness to go deep in one's spiritual practice, even if the nature of humility is to assume one is not worthy. Here, as in every place along the spiritual path where discernment is necessary, the wise counsel of your trusted peers or a spiritual director will be invaluable.

The wisest of spiritual guides recognize that contemplation, like prayer in general, can manifest in many different ways. Thomas Merton, in his book *The Inner Experience*, wrote about what he called "masked contemplatives"— ordinary people who, although they may never have a formal spiritual practice like daily lectio or silent prayer, nevertheless cultivate a spirit of openness, of wonder, of resting in God in a place deeper than thought. This kind of masked contemplation can happen at any time throughout the day and need not be linked to any particular exercise or practice. Merton gives us an important reminder here that we should never put limits on the action of the Spirit or judge others because they fail to fit in with what we consider to be a normal expression of spirituality. The moral of the story: God can appear to anyone at any time, inviting us deeper into God's silence—and love; often in very unique and surprising ways. Our job, therefore, is to always pay attention: the call of grace may arrive at any moment.

CHAPTER TWENTY

The Other Side of Silence

In returning and rest you shall be saved; in quietness and in
trust shall be your strength.
—Isaiah 30:15

The fullness of joy is to behold God in all.
—Julian of Norwich

Have you noticed the subtle shift in our exploration of mysticism and
contemplation?

We began our journey into the contemplative life by considering the
three classic stages of spiritual growth: purification, illumination, and
union. Acknowledging that these dimensions of the inner life are not
merely rungs on a ladder but also are cyclical like waves crashing on a
shore, we nevertheless began at the beginning, looking at how the life of
spiritual purification involves such down-to-earth tasks as finding our
spiritual community and working on inner growth, seeking to foster in
our hearts the virtues of holiness, based on the liberating teachings of
Jesus (the two great commandments), Moses (the Ten Commandments,
which I like to think of as a road map to spiritual freedom), and Paul (the
fruit of the Spirit).

Then we turned to the way of illumination, beginning with a recognition that the language of spirituality helps to form and shape our mystical

imagination. In the Christian tradition, we find this language in a variety of ways, from the tradition of communal prayer (the liturgy) and the Bible to the wisdom teachings of the great mystics. This in turn brought us to one of the great spiritual disciplines of contemplative spirituality: lectio divina, which combines prayerful reading of the sacred words (biblical or otherwise), with meditation on those words, leading to a prayer response (often in our own words) that culminates at the threshold of contemplative prayer: the prayer of silent, wordless adoration.

So, what subtle shift am I referring to: we've gone from an orientation toward *light* (illumination) to *silence* (contemplation). This is not inconsistent with traditional mystical teachings, where the way of illumination has traditionally been equated with a contemplative life—in contrast to the way of purification which is understood as involving more of an active (service-oriented) life.

Once again, I can't emphasize this enough: these dimensions of mystical spirituality dance in a circle. You don't graduate from one to get to the other.

But why do we begin with a hunger for the light of illumination, only to be taken to a place where we are invited to drink the thirst-quenching waters of contemplative silence? Have we given the eyes the night off, and now the ears are running the show?

Here's a way to understand this shift. Equivalent with *illumination* is the imaginative wonder that comes to us through language—through words, ideas, thoughts, concepts. Christ is the Word, and Christ is the Light of the World (we are also the light of the world, remember). So we bask in the illumination of divine light as brought to us by the Word who is Love-with-a-capital-L.

But now, we are asked to set words aside and orient our hearts and souls to love beyond language: wordless adoration. By doing so, we are not abandoning the light of illumination. Rather, we are preparing ourselves for the scariest element of the mystical life.

The dark night of the soul.

Illumination comes to us through the words of mystical love and wisdom, and those words paradoxically point us beyond themselves to the silence where—without abandoning the light of the world that shines paradoxically from both Christ and us—we encounter what has been called the "dazzling darkness."

Every day is followed by night, and each night is followed by day. We are children of the word, shaped and formed by words of compassion, love, mercy, and hope. And each word invites us into the silence that surrounds and supports it. Words need silence like day needs night; night needs day like silence needs the word. When we embrace the mystical life of brilliant wonder, brought to us through words of wisdom, intimate prayer, and ultimately an invitation to silence, we are invited into the way of illumination that is simultaneously a path into the divine darkness. There is silence in every word, and the divine word rests hidden within all silence. There is darkness in the midst of all light, and illuminating light that carries through the darkest nights.

A SEA OF SILENT LIGHT

As we explore this dimension of the mystical life, here's a quotation from one of my favorite mystical classics: a wondrous, playful, and flawed children's masterpiece, C. S. Lewis's *The Voyage of the Dawn Treader*. The book, one of the seven Narnia novels, tells the adventures of three English children who are whisked away to the magical land of Narnia, where they join the king of Narnia on a quest at sea, on the good ship *Dawn Treader*. The story is a metaphor for the spiritual life, and while Lewis always he insisted he was not a mystic, we know that he avidly studied the writings of the mystics, corresponded with at least one great mystic (Evelyn Underhill), and clearly used the map of purification/illumination/union to structure this charming children's tale. Toward the end of the adventure there is an obvious "dark night of the soul" experience, and after that comes the beauty of the final sea at the very end of the world, a sea radiant with light—and silence. Even the water is described as "drinkable light," and when the sailors and the children drink this luminous water, they become even more silent and more accustomed to the ever-growing light. Here's how Lewis describes it:

> For a long time they were all silent. They felt almost too well and strong to bear it, and presently they began to notice another result. As I have said before, there had been too much light ever since they left the island of Ramandu—the sun too large (though not too hot), the sea too bright, the air too shining. Now, the light grew no less—if anything,

it increased—but they could bear it. They could look straight up at the sun without blinking. They could see more light than they had ever seen before. And the deck and the sail and their own faces and bodies became brighter and brighter and every rope shone. And next morning, when the sun rose, now five or six times its old size, they stared hard into it and could see the very feathers of the birds that came flying from it. Hardly a word was spoken on board all that day.[1]

The light of Christ, the light of the world, impels us into silence. Silence draws us through darkness into greater light. In all of this, below the threshold of our conscious awareness, the Spirit is at work in our hearts, slowly transforming us into the persons we were created to be: the very image and likeness of God—which is to say, of divine love. All we have to do is consent to that transformation.

IT'S ALL ABOUT GOD NOW

Everyone knows someone who is a bit narcissistic: someone who always manages to bring the conversation back to themselves. I sometimes wonder if most of us have a narcissistic streak inside us. There's a part of us that likes to be the center of attention, even though there's also a part of us that wants anything *but* attention.

I believe there's a God-shaped paradox here: we are all created to both enjoy attention and to shun it. The healthy love of attention comes to play when we humbly accept God's infinite love for us, and our equally healthy tendency to avoid attention is calibrated to our desire to share that divine love with others.

It's easy to get this out of balance some way or another. Some of us are spotlight hogs, and others work really hard to always hide in the corner. Anyone who knows how to facilitate a small group learns the skills of diplomatically getting the attention hogs to simmer down to create a space where the more reclusive folks might be gently drawn out of their shells.

Your story may be different from mine, but my journey into contemplative spirituality has been a long slow process of recalibrating my relationship to both attention and hiddenness. I've slowly learned to accept the love that God wants to lavish on me (the one love God wants to lavish on everyone).

And I've also slowly learned that the contemplative life ultimately takes us to a place where, in the relationship of human/divine intimacy, God (love) always and ultimately belongs in the center—the center of the heart, the center of the soul, the center of attention.

The mystical life is learning to calibrate our entire lives to God's will, God's desire, God's design. To be a contemplative is to allow God to direct our hearts, our minds, our wills.

None of this happens overnight, of course. And even as I write these words, I am struck by how easily they can be misunderstood or misconstrued. We human beings love being in the center of things, which means we are always trying to steal the center of our egos back from God. This is one reason why I believe that God operates in our hearts in deep silence. The less God talks to us about what God is doing, the less likely we will try to wrestle control back from God and seek to run things our way.

It's a long, slow process of loving consent. A long slow listening in the same direction. A long slow silence. A long slow learning to trust the darkness—the darkness of unknowing, of uncertainty, of twilight. Always trusting that God is in charge, that love is guiding our hearts, and that compassion and mercy are reprogramming the operating systems of our lives.

As we journey deeper into illumination, into silence, into darkness, and back into the words of love and the light of a maturing faith, we basically say yes, over and over again, to allow God to slowly finish what God has started in our hearts: the adventure of making us into beings luminous with light, radiant with love, overflowing with kindness and compassion and mercy, generous with joy.

In other words, the image and likeness of divine love in human form.

THE SHADOW SIDE OF CONTEMPLATIVE PRACTICE

I have a friend who playfully jokes, "I'm too deep to worry about paying my bills." She's kidding (and as best I can tell, is very responsible with her money!), but her snark is directed at an all-too-common situation that can show up in the lives of even the most sincere spiritual seeker. We can become so engrossed in the time and effort required to study and practice our chosen spiritual path (like contemplative or mystical Christianity) that we neglect other important dimensions of our life—from paying the bills to doing the housework to making sure our meaningful relationships are being nurtured. I can become so focused in my daily practice of lectio divina and Centering Prayer that I risk using spirituality as a way of avoiding other real but difficult demands for my time and attention. When I was exploring the idea of becoming a lay Cistercian, the monks who oversaw the program made it clear that if there were ever a conflict between my responsibilities to my family and my interest in spirituality, the family needed to come first (this was especially relevant in my case, as I had a special needs child). The temptation to lose myself in the bliss of a spiritual practice was something I needed to be mindful of; indeed, my wife and I made a point of talking about any circumstances where she felt as if I were using spirituality as an unconscious way of avoiding the challenge of being a caregiver, and one time in particular, it was important for me to make a change in my daily spiritual practice in order to be more faithful to my family.

The Buddhist psychotherapist John Welwood came up with the idea of *spiritual bypassing*, which he describes as a "tendency to use spiritual ideas and practices to sidestep or avoid facing unresolved emotional issues, psychological wounds, and unfinished developmental tasks."[2] For contemplatives and other spiritual seekers, this is a helpful concept to keep in mind as we reflect on how our spiritual practice makes a difference in our lives. Is our exploration of mystical wisdom, contemplative practices, and the spirituality of deep silence a way to more fully embrace life—or a subtle strategy we use to avoid the demands and challenges that life gives us to grow, become more loving, more compassionate, more present to our relationships? Do we embrace silence and solitude to more fully respond to love, or as a way to escape the problems and pitfalls of being human and being in relationship with others? Our efforts to cooperate with the Spirit and seek the holiness and inner blossoming we associate with purification—are such efforts expressions of a deep desire to embody divine love, or could such efforts actually be a subtle form of self-aggression, motivated by a deeply held belief that "I'm not okay unless I change"?

These are broad, theoretical questions. I pose them here simply as a reminder that the spiritual journey, at every stage along the way, requires careful discernment, gentle but uncompromising honesty, and the courage that is necessary to face self-deception as well as the tendency we all have to avoid challenging circumstances rather than vulnerably facing them head on. Becoming a contemplative is not about putting an end to conflict or avoiding difficult situations: if anything, the integrity that is required to be present to God will also require that we be truly present to ourselves, honest with ourselves and with the others who have a meaningful presence in our lives. There's no one-size-fits-all way to determine if we are indulging in spiritual bypassing, or what we need to do to stop such avoidant behavior. But if we are vulnerable, honest with ourselves and our close relations, willing to listen to the needs and concerns of others, and mindful of the principle that spirituality is not meant to escape from life's messiness but rather to encourage us to meet our challenges so that they might be healed and transformed, then we are less likely to derail our life through bypassing.

AN ORDINARY AND OBSCURE WAY OF LIFE

An old Zen Buddhist tale recounts the story of a young student of meditation who approaches his teacher with a question: "Roshi, what did you do before you were enlightened?" The old master thinks for a moment and then says, "Mostly I just chopped wood and carried water," referring to the normal chores of his agricultural existence. "And now that you have received enlightenment, how do you pass your time?" continued the student. The teacher smiled and said, "Well, I chop wood and carry water."

This story carries two lessons for those who follow the Christian path of contemplation. First, it highlights the sheer ordinariness of the spiritual life. Perhaps the young student was hoping to hear about a daily regimen of meditation, chanting, study, and other "spiritual" pursuits. It must have been a surprise to hear the master speak instead about everyday household chores. Likewise, for most people, the concept of Christian mysticism probably brings to mind images of monks in contemplation or nuns in ecstasy, rather than more humdrum activities like balancing the checkbook, dealing with rush-hour traffic, or mowing the lawn. And yet, those tasks are exactly what ordinary Christian spiritual seekers and contemplatives are called to do. Indeed, the constitution of the Trappist Order of Monks notes that their way of life is "ordinary, obscure and laborious."[3] In other words, the contemplative life is down-to-earth, unglamorous, and frequently involves plenty of hard work.

The second lesson in the Zen story is perhaps even more important. The roshi is cautioning his student against expectations that the spiritual life will quickly or automatically change him in radical or remarkable ways. Although Christian spirituality does not speak of enlightenment in the same way the Buddhists do, the parallel is clear. Before I fell in love with God, I washed the dishes and folded the laundry. After I fell in love with God, I washed the dishes and folded the laundry. Before I experienced a call to the life of contemplation, I lived an ordinary life—and after receiving that call, my life remains as down-to-earth as ever.

A daily practice of lectio divina, prayer, and contemplation can, in subtle ways and over time, change our attitude toward life, help us see the evidence of the Holy Spirit in the most unlikely places, and even propel us, when you least expect it, into moments of profound joy—even ecstasy. There can be moments when everything falls away and you taste the sweetness of union with God. But daily Christian spiritual practice also leads through periods of boredom, restlessness, and questioning: "Why am I doing this every day? It seems so meaningless." Christian teachings are clear that the Spirit is always united with us in our hearts, but sometimes God simply feels absent, just as surely as sometimes it's easy to sense the divine presence. Anyone who is serious about exploring the Christian mysteries will, sooner or later, receive both of these gifts.

Aspiring mystics and contemplatives can place such a strong emphasis on the importance of direct, personal experience with God that we run the risk of rejecting mere faith as somehow second-rate. People who merely believe in God without actually having experiences of the divine presence are somehow missing out, or so we think. But perhaps we're missing an important detail: in our quest for spiritual experience, perhaps we have traded "belief in God" for "belief in experience." In the words of the French mystic Francis de Sales, "There is a great difference between being occupied with God, who gives us the contentment, and being busied with the contentment which Gods give us."[4]

Experience is only part of the mystical story. When meditation and contemplation lead to the cloud of unknowing, perhaps this points to the fact that God loves us enough to shield us from mystical experiences, most if not almost all of the time. Maybe a mystical relationship with God would soon implode if we were shouldered with the burden of continual, or even regular, experiences of ecstasy.

This is not to say that we must go through life with no sense of God's love or presence or activity whatsoever. But here is another mystical paradox. The hidden point behind the Zen story is that, while, on the one hand, nothing changes as a result of embracing the mystical life, on the other, everything changes. We do the same chores, perform the same tasks, enjoy the same pleasures, and struggle against the same sins. And yet, now we do all of this in the light of a disciplined commitment to seek intimacy with God. This illuminating light subtly informs who you are, regardless of whether you are bored or energized by your spiritual exercises on any given day. And the light of your daily practice is the light by which you can see, if not the face of God, then at least the subtle traces of the divine presence in your life, in your heart, and indeed in all your relationships and activities.

The Greek philosopher Heraclitus said, "You cannot step into the same river twice." This koan-like insight into the impermanence of existence can serve as a clue to the question of how to live a truly contemplative life. "See, I am making all things new," promises Jesus toward the end of the Christian scriptures.[5] Is Jesus just echoing Heraclitus, promising us we can never step into the same river twice because of the bracing action of God in the universe, creating new possibilities and new realities every moment of our lives?

What this means, of course, is that, even on days when you can barely stand the thought of slogging through a half-hour of meditative Bible reading, and praying to God about the boring details of your life, and sitting in silence that feels like little more than a continual struggle against your incessant mental chatter—even on those less-than-exciting days, God remains present, hidden in the mystery of your own inability to see, your own willful refusal to see, your own hidden but very real need to be ordinary and restless rather than ecstatic and joyful. But just as every winter yields to spring and every night yields to a new dawn, every restless moment in prayer promises to take us back into a more direct experience of God. Any and every moment may be the one in which, suddenly, the scales fall from your eyes and the tiniest and most undramatic things in your life become radiant and luminous with the presence of divine love. Living a contemplative life means, in large measure, living in continual expectancy of receiving an unexpected kiss from God—on good days as well as bad.

HUMBLE WISDOM FROM AN ANCIENT GUIDE

One of the wisest guides for living a contemplative life is Benedict of Nursia, the monk whose *Rule for Monasteries* became the standard for governing monastic communities in the Western church. Even though few Christians today would even think about living in a monastery, Benedict's rule is surprisingly adaptable to life in the world, largely because of the common-sense advice within the specific instructions for managing an intentional community of monks.

At first glance, Benedict's writing can strike the reader as surprisingly *un*spiritual in its focus. He comes across as mostly concerned with mundane issues like how the community is organized and which psalms will be prayed each day. He seems unconcerned with questions like how to pray, how to meditate, or how to contemplate. Benedict is utterly down to earth and his writing reflects this. And Benedictine monasticism has been shaped by his "chop wood, carry water" approach to spirituality ever since. Indeed, the motto of Benedictine spirituality is *ora et labora*, which means "pray and work." Yes, pray, in the midst of a life that is ordinary, obscure, and laborious.

The utter simplicity of this motto corresponds beautifully to the two great commandments of Jesus, which we have already seen, but which always bear repeating.

Love the Lord your God with all your heart and with all your soul and with all your mind.
Love your neighbor as yourself.[6]

The call to love God is a call to prayer; to the practice of fostering or deepening a loving relationship with God. The call to love neighbors is a call to work; as Kahlil Gibran said, "Work is love made visible."[7] We work because we love. And we love because it is essential to a truly spiritual life.

When we desire to respond to the love of God that calls us to live a truly spiritual and contemplative life, we open our hearts to the Spirit who can foster within us the splendor of mystical consciousness. Likewise, it is through the love we seek to share with our neighbors that we have the opportunity to anchor that contemplative spirituality in the most humble, down-to-earth, and ordinary of ways—by embracing the effort required to truly serve and care for one another, no matter how laborious, tedious, or exhausting that work may be.

Mystics recognize that we cannot separate the desire to love God from the commandment to love others. To live a contemplative life requires both expressions of love. This is why so many of the greatest mystics have also been deeply involved in the social and political conflicts of their time, working as hard for justice and equality and peace as for intimacy with God. This is why people today who are so dedicated to activist expressions of faith—from dismantling racism, fighting economic inequality, seeking to make society and Christianity more inclusive of queer and transgender people, and working to preserve the natural environment and reduce humanity's overconsumption of resources—need to be nurtured, supported and empowered by a meaningful interior bond with the infinite love of God.

Some people will always be more naturally contemplative, or more naturally activist. But wherever we find ourselves on this spectrum, we need both the divine love of contemplation and the human love of social activism; we each need to find our own balance between the two dimensions of love—and expression of faith.

Richard Rohr sums this up nicely in his book *The Naked Now*: "When you honor and accept the divine image within yourself, you cannot help but see it in everybody else, too, and you know it is just as undeserved and unmerited as it is in you. That is why you stop judging, and that is how you start loving unconditionally and without asking whether someone is worthy or not."[8]

The life of a mystical Christian is the life of love and, equally the life of love-made-visible work—regardless of whether that's exciting and creative work, or dull and repetitive work. The daily chores we complete in order to keep our lives and our relationships in good order are all spiritual practices in their own right: heart-centered expressions of the call to a truly spiritual life.

AFTER EACH DAY COMES THE NIGHT

It's good to see the role of ordinary labor as part of the spiritual life in perspective. Work is part of the normal rhythm of being alive, alongside the human need for rest, relaxation, recreation, connection with others, the pursuit of leisure or hobbies—and, of course, time devoted to contemplative practices like lectio divina and Centering Prayer. Rhythm is the key word here. In a similar way, the life of prayer also involves a rhythm—of those times when God feels keenly present, or close, or blissfully united with us, balanced against those times when God is known to us only in terms of absence, or distance, or simply silence.

Larger rhythms are at work in the Christian spiritual life as well— rhythms that unfold over time. We see these macrorhythms in two of the most powerful metaphors used by mystics to describe the contemplative life: the cloud and the dark night. The cloud, as immortalized in *The Cloud of Unknowing*, covers every seeker with mist and fog and renders all of our attempts to "know" God (in a mental, cognitive sense) ultimately limited if not useless. Meanwhile, the dark night, as explained by John of the Cross, can visit you more than once. John distinguishes between various "nights" of the spiritual life, looking at different ways in which God works in our hearts to strip us of our attachments and resistances to the freedom that comes only in the Spirit. At the risk of oversimplifying John's profound teaching, I'd like to suggest a simple way to differentiate between two "dark night" experiences: first, a dark night of the senses, in which we are called to surrender inordinate attachments to the things of this world in order to love God more fully, and then a dark night of the soul, a far more comprehensive (and unsettling) process in which even the pleasure we take in spiritual and religious experience must ultimately be surrendered. To love God fully, we must let go of even the "things of God" (religious or spiritual experiences), or else we risk falling into the trap of loving the pleasure we take in God rather than loving God for God alone.

The images of darkness, night, and the cloud can be discouraging if not terrifying, and they are easily misunderstood. The cloud of unknowing is not an excuse to retreat into some sort of snarky spiritual anti-intellectualism, where we refuse to wrestle with the challenges of faith because there's no way anyone can ever figure it all out anyway. The commandment to love God with all our mind still stands, even once we enter the cloud of unknowing. The cloud simply reminds us humbly that the keenest mind will still ultimately fail before the profound silence of the ultimate mystery.

Likewise, the dark night experiences are not meant to imply we should hate the things of this world. Much misery has come out of a false, dualistic interpretation of the gospel that suggests that, to be truly spiritual, you must renounce, reject, and even hate your body, your sexuality, and the material pleasures of earthly existence. This kind of thinking is particularly pernicious because it historically has been an expression of sexism. The same logic that deems the human body and sexuality to be evil also regards women as inherently inferior to men, implying that men are more "spiritual" and women more "carnal."

The dark night's call to nonattachment is meant to teach us a light, spacious relationship to our own embodiment and materiality, to enjoy the good gifts that God has given us without fusing our identity with them or thinking that happiness is bound up only with material well-being. When we allow the Spirit to free us from attachment to material things, we are better positioned to share our resources with those in need, or to roll with life's punches as we experience the losses that, sooner or later, we all face— financial setbacks, loss of loved ones, loss of health. When we recognize that the true center of our lives is always and only the God who is love, we are empowered to suffer life's challenges with grace and at least a degree of serenity. With God at our center, our task is not to reject all other things and relationships, but to love and care for God's creation in a manner consistent with living a God-centered life. But when we make the mistake of rejecting all that is "not God," we run the risk of choosing a life of judgment, or resentment, or even hatred, which, in turn, leads only to suffering.

As for the dark night process that strips away anything that comes between you and God—even religious or spiritual experience—it can be a temptation to abandon our faith in divine love, or to withdrawn from participation in spiritual community. Often when we are new to the contemplative path, it is easy to find joy in religious activities like receiving the sacraments, participating in public worship, reading the Scripture, and of course contemplative exercises like lectio and silent prayer. But the journey through the dark night of the soul creates the conditions in our hearts where the Spirit replaces that earlier sense of happiness and pleasure with a profound, wordless, imageless, feeling-transcending trust in God and God alone. In the midst of the dark night, we may be tempted to think that the mystical tradition itself has lost all purpose and meaning, and that the wisdom of the mystics no longer matters; for those who participate in Christian church communities, especially ones that are not particularly "mystical" in their character, it can seem as if contemplative spirituality has become entirely pointless, nothing more than an imaginary daydream. But it is precisely when we begin this descent into the darkness, that we need to lean on the love and support of others, even if those relationships seem to bring us nothing more than a same sense of boredom and ennui that every other aspect of spirituality seems to entail.

The experiences of darkness, of the cloud, of unknowing, of radical letting-go can tempt us to abandon the spiritual journey—to retreat into cynicism, into despair, or into ego-driven fantasy. The best safeguard against this derailing of your spiritual journey is continual prayer, counterintuitive as that may seem. This is because contemplative practice is, at its heart, a gesture of consent, an allowing of the Spirit to bring healing and transformation into our lives even below the level of our conscious awareness. To persevere in prayer—even and especially silent prayer—during the dark night experience is a gesture of radical trust, and of hope that beneath the restlessness and boredom of the night is a deeper reality where God remains hidden (mystical) yet active in our lives. Trust in God, even when it feels as if you're barely hanging on, and rely on the love, support, and guidance of others—your spiritual friend(s) or director, and your larger community of faith.

The spirituality of knowing God only through a sense of God's hiddenness, absence or the inability of images and concepts to connect with God is known as *apophatic* spirituality, from a Greek word meaning denial or negation. An apophatic spirituality is a spirituality where silence and darkness are more reliable ways of finding God than language or images. By denying or negating the normal "stuff" of spiritual meaning, we clear our hearts to foster the openness where the encounter with divine love may take place. In the words of the Russian Orthodox theologian Vladimir Lossky, "Apophaticism is not necessarily a theology of ecstasy. It is, above all, an attitude of mind which refuses to form concepts about God."[9] This has roots all the way back to the earliest centuries of Christian mysticism, as evidenced by this observation from the anonymous monk known as Pseudo-Dionysius the Areopagite: "God is known in all, and apart from all. God is known through knowledge, and through unknowing."[10]

Dark-night experiences sometimes seem to be similar to the symptoms of depression. Contemplative psychologists like Gerald May draw helpful distinctions between clinical depression and spiritual dark nights; but it's not always easy for laypersons to tell the difference. It's good to be careful, whenever we enter the darkness, to discern whether the sense of profound loss and sadness we are feeling may need the care of a qualified mental healthcare provider. Trained spiritual directors and spiritually informed psychologists are usually able to help us to sort out whether we may need psychological care or spiritual support. Sometimes, we may require both.

The journey of a maturing spiritual life has many seasons and nuanced changes. No matter how deeply we fall in love with God, we never stop being embodied human beings with material needs and earthly concerns—not, at least, on this side of death. Each stage of life—childhood, adolescence, young adulthood, midlife, and old age—carries its own set of spiritual issues and life concerns. A young person's need to establish a sense of self or discern their life calling differs considerably from a retiree's quest to find grace and humility in facing the limitations of age and the need to provide a legacy to the next generation. Our political and social beliefs, our sexual orientation, gender identity and expression, our experience with addiction or illness, our ethnicity and level of education and socioeconomic status—all these factors contribute to the unique flavor of our own dance with God. As you persevere on the long road to faithful love of God, you will experience both joy and sadness, both breathtaking moments of God's felt presence and other times marked by a sense of God's silence or absence. Times of confident growth and peaceful contentment give way to seasons of loss or unknowing. But through all of life's changes and uncertainties, when you balance the quest for the love of God with a commitment to love your neighbors as yourself, you anchor yourself in the resources and support systems necessary to live the spiritual life well.

WOOD, WATER . . . AND WINE

Since I've quoted a Buddhist psychologist and recounted a Zen tale, let's balance this chapter out with a beloved Christian tale, from the second chapter of the Gospel of John:

> On the third day there was a wedding in Cana of Galilee, and the mother of Jesus was there. Jesus and his disciples had also been invited to the wedding. When the wine gave out, the mother of Jesus said to him, "They have no wine." And Jesus said to her, "Woman, what concern is that to you and to me? My hour has not yet come." His mother said to the servants, "Do whatever he tells you." Now standing there were six stone water jars for the Jewish rites of purification, each holding twenty or thirty gallons. Jesus said to them, "Fill the jars with water." And they filled them up to the brim. He said to them, "Now draw some out, and take it to the chief steward." So they took it. When the steward tasted the water that had become wine, and did not know where it came from (though the servants who had drawn the water knew), the steward called the bridegroom and said to him, "Everyone serves the good wine first, and then the inferior wine after the guests have become drunk. But you have kept the good wine until now." Jesus did this, the first of his signs, in Cana of Galilee, and revealed his glory; and his disciples believed in him.[11]

Even before the miracle at the center of this story, this relates a marvelously human tale. Jesus responds irritably when his mother prods him to help out, and we catch a glimpse of the kind of behind-the-scenes action that takes place at just about any party or social event. Jesus, one of the guests, takes on the role of servant, following his mother's suggestion that he do something to make an ordinary day extraordinary. A miracle occurs, but it slips by when the steward suggests to the groom merely that there's been a mix-up with the wine.

This story can remind us that, whenever we talk about the night-time dimension of mystical spirituality, we ought to keep in mind that, following every night, comes a new dawn. This, then, is the other side of "chop wood, carry water." Living the contemplative life is not only about carrying water, it's also all about changing water into wine. While the exercises of the contemplative life cannot guarantee anyone any kind of supernatural or extraordinary encounters with God, for those who are willing to see the possibilities within them, they can help us to see all of life in an entirely new way. And so we arrive at yet another paradox: become a contemplative, and nothing will change; become a contemplative, and everything changes.

The dark-night experience—whether of the senses or of the soul— transforms you as certainly as Jesus changed the water into wine. The night never lasts forever, and it yields to a new dawn, a new day in which everything is changed. When you accept the boredom and confusion, the pain and letting-go that lies at the heart of the dark night, you are, in effect, yielding to the possibility that God is working something wondrous within you. And in accepting the possibility of deep transformation, you choose to embrace the promise of the new dawn.

Like chopping wood and carrying water, however, changing water into wine is not a one-time event. The wisdom of the Christian mystics does not promise that if you, say, spent a year or two in daily prayer and contemplation, then you'll wake up one morning to see everything glowing with an unearthly light because you have been totally and permanently enlightened. What is far more likely to happen after two years of prayer is that you'll wake up one morning with your heart aching for God more than ever before, along with an increasing desire to serve your neighbors, particularly those in the greatest of need.

Contemplation is a gift, a gift that requires our cooperation and participation in order for the alchemy to work. Every day, we invite Christ to turn the water of our hearts into wine. And we choose to keep our eyes and ears open for glimpses and whispers of the giver. In making that choice, we create the space for the Spirit to make a difference in your life—which, in turn, changes everything.

ALL YOU NEED IS LOVE

A Christian rock singer named Larry Norman once made fun of the Beatles for singing "All you need is love," and then breaking up shortly thereafter. There's a cautionary tale here: yes, all we need is love, but just knowing that isn't enough. We need to embody this truth, not merely by understanding it, but by giving our lives to the expression of the love that is all we need. Without such an active commitment, it's far too easy to slip into less-than-loving choices and actions.

But all in all, this is good news. Yes, it's true: all you need *is* love. And every time you choose love, every time you lay down your resistance to God's love, you allow the water of your life to be slowly but surely turned into wine. Accepting love, and choosing love, and making choices both large and small that, to the best of your knowledge, are in alignment with the love of God and the love of your neighbors—this is the heart of the heavenly contemplative life. Orienting ourselves to love will not magically solve all our problems or instantly set us free from your addictions or our imprisonment (real or metaphorical). However, choosing love will, sooner or later, create the space in our lives where the Spirit can begin changing the water of our ordinary, messy, wood-chopping lives into the wine of a truly mystical life radiant with the fruit of the Spirit.

This is how love works within us. God's love for us is unconditional, but not undemanding. Love insists that we take responsibility for our actions, if not now, then someday. But love also creates space in our life—space where light can shine, where hope can emerge, and where a sense of God's joyous and peaceful and playful presence can be felt. We can find the love within us, if we only pay attention. And every time you choose love, that spaciousness within you grows a little bigger. Little by little, the mystery of divine love will transform your life, even while you are busy chopping wood and carrying water and turning water into wine—this is the promise of the contemplative life.

CHAPTER TWENTY-ONE

The Heart of the Mystery

Take delight in God, and God will give you
the desires of your heart.
—Psalm 37:4 (adapted)

We shall not cease from exploration
And the end of all our exploring
Will be to arrive where we started
And know the place for the first time.
—T. S. Eliot

"To comprehend and understand God," remarked the Flemish mystic John Ruusbroec, "is to be God with God.... Contemplative persons will go out in accordance with the mode of their contemplation, above and beyond reason and distinction and their own created being. Through an eternal act of gazing accomplished by means of the inborn light, they are transformed and become one with that same light with which they see and which they see." This great mystic goes on to say, "The contemplative life is a heavenly life."[1]

To be a mystic is to be an artist, a musician, a poet. God is Creator, and humanity is fashioned in the "image and likeness" of God because, at heart, we are creators too. If the contemplative life is a heavenly life, then the mystical life is a generative life. When we join the circle dance we are called into our own creativity (however unique or unusual it might be). Each act of creation becomes a new verse in the song, a new chapter in the story, and we discover that the story is not finished, because our divine lover wants us to keep telling the tale. We need God, and we need each other, and God needs us! Julian of Norwich reports that Christ thanks us for all our acts of compassion, kindness, and mercy: so from the heart of God flows ever-expanding circles of gratitude and felicity, and with each wave of divine joy, we become yet more transfigured into our eternal birthright of divine communion. This, then, is the promise of the mystical life: each new adventure into silence and love reveals that the universe continues to expand, so each new unfolding makes our cosmos larger and more adventurous, where, emboldened by love and fortified by joy and peace, we journey on into the unfathomable heart of God.

THE RAIN AND THE SUN

Beyond purification and illumination, we are called into union—or, if you want to keep using words that end in -*ation*, we dance into deification or divinization, what in Greek is called *theosis*, meaning "the state of being divine." Christianity, as a religion, has been so focused on the problem of sin—of resistance to love, of actions that thwart love or cause harm—that we have lost sight of the foundational teaching that we are, in fact, one with God. We are not bad people who somehow managed to get saved because God has pity on us; we are divine people who are learning how to overcome the mistakes that we and our ancestors have made, mistakes that unfortunately have created the suffering in the world as we know it. If we lead with how *bad* we are, we're pretty much defeated out of the gate. But if we trust the tradition that proclaims God's love for us, God's dwelling in our hearts, God's abiding in us, then we can place our human problems in perspective and we become empowered to do something about it.

What does it mean to be the temple of the Spirit, to have hearts poured full of divine love, to be partakers of the divine nature? Remember the thought experiment from chapter 3: when you stand at the north pole; every direction you face is south. Likewise, if you are one with God, every direction you face is an invitation to love. This is related to Jesus's challenge for us to love our enemies (a radical teaching if there ever were one), for such unconditional love makes us children of our heavenly creator, "for

God makes the sun rise on the evil and on the good, and sends rain on the righteous and on the unrighteous."[2] Love everyone, and let God sort them out. Love everyone, whether they deserve it or not. Jesus finishes by saying in this we will be "perfect"—that has become a loaded word in our culture, since we associate perfection with an almost sterile, antiseptic lack of blemish or flaw. The Greek word we translate as perfect suggests becoming complete or reaching our fullest potential. Using a concept we find in Eastern mysticism: this is Jesus calling us to be *nondual*—when we inhabit that "one with God" place where the lines separating Creator from creature, worthy from unworthy, friends from enemies, all fall away, we are left only with love. Which means, only with God, for God is love.

Christian mysticism is a path without a destination, for the point behind the journey is not to reach a goal, but rather to be reached—by God. The only reason to embrace the mystical life is to foster intimacy with God, the ultimate mystery. Mysticism does not dangle benchmarks or objectives in front of us, like celestial carrots for which we must continually strive. The purpose of contemplation is only to make ourselves available for God and to open ourselves up to the Spirit's elusive presence. The contemplative life is not about becoming someone different from who you are, but rather about being who you really are to begin with. Many contemplative and mystical teachers call this "the true self."

Within contemplative spirituality exists a tension between being and becoming. In a very real sense, mysticism has no incremental objectives or measurable goals, nothing to strive for, since God is always present and already loves you regardless of what you do or don't do to cultivate or accept that love. And yet, you can only experience contemplation in the context of your human life, played out in a universe that is continually changing, evolving, expanding, and mutating. There is, therefore, an aspect of change—and hopefully, growth and development—to the ongoing process of the mystical life. The triune God may be, in the words of *The Book of Common Prayer*, an "eternal changelessness,"[3] and yet it seems that, built into the very structure of the ultimate mystery, is the ever-renewing, always-blossoming flower of continual dynamic activity—in other words, at the heart of eternal being is ever-evolving becoming.

Creation, it seems, is the key. The Trinity may be changeless, but is hardly static. The boundless source of unconditional love may have at its center an immovable serenity, yet like all love, divine love is hardly unmoving or unyielding. In the Hebrew Scriptures, God first appears in the act of creation, separating wind from water and giving form to chaos, working in a mythic six-day timeline to bring all of the world and the cosmos as we know it into being. And anyone familiar with scientific theories like evolution, mutation, and the continual expansion of the universe can see that God has been at it ever since.

The contemplative life opens the door to two simultaneous, and yet clearly paradoxical, possibilities: a state of being, and a state of becoming. In the state of being, you are always, already, one with God, immersed in the divine presence, always and already, here and now. No one can earn this, for it is freely given; nor do we create it; we do not make it more real by dint of effort or stretch of mind. It simply is; it always has been, and always will be. Still, the words we use to describe this state of being are words that imply a process of change (in other words, becoming)—*sanctification, deification, divinization, theosis.* As these process words imply, we are called to a dance of continual change, growth, and development through creativity, expression, and the work of love made visible. This state of becoming can be described in a way that returns us to the eternality of being: it is the state of "being creative."

Like everything about the contemplative life, the best approach for reconciling the being-becoming paradox is simply to try to live it, without necessarily figuring it out in a rational or logical way. Think of this as a practice for embracing nonduality: inhabit both simultaneously. Becoming united with God, and being eternally in God's presence. Becoming more creative, and yet relaxing into our always-already deified being, this process state is the summit to which purification, holiness, illumination, imagination, meditation, contemplation, silence, darkness, and simply living out the Christian life as best we can, leads. It leads us to where we already are.

THE ARTISTRY OF MYSTICISM

Evelyn Underhill suggested that of all people, artists are those who come closest to being natural mystics.[4] And, indeed, many mystics throughout history were, and still are, great artists—or creators in some way. Augustine,

Aquinas, Bonaventure and Simone Weil were world-class philosophers, while George Herbert, John Donne, Hadewijch, and John of the Cross were great poets. And it's not just mystics who are also great artists—many people who were renowned for their creative genius have been mystics as well. Consider musicians like John Coltrane, Johann Sebastian Bach, and Ralph Vaughan Williams; artists like Botticelli, Raphael, and Henry Ossawa Tanner; writers and poets like Dante, T. S. Eliot, Mary Oliver, and Maya Angelou; and the enigmatic artist/poet William Blake. I am conscious of how this list is skewed toward white men; that's simply an indictment of both my ignorance and the racism and sexism that has hobbled Christian history. The nondual unity of mysticism and art extends to people of all colors, genders, nationalities, and sexual orientations, and I for one am excited to discover how mystical beauty will continue to be made manifest in diverse people from all around the world.

Those who work and agitate for peace and justice also deserve to be recognized as creative: they work to create a more human and egalitarian world. Some mystics of creative justice include Mother Teresa, Howard Thurman, Thea Bowman, Harriet Tubman, Sojourner Truth, Black Elk, Pauli Murray, and Martin Luther King Jr. Although on the surface not all of these people are known as mystics or contemplatives, their words and their wisdom reveal a deep knowing of their own inner divinity, directing and guiding them in their work for the liberation of all.

The implication of this connection between art and spirituality is fairly clear: creativity supports contemplation—and vice versa. Anyone who yearns to live a contemplative life, sooner or later is likely to find God seeking to manifest in them through some form of creative expression. To the extent that contemplation opens us up to participation in the divine nature, one way to support this realization of the divine mystery is to develop our own capacity to create. Exploring some form of authentic, soulful creativity can be an important part of the overall commitment to ever-deepening intimacy with God. For many of us, this may be a challenge, since we live in a society that often does more to undermine our innate creativity than to nurture it. We think that because we don't have an extraordinary, innate talent, we are not meant to be creative. But that is just a lie given to us by a culture that wants us to be passive consumers. So as we consent to the Spirit's action in our hearts, one of the possible futures we are consenting to is a future in which we will express divine love in a meaningful and creative way.

I'm not suggesting that in order to be a mystic one must become an artist, writer, or musician. Granted, creative expression will often involve the performing arts like music, dance, or theater; or the visual arts like drawing, painting, sculpture, or computer-generated imagery; or literary arts such as poetry, fiction, or playwriting. There are many other ways to embody creativity, and each of us must find our unique call. It may be to develop some other form of talent: in domestic arts like cooking, interior design, or scrapbooking; in crafts like carpentry or wood turning; or in mechanical or technical skills. Creativity might find expression through business, social work or nonprofit advocacy, politics or public service, or a healing profession. And divine creativity is larger than the need to earn money. The key to the spirituality of creation lies not so much in artistry-as-livelihood, but in the pure pursuit of creativity for its own sake. When you open yourself up to the delight that comes from creating for the sake of creating and no other purpose, you more readily participate in God's own felicity.

Your creative play does not have to be "religious" or "spiritual" in nature. A poem or painting or some other work need not be concerned with the resurrection or the ascension in order for its artistry to be anchored in contemplation. When we keep our creative efforts honest and grounded, they will not contradict the hope and love that comes from the heart of God—even if these themes are not explicit in our work.

The first book of the Bible, Genesis, not only reveals that creativity is essential to God, it also describes the fundamental link between creativity and contemplation. In the initial creation story, God manifests everything— the entire cosmos, the solar system, the earth, the ecosystems within the biosphere, eventually even the plants and animals and humankind itself— over the course of six "days." On the seventh day, God rested. In this divine rest, the Creator contemplated the fruits of this divine artistry. From this we see that creative effort and contemplative rest naturally complement one another. In fact, they complete each other. A work of art is not complete until the artist stands back from it, gazes upon it, and hopefully smiles in approval—just as God gazed upon the cosmos and "saw that it was good."

Likewise, contemplation is not "completed" until you rise from your repose, and, nourished and refreshed by the silence and the resting in

God's presence, are capable of responding to the universal call to bring new creativity—and healing, hope, and love—to the world. Contemplative spirituality does not limit itself to an impulse to endlessly gaze on the beauty of God with no regard for participating in that beauty by creating art, or justice, or wisdom, or love. Even those who retreated into desert solitude or monastic community found that a life shaped and seasoned by contemplation is a life meant to be given away—through love, service, peacemaking, activism, creativity, and care for family, friends, fellow members of a faith community, and the larger human family in all its need, hunger, and longing for God. Sharing our talents with others is, like resting in contemplative silence, a part of the overall process.

The spiritual path thus incorporates creativity, community, and contemplation in an integral mystical practice that includes seeking after, experiencing, and letting go of the presence of God, who is the object of our contemplation, the inspiration of our creativity, and the love that binds the members of our community together. And in this mysterious relationship between contemplation and creativity, we continually cross the threshold of unknowing, the doorway to the deepest mystery of mysticism: the mystery of theosis, of en-God-hood, of nondual recognition that "God and I are not-two."

Earlier on, I wrote about a monk who doesn't like the idea of the beatific vision, because it seems to make union with God sound like a spectator sport; instead, he sees the mystery of human destiny in God as the *beatifying communion*, in which we join in the very heart of the loving relationships within the Trinity. This holds true not just for eternity, but equally for the contemplative life here and now. We are called not only *to* contemplation, but even *beyond* contemplation. We are called to the deifying life precisely so that we can share the presence of God with others. We receive the gifts of God's love and presence so that we can pass those same gifts on to our neighbors—those we love as ourselves.

Guigo II described lectio divina as involving four steps: reading, meditation, prayer, and contemplation. But his is not the final word on the spiritual exercise. In his book *Conversing with God in Scripture*, Stephen J. Binz suggests that *contemplatio* leads beyond itself to additional practices, such as *operatio* ("faithful witness in daily life") and *collatio* (forming community). When we offer to God our capacity to create, we are given the opportunity to witness to God's love through our prayerful activity, which includes the opportunity to help establish truly loving community here on earth. In a very real way, then, the spiritual life brings us full circle: we begin by finding nurture in community and in the wisdom of those who have gone before us, and in that wisdom we discern the call to enter ever more deeply into the loving mystery of God through prayer and contemplation, only to find that our highest destiny as contemplatives is to give back to our community, by the operation of our creative skill—arising out of God's transforming and healing love.

THE EVER-EXPANDING JOURNEY INTO GOD

When she wrote about mysticism over a century ago, Evelyn Underhill exhibits a wise reticence when describing what she calls "the unitive life." She knew that her critics would pounce if she tried to recount her own experience of the summit of Christian mysticism, so she prudently played the role of a journalist reporting what others had said (or done) as evidence of where the mystical journey promises to take us. Her writing shows its age, as she uses gendered language for both God and humanity, and lacks terminology we might be more comfortable with (like nonduality), but her words are still worth pondering.

> The language of "deification" and of "spiritual marriage," then, is temperamental language: and is related to subjective experience rather than to objective fact. It describes on the one hand the mystic's astonished recognition of a profound change effected in his own personality—the transmutation of his salt, sulphur, and mercury into Spiritual Gold—and on the other, the rapturous consummation of his love. Hence, by a comparison of these symbolic reconstructions, and by the discovery and isolation of the common factor latent in each, we may perhaps learn something of the fundamental fact that each is trying to portray.[5]

Likewise, Robert Hughes accompanies his description of "waves of glory" —his name for the state of union—with a disclaimer acknowledging that it is a topic of which little can be said. "The witness of all those who have tasted it, however, is that it cannot really be spoken but only alluded to by analogies and art."[6]

Underhill and Hughes agree that the unitive, nondual life is characterized primarily by humility, which in this context can be defined as "self-forgetfulness." In other words, the truly divinized mystics are those who are the least likely to waste a lot of time recounting their experience.

It's not that mystics necessarily think their experience is unimportant. It's just that divine intimacy is, in the final analysis, a tender, precious, and delicate matter. This is a personal, and deeply secluded, dimension to the mystical life, as Jesus himself acknowledged: "Whenever you pray, go into your room and shut the door and pray to your Father who is in secret; and your Father who sees in secret will reward you" (Matthew 6:6). What begins as a closet where prayer is offered in secret becomes, entirely by the grace of God, the most beautiful and intimate marriage chamber, where you give yourself fully, completely, entirely to God.

We have come back to the erotic wonder of the Song of Songs—a theme that is picked up again and again by mystics and contemplatives throughout the history of Christian spirituality. The spiritual marriage that emerges from the heart of our intimacy with God is far more than just a cozy experience of love given and received. By the very nature of this contemplative encounter with God, the mystical marriage urges you to join in a joyful circle of love and generativity with God-as-relationship: the Creator, the Redeemer, and the Sustaining Spirit of Holy Love. We do not just imagine this circle of creative love, we are invited to embody it. This sacred embodiment is the root of Christian wisdom teachings concerning the body of Christ or the communion of saints. This is radically inclusive, radically egalitarian: this profound relationship is open to every human being who says yes in response to that call. The seeds of mystical love may be rooted in the privacy of intimate contemplation, but they blossom into the joyful ecstasy of a communion that lasts forever—with the God in three persons beginning, sustaining, and completing the dance.

THE DANCE BELONGS TO ALL OF US

In this fully blossomed mystical life, the ecstasies and pleasures of knowing God intimately and fully are, as best I can tell, simply a small element of the entire experience. The beauty and splendor of mystical intimacy in some ways must forever remain hidden, to be shared privately between a contemplative and God. But this beauty will also, in very real ways, spill endlessly over to others. Through the splendor of intimacy with God, mystics and contemplatives find wisdom to share with others. Through this beauty, we are called to serve those in need and care for those who suffer; we are inspired to work hard to dismantle systems of injustice and create a world shaped by a truly beloved community. The full weight of the glory of the Christian mysteries finds expression in the contemplative's creative work, in whatever form that might take. Out of the silence that is the natural habitat of mystical contemplation, God leads all who have given themselves to love to carry that love to others, even as they return again and again to the silence, for their own rest and renewal.

More than one contemporary contemplative writer has remarked that "the mystic is not a special kind of person; each person is a special kind of mystic." This means that every one of us is, to a greater or lesser extent, already a participant in the unitive life. Consider this last, delicious, nondual paradox: mysticism is a gift lavishly given to anyone, even those who have never bothered to seek a holy life, who have never made a disciplined effort to pray or meditate, or who have not shown any particular interest in pursuing any kind of spiritual practice or relationship with God. If God can give amazing mystical experiences to anyone, who are we to say that God cannot give some sort of mystical life to everyone?

It's important to pair "each person is a special kind of mystic" with Karl Rahner's statement that "the Christian of the future will be a mystic or will not exist." With these ideas in mind, we need to let go of any idea that some Christians get to be mystics while others do not; that only certain contemplatives receive union with God while others never do; that only the worthy few become deified or get to enjoy the nondual unitive life. Both the wisdom teachings of Jesus and the wisdom of the mystics point to a unifying spiritual reality beyond such limited thinking. All who seek to be the lovers of God, to some extent and on some level, are "partakers of the divine nature." Just as it is a puzzle why some people are more musically or athletically talented than others, it is a mystery how some may enjoy the awareness of union with God, or the conscious presence of God, more fully or abundantly than others. But this is a difference of degree, not of kind. I rather suspect that anyone who feels like they have never had any kind of mystical or profound spiritual experience at all may simply have never learned how to recognize the powerful, but hidden and subtle, action of the Spirit in their lives.

We know enough about the reality of the unconscious and subconscious dimensions of the human mind to recognize that God, in God's limitless sovereignty, can easily pour divine love and gifts into us on a deeper-than-conscious level. Perhaps if we want to learn about the mystery of theosis—the mystery of the unitive life or, for that matter, any aspect of the divine mystery and its place in our hearts—we primarily need to inquire within.

As contemplatives, we can turn to the great mystics of history for guidance and inspiration: Julian of Norwich, Meister Eckhart, Howard Thurman, John Ruusbroec, Evelyn Underhill, Simone Weil, Teresa of Ávila, John of the Cross, and so many others. And whether or not we can ever articulate our experience of the mystery as lyrically as these giants of the spiritual life, we can learn from and appreciate the treasury of wisdom they have handed to us. Through silence, prayer, and contemplative practice, we can allow their living wisdom to shape us, form us, and nurture our temperament for the ultimate contemplative task: falling, and staying, in love with God. It lets us open our hearts to receive the vast and limitless love given to us—luscious love that the Spirit eagerly pours into us, love that will fill us up and overflow from us to a world that so desperately needs it, love that will transfigure our values, revolutionize our ethics, and recalibrate our sense of right and wrong so that we reorient our entire lives to the expression of grace and joy in ways both large and small.

THE END (AND THE BEGINNING)

There is a point in the Catholic Mass when the priest pours water into the wine that will be consecrated as the blood of Christ. As he pours that water, he is instructed to quietly say this blessing, "By the mystery of this water and wine may we come to share in the divinity of Christ, who humbled himself to share in our humanity."[7] Because these words are inaudibly spoken, they are *hidden* from the average person participating in the Mass. But in these hidden words lie the heart of the Christian mystery. Christ, who is one with God, comes to us and shares divinity with us.

Psalm 82 contains this rather explosive verse: "You are gods, children of the Most High, all of you."[8] We live in an age where plenty of people are inspired to say "I am one with God," but it seems that such statements can be tossed off in such a glib and cavalier way that we may have difficulty recognizing just how awe-inspiring these words really are.

As a religion, Christianity insists that God is transcendent: greater than all things, larger than the cosmos, infinitely beyond what the human mind and heart can grasp. Mystical wisdom does not deny this teaching, but the mystics would say it is incomplete. By stressing only God's otherwise and remoteness, religion has too often transmitted another, less helpful message: that God is God, and we are not. Christian mystics, by contrast, merrily aim to deconstruct the dualistic walls that separate the immanence of God from the divine transcendence. Of all the paradoxes that mysticism helps to bring together, this may be the most important of all. God is greater than the universe, and God is present, right here and right now, in you and me. We are partakers of the divine nature, temples of the Spirit. God will always remain as different from us as the ocean is different from a single drop of water, and yet that water *is* the ocean in minute form.

How can we sort this out and make it relevant to our daily lives? The answer is encoded in Psalm 82, where we are called "the children of the Most High." And Jesus said it even better, "Unless you change and become like children, you will never enter the kingdom of heaven."[9] In the English language this teaching might be more powerful if we reframe it as a positive: to enter heaven, consent to the transformation that will manifest as a divine child within you.

If, in fact, the mystical life can be likened to a sacred, spiritual marriage between your soul and God, it is fitting that a child be born out of that union of love. This heavenly love child is born inside of you and is, in fact, a part of you—the part who knows that you are a "god" and a child of the Most High, a child who, by knowing this, resides already in the unspeakable glories of heaven, right here, right now.

Christian mysticism is, ultimately, simply the art of going to heaven before you die—or, perhaps better said, the art of letting heaven emerge within you now. This doesn't magically eliminate our sins, or our pain and suffering, or our woundedness. Nor does it take away the brokenness of the world in which we dwell, and will continue to live on this side of eternity.

But it does transform all these things, and it does enable us to respond to the pain and suffering and brokenness we encounter in the light of eternity and with the luminosity of paradise within. Our mystical divine union empowers us to make God-infused choices and responses to all that life throws our way—and to do it all with an unself-conscious freedom that characterizes every reasonably well-adjusted child. To be fully aware that you partake of the divine nature, to accept that simply and naturally, and to calibrate your life accordingly—this, perhaps, is what you and I and everyone can hope to find at the culmination of the contemplative journey.

And of course, the end simply unfolds into ever-new beginnings.

"KEEP YOUR EYES OPEN"

Since we can more readily access heaven within by becoming like children, it seems appropriate to finish this chapter with words of advice offered to kids. From C. S. Lewis's Narnia books, here's what a wise old professor had to say to four youngsters who, having visited the wondrous and mystical land of Narnia, wonder if they'll ever return.

> Yes, of course you'll get back to Narnia again some day. . . . But don't go trying to use the same route twice. Indeed, don't try to get there at all. It'll happen when you're not looking for it. And don't talk too much about it even among yourselves. And don't mention it to anyone else unless you find that they've had adventures of the same sort themselves. What's that? How will you know? Oh, you'll know all right. Odd things, they say—even their looks—will let the secret out. Keep your eyes open.[10]

May we all remain open-eyed with wonder, trust, and love.

CHAPTER TWENTY-TWO

Living a Mystical Life

Every now and then someone will ask me, "How do I become a mystic?" It's a great question. Just as I don't have a snappy soundbite definition of mysticism, likewise there is no handy, tried-and-true formula for becoming the mystic you have always wanted to be. But it's still worth reflecting on as we bring our exploration of mystical Christianity to a close.

I'll make a confession: sometimes I'm tempted to reply to that question with a witty one-liner, like, "It's God's decision whether or not you become a mystic, so your job is to seek the will of God" or perhaps, "Remember, every person is a special kind of mystic, so you already are one, now your job is to figure out your unique mystical identity." But while such mildly snarky comments may be true in a basic literal sense, they are too simplistic to allow for the rich paradox and nuance that accompanies any serious exploration of the contemplative life.

For yes, you already are a mystic, just like we all are. And yes, it is up to God to form in your heart a unique expression of mystical awareness or contemplative living. Meanwhile, just like every child is born with potential talents—say, for athletics or making music—but must nurture those potentials in order to turn their aptitude into skill, so we who are mystics by grace must show up in terms of making choices and commitments to truly embody the contemplative life, right here in our own minds and hearts, bodies and souls. Just because you've been given a gift doesn't mean you are going to unwrap the present and put it to use in your life. God will respect your freedom, and never force the heart-transforming, mind-expanding joy of mystical spirituality onto you, without your consent and cooperation.

So we can rephrase our question: How do I consent to God's action in my heart? How do I cooperate with the Spirit's slow work in my life, to transform me into the radiant incarnation of divine love that each of us can potentially become? In other words, how do I become a mystic?

My (more serious and respectful) answer to this question is inspired by the teachings surrounding the practice of Centering Prayer. Thomas Keating and others who developed the spiritual practice of Centering Prayer would often emphasize that Centering Prayer, in itself, is not necessarily the same thing as contemplative prayer, but rather it is a method of *preparation* for the God-given gift of contemplation.

So, once again, let's rephrase our question: How do I prepare myself for the gift of a mystical life? Trusting, of course, that God wants each of us to embody contemplative and mystical spirituality in the manner that is best for us as individuals. In other words, not everyone becomes a visionary like Julian of Norwich, or an ecstatic like Teresa of Ávila, or a prophetic voice for social justice like Howard Thurman, or a gifted theologian like Meister Eckhart, or a great poet like John of the Cross, or a respected philosopher like Simone Weil. Every mystic is unique, and just like we each have a one-of-a-kind DNA pattern, so everyone who responds to divine love and the call to union with God will experience and express that call and response in a unique, one of a kind way.

Your job is to become the perfect expression of God's love that *you* can become. You are a one-of-a-kind artistic masterpiece. And to become that unique expression of divine love, you (like all of us) begin by consenting to God's presence and action in your life, in your heart, in your mind and body.

How do we express this consent in real, concrete ways? Traditionally, the means by which mystics have lived a mystical or contemplative life has been through regular spiritual practices. And while different mystics have focused on or emphasized different practices, all in all there are just a few basic ways of responding to the mystical call. Most of these practices we have already touched on over the course of this book; in this final chapter I'd like to summarize the practices of contemplative spirituality and create a basic list that hopefully can inspire you to form your unique *rule of life*—in other words, your unique game-plan for nurturing a contemplative spirituality in your day-to-day life.

No one needs to do (or even try) all of these practices in order to cultivate a mystical spirituality. But in Christian terms, it's safe to say that anyone seriously intentional about fostering a contemplative or mystical practice needs to consider making at least some of the following practices a regular, ongoing part of your spiritual life.

TWENTY ESSENTIAL MYSTICAL PRAYER PRACTICES

Lectio Divina. Feasting on the word of God as found in Scripture, not only as a way to more fully be immersed in the story of Christian faith and practice, but as a doorway to deeper prayer, meditation, and contemplation.

The Daily Office. We perform ordinary routine tasks every day simply to care for our home and family, from personal hygiene to washing the dishes to walking the dog. Does our intimacy with the mystery we call God deserve anything less? Whether it's twice a day, seven times a day, or some other regular rhythm, contemplative spirituality is nurtured by fixed daily prayer.

Participation in the sacraments. Most Christians recognize that baptism and communion are essential elements of the Christian life. Some churches consider other rites, including marriage, confession of sins, and anointing for those who need healing, also as sacramental expressions of God's grace. The sacraments bring spirituality down to earth, and remind us that God can meet us in the ordinary stuff of life, like water, bread, wine and oil. Different forms of Christianity have different understandings of the role of sacraments; for example, the Religious Society of Friends (the Quakers), a deeply contemplative expression of Christianity, does not observe sacramental rituals like baptism or the Eucharist; to Quakers, all of life is sacramental, so there is no need for special sacramental rites. The common thread seems to be a way of acknowledging the divine presence in the ordinary stuff of life—whether through sacramental rites, or through a broader appreciation of the Spirit's indwelling in matter.

Disciplines of renunciation. Our culture operates under the unstated assumption that "if it feels good, do it"—but spirituality thrives when we also embrace appropriate forms of renunciation or self-denial. We fast to remind ourselves of our deep hunger for the love of God. We embrace simplicity or abstinence (like forgoing meat on Fridays) not because such practices are necessary to win God's approval, but because they can be expressions of our solidarity with Christ's suffering—and our desire to calibrate our lives to love and service rather than simply to personal comfort.

Generosity and giving. The apostle Paul wryly commented that "God loves a cheerful giver"[1]—and while many people struggle with the fact that the church, like any nonprofit organization, seems to be always fund-raising, there's a solid spiritual truth in that generosity can breed both happiness and holiness. When we find it in our heart joyfully to share our resources with those who are in need, it fosters our capacity to orient our lives toward trust in God rather than grasping of our resources.

"The gift of tears." Lament and sorrow is a core part of being human, even if it's not something we particularly relish. Jesus said that those who mourn are blessed, "for they shall be comforted." We mourn for many reasons: we lose someone we love, we experience some other form of loss or setback, or we may face difficult truths about ourselves, including acknowledging our own brokenness and sinfulness. Classical theological terms for this process include *compunction* (feeling the pang of remorse) and *contrition* (feeling sorrow for our wrongdoing). Sometimes compunction and contrition can also bring us to tears. Not all tears are related to sorrow, of course: we may shed tears of happiness or joy as we consider the depths of God's love for us. Although tears are not something most of us can produce at will, being open to life's sorrows (and the humility of acknowledging our own limitations) can be a meaningful doorway into a closer sense of intimacy with God.

The rosary. This method of prayer involving the repetitive recitation of memorized prayers like the Our Father and the Hail Mary, paired with meditative reflection on key events from the lives of Jesus and Mary, is associated especially with Catholicism but can be blessing for all types of Christians. Like lectio divina, the rosary combines prayer and meditation and can foster a contemplative silence in the hearts of those who pray it.

The Jesus Prayer. As the rosary is associated with Catholicism, so the Jesus Prayer—also known as the Prayer of the Heart—is associated with Eastern Orthodoxy, but again, it is a prayer practice available to all. Reciting the name of Jesus, or a brief prayer like "Lord Jesus Christ, son of God, have mercy on me" in such a way as to focus our attentiveness on the love in our hearts rather than the chatter in our minds, can be a rich way of preparing for the grace of contemplation.

Conversational prayer. One could say this is the Protestant equivalent to the rosary or the Jesus Prayer, but again, it's for everyone. This is the way of prayer that entails simply sharing what's on our mind with God in an unscripted, candid, verbal way. Such prayer can include giving thanks for our blessings, confessing our sins, expressing adoration and love for God, and praying for the needs of others (intercession) or ourselves (petition). Regular conversational prayer not only can help us feel God's intimate presence, but it can foster our own sense of humility and dependence on God as our provider and caretaker.

Mental (mind-in-heart) prayer. I learned this phrase "mind-in-heart" from the contemplative teacher Tilden Edwards; it also has roots in Orthodox spirituality. It's a simple recognition that sustained prayer ultimately is a matter of the heart as much as the head. While practices like the rosary, the Jesus Prayer or Centering Prayer can help us to foster a more heart-centered prayer, even in the Daily Office or conversational prayer we can be intentional about letting our "mind" (awareness) sink into our "heart" (our capacity to love). The *Catholic Catechism* describes contemplation as "wordless adoration"—in other words, prayer from the heart, shaped by love, where words become unnecessary.

Imaginative prayer. Today this way of praying is especially associated with the spirituality of St. Ignatius of Loyola, founder of the Jesuits and the creator of the Spiritual Exercises. But Ignatius is not the only Christian teacher to promote this way of praying (a Cistercian monk from the twelfth century, Aelred of Rievaulx, also advocated using the imagination in prayer). At its simplest, imaginative prayer is simply allowing your imagination to carry you, in your mind's eye, into the presence of God and Christ, and in that divine presence, to imaginative interact. This visualization prayer can be deeply moving, surprisingly insightful, and a rich way to grow closer to the God of love.

Ora et labora. There are other ways to pray than simply by reciting words, fostering inner silence, or cultivating an imaginative encounter with God. From the earliest centuries of the Christian era, it has been understood that labor—the work of our hands—can itself be a way of praying. When we dedicate our physical labor to expressing our love for our family, community, or those in need, we are fostering a humble act of making our spiritual yearning concrete in the service we offer to others.

"Whatsoever you do to the least of these." In Matthew 25, Jesus makes it clear that serving others, especially those who are sick, hungry, imprisoned, or otherwise in need, can be an essential way of expressing worship and adoration toward him. "What you do to the least of these, you do to me." When we care for others, we care for Christ. When we serve others, we serve Christ. When we relate to others out of compassion rather than competition, we are cultivating our love for Christ. Once again, for Christians mystical union is not some pie-in-the-sky, but a down-to-earth expression of love, given away to our human neighbors.

Practicing mercy and forgiveness. Jesus prayed "forgive us our sins, as we forgive those who sin against us." The archaic word *trespasses* found in the most common version of the Lord's Prayer still means "sins"—so forgiveness is truly a central element of the Christian spiritual life, whether forgiveness received or given. A life calibrated toward forgiveness and mercy is a life built on kindness and compassion to others. It's not about "anything goes"—we can and should set healthy boundaries in our lives—but it is an important recognition that union with Christ necessarily involves becoming the same kind of merciful, compassionate, forgiving figure that Christ himself is. We can only do this by grace, but the Christian faith assures us that such grace is always available to those who sincerely seek to orient their lives to divine love.

Keeping a spiritual journal. You don't have to be a writer or a poet to be a mystic, but keeping a personal journal (even if just for your eyes only) can be a meaningful and rich way to grow spiritually. Your journal can be a record of your prayer, your meditation, your experience of God. In it you can document your heart's deepest longings and your sense of how God answers your petitions. Just as keeping a diary in a secular sense can be a meaningful way to cultivate meaning in your life, so keeping a spiritual journal can be a profound way to understand and reflect on your relationship with God.

Silence as prayer. Many of the practices we have already considered include silence, but arguably fostering some sort of specifically silent practice is the single most important way of cultivating a contemplative heart.

Centering Prayer, Christian meditation, adoration of the blessed sacrament, and even walking a labyrinth or examples of ways to consciously integrate prayerful silence into your spiritual life. As Thomas Keating pointed out, "Silence is God's first language."[2] Making time to enter into silence-as-prayer is learning that language of the heart for yourself.

Acquired contemplation. This rather technical theological term refers to practices in which we seek, on a natural level (although aided by divine grace) to foster contemplation in our own hearts. Such natural contemplation is "acquired" through our God-assisted efforts. Practices such as intentional silence, heart-centered adoration, and serving others can all be ways to foster that contemplative spirit within us. Remember the Catechism definition of contemplation: wordless adoration. Bring silence and love together in your heart, and you are opening yourself to the grace of acquired contemplation. This is something we can all choose to do, and (by God's grace) make that intention a regular part of our daily spiritual practice.

Infused contemplation. If acquired contemplation is natural and intentional, infused contemplation takes us beyond the frontier where our human capacity for control falls away. This is the kind of contemplation that is always a gift: God's graced way of ushering us more deeply into the blessings of divine union as experienced through wordless adoration (or even through more supernatural experiences, like ecstasy or rapture, although such extraordinary phenomena are rare). We do not set out to achieve infused contemplation, for it is always God's gift, beyond our control. But we can pair our efforts to foster acquired contemplation with a radical, humble openness to receive whatever grace God may seek to give us—even the grace of non-dual experiential union with God. Our "practice" in regard to infused contemplation is a practice of willing readiness to receive, and trusting God to give us whatever experience we need, no matter how dramatic, ordinary, or humble.

Making a retreat. Most of the practices in this list lend themselves to a daily rule of life: a daily commitment to prayer, meditation, and contemplation for the purpose of growing closer to God and more fully expressing the fruits of divine union. But to support that kind of daily discipline, contemplatives over the centuries have discovered the beauty and power of making a retreat—several days or even a week or more removed from the normal duties of everyday life, where we can more fully immerse ourselves in an intensive experience of prayer, worship, silence, and reflection. Monasteries and retreat centers provide hospitality for those seeking to make a retreat, and spiritual directors and retreat leaders can guide retreatants in making the best use of their time while on retreat, in order to draw closer to God.

Receiving spiritual direction. Finally, I would strongly encourage anyone who is serious about a sustained, daily practice of meditative, contemplative or silent prayer to seek the caring companionship of a spiritual director—who, despite the name, will not "direct" you so much as *accompany* you as you seek to grow in your response to divine love. Spiritual directors are typically people who are themselves experienced in prayer and usually have received training in the skills necessary for effective spiritual guidance and companionship. The spiritual life can sometimes lead us down blind alleys of egotism, scrupulosity, false humility, and other spiritual detours. A caring companion in the life of prayer can affirm us as we grow, and gently challenge us to avoid the pitfalls along the way.

In the Middle Ages, monks would invoke the Virgin Mary and her role as the mother of Christ, to suggest that all Christians—regardless of your gender, your age, your station of life—are called to "give birth" to Christ in our hearts and in our lives. God wants to "impregnate" us with the spirit of Christ, just as surely as Mary was impregnated with Jesus so many centuries ago. While this is obviously a spiritual, rather than physical, gestation, it is no less real. We are asked to bring Christ into the world, not through a physical pregnancy and maternity, but through a spiritual commitment formed by prayer and meditation and intimacy with God, where we commit to the same measure of intimacy and union that exists between a pregnant mother and the child within her. Mary's motherhood of Christ is a paradox: How could she be the mother of the one who ultimately created her (and all things)? Yet this paradox is spiritually available to all of us. The Creator of the entire universe is willing to take up residence in the tiny chambers of our hearts, if we simply are willing to host such a divine guest. Of course, making room for God in your heart will completely transform your life, your personality, your moral compass, your capacity for compassion and caring and joy. Sounds risky, but oh, what a risk worth taking! And these twenty practices are the "nutrients" we can draw on to nourish the life of the divine baby within us.

There is so much more to say about mystical Christianity and the contemplative life. But sooner or later, words get in the way. You do not need me or this book to usher you into the mystical life. All you need is to open your heart to the Spirit who loves you and wishes to guide you.

Blessings to you on your journey.

Appendix A:
The Communion of Mystics

It has been said that religion—and, by extension, spirituality—is not meant to be a museum. In other words, the purpose behind following Christ, or the Buddha, or any major wisdom teacher, is not just to become immersed in the lives and teachings of spiritual masters from the past. Rather, the point behind mystical Christianity—like any mystical tradition—is to encounter the transforming insight, wisdom, and grace of God in the present moment, here and now, in our own lives. In other words, mysticism is not a spectator sport. The mystical life is meant to be lived from the heart, in a real way that makes a real difference in real people's lives.

The other side of this is that whenever we try to learn something new, it is a normal human strategy to seek out the wisdom, counsel, and instructions of someone who has already mastered whatever it is we seek to learn. If you want to become a plumber, you apprentice yourself to a knowledgeable plumber. To learn a musical instrument, you find a teacher who can guide you as you strive to understand music in general but also the specific tricks to playing your chosen instrument well.

Mystical spirituality is no different. When we study the teachings of the mystics, the methods of contemplative exercises like lectio divina or Centering Prayer, and apply these insights to our own spiritual practice, we can benefit from the wisdom of the great mystics who have gone before. In theory, mystics can learn everything they need to know directly from the Holy Spirit in their hearts. But why wouldn't the Spirit also direct us to learn from the wisdom of the mystics of the past who have left teachings to guide us along the way? It is for this reason that one of the joys of exploring mystical spirituality is getting to know the words and wisdom of the great mystics—not only of Christianity, but of all the world's wisdom traditions.

Since this is a book specifically about Christian mysticism, we'll keep our eyes on the riches of mystical Christianity. From the time of Jesus to the present day, every century—I suppose you could say every generation—has given to the church and to the world the voices of contemplatives and mystics who share their wisdom and experience of union with God through their poetry, theology, philosophy, memoir and spiritual writings. Not every mystic is a writer, of course, but those mystics who did commit their insights into written form have bequeathed a priceless gift to every succeeding generation. When you and I sit down to read the words of Meister Eckhart, Julian of Norwich, Teresa of Ávila, or Howard Thurman, the years melt away and these great spiritual masters, no longer present on earth in the flesh, nevertheless touch our hearts with their words of insight and encouragement. To pick up a book of mystical writings is to gain access to the teaching ministry of a skilled person of prayer.

But before I paint too rosy a picture, let me also hasten to point out that it can be challenging to read the writings of the mystics. Many of them, living decades or centuries or even millennia ago, held theological or philosophical values that can seem very much at odds with the best spiritual wisdom of our time. Mystics of ancient times lacked the social, psychological, or organizational insights that most people today take for granted. Many of the mystics were dualistic (seeing spirit as good but "the world" as corrupt or evil), patriarchal and sexist, and exhibited other problematic qualities such as racism, homophobia, anti-Semitism, and Islamophobia. Finally, many mystics regarded the structure of institutional Christianity as above questioning, and submitted themselves to church authorities in a way that many of us today would find deeply questionable.

So reading the mystics is not always an easy task. It requires an ability to sort through the cultural baggage of previous centuries, while discerning the wisdom that is truly timeless and eternal, that can speak to every generation including our own. For this reason, you might find that you'd like to begin your exploration of mystical writings with voices from the present day or the recent past—for example, Thomas Merton, Cynthia Bourgeault, Evelyn Underhill, and Howard Thurman are more accessible to beginning contemplatives than the often difficult writings of ancient figures like John of the Cross, John Ruusbroec, Meister Eckhart, or Hildegard of Bingen. Some people find they prefer reading "curated" or edited anthologies of mystical writings, where an editor or team of editors have selected specific passages, often organized around specific themes or for devotional use, and sometimes published with commentary or annotations that make reading the old texts easier.

Another approach is to enjoy writings *about* the mystics, instead of or in addition to the ancient writings themselves. Take, for example, a charming book recently published called *The Mystics Who Came to Dinner* by Carmel Bendon. It's a novel about a woman who hosts a dinner party where six mystics from the past time travel to the present day and join the evening's fun. It's a fantasy, of course, but woven into this accessible and whimsical tale is plenty of helpful insight into the teachings of the mystics. Especially for the most well-known mystics, many books *about* the mystics are available, and often function as the best way to get to know their wisdom. Other novels that explore the lives and wisdom of the mystics include *Revelations* by Mary Sharratt, *Lady at the Window* by Robert Waldron, and *Sister Teresa* by Bárbara Mujica.

Meanwhile, who *are* the mystics? Who are the great exemplars of the contemplative life?

To answer this question, let me refer you to the two companion volumes to this book: *Christian Mystics: 108 Seers, Saints and Sages* and *The Little Book of Christian Mysticism.* Just as *The New Big Book of Christian Mysticism* seeks to answer the question, "What is Christian mysticism?" *Christian Mystics* explores "Who are the mystics?" and *The Little Book of Christian Mysticism* offers the wisdom of the mystics in their own words. Few of the mystics are particularly well known in a popular sense—I doubt if we are going to see major motion pictures about Ramon Panikkar or Hadewijch of Antwerp anytime soon. Some, who have been declared saints by the Catholic Church, have the kind of visibility that their canonization provided them. Francis of Assisi, Thomas Aquinas, and Augustine of Hippo are famous (or infamous) as Catholic saints, but one would need to be familiar with their life stories to realize they are renowned as mystics as well.

To become a saint, one must be officially recognized as such by the Vatican; but there is no similar vetting process for identifying who the great mystics are. Mystics do, however, have a habit of writing about each other, so we can find the mystics through the words of other mystics (or scholars of mysticism). Evelyn Underhill provided in-depth survey of the greatest mystics at the end of her book *Mysticism;* several years later she published a history of the topic, *Mystics of the Church.* Thomas Merton's *An Introduction to Christian Mysticism* (later reissued in an abridged edition called *A Course in Christian Mysticism*) also provided a rich introduction to the contemplative tradition. Meanwhile, scholars of mysticism and spirituality have issued several useful anthologies of mystical writings (see Bernard McGinn's *The Essential Writings of Christian Mysticism*, Harvey D. Egan's *An Anthology of Christian Mysticism*, and Louis Dupré's and James Wiseman's *Light from Light: An Anthology of Christian Mysticism*). One of the best ways to get to know the mystics is to read a history of the topic. Here, the essential resource is Bernard McGinn's nine-volume opus *The Presence of God: A History of Western Christian Mysticism.* If you want to begin with something a little less ambitious, try Harvey Egan's *Soundings in the Christian Mystical Tradition*, Ursula King's *Christian Mystics: Their Lives and Legacies Throughout the Ages*, and John MacQuarrie's *Two Worlds Are Ours: An Introduction to Christian Mysticism.*

Finally, if you find the writings of a particular mystic challenging, consider reading a book of commentary or devotional reflection about that mystic's teachings. Some excellent examples of this genre include Lerita Coleman Brown's *What Makes You Come Alive* (about Howard Thurman), Sophfronia Scott's *The Seeker and the Monk* (Thomas Merton), or Claudia Mair Burney's *God Alone is Enough* (Teresa of Ávila).

I get asked all the time who my favorite mystics are. Evelyn Underhill made no secret that her favorite mystic was the obscure Flemish theologian John Ruusbroec. If I could only read one mystic for the rest of my earthly life, it would probably be Julian of Norwich, whose optimism, lyrical writing, and clear-eyed theology of love I find simply compelling. And I would agree with Underhill that Ruusbroec is one of the greats; he is probably the most underrated of all the major contemplatives—his writing shows a clear sense of nondual consciousness that represents the ultimate flowering of the mystical life. But let me go ahead and round out a list of a dozen figures; this list simply represents the mystics whose writing I keep returning to, again and again. Such a list can never be considered complete, and anyone who studies the mystics for very long will be unhappy that this or that figure didn't make the cut. So think of this list not as a final word about the greatest mystics, but merely a snapshot of the mystics I especially love as I'm writing these words (in 2022). A decade from now, my list may look different. So see this is a starting point. If you want to spend just a few months or the rest of your life studying the wisdom of the Christian mystics, I encourage you to place these twelve writers near the top of your reading list:

- Meister Eckhart (1260–1328)
- John Ruusbroec (1293–1381)
- Anonymous author of *The Cloud of Unknowing* (late fourteenth century)
- Julian of Norwich (1342–1416)
- Teresa of Ávila (1515–1582)
- John of the Cross (1542–1591)
- Evelyn Underhill (1875–1941)
- Caryll Houselander (1901–1954)
- Thomas Merton (1915–1968)
- Howard Thurman (1899–1981)
- John O'Donohue (1956–2008)
- Kenneth Leech (1939–2015)

I am conscious, and frankly rather embarrassed, by how predominantly white/male this list is. That is very much an indictment of my own limitations. But it's also the legacy of how mysticism, as a category of spirituality, has roots in medieval patriarchal European culture and therefore many of the better known historic exemplars of mysticism were white, and male. Women who expressed their mystical spirituality in medieval Europe were truly courageous; for they lived in a time when women had no official voice in the church, and at least one woman mystic (Marguerite Porete) was killed because her spirituality did not meet with the approval of the (male) religious establishment. So while there are fewer historical women mystics than male mystics, the women mystics who did write down their wisdom and stories deserve to be seen as spiritual foremothers of feminism.

It's important in our time to celebrate contemplatives and mystics who are Black, Indigenous, and other persons of color (BIPOC). Alongside Howard Thurman, other non-white mystics include Anthony De Mello, Raimon Panikkar, and Desmond Tutu. Historically, it's important to keep in mind that many of the desert mothers and fathers, and for that matter Augustine of Hippo, were African — indicating that the origins of Christian mysticism took place outside of white European culture. Students of contemplative and mystical spirituality also may wish to take a closer look at BIPOC persons who may not be "known" as mystics but who nevertheless expressed a meaningful, experiential faith which informed their spiritual practice and social activism. In this category we could include persons like Martin Luther King Jr., Thea Bowman, Harriet Tubman, Sojourner Truth, Cyprian Michael Iwene Tansi, Black Elk, Pauli Murray, Watchman Nee, and many others. As Christians and others of goodwill seek to dismantle systems of racism and privilege in our society, it's important that we recognize and amplify the often hidden voices of mystics and contemplatives who did not "fit in" with the expectations of Eurocentric white Christianity. Scholars and theologians like Barbara Holmes, Joy Bostic, Therese Taylor-Stinson and Lerita Coleman Brown are doing vital and important work celebrating contemplatives and mystics of color, both of the past and the present.

Mystical spirituality belongs to everyone, not just college-educated people of European descent. I hope and trust that in the years to come more mystical voices from around the world will become better known to all people, and I look forward to discovering such wisdom for myself.

Appendix B:
A Contemplative Reading List

One does not need to read a lot of books to explore the mysteries. Nevertheless, the wisdom of the great mystics—and people who have studied them and written insightful commentaries on their words—can help anyone who seeks to more fully respond to divine love. The Christian tradition has been blessed with numerous contemplatives and mystics who have documented their experiences and their life stories, and left advice and direction for those of us who follow in their footsteps.

This reading list is meant only to get you started on your own journey of contemplative reading. It's divided into several sections: anthologies of great mystical writings, contemplative classics from the great mystics of the past, insightful instructions from living contemplative teachers, and helpful commentaries and academic studies of mystical spirituality. This is very much a subjective list—it features authors and works that I myself have found useful or inspiring.

In each category the books are presented alphabetically by author, which means I'm not offering any particular order for reading these titles. Follow your own intuition. If you are drawn to a particular book, trust your hunch and read that one first. If you want even more ideas on books that may be of help to you as you continue your exploration of Christian mysticism, please consult my bibliography.

I encourage you to approach these books, like all mystical and contemplative writing, in the spirit of lectio divina. Read them slowly and with an open heart, not only savoring the wisdom they contain, but also taking time to ponder the often challenging or paradoxical insights they give into the nature of God and the dynamics of the spiritual life. Naturally, there is more to being a contemplative than learning how to read meditatively. But as you embrace the prayerful rhythm of lectio divina, your journey into the world of mystical wisdom will be so much the richer for it.

This list is hardly exhaustive, and probably anyone with more than a passing knowledge of Christian mysticism and spirituality will be able to list plenty of worthy books I did not include. My purpose is simply to whet your appetite. There are enough interesting and provocative writings by the great mystics—and about their wisdom—to fill a lifetime of study. Even in this relatively short list, you will find many different styles of writing and approaches to mysticism. Some are academic; some are informal; some emphasize the experiential side of mysticism; some focus on the values and teachings that undergird such experience. Only by exploring the literature for yourself can you discern which authors and writings speak most richly to you. Take the time to explore. One final (but important) note: as good as it is to read about prayer, it is even better to set aside whatever book you're reading—and give God your undivided attention.

THE ONE ESSENTIAL BOOK FOR EXPLORING CHRISTIAN MYSTICISM

- **The Holy Bible.** Not only is the Bible the text *par excellence* for lectio divina, it is also the single most important document for Christian mysticism. Reading the Bible can be challenging in our time, particularly because of its images of God as angry or vengeful, or the passages on gender and sexuality that come across as patriarchal, misogynistic, or homophobic. But for those who are willing to wrestle with the text, the Bible contains luminous passages of mystical insight. Start with the Gospel of John, then move on to Ephesians, Colossians, Philippians, the First Letter of John, the Psalms, and the Song of Songs. And don't stop there; shimmering glimpses of mystical insight can be found throughout this essential book. For the purposes of both study and devotional reading, I recommend you avoid historical Bibles like the King James and the Douay-Rheims versions; newer translations are easier to read and generally more accurate. The New Jerusalem

Bible and the New Revised Standard Version are both excellent, respected translations, worthy for both Bible study and for use in lectio. If you're looking for a helpful edition of the Bible that can be particularly useful for contemplatives, consider *The Life with God Bible* from Renovaré, or the *Saints Devotional Bible* (especially the New Jerusalem version).

<h2 style="text-align:center">ANTHOLOGIES OF MYSTICAL AND
CONTEMPLATIVE WRITING</h2>

- **Karen Armstrong (editor), *Visions of God: Four Medieval Mystics and Their Writings.*** Since it only features the writings of four mystics, all from the same century and country—Richard Rolle, Julian of Norwich, Walter Hilton, and the author of *The Cloud of Unknowing*—this seems to be quite a limited compilation. But it's a great read not only because of Armstrong's helpful commentary and the excellent translation of the source writings, but also because it's a great case study of how diverse the voices of the different mystics really are. Seeing firsthand the distinctions between these four mystics is a good way to begin to appreciate how different *all* the mystics are.
- **Carmen Acevedo Butcher (editor), *A Little Daily Wisdom: Christian Women Mystics.*** Although best known for her luminous translations of contemplative classics, Butcher here provides a devotional anthology of 366 writings, all from female mystics like Julian of Norwich or Teresa of Ávila, arranged for daily prayer and reflection.
- **Louis Dupré and James A. Wiseman, OSB (editors), *Light from Light: An Anthology of Christian Mysticism*.** After an informative introductory essay, this chronological collection features lengthy selections of writings from over twenty mystics, from Origen in the second century to Merton in the twentieth.
- **Harvey Egan (editor), *An Anthology of Christian Mysticism.*** Like *Light from Light*, another survey of the writings of over fifty great mystics in chronological, rather than topical, order—an

in-depth anthology that allows the reader to get a feel for how mystical literature has evolved over the past two thousand years.

- **Nikodimos of the Holy Mountain and Makarios of Corinth (compilers), *The Philokalia.*** This multivolume anthology of writings from contemplatives of the Eastern Orthodox churches provides detailed instructions on asceticism and the life of prayer, particularly the Prayer of the Heart. Among the great mystics whose writings are included in *The Philokalia* are John Cassian, Evagrius Ponticus, Maximus the Confessor, and Gregory Palamas. A one-volume anthology, *Writings from the Philokalia on the Prayer of the Heart*, features the writings that were mentioned in the anonymous Russian classic *The Way of a Pilgrim*.

- **Shawn Madigan, CSJ (editor), *Mystics, Visionaries, and Prophets: A Historical Anthology of Women's Spiritual Writings.*** As the title implies, this is a broader anthology of spiritual writing that includes not only mystical/contemplative women, but also significant women theologians and activists. Still, plenty of mystics are included, and this collection invites us to consider the important relationship between mystical spirituality and faith-based activism for a better and more just world.

- **Carl McColman (compiler), *The Little Book of Christian Mysticism.*** Over three hundred quotations from the Bible and the great mystics, arranged according to the process of purification, illumination, and deification, and selected for devotional use.

- **Bernard McGinn (editor), *The Essential Writings of Christian Mysticism.*** Numerous anthologies of writings by the great mystics have been published over the years, but this one towers over them all. It includes lengthy selections from the writings of the mystics arranged topically, as well as insightful introductions and commentaries on the various selections.

- **H. A. Reinhold (editor), *The Soul Afire: Revelations of the Mystics.*** Dating from the 1940s, this is an older compilation of mystics, and long out of print so you'll have to find a used copy. But it's an interesting assortment of quotations and a reminder that interest in Christian mysticism is not just some fad from the last few decades.

- **Douglas V. Steere (editor),** *Quaker Spirituality.* This installment in the Classics of Western Spirituality series[1] presents key writings from the Religious Society of Friends, including works by George Fox, Isaac Penington, Caroline Stephen, John Woolman, Rufus M. Jones, and Thomas R. Kelly, all of whom celebrate the rich Quaker tradition, whose profound attentiveness to contemplative silence and to God's presence within has resulted in a strong heritage of social justice.

KEY WRITINGS OF THE GREAT MYSTICS

- **Anonymous,** *The Cloud of Unknowing with The Book of Privy Counsel.* These two classic manuals on contemplative spirituality date from the fourteenth century. *The Cloud of Unknowing* affirms the primacy of love over thought in the mystical life, and served as a direct inspiration for the Centering Prayer movement in our time. *The Book of Privy Counsel* offers additional instruction for the serious student of silent prayer. Carmen Acevedo Butcher's translation is the one to get, although Ira Progoff's version of *The Cloud* is also respected.
- **Anonymous,** *Meditations on the Tarot: A Journey into Christian Hermeticism.* Don't let the title fool you: this is not a book about divination or fortune-telling; rather, it uses imagery from the twenty-two major Tarot cards to illustrate a brilliant synthesis of mystical Christianity with esoteric philosophy. Although flawed by the author's chauvinism, it is nevertheless a deeply imaginative and ultimately generous expression of mysticism's continued relevance even in the postmodern era.
- **Anonymous,** *The Way of a Pilgrim and The Pilgrim Continues His Way.* These nineteenth-century Russian novels provide an accessible explanation of the spirituality of the Prayer of the Heart—the Eastern Orthodox practice of repeating the Jesus Prayer continually, thereby cultivating an ongoing awareness of Christ's presence.
- **Jean-Pierre de Caussade,** *Abandonment to Divine Providence.* This short eighteenth-century mystical text, originally written as

letters of spiritual direction for a convent of nuns, promotes the freedom that arises from living in the present moment and joyfully offering all our concerns to the loving care of God.

- **Meister Eckhart, *Selected Writings*.** One of the most celebrated, but also controversial, of Christian mystics, Eckhart, a thirteenth-century Dominican theologian, wrote scholarly works but also preached in both Latin and his native German about the experience of union with God available to the ardent contemplative. Clearly a mystic who himself knew nondual union with God, Eckhart unfortunately lived in a time when the church hierarchy did not know how to appreciate such wisdom. The Penguin Books anthology of his writings includes three treatises, along with a selection of the sermons, which is where his most daring mystical ideas were expressed.

- **Evagrius Ponticus, *The Praktikos & Chapters on Prayer*.** Perhaps the most important of the desert fathers, Evagrius influenced later monks like John Cassian and Benedict, thereby influencing monasticism as a whole. This book gathers his pithy, concise writings about the struggle to overcome sin, become holy, and enter into the serene state where true contemplation may occur.

- **Hildegard of Bingen, *Selected Writings*.** This twelfth-century nun was a renaissance woman before the Renaissance. Celebrated in our time because of her beautiful music, Hildegard was a renowned visionary who wrote of her mystical experiences and corresponded with some of the leading figures of her day, including Bernard of Clairvaux. She instructed an artistically talented nun to create stunning visual images inspired by her visions, including a beautiful image of the Holy Trinity where a sapphire-blue Christ is surrounded by rings of flame and light, representing God the Creator and the sustaining Spirit.

- **Walter Hilton, *The Scale of Perfection*.** A contemporary of both Julian of Norwich and *The Cloud of Unknowing*, Hilton is not as well-known now, but, during their lifetime, his work was the most widely circulated of the three. This may be because *The Scale of Perfection* is an astute study of the psychology of spiritual development that explains the dynamics of the inner life in a down-to-earth, practical style.

- **Caryll Houselander, *Essential Writings*.** This British Catholic author, who lived at the same time as Evelyn Underhill and C. S. Lewis, wrote deeply devotional books with a truly incarnational sense of divine presence. Read *Essential Writings* to get to know her, but follow it up with her masterpiece about the Virgin Mary, *The Reed of God* and her insightfully surprising reflections on the nativity of Jesus, *The Passion of the Infant Christ*.

- **John of the Cross, *Collected Works*.** One of the most renowned of Christian mystics, John of the Cross was a world-class Spanish poet and a gifted writer with a keen understanding of the psychology of the inner life. His collected works include his four major mystical treatises, the best known being *The Ascent of Mount Carmel* and *The Dark Night of the Soul*. His mystical writings were created as commentaries on his sublime poetry. He has a reputation for being stern, likely due to his ideas about the "dark nights" that a soul must undergo to give up everything that holds us back from complete union with God. But John's writing is also filled with light and love, more readily apparent in his lesser known works *Living Flame of Love* and *The Spiritual Canticle*.

- **Julian of Norwich, *The Showings (Revelations of Divine Love)*.** In my opinion, this is the single most important written record of Christian mystical experience (at least so far). On the surface, it is the tale of a devout woman who experienced visions while suffering from illness; but as Julian shares the details of her visions, a powerful theology of divine love and transforming grace emerges that supports her central conviction that, in Christ, "all shall be well." There are a number of excellent translations available; I particularly love the versions by Mirabai Starr, M. L. del Mastro, John Skinner, and Halcyon Backhouse & Rhona Pipe.

- **Brother Lawrence, *The Practice of the Presence of God*.** This is a slender volume of collected papers by and about a seventeenth-century Carmelite friar that captures his simple spirituality of intentionally and continually choosing awareness of God's presence moment by moment throughout the day. Once again, Carmen Acevedo Butcher's translation is superb.

- **C. S. Lewis, *The Voyage of the Dawn Treader*.** This installment from C. S. Lewis's beloved Narnia books is a superb introduction to the mystical life under the charming guise of a children's book. It is a masterful integration of an ancient Celtic myth (the *immram*, or the wondrous sea voyage that leads to paradise) with the key elements of the Christian mystical journey. All the important dimensions of the contemplative life are here: conversion, repentance, and growth in holiness, the embrace of silence, the encounter with darkness, and finally, the glorious union with God in light.

- **Thomas Merton, *The Inner Experience: Notes on Contemplation*.** In the 1940s, Merton wrote a short book called *What Is Contemplation?*, which he revised and expanded in the 1950s. That manuscript was revised yet again shortly before he died in 1968. Now published as *The Inner Experience*, it offers an in-depth look at Merton's understanding of contemplation, and how all people, including those who are *not* called to monastic life, can embrace the path of contemplation in our day. Also check out *New Seeds of Contemplation*.

- **John O'Donohue, *Anam Ċara: A Book of Celtic Wisdom*.** A surprise bestseller when published in 1997, this book celebrates the living spirituality of Ireland and the other Celtic lands; O'Donohue, at the time a Catholic priest and a student of mysticism, brings both beauty and depth to his poetic evocation of the spirituality of his homeland.

- **Pseudo-Dionysius, *The Complete Works*.** The Classics of Western Spirituality has published a one-volume edition of all the known writings by the elusive and mysterious sixth-century theologian who took for a pseudonym Dionysius the Areopagite, the name of a minor figure in the Acts of the Apostles. There is evidence in Pseudo-Dionysius's writings to indicate he actually lived around the year 500, centuries after Acts was written. What this author has to say is just as mysterious (and controversial) as his identity. He expresses his understanding of God, the angels, and even the church using language and concepts that are clearly derived from pagan Greek philosophy. Pseudo-Dionysius has had an enormous impact on the mystical tradition as a whole, influencing figures as diverse as Thomas Aquinas, the author of *The Cloud of Unknowing*, and lesser-known mystics like John Scotus Eriugena. Of the four works included in his collected works, *The Divine Names* and *The Mystical Theology* are profound, significant works of apophatic (imageless) theology.

- **John Ruusbroec, *The Spiritual Espousals and Other Works.*** Evelyn Underhill considered Ruusbroec her favorite mystic, and it's easy to see why. His spirituality is deeply trinitarian, and his understanding of the mystical summit of union with God that nevertheless does not erase the distinction between Creator and creature makes him one of the most articulate Christian mystics. *The Spiritual Espousals* is generally regarded as his masterpiece. Three minor works are also included in the Classics of Western Spirituality edition.

- **Pierre Teilhard de Chardin, *Hymn of the Universe.*** As a Jesuit scientist, Teilhard de Chardin's writing is deeply philosophical, but for an accessible introduction to his deeply embodied and earth-friendly spirituality, try this collection of his shorter writings, especially "The Mass on the World," a eucharistic meditation that celebrates the indwelling presence of God in nature.

- **Teresa of Ávila, *Collected Works,* volumes 1–3.** Not only was she John of the Cross's mentor, but Teresa herself remains one of the greatest of Christian mystics; she was the first woman to be declared a Doctor of the Universal Church, meaning her writings are considered exemplary sources of spiritual wisdom. The first two volumes of Teresa's collected works include three mystical classics: her autobiography, one of the finest statements of personal spiritual experience; *The Way of Perfection*, her commentary on prayer and particularly on the Lord's Prayer; and *The Interior Castle*, a survey of the mystical life built around the metaphor of the soul as a castle fashioned out of a glittering diamond, in whose center God reigns. As we travel through the rooms or "mansions" of the castle, we are called to grow in virtue and holiness. Volume

3 of the collected works includes more autobiographical material that is well worth exploring, and her collected letters reveal the human side of this renowned saint.

- **Thérèse of Lisieux,** *The Story of a Soul.* Immensely popular when published, this autobiography of a nineteenth-century French nun who died of tuberculosis while still in her twenties has become a modern classic. Thérèse promotes what she calls "the little way" of serving God in humble and ordinary ways, acknowledging that the spiritual life is not just for martyrs or others who are heroic in their stature, but also for even the most down-to-earth people in the lowliest of circumstances who nevertheless have a loving heart to offer to God and their neighbors.

- **Howard Thurman,** *With Head and Heart: The Autobiography of Howard Thurman.* Thurman, the grandson of a slave who grew up in the Jim Crow South and went on to become a world-renowned pastor and the mentor to Martin Luther King Jr., is one of the greatest Christian theologians of the twentieth century—but also a great mystic and contemplative. This beautifully written memoir recounts the beauty and power of his singular life, while in a humble and matter-of-fact way describes how he embodied a lovely, ordinary mystical spirituality, down to earth and accessible to all.

- **Evelyn Underhill,** *Practical Mysticism.* Many of Underhill's books on mysticism and Christian spirituality are scholarly in tone, but this short book presents her understanding of how Christian mysticism can be applied to ordinary life in the modern world. A century after its publication, it feels a bit dated, but nevertheless contains keen insight on how mysticism can transform the spirituality of anyone, no matter how "practical" he may be. I also especially love Underhill's letters, available in two different editions: they reveal not only her warm personality but also her skill as a spiritual director.

- **Adrienne von Speyr,** *The Boundless God.* This prolific twentieth-century mystic wrote about many topics related to the spiritual life, but to appreciate the depth of contemplative knowing, begin with this book, which is her meditation on the limitlessness of

God. Follow it up with *The World of Prayer* and *Light and Images: Elements of Contemplation*.

- **Benedicta Ward (translator), *The Sayings of the Desert Fathers: Sayings of the Early Christian Monks*.** Most of the early Christian hermits and monks who retreated into the deserts of Egypt and Syria to surrender their lives to prayer did not write about their experiences, but tales of their teachings were eventually collected and anthologized. Today, the sayings of the desert read like parables and sometimes even riddles, offering insight into lives where everything was held secondary to the quest for God.
- **Simone Weil, *Waiting for God*.** One of the twentieth century's most enigmatic figures, Weil was a Jewish philosopher who had mystical experiences of Christ and who explored the teachings of the Christian faith. Her masterpiece, *Waiting for God*, collects a number of her essays and letters, including a powerful reflection on the various forms of the implicit (not readily visible) love of God.

RECENT AND CONTEMPORARY WRITINGS ON THE CONTEMPLATIVE LIFE

- **Bruno Barnhart, *The Future of Wisdom: Toward a Rebirth of Sapiential Christianity*.** Barnhart, who was a monk of New Camaldoli Hermitage in Big Sur, offers a reflection on how the wisdom or sapiential tradition within Christianity can be restored and recovered in our time, illuminated by East-West dialogue and a recognition that contemplative consciousness is being set free from behind monastic walls so that it might transform not only all Christians, but indeed the entire human family.
- **Anthony Bloom, *Beginning to Pray*.** Most of the books on this list are concerned primarily with contemplation, but this book takes us back to the basics of prayer in its most elementary form (even including recited or memorized prayer). Written by an Orthodox archbishop, this introductory work offers gentle encouragement and insight into practical questions (and common obstacles) for

anyone wishing to foster a greater sense of intimacy and connection with God.

- **Beatrice Bruteau, *Radical Optimism: Rooting Ourselves in Reality.*** Bruteau wrote about contemplative spirituality from both Christian and interfaith perspectives; in *Radical Optimism* she describes how the cultivation of contemplative consciousness helps us to see reality clearly and deeply, while also empowering our efforts to respond to the challenges of our time and bring about transformation of both the self and the world in Christ.

- **Cynthia Bourgeault, *Centering Prayer and Inner Awakening.*** Bourgeault brings to this book a keen insight, not only of Centering Prayer itself, but also of the dynamics of inner growth and healing that can occur as part of a sustained contemplative practice. See also her subsequent book, *The Heart of Centering Prayer*, which contains insightful commentary on *The Cloud of Unknowing* and an excellent introduction to nonduality from a Christian perspective.

- **Ruth Burrows, *Guidelines for Mystical Prayer.*** Drawing on the rich wisdom of Carmelite spirituality, Burrows describes what contemplative prayer is, and why it is ultimately a spirituality that involves a deep, radical surrendering to Christ—trusting Christ's initiative to draw us into union with God, even at a level deeper than our conscious awareness.

- **Michael Casey, *Fully Human, Fully Divine.*** The mystery of deification is explored and, as much as possible, explained in this meditative commentary on the Gospel of Mark—and how Mark's story of Christ can, in turn, illuminate our own experience as members of Christ's body, here and now. By commenting on the words of the Gospel in the light of his own wisdom as well as the insights from great Cistercian writers like Bernard of Clairvaux, Casey provides an excellent model for reading Scripture in a contemplative way, not only for devotional purposes (lectio divina) but for study as well.

- **Joan Chittister, *Radical Spirit: 12 Ways to Live a Free and Authentic Life.*** Chittister, a Benedictine nun, has written several books that interpret the Rule of Saint Benedict (and Benedictine spirituality in general) for our time. This book looks at Benedictine teachings on humility, exploring how such teachings can bring freedom and peace into everyday life.

- **Tilden Edwards, *Living Simply Through the Day: Spiritual Survival in a Complex Age.*** Edwards, an Episcopal priest and the founder of the Shalem Institute, recounts how his encounter with Tibetan Buddhism initiated his own rediscovery of the Christian contemplative tradition. Edwards's vision of spirituality is spacious, gentle, and open, and his appreciation for Eastern spirituality in dialogue with Christianity makes his vision especially relevant for our time.
- **Hugo Enomiya-Lassalle, *Living in the New Consciousness.*** This German Jesuit priest spent many years in Japan and immersed himself in Zen Buddhism, eventually becoming recognized as a Zen master. In this book he offers his vision for a renewed mystical heart in Christian spirituality.
- **Barbara Holmes, *Joy Unspeakable: Contemplative Practices of the Black Church.*** Dr. Holmes is one of the leading scholars dedicated to reclaiming and celebrating the often forgotten contemplative dimension of African-American Christianity, showing not only how deeply mystical Black Christianity is, but also offering helpful insights for a broader understanding of contemplation and mysticism than what has traditionally been linked to white/European spirituality.
- **Thomas Keating, *Open Mind Open Heart: The Contemplative Dimension of the Gospel.*** Before his death in 2018 Keating had become the leading advocate for Centering Prayer; this book is probably the single best introduction to the topic, at least in his words. He offers sage advice on how to deal with distracting thoughts and what to expect as a deepening practice of silent prayer can facilitate healing in the unconscious.
- **Martin Laird, *Into the Silent Land, A Sunlit Absence* and *An Ocean of Light.*** Ideal for both beginners and proficients in the spiritual life, these three beautifully written books examine the landscape of interior prayer, drawing on both the Eastern and Western traditions of Christian wisdom. Laird offers practical

advice on such topics as attentiveness to the breath as an aid to contemplation, dealing with distractions, and learning how to pray through suffering.

- **Kenneth Leech, *Prayer and Prophecy: The Essential Kenneth Leech.*** Leech, a priest of the Church of England, was probably best known in America for his work on the revival of spiritual direction (one-on-one guidance and accompaniment for those engaged in a committed prayer practice). But this anthology of his key writings reveals the breadth of his work: strong advocacy for social justice, a keen understanding that theology and spirituality always happen in a community context, and yes, a deep appreciation for the beauty of silence and prayer. Be sure to read the section on "Subversive Contemplation."

- **Gerald May, *Will and Spirit: A Contemplative Psychology.*** Combining the scientific thinking of a psychiatrist with the deep interior knowingness of a mature contemplative, May explores how the prayerful process of surrendering to God in a spirit of "willingness" can transform us both psychologically and spiritually.

- **Carl McColman, *Answering the Contemplative Call: First Steps on the Mystical Path.*** How does one begin to walk the path of mystical spirituality? This book explores that question, recognizing that a desire for contemplation is evidence of being called into the silence and beauty of the inner life.

- **Carl McColman, *Eternal Heart: The Mystical Path to a Joyful Life.*** So many of the mystics speak about the heart as the center of our spiritual lives; and indeed, the Bible repeatedly refers to gifts that the Spirit places in our hearts. By meditating on those gifts and their power to transform our lives, we can discern a path to God's joyful presence within.

- **Bernadette Roberts, *The Experience of No-Self: A Contemplative Journey.*** Thomas Keating called this "one of the best books on this subject since St. John of the Cross." In this book Roberts recounts her own journey through a decade living as a nun, eventually returning to secular life, but experiencing the profound inner transformation that has traditionally been described as "dying to self."

- **Richard Rohr,** *Everything Belongs: The Gift of Contemplative Prayer.* This is a general introduction to the beauty of contemplative spirituality, in which Rohr poetically explores how contemplation fosters new ways of seeing and thinking and understanding. His message, that contemplation transforms us from ordinary consciousness (which is dualistic, competitive, and oppositional) to unitive consciousness (a holistic recognition of God's grace and presence in all things), falls squarely in the heart of mystical wisdom. Many of Rohr's books are worth reading; especially *The Naked Now* and *The Universal Christ.*
- **Margaret Silf,** *Companions of Christ: Ignatian Spirituality for Everyday Living.* Some readers may wonder why Ignatius of Loyola's *Spiritual Exercises* is not included in the "Key Writings" section above. While Ignatius's book is certainly a mystical classic, it is dense, technical, and written for spiritual directors who are *leading* the spiritual exercises, not individual participants. So to truly appreciate the spirituality of Ignatius, it's better to begin with a book that introduces his spirituality to our age. Many such titles are available, but I particularly recommend Margaret Silf's accessible invitation into the Ignatian approach to prayer and spiritual growth.
- **Dorothee Soelle,** *The Silent Cry: Mysticism and Resistance.* Soelle was better known as a theologian than a mystic, and especially for her strong commitment to peace and social justice. This book reveals her understanding of the intimate connection between contemplation and action: how mystical spirituality provides a foundation for the struggle for a better world, and how that struggle in turn helps to clarify the nature and blessings of the contemplative life.

RESOURCES FOR FURTHER STUDY

- **Amy Hollywood and Patricia Z. Beckman (editors),** *The Cambridge Companion to Christian Mysticism.* Twenty-two essays by a variety of scholars consider the history of mysticism, key concepts in the study of it, and significant issues such as the relationship of mysticism to gender, sexuality, authority, and the body.

- **Edward Howells and Mark A. McIntosh (editors),** *The Oxford Handbook of Mystical Theology.* What is the relationship between mysticism and theology (Christian or otherwise)? This book offers an in-depth exploration of mystical theology, patterns of mystical thought, key sources and contexts, and special topics ranging from metaphysics to anthropology to interreligious dialogue.

- **Robert Davis Hughes III,** *Beloved Dust: Tides of the Spirit in the Christian Life.* This award-winning book offers a constructive theology of the Holy Spirit (and therefore, of spirituality and mysticism) in an academically rigorous yet accessible text. Hughes uses the classic model of purgation/illumination/union, but applies to it the metaphor of tides (water flowing in and out) to suggest that the spiritual life is circular rather than linear in the way most people experience it.

- **Grace Jantzen,** *Power, Gender and Christian Mysticism.* It's no secret that Christianity, like most historical elements of Western culture, has been rooted in sexism and therefore complicit in the oppression of women. But Jantzen methodically shows how mystical literature, especially by men, has its own long shadow of patriarchal bias. It's important not only as a reminder that mysticism needs to be criticized like any other element of our culture, but also because Jantzen's highlighting of the resilient and courageous women mystics offers insight into how mystical Christianity can move beyond its limited past to more fully embody a radical grace that transcends sexism or other systems of power and privilege.

- **Julia A. Lamm (editor),** *The Wiley-Blackwell Companion to Christian Mysticism.* Another collection of scholarly essays on a variety of topics related to the study of mysticism, including an in-depth survey of the history of mysticism and critical perspectives on the academic study of mysticism today.

- **Mark A. McIntosh,** *Mystical Theology: The Integrity of Spirituality and Theology.* McIntosh, an Episcopal priest who taught at

Loyola University of Chicago, developed this survey of current issues in mystical theology in response to how many of his students identified as "spiritual but not religious." He makes the case that spirituality and theology need to be reintegrated in our time.

- **Bernard McGinn, *The Presence of God: A History of Western Christian Mysticism* (nine volumes).** An in-depth study of Christian mysticism, beginning with the New Testament and the Jewish and Greek backgrounds, and continuing on through to the crisis of mysticism in seventeenth-century Europe, when popular mystics like Jeanne Guyon and Miguel de Molinos were accused of heresy. McGinn is scholarly but his writing is clear and accessible, making this a profoundly valuable resource for anyone interested in the big picture of mystical history.

- **Louise Nelstrop with Kevin Magill and Bradley B. Onishi, *Christian Mysticism: An Introduction to Contemporary Theoretical Approaches.*** One of the most accessible of academic surveys of mysticism, this book, written with undergraduate students in mind, should be useful for anyone interested in a scholarly overview of mystical Christianity. The authors review a variety of philosophical and theoretical perspectives on the subject, demonstrating how mysticism can be understood in a variety of ways.

- **Janet K. Ruffing (editor), *Mysticism and Social Transformation.*** How does mysticism make a difference in the real world? That's the question that the essays in this book explore. Beginning with the social implications of the teachings of historical mystics like Teresa of Ávila or George Fox, the book considers mysticism's relation to a variety of social issues, including environmentalism, racism and sexism.

- **Denys Turner, *The Darkness of God: Negativity in Christian Mysticism.*** By "negativity" this does not mean a poor attitude, but rather the apophatic tradition, which emphasizes God's hiddenness and ultimate unknowability. Surveying mystics from Augustine to John of the Cross, the book considers issues related to the topic of mystical negativity, including depression, detachment, and the dark nights of the senses and soul.

Let me reiterate, this list is hardly complete or comprehensive. It certainly displays the idiosyncrasies of my own reading and research over the years. Let this be an invitation for you to begin doing your own reading and exploration of the mystics, past and present, and those who reflect on their wisdom. Remember, you do not need to read a lot of books to be a mystic or a contemplative, but reading books like these can be a blessing as you continue your own lifelong journey of responding to divine love.

Appendix C: The Charter of Christian Mysticism

To appreciate the early origins of Christian mysticism, I'd like to reflect on one particular passage in the Christian Scriptures, Ephesians 3. This brief chapter provides essential insights for understanding the roots of this wisdom tradition, charting a template of the mystical dimension of Christian spirituality which remains relevant today. For understanding the scriptural basis of mystical Christianity, the third chapter of Ephesians is probably more important than any other segment in the New Testament, if not the Bible as a whole.

The Letter to the Ephesians, traditionally attributed to the apostle Paul,[1] is one of the shortest, but most lyrical, of the early Christian writings. The third chapter of this letter explains how Jesus came, not just for Israel, but for all the world—to proclaim and share God's love and healing for all people. The letters speak of the mystery of God made known to Paul through divine revelation and goes on to point out that this mystery "made known by revelation" is, in fact, Christ. Later in the chapter, the author maintains that this "mystery of Christ" had been hidden all along "in God who created all things."[2]

In its poetic description of the mystery of Christ, Ephesians 3 lays the foundation for Christian mystical theology, introducing ideas and beliefs that inspired generations of contemplatives who sought to unite their lives with the love of God. Indeed, this single chapter of the New Testament reveals how mysticism was a part of Christianity from the very beginning. It is the "charter," if you will, of the Christian tradition of seeking to enter the hidden, loving, and transformative splendor of God.

The chapter begins with the author declaring how God has entrusted him with a revelation of the mystery of Christ:

This is the reason that I Paul am a prisoner for Christ Jesus . . . for surely you have already heard of the commission of God's grace that was given me for you, and how the mystery was made known to me by revelation, as I wrote above in a few words, a reading of which will enable you to perceive my understanding of the mystery of Christ.

"Wrote above" refers to Ephesians 2:22, where Paul describes the mystery of Christ: "in whom you also are built together spiritually into a dwelling place for God." The author makes the amazing statement that God, in the Spirit, will dwell *in us* because we, the community of believers, are "*in Christ.*" We are actually immersed in the divine spiritual presence.

The mystery that Paul describes might be restated like this: "God is in us, because we are in Christ." As we have already seen, Jesus is one with God and the community of Christians are known as the body of Christ, and in that body dwells the Spirit of God.³ It's a dance, in which the divine mystery, the anointed one, the sacred breath, and the people of faith all are immersed in each other's presence—and love.

The next verses lay out the main point of this chapter.

In former generations this mystery was not made known to humankind, as it has now been revealed to his holy apostles and prophets by the Spirit: that is, the Gentiles have become fellow heirs, members of the same body, and sharers in the promise in Christ Jesus through the gospel.

The mystery of Christ is available to all, not only (as some expected) just to Jesus's Jewish disciples. The author proclaims that the liberating presence of the Christian mystery (a concept familiar to the readers, since they were already believers) is not limited to just one ethnic group. Even though Paul's main point is not to describe what the mystery is, he does so nonetheless, providing valuable information for those of us who want to explore this ultimate mystery in our lives today. By explaining "the mystery of Christ," Paul reveals the heart of Christian mysticism, and points out his own mission to spread the good news of Christ to all people.

Of this gospel I have become a servant according to the gift of God's grace that was given me by the working of his power. Although I am the very least of all the saints, this grace was given to me to bring to the Gentiles the news of the boundless riches of Christ, and to make everyone see what is the plan of the mystery hidden for ages in God who created all things . . .

Both the purpose and the beauty of the mystical path, therefore, is to embody the ineffable splendors of the mutual indwelling of the soul in Christ.

. . . so that through the church the wisdom of God in its rich variety might now be made known to the rulers and authorities in the heavenly places.

The author engages in some subtle humor here. The ancient community of believers who followed Jesus was hardly in a position to instruct the "rulers and authorities" of either heaven or earth. On the contrary, in those days, Christianity was a marginal, minority religion. Several centuries would pass before this spiritual movement would become part of the cultural mainstream. Paul's point is that Christians, even if they lack any social standing whatsoever, have access to wisdom that can be a true revelation to both human and spiritual powers (whether they pay attention to this wisdom or not). Paul lauds "the wisdom of God in its rich variety," suggesting that the mystery (of God's indwelling presence) cannot be reduced to a simple equation or formula.

This was in accordance with the eternal purpose that he has carried out in Christ Jesus our Lord, in whom we have access to God in boldness and confidence through faith in him. I pray therefore that you may not lose heart over my sufferings for you; they are your glory.

The apostle colors his subtle but important commentary with political as well as spiritual overtones. Today, in the United States and other parts of the world, we tend to think of God as available to everyone, accessible to all. It may be impossible to set up an appointment with the president of the United States or the king of England, but the God of all creation is always immediately present in our hearts.

Paul reminds us that people did not always have this kind of confidence about approaching God. In the days of imperial power, God was seen as even less accessible than the emperor. But Paul depicts Christ as the great demolisher of red tape. Through Jesus, God becomes accessible to everyone. This was a revolutionary idea for the time, although one we take for granted today. It is also a foundational principle at the heart of Christian mysticism.

For this reason I bow my knees before the Father, from whom every family in heaven and on earth takes its name.

Paul then tells us what he himself prays for—that all believers have this immediate encounter with Christ (in other words, that they all be mystics).

I pray that, according to the riches of his glory, he may grant that you may be strengthened in your inner being with power through his Spirit, and that Christ may dwell in your hearts through faith, as you are being rooted and grounded in love. I pray that you may have the power to comprehend, with all the saints, what is the breadth and length and height and depth, and to know the love of Christ that surpasses knowledge, so that you may be filled with all the fullness of God.

In a burst of mystical eloquence to rival (if not surpass) anything that came from the hand of the great contemplatives over the following centuries, Paul describes the breadth and depth of this sacred mystery in lyrically poetic language:

According to the riches of his glory: What is being described here is replete with the beauty, splendor, honor, and praiseworthiness of God.

God may grant that you may be strengthened in your inner being with power through his Spirit: the mystical life is the opportunity to receive power, internally, which means growing into a dynamic spiritual life, rooted in Christ through his Spirit.

And that Christ may dwell in your hearts through faith: This powerful spiritual life isn't just some sort of inner entertainment. It opens our hearts to receive the presence of Christ, who lives within us.

As you are being rooted and grounded in love: Christ living within us means we will be immersed in love, will rest on love, and will embrace and be embraced by the fullness of love.

I pray that you may have the power to comprehend, with all the saints, what is the breadth and length and height and depth: This is a mysterious verse. I suspect Paul here refers to the love of Christ and the fullness of God, which he goes on to mention.

And to know the love of Christ that surpasses knowledge: The love of Christ (which has just taken up residence in our hearts) surpasses knowledge (the Greek word is *gnosis*). Whatever we may comprehend or "know" in terms of God's presence in our lives will be only a tiny fraction of what is truly being offered to us in the Mystery.

So that you may be filled with all the fullness of God: In other words, true union with God. The author of this letter promises that the mystery of Christ leads to the glorious end that so many mystics since have described—nondual union with God, the beatific vision, communion with the Holy Trinity, deification, to be filled with the utter fullness of God.

Ephesians 3 acknowledges that the mystery of Christ (i.e., mysticism) emerges from the "inner self," where "Christ may dwell . . . rooted and grounded in love." We are given the ability to grasp all the dimensions of this supernatural love, thereby integrating heart and mind in a unitive experience. This love of Christ is ineffable: it can't be put into words. It's divine love that "surpasses knowledge"—a knowledge beyond knowledge— "so that you may be filled with all the fullness of God."

Now to him who by the power at work within us is able to accomplish abundantly far more than all we can ask or imagine, to him be glory in the church and in Christ Jesus to all generations, forever and ever. Amen.

This stirring conclusion simply voices praise for the One in whom we are mystically united. In offering this praise, Paul notes that Christ immerses us in divine mystery on a level far beyond "all we can ask or imagine"—in other words, as good as you think union with God in Christ can be, it is far, far better than that.

Alfred North Whitehead once suggested that all of Western philosophy is little more than an extensive collection of footnotes to Plato. The more I read Ephesians 3, the more convinced I am that the entire sweep of Christian mysticism is, likewise, simply two thousand years' worth of annotations on this profound chapter, a story told as generation after generation has sought to explore the radiant splendor of the mystery it describes—the mystery of the indwelling presence of God in Christ, embodied and encountered in communion with other Christians, something that can be powerfully known and yet is ultimately beyond knowledge, for its true nature takes us beyond language, beyond thought, to the silent splendor of love.

Acknowledgments

Christianity is a communal spirituality, and writing a book certainly takes a village. Many people have helped in the creation of this book, in small and large ways. The first edition of *The Big Book of Christian Mysticism* was published in 2010. It is a rare honor for an author to revisit a book previously released. For this edition, my gratitude extends to those who supported and accompanied me fifteen years ago when working on the original book, along with those who have supported the process of revising, updating and enlarging the book.

Here are my words of thanks from the first edition:

Thanks to Greg Brandenburgh for his insight, challenge, and support, and to Linda Roghaar for making the connections (and for playing amateur counselor when necessary). Thanks to Meg Anderson, Nancy Carnes, Claudette Cuddy, Cliff Post, Michael Morrell, Gini Eagen, Bob Hughes, Greg Kenny, Darrell Grizzle, Phil Foster, Kenneth Leech, Emmett Jarrett, Natalia Shulgina, John Skinner, Brittian Bullock, Peter Rollins, Richard Rohr, Brian McLaren, and Jon Sweeney for your feedback, insight, encouragement, and suggestions.

Thanks to the readers of my blog (www.anamchara.com), who have, in many cases, been the first people exposed to the ideas and perspectives that eventually shaped this book. Your comments, questions, and support inspired me to persevere and made the final project much more valuable. Its limitations, naturally, remain my responsibility.

I especially want to thank the Trappist monks of the Monastery of the Holy Spirit in Conyers, Georgia, where I am blessed to be both a member of the lay associates community and an employee of the monastery's business division (I work in the bookstore). I owe immense thanks, not only for their witness as a community of faith, but also for the many small gestures of kindness and hospitality they offered as I worked and prayed alongside them. Members of this community have related to me as mentors, spiritual directors, confessors, teachers, business colleagues, and—most rewarding of all—friends. In particular, I wish to mention Fr. Tom Francis, Fr. Anthony Delisi, Br. Elias Marechal, Fr. Matt Torpey, and Fr. James Behrens, each of whom patiently endured my endless questions and occasional whining as I sought to understand the splendor of Christian mystical spirituality and to capture its beauty in the written word.

Because of my relationship with the monastery, I feel I must emphasize that this book represents my personal views and thoughts on Christian mysticism. Any errors or distortions within it are entirely my own fault. Of course, what little wisdom may be present in these pages is very much the result of my having access to a living contemplative community. For this, I am profoundly grateful.

Thanks also to the members of the Lay Cistercians of Our Lady of the Holy Spirit, especially Paco Ambrosetti, Jacquie Johnston, Linda Mitchell, Jacki Rychlicki, and Rocky Thomas, and to my colleagues at the Abbey Store and Monastery Industries. I'm always afraid when I write my acknowledgments that I will leave out someone who has really made an important contribution to my life or the project at hand. To such an unknown contributor, I can only offer my gratitude and beg for your forgiveness. You know who you are.

During the coronavirus pandemic of 2020–2021 I began conversations with Linda Roghaar, my literary agent; Greg Brandenburgh, the original editor of this book; Lil Copan, the editor of several of my books including *Eternal Heart*; and the publishing director of Broadleaf Books, Andrew DeYoung, about revising and expanding this book. Their enthusiasm and support for creating a "new" *Big Book of Christian Mysticism* has been a source of joy and a cause for deep gratitude.

My hope is that this newly revised edition of the book will be even more useful to everyone, of any faith identity, who approaches the Christian expression of the hidden source of the mysteries of love, not only with the curiosity of a scholar, but with the longing of a seeker. With that in mind,

I have endeavored to focus each chapter of the book more on the joys and challenges of contemplative living.

This time around, I particularly wish to express gratitude to Linda Boland, Laverne Brown, Lerita Coleman Brown, Maria Cressler, Mark Dannenfelser, Cassidy Hall, Kevin Johnson, Rosary Mangano, Debonee Morgan, Kay Satterfield, Therese Taylor-Stinson, and Maggie Winfield, for your support, encouragement, and advice. Deep appreciation goes out to all those who support my writing work through Patreon—you literally make this work possible. A special bow of gratitude goes out to everyone who has offered feedback and questions or insights in response to the first edition of this book; your input has given me a map toward what I hope will make this a much improved version of the book. A special word of appreciation to my community of contemplatives, here in Atlanta and beyond; especially those who participate in Contemplative Outreach Atlanta, Ignatius House, St. Thomas More Catholic Church, Zeitgeist Atlanta, and the spiritual direction community. Your friendship, prayers, and encouragement has continued to bring me great joy.

In the first edition of this book I also made special mention of the love and support of my wife, Fran, and our daughter Rhiannon, whose love, encouragement, and companionship made the writing process not only possible, but meaningful. Rhiannon passed from this earthly life in 2014 after a long sojourn with polycystic kidney disease. Fran and I have had to reinvent our lives and learn the ways of the empty nest. We try to take good care of one another and be each other's best friend. I am sure I fail at this often, but Fran is nearly flawless in her tenderness and love. Fran, your caring and support makes it possible for me to write, so I truly can say this book would not have been possible without you. Thank you, from the deepest place in my heart.

Carl McColman
Thursday of the Mysteries (Maundy Thursday), 2023

Selected Bibliography

Abhishiktananda. *Prayer.* Delhi: ISPCK, 1989.

———. *Saccidananda: A Christian Approach to Advaitic Experience.* Delhi: ISPCK, 1984.

———. *Swami Abhishiktananda: Essential Writings.* Edited by Shirley DuBoulay. Maryknoll, NY: Orbis Books, 2006.

Aelred of Rievaulx. *Spiritual Friendship.* Kalamazoo, MI: Cistercian Publications, 1977.

Ahlgren, Gillian T. W. *Entering Teresa of Avila's Interior Castle: A Reader's Companion.* New York: Paulist Press, 2005.

Allchin, A. M. *Participation in God: A Forgotten Strand in Anglican Tradition.* London: Darton, Longman & Todd, 1988.

Anonymous. *The Cloud of Unknowing with The Book of Privy Counsel.* Translated by Carmen Acevedo Butcher. Boulder, CO: Shambhala Publications, 2009.

Anonymous. *Meditations on the Tarot: A Journey into Christian Hermeticism.* Brooklyn, NY: Angelico Press, 2019.

Anonymous. *The Way of a Pilgrim and The Pilgrim Continues His Way.* Blanco, TX: New Sarov Press, 1993.

Armstrong, Christopher. *Evelyn Underhill: An Introduction to Her Life and Writings.* Oxford: A. R. Mowbray, 1975.

Arseniev, Nicholas. *Mysticism and the Eastern Church.* Crestwood, NY: St. Vladimir's Seminary Press, 1979.

Augustine of Hippo. *Selected Writings.* New York: Paulist Press, 1984.

Bailey, Raymond. *Thomas Merton on Mysticism.* Garden City, NY: Image Books, 1976.

Baillie, John. *The Sense of the Presence of God.* New York: Charles Scribner's Sons, 1962.

Baker, Augustine. *Holy Wisdom.* Wheathampstead, UK: Anthony Clarke Books, 1972.

Barker, Margaret. *Temple Mysticism: An Introduction.* London: Society for Promoting Christian Knowledge, 2011.

Barnhart, Bruno. *The Future of Wisdom: Toward a Rebirth of Sapiential Christianity.* Rhinebeck, NY: Monkfish, 2018.

———. *Second Simplicity: The Inner Shape of Christianity.* Mahwah, NJ: Paulist Press, 1999.

Barry, William A. and William J. Connolly. *The Practice of Spiritual Direction.* San Francisco: HarperCollins, 1986.

Batterson, Mark. *Wild Goose Chase: Reclaim the Adventure of Pursuing God.* Colorado Springs, CO: Multnomah Books, 2008.

Baxter, Jason M. *An Introduction to Christian Mysticism: Recovering the Wildness of Spiritual Life.* Grand Rapids, MI: Baker Academic, 2021.

Behrens, James Stephen. *Portraits of Grace: Images and Words from the Monastery of the Holy Spirit.* Skokie, IL: Acta Publications, 2007.

Bendon, Carmel. *The Mystics Who Came to Dinner*. Maryknoll, NY: Orbis Books, 2022.

Benson, Robert. *In Constant Prayer*. Nashville: Thomas Nelson, 2008.

Bergström-Allen, Johan. *Climbing the Mountain: The Carmelite Journey*. Faversham, UK: Saint Albert's Press, 2014.

Bernard of Clairvaux. *Selected Works*. New York: Paulist Press, 1987.

Bielecki, Tessa. *Holy Daring: The Earthy Mysticism of St. Teresa, the Wild Woman of Ávila*. Rhine-beck, NY: Adam Kadmon Books, 2016.

———. *Wild at Heart: Radical Teachings of the Christian Mystics*. Boulder, CO: Sounds True, 2006.

Binz, Stephen J. *Conversing with God in Scripture: A Contemporary Approach to Lectio Divina*. Ijamsville, MD: The Word Among Us Press, 2008.

Birgitta of Sweden. *Life and Selected Works*. New York: Paulist Press, 1990.

Blake, William. *The Complete Illuminated Books*. Introduction by David Bindman. New York: Thames & Hudson, 2,000.

Bloom, Anthony. *Beginning to Pray*. New York: Paulist Press, 1982.

Boers, Arthur. *Day by Day These Things We Pray: Uncovering Ancient Rhythms of Prayer*. Scottdale, PA: Herald Press, 2010

Bonaventure. *The Soul's Journey into God and Other Works*. New York: Paulist Press, 1978.

Bondi, Roberta. *To Love as God Loves: Conversations with the Early Church*. Philadelphia: Fortress Press, 1987.

———. *To Pray and to Love: Conversations on Prayer with the Early Church*. Minneapolis: Fortress Press, 1991.

Borg, Marcus. *The Heart of Christianity: Rediscovering a Life of Faith*. San Francisco: HarperCollins, 2003.

Borys, Peter N., Jr. *Transforming Heart and Mind: Learning from the Mystics*. New York: Paulist Press, 2006.

Bourgeault, Cynthia. *Centering Prayer and Inner Awakening*. Cambridge, MA: Cowley Publications, 2004.

———. *The Heart of Centering Prayer: Nondual Christianity in Theory and Practice*. Boulder, CO: Shambhala Publications, 2016.

———. *Mystical Hope: Trusting in the Mercy of God*. Cambridge, MA: Cowley Publications, 2001.

———. *The Wisdom Way of Knowing: Reclaiming an Ancient Tradition to Awaken the Heart*. San Francisco: Jossey-Bass, 2003.

Bouyer, Louis. *The Christian Mystery: From Pagan Myth to Christian Mysticism*. Edinburgh: T & T Clark, 1991.

Bouyer, Louis, Jean Leclercq, and Francois Vandenbroucke. *A History of Christian Spirituality*. Minneapolis: Winston Press, 1963–1969. Volume 1: *The Spirituality of the New Testament and the Fathers*. Volume 2: *The Spirituality of the Middle Ages*. Volume 3: *Orthodox Spirituality and Protestant and Anglican Spirituality*.

Boylan, Eugene. *The Mystical Body*. Westminster, MD: The Newman Bookshop, 1948.

———. *Partnership with Christ: A Cistercian Retreat*. Edited with a preface by Chaminade Crabtree. Kalamazoo, MI: Cistercian Publications, 2008.

Bradley, Ritamary. *Julian's Way: A Practical Commentary on Julian of Norwich*. London: HarperCollins, 1992.

Brett, Jesse. *Via Mystica: A Devotional Treatise on the Life of Prayer Based upon the Song of Songs*. London: Society for Promoting Christian Knowledge, 1925.

Brother Lawrence. *The Practice of the Presence of God*. Washington, DC: ICS Publications, 1994.

Brown, Lerita Coleman. *What Makes You Come Alive: A Spiritual Walk with Howard Thurman*. Minneapolis: Broadleaf Books, 2023.

Bunta, Silviu Nicolae. *The Lord God of Gods: Divinity and Deification in Early Judaism*. Piscataway, NJ: Giorgias Press, 2021.

Burrows, Ruth. *Guidelines for Mystical Prayer*. Mahway, NJ: Paulist Press, 2007.

Carmichael, Alexander, ed. *Carmina Gadelica: Hymns and Incantations*. Hudson, NY: Lindisfarne Press, 1992.

Carter, Sydney. *Dance in the Dark*. New York: Crossroad, 1982.

Cary, Phillip. *The History of Christian Theology*. Chantilly, VA: The Learning Company, 2008.

Casey, Michael. *Fully Human Fully Divine: An Interactive Christology*. Liguori, MO: Liguori/Triumph, 2004.

———. *Sacred Reading: The Ancient Art of Lectio Divina*. Liguori, MO: Liguori/Triumph, 1996.

———. *Strangers to the City: Reflections on the Beliefs and Values of the Rule of Saint Benedict*. Brewster, MA: Paraclete Press, 2005.

———. *Toward God: The Ancient Wisdom of Western Prayer*. Liguori, MO: Liguori/Triumph, 1996.

———. *The Undivided Heart: The Western Monastic Approach to Contemplation*. Petersham, MA: St. Bede's Publications, 1994.

Cassian, John. *Conferences*. New York: Paulist Press, 1985.

Castelo, Daniel. *Pentecostalism as a Christian Mystical Tradition*. Grand Rapids, MI: Eerdmans, 2017.

Catherine of Genoa. *Purgation and Purgatory: The Spiritual Dialogue*. New York: Paulist Press, 1979.

Catherine of Siena. *The Dialogue*. New York: Paulist Press, 1980.

Chesterton, G. K. *Orthodoxy*. Garden City, NY: Image Books, 1959.

———. *Saint Thomas Aquinas: The Dumb Ox*. Garden City, NY: Image Books, 1956.

Chittister, Joan. *Called to Question: A Spiritual Memoir*. Lanham, MD: Sheed & Ward, 2009.

———. *The Monastic Heart: 50 Simple Practices for a Contemplative and Fulfilling Life*. New York: Convergent, 2021.

———. *Radical Spirit: 12 Ways to Live a Free and Authentic Life*. New York: Convergent, 2017.

Chu-Cong, Joseph. *The Contemplative Experience: Erotic Love and Spiritual Union*. New York: Crossroad, 1999.

Claiborne, Shane. *The Irresistible Revolution: Living as an Ordinary Radical*. Grand Rapids, MI: Zondervan, 2006.

Claiborne, Shane, and Jonathan Wilson-Hartgrove. *Becoming the Answer to Our Prayers: Prayer for Ordinary Radicals*. Downers Grove, IL: InterVarsity Press, 2008.

Clément, Olivier. *The Roots of Christian Mysticism*. London: New City, 1993.

Climacus, John. *The Ladder of Divine Ascent*. New York: Paulist Press, 1982.

Coakley, Sarah. *The New Asceticism: Sexuality, Gender and the Quest for God*. London: Bloomsbury, 2015.

Cole, David. *The Mystic Path of Meditation: Beginning a Christ-Centered Journey*. Vestal, NY: Anamchara Books, 2013.

Colledge, Eric, ed. *The Mediaeval Mystics of England*. New York: Charles Scribner's Sons, 1961.

Cook, Christopher C. H., Julienne McLean, and Peter Tyler, eds. *Mystical Theology and Contemporary Spiritual Practice: Renewing the Contemplative Tradition.* London: Routledge, 2018.

Countryman, L. William. *The Mystical Way in the Fourth Gospel: Crossing Over into God.* Valley Forge, PA: Trinity Press International, 1994.

Cron, Ian Morgan. *Chasing Francis: A Pilgrim's Tale.* Colorado Springs, CO: NavPress, 2006.

Cross, F. L. and E. A. Livingstone, eds. *The Oxford Dictionary of the Christian Church.* Oxford: Oxford University Press, 1983.

Cupitt, Don. *Mysticism after Modernity.* Oxford: Blackwell Publishers, 1998.

Davies, Oliver. *God within: The Mystical Tradition of Northern Europe.* Hyde Park, NY: New City Press, 1988.

Davies, Oliver, and Denys Turner, eds. *Silence and the Word: Negative Theology and Incarnation.* Cambridge: Cambridge University Press, 2002.

de Caussade, Jean-Pierre. *Abandonment to Divine Providence.* Translated by John Beevers. New York: Image Books, 1975.

de Dreuille, Mayeul. *The Rule of Saint Benedict: A Commentary in Light of World Ascetic Traditions.* New York: The Newman Press, 2,000.

Delio, Ilia. *Franciscan Prayer.* Cincinnati: Saint Anthony Messenger Press, 2004.

———. *The Humility of God: A Franciscan Perspective.* Cincinnati: Saint Anthony Messenger Press, 2005.

———. *The Unbearable Wholeness of Being: God, Evolution, and the Power of Love.* Maryknoll, NY: Orbis Books, 2013.

Delisi, Anthony. *Praying in the Cellar: A Guide to Facing Your Fears and Finding God.* Brewster, MA: Paraclete Press, 2005.

———. *What Makes A Cistercian Monk? Chapter Talks on the Charism of the Cistercian Order of the Strict Observance.* Conyers, GA: Our Lady of the Holy Spirit Monastery, 2003.

DeMello, Anthony. *Awareness: Conversations with the Masters.* New York: Image Books, 1992.

———. *Contact with God: Retreat Conferences.* New York: Image Books, 1991.

———. *Sadhana, a Way to God: Christian Exercises in Eastern Form.* New York: Image Books, 1984.

———. *The Song of the Bird.* New York: Image Books, 1984.

Doherty, Catherine De Hueck. *Molchanie: The Silence of God.* New York: Crossroad Publishing Company, 1982.

Downey, Michael, ed. *The New Dictionary of Catholic Spirituality.* Collegeville, MN: The Liturgical Press, 1993.

Downing, David C. *Into the Region of Awe: Mysticism in C. S. Lewis.* Downers Grove, IL: InterVarsity Press, 2005.

Dubay, Thomas. *Deep Conversion, Deep Prayer.* San Francisco: Ignatius Press, 2006.

Dupré, Louis. *The Common Life: The Origins of Trinitarian Mysticism and Its Development by Jan Ruusbroec.* New York: Crossroad, 1984.

Eaton, John. *The Contemplative Face of Old Testament Wisdom.* London: SCM Press, 1989.

Edwards, Tilden. *Embracing the Call to Spiritual Depth: Gifts for Contemplative Living.* New York: Paulist Press, 2010.

———. *Living in the Presence: Spiritual Exercises to Open Our Lives to the Awareness of God.* San Francisco: HarperCollins, 1994.

———. *Living Simply through the Day: Spiritual Survival in a Complex Age.* New York: Paulist Press, 1977.

Egan, Harvey D., ed. *An Anthology of Christian Mysticism.* 2nd ed. Collegeville, MN: The Liturgical Press, 1996.

———. *Soundings of the Christian Mystical Tradition*. Collegeville, MN: Liturgical Press, 2010.

———. *What Are They Saying about Mysticism?* New York: Paulist Press, 1982.

Enomiya-Lassalle, Hugo. *Living in the New Consciousness*. Boston: Shambhala, 1988.

Ephrem the Syrian. *Hymns*. New York: Paulist Press, 1989.

Evagrius Ponticus. *The Praktikos and Chapters on Prayer*. Kalamazoo, MI: Cistercian Publications, 1980.

Fanning, Steven. *Mystics of the Christian Tradition*. London: Routledge, 2001.

Fanous, Samuel and Vincent Gillespie, eds. *The Cambridge Companion to Medieval English Mysticism*. Cambridge: Cambridge University Press, 2011.

Finlan, Stephen, and Vladimir Kharlamov, eds. *Theosis: Deification in Christian Theology*. Eugene, OR: Pickwick Publications, 2006.

Fisher, Barbara LeVan. *The Spirit of Saint Hildegard: A Treasury of Wisdom from the Life of Hildegard of Bingen—12th Century Mystic, Author, Composer, Scientist and Revolutionary*. Fairfield, CA: Viriditas Press, 2022.

Fitzgerald, Constance, Laurie Cassidy and M. Shawn Copeland. *Desire, Darkness and Hope: Theology in a Time of Impasse*. Collegeville, MN: Liturgical Press, 2021.

Flinders, Carol. *Enduring Grace: Living Portraits of Seven Women Mystics*. San Francisco: HarperCollins, 1993.

Foster, David. *Deep Calls to Deep: Going Further in Prayer*. London: Continuum, 2007.

Fox, George. *The Journal*. London: Penguin Books, 1998.

Francis and Clare. *The Complete Works*. New York: Paulist Press, 1982.

Freeman, Laurence. *Christian Meditation: Your Daily Practice*. Alresford, UK: Hunt & Thorpe, 1994.

———. *Jesus, the Teacher within*. Foreword by the Dalai Lama. Norwich, UK: Canterbury Press, 2008.

———. *Light Within: Meditation as Pure Prayer*. Norwich, UK: Canterbury Press, 2008.

———. *The Selfless Self: Meditation and the Opening of the Heart*. Norwich, UK: Canterbury Press, 2009.

Freke, Timothy, and Peter Gandy. *The Complete Guide to World Mysticism*. London: Piatkus, 1997.

Fremantle, Anne, ed. *The Protestant Mystics: An Anthology of Spiritual Experience from Martin Luther to T. S. Eliot*. Introduction by W. H. Auden. Boston: Little, Brown and Company, 1964.

Frost, Bede. *The Christian Mysteries*. London: A. R. Mowbray, 1950.

Fruehwirth, Robert. *The Drawing of This Love: Growing in Faith with Julian of Norwich*. Norwich, UK: Canterbury Press, 2016.

Fry, Timothy, ed. *RB 1980: The Rule of St. Benedict in Latin and English with Notes*. Collegeville, MN: The Liturgical Press, 1981.

Funk, Margaret. *The Matters Series*. Collegeville, MN: Liturgical Press, 2013. Volume 1: *Thoughts Matter: Discovering the Spiritual Journey*. Volume 2: *Tools Matter: Beginning the Spiritual Journey*. Volume 3: *Humility Matters: Toward Purity of Heart*. Volume 4: *Lectio Matters: Before the Burning Bush*. Volume 5: *Discernment Matters: Listening with the Ear of the Heart*.

Furlong, Monica. *Contemplating Now*. Cambridge, MA: Cowley Publications, 1983.

Garrison, Becky. *Rising from the Ashes: Rethinking Church*. New York: Seabury Books, 2007.

Gatta, Julia. *Three Spiritual Directors for Our Time: Julian of Norwich, The Cloud of Unknowing, Walter Hilton*. Cambridge, MA: Cowley, 1986.

Giordano, Silvano, ed. *God Speaks in the Night: The Life, Times, and Teaching of St. John of the Cross*. Translated by Kieran Kavanaugh. Washington, DC: ICS Publications, 1991.

Grant, Sara. *Lord of the Dance*. Bangalore: Asian Trading Corporation, 1987.

———. *Toward an Alternative Theology: Confessions of a Non-dualist Christian*. Notre Dame, IN: University of Notre Dame Press, 2002.

Greeley, Andrew M. *The Great Mysteries: Experiencing Catholic Faith from the inside Out*. Lanham, MD: Sheed & Ward, 2003.

Gregory of Nyssa. *From Glory to Glory*. Selected and introduced by Jean Daniélou; translated and edited by Herbert Musurillo. New York: Charles Scribner's Sons, 1961.

———. *The Life of Moses*. Translated by Everett Ferguson and Abraham J. Malherbe. New York: Paulist Press, 1978.

Gregory Palamas. *The Triads*. New York: Paulist Press, 1983.

Griffiths, Bede. *The One Light: Bede Griffiths' Principal Writings*. Edited and with commentary by Bruno Barnhart. Springfield, IL: Templegate Publishers, 2001.

Guigo II. *Ladder of Monks and Twelve Meditations*. Kalamazoo, MI: Cistercian Publications, 1979.

Haase, Albert. *Becoming an Ordinary Mystic: Spirituality for the Rest of Us*. Downers Grove, IL: IVP Academic, 2019.

Haggerty, Brian A. *Out of the House of Slavery: On the Meaning of the Ten Commandments*. New York: Paulist Press, 1978.

Harmless, William. *Desert Christians*. Oxford: Oxford University Press, 2004.

———. *Mystics*. Oxford: Oxford University Press, 2008.

Hardy, Richard P. *John of the Cross: Man and Mystic*. Boston: Pauline Books & Media, 2004.

Harrington, Joel F. *Dangerous Mystic: Meister Eckhart's Path to the God Within*. New York: Penguin Press, 2018.

Harton, F. P. *The Elements of the Spiritual Life: A Study in Ascetical Theology*. London: SPCK, 1957.

Heath, Elaine A. *The Mystic Way of Evangelism: A Contemplative Vision for Christian Outreach*. Grand Rapids, MI: Baker Academic, 2008.

Henry, Patrick, ed. *Benedict's Dharma: Buddhists Reflect on the Rule of Saint Benedict*. New York: Riverhead Books, 2001.

Herbert, George. *The Country Parson and the Temple*. New York: Paulist Press, 1981.

Herman, Nicolas (Brother Lawrence of the Resurrection). *Practice of the Presence*. Translated by Carmen Acevedo Butcher. Minneapolis: Broadleaf Books 2022.

Hildegard of Bingen, *Selected Writings*. London: Penguin Books, 2001.

Hilton, Walter. *The Goad of Love*. London: Faber and Faber, 1952.

———. *The Stairway of Perfection*. Translated by M. L. Del Mastro. Garden City, NY: Image Books, 1979.

Hoffman, Bengt R. *Theology of the Heart: The Role of Mysticism in the Theology of Martin Luther*. Minneapolis: Kirk House Publishers, 1998.

Holdaway, Gervase, ed. *The Oblate Life*. Collegeville, MN: Liturgical Press, 2008.

Hollywood, Amy. *Sensible Ecstasy: Mysticism, Sexual Difference, and the Demands of History*. Chicago: University of Chicago Press, 2002.

Hollywood, Amy, and Patricia Z. Beckman, eds. *The Cambridge Companion to Christian Mysticism*. Cambridge: Cambridge University Press, 2012.

Holmes, Barbara. *Joy Unspeakable: Contemplative Practices of the Black Church*. Minneapolis: Fortress Press, 2017.

Holmes, Urban T. *A History of Christian Spirituality: An Analytical Introduction*. New York: The Seabury Press, 1980.

Houselander, Caryll. *Essential Writings*. Selected with commentary by Wendy M. Wright. Maryknoll, NY: Orbis Books, 2005.

———. *The Reed of God.* New York: Sheed and Ward, 1944.

Howells, Edward, and Mark A. McIntosh, eds. *The Oxford Handbook of Mystical Theology.* Oxford: Oxford University Press, 2020.

Huggett, Joyce. *The Joy of Listening to God.* Downers Grove, IL: InterVarsity Press, 1986.

Hughes, Robert Davis, III. *Beloved Dust: Tides of the Spirit in the Christian Life.* New York: Continuum, 2008.

Hunt, Anne. *The Trinity: Insights from the Mystics.* Collegeville, MN: Liturgical Press, 2010.

Huxley, Aldous. *The Perennial Philosophy.* New York: Harper and Brothers, 1945.

Ignatius of Loyola. *Letters and Instructions.* St. Louis: Institute of Jesuit Sources, 2006.

———. *Personal Writings.* London: Penguin Books, 2004.

———. *The Spiritual Exercises of Saint Ignatius of Loyola, translated from the Spanish with a Commentary and a translation of the Directorium in Exercita.* Translated by W. H. Longridge. London: A.R. Mowbray, 1919.

Jantzen, Grace M. *Julian of Norwich: Mystic and Theologian.* New York: Paulist Press, 2000.

———. *Power, Gender, and Christian Mysticism.* Cambridge: Cambridge University Press, 1995.

John of the Cross. *Collected Works.* Washington, DC: ICS Publications, 1991.

Johnson, Elizabeth A. *Quest for the Living God: Mapping Frontiers in the Theology of God.* New York: Continuum, 2007.

Johnson, Luke Timothy. *Mystical Tradition: Judaism, Christianity, and Islam.* Chantilly, VA: The Learning Company, 2008.

Jones, Cheslyn, Geoffrey Wainwright, and Edward Yarnold, eds. *The Study of Spirituality.* New York: Oxford University Press, 1986.

Jones, Rufus. *Essential Writings.* Maryknoll, NY: Orbis Books, 2001.

Julian of Norwich. *The Showings.* Translated by Mirabai Starr. Charlottesville, VA: Hampton Roads, 2022.

Kadloubovsky, E., and G. E. H. Palmer, trans. *Writings from the Philokalia on Prayer of the Heart.* London: Faber and Faber, Ltd., 1951.

Kaplan, Aryeh. *Meditation and the Bible.* York Beach, ME: Weiser Books, 1978.

Keating, Daniel A. *Deification and Grace.* Naples, FL: Sapientia Press, 2007.

Keating, Thomas. *Intimacy with God: An Introduction to Centering Prayer.* New York: Crossroad, 2009.

———. *Invitation to Love: The Way of Christian Contemplation.* London: Bloomsbury, 2011.

———. *Manifesting God.* Brooklyn, NY: Lantern Publishing & Media, 2021.

———. *The Mystery of Christ: The Liturgy as Christian Experience.* Rockport, MA: Element, 1991.

———. *Open Mind, Open Heart: the Contemplative Dimension of the Gospel.* London: Bloomsbury Continuum, 2006.

———. *Reflections on the Unknowable.* Brooklyn, NY: Lantern Publishing & Media, 2020.

———. *Spirituality, Contemplation and Transformation: Writings on Centering Prayer.* New York: Lantern Books, 2008.

———. *St. Therese of Lisieux: A Transformation in Christ.* Brooklyn, NY: Lantern Publishing & Media, 2020.

———. *The Thomas Keating Reader.* Woodstock, NY: Lantern Publishing & Media, 2022.

Kelsey, Morton. *The Christian and the Supernatural.* Minneapolis: Augsburg Publishing, 1976.

———. *Dreams: A Way to Listen to God.* New York: Paulist Press, 1978.

———. *The Other Side of Silence: Meditation for the Twenty-First Century.* New York: Paulist Press, 1997.

Kempe, Margery. *The Book of Margery Kempe.* London: Penguin Books, 1985.

King, Ursula. *Christian Mystics: Their Lives and Legacies throughout the Ages.* Mahwah, NJ: HiddenSpring, 2001.

Kripal, Jeffrey J. *Roads of Excess, Palaces of Wisdom: Eroticism and Reflexivity in the Study of Mysticism.* Chicago: University of Chicago Press, 2001.

Kushner, Lawrence. *Honey from the Rock: An Introduction to Jewish Mysticism.* Woodstock, VT: Jewish Lights, 2003.

———. *Jewish Spirituality: A Brief Introduction for Christians.* Woodstock, VT: Jewish Lights, 2001.

Laird, Martin. *Into the Silent Land: A Guide to the Christian Practice of Contemplation.* Oxford: Oxford University Press, 2006.

———. *An Ocean of Light: Contemplation, Transformation and Liberation.* Oxford: Oxford University Press, 2018.

———. *A Sunlit Absence: Silence, Awareness and Contemplation.* Oxford: Oxford University Press, 2011.

Lamm, Julia A., ed. *The Wiley-Blackwell Companion to Christian Mysticism.* Oxford: Wiley-Blackwell, 2013.

Lamott, Anne. *Bird by Bird: Some Instructions on Writing and Life.* New York: Pantheon Books, 1994.

Lanzetta, Beverly. *The Eye of the Storm: Living Spiritually in the Real World.* San Francisco: HarperCollins, 1992.

———. *A New Silence: Spiritual Practices and Formation for the Monk Within.* Sebastopol, CA: Blue Sapphire Books, 2020.

———. *The Other Side of Nothingness: Toward a Theology of Radical Openness.* Albany: State University of New York Press, 2001.

———. *Path of the Heart: A Spiritual Guide to Divine Union.* San Diego, CA: Blue Sapphire Books, 2014.

———. *Prayer and Prophecy: The Essential Kenneth Leech.* New York: Seabury Books, 2009.

———. *Radical Wisdom: A Feminist Mystical Theology.* Minneapolis: Fortress Press, 2005.

Leech, Kenneth. *Experiencing God: Theology as Spirituality.* San Francisco: Harper & Row, 1985.

———. *The Social God.* London: Sheldon Press, 1981

———. *Soul Friend: The Practice of Christian Spirituality.* San Francisco: Harper & Row, 1977.

———. *Subversive Orthodoxy: Traditional Faith and Radical Commitment.* Toronto: Anglican Book Centre, 1992.

———. *True Prayer: An Invitation to Christian Spirituality.* San Francisco: Harper & Row, 1980.

Leloup, Jean-Yves. *Being Still: Reflections on an Ancient Mystical Tradition.* Translated by M. S. Laird. Leominster, UK: Gracewing, 2003.

Lewis, C. S. *Letters to Malcolm: Chiefly on Prayer.* London: Geoffrey Bles, 1964.

———. *The Lion, the Witch and the Wardrobe.* New York: Macmillan Books, 1950.

———. *The Voyage of the Dawn Treader.* New York: Macmillan Books, 1952.

Linn, Dennis, Sheila Fabricant Linn, and Matthew Linn. *Good Goats: Healing Our Image of God.* Mahwah, NJ: Paulist Press, 1994.

Llewellyn, Robert. *Why Pray?* Brewster, MA: Paraclete Press, 2019.

———. *With Pity Not with Blame: The Spirituality of Julian of Norwich and The Cloud of Unknowing for Today.* London: Darton, Longman and Todd, 1982.

Louf, André. *The Cistercian Way.* Translated by Nivard Kinsella. Kalamazoo, MI: Cistercian Publications, 1983.

Louth, Andrew. *The Origins of the Christian Mystical Tradition from Plato to Denys*. Oxford: Clarendon Press, 1981.

Mabry, John. *Growing into God: A Beginner's Guide to Christian Mysticism*. Wheaton, IL: Quest Books, 2012.

Macleod, George F. *Daily Readings with George Macleod*. Edited by Ron Ferguson. London: HarperCollins, 1991.

———. *The Whole Earth Shall Cry Glory*. Glasgow: Wild Goose Publications, 1985.

MacQuarrie, John. *Two Worlds Are Ours: An Introduction to Christian Mysticism*. Minneapolis: Fortress Press, 2004.

Main, John. *Fully Alive: An Introduction to Christian Meditation*. Maryknoll, NY: Orbis Books, 2014.

———. *John Main: Essential Writings*. Maryknoll, NY: Orbis Books, 2002.

———. *The Way of Unknowing: Expanding Spiritual Horizons through Meditation*. Norwich, UK: Canterbury Press, 2011.

———. *Word into Silence: A Manual for Christian Meditation*. Norwich, UK: Canterbury Press, 2006.

Maitland, Sara. *A Book of Silence*. Berkeley, CA: Counterpoint, 2008.

Maloney, George A. *Abiding in the Indwelling Trinity*. New York: Paulist Press, 2004.

———. *Invaded by God: Mysticism and the Indwelling Trinity*. Denville, NJ: Dimension Books, 1979.

———. *The Mystery of Christ in You: The Mystical Vision of Saint Paul*. New York: Alba House, 1998.

———. *The Mystic of Fire and Light: St. Symeon, the New Theologian*. Denville, NJ: Dimension Books, 1975.

Manser, Martin H. *The Westminster Collection of Christian Quotations*. Louisville, KY: Westminster John Knox Press, 2001.

Marechal, Elias. *Tears of an Innocent God: Conversations on Silence, Kindness and Prayer*. Mahway, NJ: Paulist Press, 2015.

Marechal, Paul. *Dancing Madly Backwards: A Journey into God*. New York: Crossroad, 1982.

Marion, Jim. *Putting on the Mind of Christ*. Charlottesville, VA: Hampton Roads Publishing, 2000.

Martin, James. *The Jesuit Guide to (Almost) Everything: A Spirituality for Real Life*. San Francisco: HarperCollins, 2010.

Mathewes-Green, Frederica. *The Lost Gospel of Mary: The Mother of Jesus in Three Ancient Texts*. Brewster, MA: Paraclete Press, 2007.

Maximus the Confessor. *On the Cosmic Mystery of Jesus Christ*. Crestwood, NY: St. Vladimir's Seminary Press, 2003.

May, Gerald G. *Living in Love: Articles from Shalem News 1978–2005*. Washington, DC: Shalem Institute for Spiritual Formation, 2008.

———. *Will and Spirit: A Contemplative Psychology*. San Francisco: Harper & Row, 1982.

McClernon, John P., ed. *Sermons in a Sentence: A Treasury of Quotations on the Spiritual Life*. Vol. 4, *St. Teresa of Avila*. San Francisco: Ignatius Press, 2005.

McColman, Carl. *Answering the Contemplative Call: First Steps on the Mystical Path*. Minneapolis: Broadleaf Books, 2013.

———. *Christian Mystics: 108 Seers, Saints and Sages*. Minneapolis: Broadleaf Books, 2016.

———. *Eternal Heart: The Mystical Path to a Joyful Life*. Minneapolis: Broadleaf Books, 2021.

———. *The Lion, the Mouse and the Dawn Treader: Spiritual Lessons from C.S. Lewis's Narnia*. Brewster, MA: Paraclete Press, 2011.

———. *The Little Book of Christian Mysticism: Essential Wisdom of Saints, Seers, and Sages.* Minneapolis: Broadleaf Books, 2018.

McGinn, Bernard, ed. *The Essential Writings of Christian Mysticism.* New York: The Modern Library, 2006.

———. *The Mystical Thought of Meister Eckhart: The Man from Whom God Hid Nothing.* New York: Crossroad, 2001.

———. *The Presence of God: A History of Western Christian Mysticism.* New York: Crossroad, 1992–2021. Volume 1: *The Foundations of Mysticism.* Volume 2: *The Growth of Mysticism.* Volume 3: *The Flowering of Mysticism.* Volume 4: *The Harvest of Medieval Germany.* Volume 5: *Varieties of Vernacular Mysticism.* Volume 6.1: *Mysticism in the Reformation.* Volume 6.2: *Mysticism in the Golden Age of Spain.* Volume 6.3: *The Persistence of Mysticism.* Volume 7: *The Crisis of Mysticism.*

McGinn, Bernard, and Patricia Ferris McGinn. *Early Christian Mystics: The Divine Vision of the Spiritual Masters.* New York: Crossroad, 2003.

McHugh, Adam S. *Introverts in the Church: Finding Our Place in an Extroverted Culture.* Downers Grove, IL: IVP Books, 2009.

McLaren, Brian D. *Finding Our Way Again: The Return of the Ancient Practices.* Nashville: Thomas Nelson Publishers, 2008.

———. *A Generous Orthodoxy.* Grand Rapids, MI: Zondervan, 2004.

McNamara, William. *Earthy Mysticism: Contemplation and the Life of Passionate Presence.* New York: Crossroad, 1987.

Mechthild of Magdeburg. *The Flowing Light of the Godhead.* New York: Paulist Press, 1998.

Meister Eckhart. *The Complete Mystical Works.* New York: Crossroad, 2010.

———. *Selected Writings.* London: Penguin Books, 1994.

Menzies, Lucy. *Mirrors of the Holy: Ten Studies in Sanctity.* London: A. R. Mowbray, 1928.

Merton, Thomas. *Contemplative Prayer.* New York: Image Books, 1971.

———. *A Course in Christian Mysticism.* Edited by Jon M. Sweeney. Collegeville, MN: Liturgical Press, 2017.

———. *The Inner Experience: Notes on Contemplation.* Edited by William H. Shannon. San Francisco: HarperSanFrancisco, 2003.

———. *An Introduction to Christian Mysticism: Initiation into the Monastic Tradition 3.* Edited by Patrick F. O'Connell. Kalamazoo, MI: Cistercian Publications, 2008.

———. *New Seeds of Contemplation.* New York: New Directions, 1961.

———. *The Seven Storey Mountain.* Garden City, NY: Image Books, 1970.

———. *Thomas Merton, Spiritual Master: The Essential Writings.* Edited by Lawrence S. Cunningham. New York: Paulist Press, 1992.

———. *The Waters of Siloe.* New York: Houghton Mifflin, 1949.

Miller, Gordon L. *The Way of the English Mystics: An Anthology and Guide for Pilgrims.* Ridgefield, CT: Morehouse Publishing, 1996.

A Monk of the West. *Christianity and the Doctrine of Non-dualism.* Hillsdale, NY: Sophia Perennis, 2004.

Moorcroft, Jennifer. *He Is My Heaven: The Life of Elizabeth of the Trinity.* Washington, DC: ICS Publications, 2002.

Murray, Pauli. *Selected Sermons and Writings.* Selected with an Introduction by Anthony B. Pinn. Maryknoll, NY: Orbis Books, 2006.

Murray, Seth. Lord, *Open My Lips: The Liturgy of the Hours as Daily Prayer.* El Sobrante, CA: North Bay Books, 2004.

Muto, Susan. *A Feast for Hungry Souls: Spiritual Lessons from the Church's Greatest Masters and Mystics.* Notre Dame, IN: Ave Maria Press, 2020.

Nelstrop, Louise, with Kevin Magill and Bradley B. Onishi. *Christian Mysticism: An Introduction to Contemporary Theoretical Approaches.* London: Routledge, 2016.

Nicholas of Cusa. *Selected Spiritual Writings.* New York: Paulist Press, 1997.

Nieva, Constantino Sarmiento. *This Transcending God: The Teaching of the Author of "The Cloud of Unknowing."* London: The Mitre Press, 1970.

Nikodimos of the Holy Mountain and Makarios of Corinth, compilers. *The Philokalia: The Complete Text.* Vols. 1–4. London: Faber and Faber, 1979, 1981, 1984, 1995.

Nolan, Albert. *Jesus before Christianity.* Maryknoll, NY: Orbis Books, 1976.

Nolan, William Michael. *Growing Up as a Trappist Monk.* New York: Vantage Press, 2003.

Norris, Kathleen. *Acedia and Me: A Marriage, Monks, and a Writer's Life.* New York: Riverhead Books, 2008.

———. *The Cloister Walk.* New York: Riverhead Books, 1996.

O'Connor, Patricia. *In Search of Thérèse.* Wilmington, DE: Michael Glazier, 1987.

O'Donohue, John. *Anam Čara: A Book of Celtic Wisdom.* San Francisco: HarperCollins, 1997.

Olivera, Bernardo. "Solus Deus Vacare Deo: Towards a Renewed Christian Mysticism." *Cistercian Studies Quarterly* 43, no. 3 (2008): 253–70.

Ó Madagáin, Murchadh. *Centering Prayer and the Healing of the Unconscious.* New York: Lantern Books, 2007.

Origen. *An Exhortation to Martyrdom, Prayer, and Selected Works.* Translated by Rowan A. Greer. New York: Paulist Press, 1979.

Paintner, Christine Valtners. *Illuminating the Way: Embracing the Wisdom of Monks and Mystics.* Notre Dame, IN: Sorin Books, 2016.

Palmer, Phoebe. *The Way of Holiness.* Charleston, SC: Bibliolife, 2009.

Panikkar, Raimon. *Christophany: The Fullness of Man.* Maryknoll, NY: Orbis Books, 2004.

———. *The Experience of God: Icons of the Mystery.* Minneapolis: Fortress Press, 2006.

———. *Opera Omnia.* Vol. 1.1, *Mysticism and Spirituality, Part One: Mysticism, Fullness of Life.* Maryknoll, NY: Orbis Books, 2014.

Papanikolaou, Aristotle. *Being With God: Trinity, Apophaticism, and Divine-Human Communion.* Notre Dame, IN: University of Notre Dame Press, 2006.

Parsons, William B., ed. *Teaching Mysticism.* Oxford: Oxford University Press, 2011.

Pascal, Blaise. *Pensées.* London: Penguin Books, 1966.

Patmore, Coventry. *The Rod, the Root and the Flower.* Freeport, NY: Books for Libraries Press, 1950.

Pennington, M. Basil. *Centering Prayer: Renewing an Ancient Christian Prayer Form.* New York: Image Books, 1980.

Perl, Eric D. *Theophany: The Neoplatonic Philosophy of Dionysius the Areopagite.* Albany: State University of New York Press, 2007.

Peterson, Christiana N. *Mystics and Misfits: Meeting God through St. Francis and Other Unlikely Saints.* Harrisonburg, VA: Herald Press, 2018.

Peterson, Eugene. *A Long Obedience in the Same Direction: Discipleship in an Instant Society.* Revised and Expanded Edition. Downers Grove, IL: Intervarsity Press, 2000.

Pizzuto, Vincent. *Contemplating Christ: The Gospels and the Interior Life.* Collegeville, MN: Liturgical Press, 2018.

Ponticus, Evagrius. *The Mind's Long Journey to the Holy Trinity: The Ad Monachos of Evagrius Ponticus.* Translated by Jeremy Driscoll. Collegeville, MN: Liturgical Press, 1994.

———. *The Praktikos and Chapters on Prayer.* Kalamazoo, MI: Cistercian Publications, 1972.

Pryce, Paula. *The Monk's Cell: Ritual and Knowledge in American Contemplative Christianity.* Oxford: Oxford University Press, 2018.

Pseudo-Dionysius. *The Complete Works.* New York: Paulist Press, 1987.

Pseudo-Macarius. *The Fifty Spiritual Homilies and the Great Letter*. New York: Paulist Press, 1992.

Rahner, Karl. *The Christian of the Future*. New York: Herder and Herder, 1967.

———. *Concern for the Church: Theological Investigations*. Vol. 20. New York: Crossroad, 1981.

———. *The Mystical Way in Everyday Life*. Maryknoll, NY: Orbis Books, 2010.

———. *Spiritual Writings*. Maryknoll, NY: Orbis Books, 2004.

Ramsey, Michael. *Be Still and Know: A Study in the Life of Prayer*. Cambridge, MA: Cowley Publications, 1993.

Reinhold, H. A., ed. *The Soul Afire: Revelations of the Mystics*. Garden City, NY: Image Books, 1973.

Richard of St. Victor. *The Twelve Patriarchs and Other Works*. New York: Paulist Press, 1979.

Roberts, Bernadette. *The Christian Contemplative Journey: Essays on the Path*. Austin, TX: Contemplative Christians, 2017.

———. *The Experience of No-Self: A Contemplative Journey*. Boston: Shambhala Publications, 1985.

———. *The Path to No-Self: Life at the Center*. Boston: Shambhala Publications, 1985.

Roden, Frederick S., and John-Julian. *Love's Trinity: A Companion to Julian of Norwich*. Collegeville, MN: Liturgical Press, 2009.

Rohr, Richard. *Everything Belongs: The Gift of Contemplative Prayer*. New York: Crossroad, 2003.

———. *The Naked Now: Learning to See as the Mystics See*. New York: Crossroad, 2009.

———. *Things Hidden: Scripture as Spirituality*. Cincinnati: St. Anthony Messenger Press, 2008.

———. *The Universal Christ: How a Forgotten Reality Can Change Everything We See, Hope for, and Believe*. New York: Convergent, 2019.

Rohr, Richard, with Mike Morrell. *The Divine Dance: The Trinity and Your Transformation*. New Kensington, PA: Whitaker House, 2016.

Rolheiser, Ronald. *The Holy Longing: The Search for a Christian Spirituality*. New York: Doubleday, 1999.

Rolle, Richard. *The Fire of Love and the Mending of Life*. Translated with an introduction by M. L. del Mastro. Garden City, NY: Image Books, 1981.

Rollins, Peter. *The Fidelity of Betrayal: Towards a Church beyond Belief*. Brewster, MA: Paraclete Press, 2008.

———. *How (Not) to Speak of God*. Brewster, MA: Paraclete Press, 2006.

Ross, Maggie. *Pillars of Flame: Power, Priesthood, and Spiritual Maturity*. San Francisco: Harper & Row, 1988.

———. *Silence: A User's Guide*. Eugene, OR: Cascade Books, 2014, 2018. Volume 1: *Process*. Volume 2: *Application*.

———. *Writing the Icon of the Heart: In Silence Beholding*. Abingdon, UK: The Bible Reading Fellowship, 2011.

Rowland, Christopher, and Christopher R.A. Morray-Jones, eds. *The Mystery of God: Early Jewish Mysticism and the New Testament*. Boston: Brill, 2009.

Ruffing, Janet K., ed. *Mysticism and Social Transformation*. Syracuse, NY: Syracuse University Press, 2001.

Russell, Norman. *The Doctrine of Deification in the Greek Patristic Tradition*. Oxford: Oxford University Press, 2004.

Ruusbroec, John. *Spiritual Espousals*. New York: Paulist Press, 1985.

Ryrie, Alexander. *Silent Waiting: The Biblical Roots of Contemplative Spirituality*. Norwich, UK: Canterbury Press, 1999.

———. *Wonderful Exchange: An Exploration of Silent Prayer.* New York: Paulist Press, 2003.

Sanford, John A. *Mystical Christianity: A Psychological Commentary on the Gospel of John.* New York: Crossroad, 1993.

Scott, Sophfronia. *The Seeker and the Monk: Everyday Conversations with Thomas Merton.* Minneapolis: Broadleaf Books, 2021.

Sellner, Edward C. *Finding the Monk Within: Great Monastic Values for Today.* Mahwah, NJ: Hidden Spring/Paulist Press, 2008.

Sells, Michael A. *Mystical Languages of Unsaying.* Chicago: University of Chicago Press, 1994.

Slade, Herbert. *Exploration into Contemplative Prayer.* London: Darton, Longman and Todd, 1975.

Smith, Brendan. *The Silence of Divine Love.* London: Darton, Longman and Todd, 1998.

Smith, Jessica M., and Stuart Higginbotham, eds. *Contemplation and Community: A Gathering of Fresh Voices for a Living Tradition.* New York: Crossroad, 2019.

Smith, Martin L. *Reconciliation: Preparing for Confession in the Episcopal Church.* Cambridge, MA: Cowley Publications, 1985.

———. *The Word Is Very Near You: A Guide to Praying with Scripture.* Cambridge, MA: Cowley Publications, 1989.

Soelle, Dorothee. *The Silent Cry: Mysticism and Resistance.* Minneapolis: Fortress Press, 2001.

Somerville, James M. *The Mystical Sense of the Gospels: A Handbook for Contemplatives.* New York: Crossroad, 1997.

Spidlík, Tomas. *Drinking from the Hidden Fountain: A Patristic Breviary.* Kalamazoo, MI: Cistercian Publications, 1994.

———. *Prayer: The Spirituality of the Christian East.* Vol. 2. Kalamazoo, MI: Cistercian Publications, 2005.

———. *The Spirituality of the Christian East.* Kalamazoo, MI: Cistercian Publications, 1986.

Starr, Mirabai. *Saint John of the Cross: Luminous Darkness.* Albuquerque, NM: CAC Publishing, 2022.

Stavropoulos, Archimandrite Christoforos. *Partakers of Divine Nature.* Minneapolis: Light and Life, 1976.

Steere, Douglas V. *Prayer and Worship.* Richmond, IN: Friends United Press, 1978.

———, ed. *Quaker Spirituality: Selected Writings.* New York: Paulist Press, 1984.

Steindl-Rast, David. *Gratefulness, the Heart of Prayer: An Approach to Life in Fullness.* New York: Paulist Press, 1984.

Stroumsa, Guy. *Hidden Wisdom: Esoteric Traditions and the Roots of Christian Mysticism.* Leiden: Brill Academic, 2005.

Sweeney, Jon. *Cloister Talks: Learning from My Friends the Monks.* Grand Rapids, MI: Brazos Press, 2009.

Sweeney, Marvin A. *Jewish Mysticism: From Ancient Times through Today.* Grand Rapids, MI: Eerdmans, 2020.

Symeon the New Theologian. *The Practical and Theological Chapters and the Three Theological Discourses.* Kalamazoo, MI: Cistercian Publications, 1982.

Tasto, Maria. *The Transforming Power of Lectio Divina.* New London, CT: Twenty-Third Publications, 2015.

Taylor-Stinson, Therese. *Walking the Way of Harriet Tubman: Public Mystic and Freedom Fighter.* Minneapolis: Broadleaf Books, 2023.

Teilhard de Chardin, Pierre. *The Divine Milieu.* New York: Harper & Row, 1965.

———. *Hymn of the Universe.* New York: Harper & Row, 1965.

Teresa of Avila. *Collected Works*. Vols. 1–3. Washington, DC: ICS Publications, 1976, 1980, 1985.

Thérèse of Lisieux. *Story of a Soul: The Autobiography*. Washington, DC: ICS Publications, 1996.

Thornton, Martin. *Christian Proficiency*. London: SPCK, 1959.

———. *English Spirituality: An Outline of Ascetical Theology According to the English Pastoral Tradition*. London: SPCK, 1963.

Thurman, Howard. *Disciplines of the Spirit*. Richmond, IN: Friends United Press, 1963.

———. *The Inward Journey*. Richmond, IN: Friends United Press, 1961.

———. *Jesus and the Disinherited*. Boston: Beacon Press, 1976.

———. *Meditations of the Heart*. Boston: Beacon Press, 1953.

———. *Mysticism and the Experience of Love*. Wallingford, PA: Pendle Hill, 1961.

———. *The Way of the Mystics*. Maryknoll, NY: Orbis Books, 2021.

———. *With Head and Heart: The Autobiography of Howard Thurman*. New York: Harcourt Brace, 1979.

Tozer, A.W. *The Pursuit of God*. Camp Hill, PA: Wing Spread Publishers, 2006.

Turner, Denys. *The Darkness of God: Negativity in Christian Mysticism*. Cambridge: Cambridge University Press, 1995.

———. *Eros and Allegory: Medieval Exegesis of the Song of Songs*. Kalamazoo, MI: Cistercian Publications, 1995.

———. *God, Mystery and Mystification*. Notre Dame, IN: University of Notre Dame Press, 2019.

Underhill, Evelyn. *An Anthology of the Love of God*. London: Mowbray, 1953.

———. *The Evelyn Underhill Reader*. Compiled by Thomas S. Kepler. New York: Abingdon Press, 1962.

———. *The Letters of Evelyn Underhill*. Edited with an introduction by Charles Williams. London: Longmans, Green, 1943.

———. *The Making of a Mystic: New and Selected Letters of Evelyn Underhill*. Edited by Carol Poston. Urbana: University of Illinois Press, 2010.

———. *Mysticism: A Study in the Nature and Development of Spiritual Consciousness*. Twelfth ed., revised. London: Methuen, 1930.

———. *The Mystics of the Church*. Cambridge: James Clarke, 1925.

———. *Practical Mysticism*. New York: E. P. Dutton, 1915.

———. *Radiance: A Spiritual Memoir*. Brewster, MA: Paraclete Press, 2004.

Upjohn, Sheila. *In Search of Julian of Norwich*. London: Darton, Longman and Todd, 1989.

Verdeyen, Paul. *Ruusbroec and His Mysticism*. Collegeville, MN: The Liturgical Press, 1994.

Vogel, Arthur A. *The Power of His Resurrection: The Mystical Life of Christians*. New York: Seabury Press, 1976.

Von Hügel, Friedrich. *The Mystical Element of Religion as Studied in Saint Catherine of Genoa and Her Friends*. 2nd ed. With an introduction by Michael Downey. New York: Crossroad, 1999.

Wakefield, Gordon S., ed. *The Westminster Dictionary of Christian Spirituality*. Philadelphia: The Westminster Press, 1983.

Ward, Benedicta, trans. *The Desert Fathers: Sayings of the Early Christian Monks*. London: Penguin, 2003.

Wathen, Ambrose G. *Silence: The Meaning of Silence in the Rule of St. Benedict*. Washington, DC: Cistercian Publications/Consortium Press, 1973.

Watts, Alan. *Behold the Spirit: A Study in the Necessity of Mystical Religion*. New York: Random House, 1947.

Weil, Simone. *Awaiting God*. Abbotsford, BC: Fresh Winds Press, 2012.

———. *Gravity and Grace*. London: Routledge, 1952.

Welch, John. *When Gods Die: An Introduction to John of the Cross*. Darien, IL: Carmelite Media, 2017.

Wesley, John. *A Plain Account of Christian Perfection*. Annotated edition by Mark K. Olson. Fenwick, MI: Alethea in Heart, 2005.

Wilber, Ken. *Integral Spirituality: A Startling New Role for Religion in the Modern and Postmodern World*. Boston: Integral Books, 2006.

William of St. Thierry. *On Contemplating God, Prayer, Meditations*. Kalamazoo, MI: Cistercian Publications, 1977.

Williams, Rowan. *The Wound of Knowledge*. London: Darton, Longman and Todd, 1990.

Woods, Richard, ed. *Understanding Mysticism*. Garden City, NY: Image Books, 1980.

Young, Wm. Paul. *The Shack*. Newbury Park, CA: Windblown Media, 2007.

Zacharias, Archimandrite. *Remember Thy First Love*. Dalton, PA: Mount Thabor Publishing, 2010.

Notes

PREFACE

1. Romans 5:5.
2. 2 Peter 1:4 KJV.

CHAPTER ONE: THE TRANSFIGURING MOMENT

1. Walnut Street was renamed Muhammad Ali Boulevard in 1978; the intersection was declared "Thomas Merton Square" in 2008.
2. Thomas Merton, *Conjectures of a Guilty Bystander* (New York: Crown Publishing, 1968), 153–56.
3. John 8:12; Matthew 5:14.
4. Mirabi Starr, *Teresa of Avila: The Book of My Life* (Boston: New Seeds, 2007), 225.
5. Ecclesiastes 3:1, 7. The famous song by Pete Seeger, "Turn, Turn, Turn" which became a hit in 1965 for the Byrds, is based on Ecclesiastes 3.
6. See *The Autobiography of Saint Teresa of Ávila*, chapter 10. At least one popular translation of the autobiography renders this as "mystical experience" but the Spanish is more accurately translated as "mystical theology."
7. Philippians 2:5; 2 Peter 1:4.

CHAPTER TWO: THE MUTE MYSTERY: MAKING SENSE OF MYSTICISM

1. Anonymous (Valentin Tomberg), *Meditations on the Tarot: A Journey into Christian Hermeticism,* trans. Robert Powell (New York: Jeremy Tarcher, 2002), 297, Kindle loc. 6207. Despite the esoteric title, this book is a profound exploration of mystical and contemplative Christianity, and has been endorsed by leading contemplative Christians like Bede Griffiths, Cynthia Bourgeault, Thomas Keating, and others.
2. Evelyn Underhill, *Mystics of the Church* (Cambridge: James Clarke, 1925), 10
3. Howard Thurman, *Mysticism: And the Experience of Love*, Pendle Hill Pamphlets Book 115 (Wallingford, PA: Pendle Hill Publications, 1961).
4. Harvey D. Egan, *An Anthology of Christian Mysticism* (Collegeville, MN: Liturgical Press, 1996), xvi.
5. Louise Nelstrop et al., *Christian Mysticism: An Introduction to Contemporary Theoretical Approaches* (Farnham, UK: Ashgate Publishing, 2009), Kindle edition, loc. 52.

6. Bernard McGinn, "Mystical Consciousness: A Modest Proposal," *Spiritus* 8 (2008): 44.
7. Timothy Freke and Peter Gandy, *The Complete Guide to World Mysticism* (London: Piatkus, 1997), 9.
8. Swami Abhayananda, *History of Mysticism: The Unchanging Testament* (Olympia, WA: Atma Books, 1996), 1.
9. F. C. Happold, *Mysticism: A Study and an Anthology* (London: Penguin Books, 1990), 16.
10. Andrew Harvey, *The Essential Mystics: The Soul's Journey to Truth* (New York: Harper-Collins, 1996), x.
11. Acts 9:3–9.
12. Philippians 2:5.
13. 1 John 4:19.

CHAPTER THREE: TO PLAY IN TEN THOUSAND PLACES: CHRIST
AS THE CENTER OF MYSTICAL CHRISTIANITY

1. Matthew 5:43–48—adapted to make the language more inclusive, less gendered.
2. John 10:30; 14:20; 17:20–23; 15:5—adapted to make the language more inclusive, less gendered.
3. See 1 Corinthians 15:12–19.

CHAPTER FOUR: OF PROPHETS AND PHILOSOPHERS: THE SOURCES
OF CHRISTIAN MYSTICISM

1. See Evelyn Underhill's *The Mystics of the Church*, Rowan Williams's *The Wound of Knowledge*, and Bernard McGinn's *The Presence of God: A History of Western Christian Mysticism*. I especially recommend McGinn's work: it consists of nine hefty volumes of richly detailed history and commentary—and even so it only covers Western Christianity, up until about the year 1700!
2. I strongly recommend the writings of Professor Amy-Jill Levine, to help Christians to understand Jesus and the Bible from a Jewish perspective.
3. 1 Samuel 10:6.
4. Exodus 3:1–17; 1 Kings 19:11–12; Isaiah 6:1–8; Ezekiel 1:1–28.
5. 2 Corinthians 12:2.
6. Ezekiel 1:4; 1 Kings 19:11–12.
7. Aryeh Kaplan, *Meditation and the Bible* (York Beach, ME: Weister Books, 1978), Kindle loc. 699–734.
8. 1 Kings 19:12.
9. Kaplan, *Meditation and the Bible*, Kindle loc. 1810.
10. Habakkuk 2:20.
11. Daniel 12:3.
12. See Jay Michaelson, *Everything Is God: The Radical Path of Nondual Judaism* (Boston: Shambhala, 2012).
13. Louis Bouyer, *Understanding Mysticism*, ed. Richard Woods, OP (Garden City, NY: Image Books, 1980), 43.
14. Philippians 4:12.

15. George Maloney's *The Mystery of Christ in You* (New York: Alba House, 1998) explains much of the meaning behind the concept of mystery in the Christian Scriptures, particularly in the writings of St. Paul.
16. John 15:4.
17. Luke 24:32.
18. 2 Corinthians 12:2–4.

CHAPTER FIVE: HERMITS, NUNS, AND POETS: THE EVOLUTION OF CHRISTIAN MYSTICISM

1. John 1:14; 10:30; Matthew 27:43.
2. John 15:26.
3. Deuteronomy 6:4.
4. Karl Rahner, *Concern for the Church* (New York: Crossroad, 1981), 149.
5. Harvey D. Egan, *Soundings in the Christian Mystical Tradition* (Collegeville, MN: Liturgical Press, 2010), 345–46.

CHAPTER SIX: PRAYS WELL WITH OTHERS: MYSTICAL CHRISTIANITY AND INTERSPIRITUALITY

1. See Catherine Swietlicki, *Spanish Christian Cabala* (Columbia: University of Missouri Press, 1986) for insight into how Teresa, John, and Luis de Leon drew upon the Kabbalah for their work.
2. Darrell Grizzle, comment left on my blog, *Anamchara*, November 18, 2007. https://anamchara.com/everything-you-always-wanted-to-know-about-christian-mysticism-but-were-afraid-to-ask/ (accessed March 25, 2023).
3. S. Abhayananda, *History of Mysticism: The Unchanging Testament* (Olympia, WA: Atma Books, 1996), 232.
4. C. S. Lewis, *Letters to Malcolm: Chiefly on Prayer* (London: Geoffrey Bles, 1964), 62

CHAPTER SEVEN: TO THE LEAST OF THESE: THE SOCIAL DIMENSION OF CHRISTIAN MYSTICISM

1. Luke 10:38–42.
2. Matthew 22:37, 39; 5:43.
3. Teresa of Ávila, *The Interior Castle*, trans. E. Allison Peers (n.p.: Dover Publications, 1961), Seventh Mansion, chapter 4. Kindle edition.
4. Teresa, *The Interior Castle*, trans. Mirabai Starr (New York: Riverhead Books, 2003), Fourth Dwelling, chapter 1. Kindle edition.
5. Matthew 6:6.
6. John 13:1–17.
7. Matthew 25:31–45.
8. *The Rule of St. Benedict in English* (Collegeville, MN: Liturgical Press, 1981), 73.
9. Evelyn Underhill, *Mysticism: A Study in the Nature and Development of Spiritual Consciousness* (1930; repr., n.p.: Dover Publications, 2002), 362. Kindle edition.
10. Howard Thurman, *Jesus and the Disinherited* (Boston: Beacon Press, 1976), 72.
11. Kenneth Leech, *The Social God* (London: Sheldon Press, 1981), 53.

12. Rowan Williams, "Archbishop's Address to the Synod of Bishops in Rome," October 10, 2012, found online at http://rowanwilliams.archbishopofcanterbury.org/articles. php/2645/archbishops-address-to-the-synod-of-bishops-in-rome.html (accessed December 16, 2022).

CHAPTER EIGHT: SINGING THE SONG OF SONGS: THE EROTIC CHARACTER OF MYSTICAL CHRISTIANITY

1. Hadewijch, *The Complete Works* (Mahwah, NJ: Paulist Press, 1980), 244.
2. St. Teresa of Avila, *Autobiography of St. Teresa of Avila* (New York: Image Books, 1960), 274–75.
3. Grace M. Jantzen, *Power, Gender and Christian Mysticism* (New York: Cambridge University Press, 1995), 136.
4. Another interesting question: how many celibate mystics down the ages were people that today would identify as asexual? In all likelihood, quite a few. The recognition of asexuality as a valid expression of sexuality could help Christians to affirm the vocation of celibacy as a possible and appropriate spiritual calling for some individuals, while others of course are called to marital intimacy — and either of these expressions of sexuality can be consistent with mystical and contemplative spirituality.

CHAPTER NINE: THE MYSTERY'S PROMISE: WHY CHRISTIAN MYSTICISM MATTERS

1. 1 John 4:16; Matthew 22:36–39; John 10:10; Philippians 2:5; 4:13.

CHAPTER TEN: THE MYSTICAL PARADOXES

1. As quoted by his son Hans Bohr in "My Father," in *Niels Bohr: His Life and Work* (Amsterdam: Elsevier, 1967), 328.
2. Jean-Yves Leloup, *Being Still: Reflections on an Ancient Mystical Tradition* (New York: Paulist Press, 2003), 59.
3. Luke 17:21; John 18:36.
4. Romans 3:28; James 2:26.
5. 1 Corinthians 13:11.
6. Traditional language for the three persons of the Trinity is unfortunately highly gendered: "The Father, Son and Holy Spirit."
7. John 8:12; Matthew 5:14.
8. 2 Corinthians 4:6.
9. Ephem the Syrian, *Hymns* (New York: Paulist Press, 1989), 464.
10. Psalm 37:4, adapted.
11. Romans 7:12; Deuteronomy 4:31.
12. Hebrews 7:26, Luke 14:16–23.
13. Matthew 5:8.
14. Matthew 5:48.
15. Jeremiah 2:7.
16. Genesis 1:10, adapted.
17. 1 John 2:15.

18. Mark 12:14.
19. Proverbs 9:10.
20. Gerald G. May, *Will and Spirit: A Contemplative Psychology* (New York: HarperCollins, 1987) 54.
21. Hebrews 11:1.
22. Isaiah 42:10, Numbers 11:12, Luke 15:8–10; Matthew 23:37.
23. Julian of Norwich, *The Showings*, trans. Mirabai Starr (Charlottesville, VA: Hampton Roads Publishing), 163.
24. Carmen Acevedo Butcher, trans. *The Cloud of Unknowing* (Boulder, CO: Shambhala Publications, 2009), 21.
25. For just a few examples, see Psalm 62:1, 65:1 (when translated literally), Habakkuk 2:20, and 1 Thessalonians 4:11 (again, when translated literally).
26. G. K. Chesterton, *What's Wrong With the World*, part 4, chapter 14. Project Gutenberg, 2008/2016, https://www.gutenberg.org/files/1717/1717-h/1717-h.htm#link2H_4_0045 (accessed March 25, 2023).
27. Sirach 24:19–21.
28. C. S. Lewis, *The Pilgrim's Regress* (New York: HarperCollins, n.d.), 202. Kindle Edition.
29. Arthur A. Vogel, *The Power of His Resurrection: The Mystical Life of Christians* (New York: Seabury, 1976), 3–4.
30. Philippians 2:7.
31. Matthew 5:39; 20:16; 16:25.
32. Psalm 46:10.
33. Gerald May, *Will and Spirit* (San Francisco: Harper & Row, 1982), 46.

CHAPTER ELEVEN: CHRISTIANITY'S BEST-KEPT SECRET

1. Pseudo-Dionysius the Areopagite, *Epistle* 9.1. Quoted in Bernard McGinn, *The Foundations of Mysticism* (New York: Crossroad, 1991), 173.
2. Bernard McGinn, *The Growth of Mysticism* (New York: Crossroad, 1994), 263.

CHAPTER TWELVE: THE EMBODIED HEART

1. Romans 5:5.
2. Luke 1:37; Matthew 19:26.
3. Matthew 6:6.
4. Bernard McGinn, *The Foundations of Mysticism* (New York: Crossroad, 1991), 141.

CHAPTER THIRTEEN: THE MYSTICAL BODY: CHRIST WITHIN US, CHRIST AMONG US

1. Teresa of Ávila, *The Book of Her Life*, in *The Collected Works of Teresa of Avila*, vol. 1, trans. Kieran Kavanaugh, and Otilio Rodriguez, (Washington, DC: ICS Publications, 1987), 22.2.
2. Matthew 18:20.
3. Matthew 19:26.
4. Visit the Spiritual Directors International (SDI) website, www.sdicompanions.org, to find an interfaith directory of spiritual directors and companions.

5. Meister Eckhart, *Selected Writings* (London: Penguin Books, 1994), 179.
6. Matthew 6:6.

CHAPTER FOURTEEN: EMPTINESS AND THE DANCE

1. 2 Peter 1:4.
2. Athanasius, *De Incarnatione*, 54. This is my poetic translation; the Greek literally reads "so that we might become deified."
3. Colossians 1:27.
4. Romans 5:5.
5. Hebrews 13:8.
6. Philippians 2:5–7.
7. Matthew 23:12.
8. Julian of Norwich, *Revelations of Divine Love*, trans. Clifton Wolters (New York: Penguin Books, 1966), 66.
9. Acts 17:28.
10. Ephesians 3:17. See also appendix C, "The Charter of Christian Mysticism."

CHAPTER FIFTEEN: BECOMING WHO YOU ALREADY ARE

1. Galatians 5:22–23.
2. Matthew 18:4.
3. Matthew 7:26–27.
4. Quoted in Paul Verdeyen, *Ruusbroec and His Mysticism* (Collegeville, MN: The Liturgical Press, 1994), 72.
5. Matthew 22:35–40.
6. Galatians 5:22–23.
7. Brian Haggerty, *Out of the House of Slavery: On the Meaning of the Ten Commandments* (New York: Paulist Press, 1978), 135–36.
8. *1 Corinthians 13:4–7.*

CHAPTER SIXTEEN: A PATHLESS PATH OF LIGHT

1. John 8:12; Matthew 5:14.
2. From Merton's Epiphany, documented in *Conjectures of a Guilty Bystander* (New York: Image Books, 2014), 154. Kindle edition.
3. Philippians 3:13–14.
4. John O'Donohue, *Anam Ċara: A Book of Celtic Wisdom* (New York: Harper Collins, 1987), 89. Kindle edition.

CHAPTER SEVENTEEN: THE WORD IS VERY NEAR YOU

1. Romans 5:5, 1 Corinthians 3:16.
2. Isaiah 45:15.

CHAPTER EIGHTEEN: THE HEAVENLY CONVERSATION

1. Marianne Williamson, *A Return to Love* (New York: HarperCollins, 1992), 190.
2. Matthew Fox, *Prayer* (New York: Tarcher/Putnam, 2001), 1.
3. Matthew 6:9–13.
4. Psalm 69:2 Douay-Rheims Version.
5. David Steindl-Rast, *Gratefulness, The Heart of Prayer* (New York: Paulist Press, 1984); Meister Eckhart, "Sermon Twenty-Seven" in *The Complete Mystical Works of Meister Eckhart* (New York: Crossroad, 2009), 173.
6. See 1 Corinthians 13:1, 14:2.
7. Acts 2: the story of the coming of the Holy Spirit at Pentecost.

CHAPTER NINETEEN: ETERNITY WITHIN

1. Quoted in *Sermons in a Sentence: A Treasury of Quotations on the Spiritual Life*, vol. 2, *St. Francis de Sales* (San Francisco: Ignatius Press, 2003), 138.
2. Libreria Editrice Vaticana, *Catechism of the Catholic Church*, 2nd ed. (Washington, DC: USCCB, 1997), 872.
3. 1 Corinthians 4:10.
4. Matthew 18:20, 1 Corinthians 3:16.
5. John 14:17; Romans 5:5.
6. Thomas Merton, *Conjectures of a Guilty Bystander* (New York: Crown Publishing, 1968), 156.
7. 1 Kings 19:12.
8. Isaiah 45:15.
9. Contemplative Outreach, "Centering Prayer," https://tinyurl.com/ek4cuvb4 (accessed December 24, 2022).

CHAPTER TWENTY: THE OTHER SIDE OF SILENCE

1. Cynthia Bourgeault's *The Heart of Centering Prayer* provides an excellent overview of how Centering Prayer helps us to cultivate a practice of objectless awareness.
2. C. S. Lewis, *The Voyage of the Dawn Treader: The Chronicles of Narnia* (New York: Macmillan Books, 1952), 223–24.
3. Quoted in John Welwood, interview with Tina Fossella, "Human Nature Buddha Nature: On Spiritual Bypassing, Relationship, and the Dharma," *Tricycle: The Buddhist Review* 20 (Spring 2011). https://tricycle.org/magazine/human-nature-buddha-nature/ (accessed March 25, 2023).
4. Constitution of the Monks of the Order of Cistercians of the Strict Observance, 1990; C.3.5. https://tinyurl.com/262r579h (accessed August 19, 2022).
5. Quoted in H. A. Reinhold, ed., *The Soul Afire: Revelations of the Mystics* (Garden City, NY: Image Books, 1973), 112.
6. Revelation 21:5.
7. Matthew 22:37–40
8. Kahlil Gibran, *The Prophet*, "On Work," https://tinyurl.com/2zc9sbac (accessed August 19, 2022).

9. Richard Rohr, *The Naked Now: Learning to See as the Mystics See* (New York: Crossroad, 2009), 159.

10. Vladimir Lossky, *The Mystical Theology of the Eastern Church* (Crestwood, NY: St. Valdimir's Seminary Press, 1957), 38–39.

11. Pseudo-Dionysius, *The Divine Names,* VII.3. *The Divine Names and the Mystical Theology,* trans. John D. Jones (Milwaukee: Marquette University Press, 1999), 178–79.

12. John 2:1–11.

CHAPTER TWENTY-ONE: THE HEART OF THE MYSTERY

1. John Ruusbroec, *The Spiritual Espousals and Other Works* (New York: Paulist Press, 1985), 146, 150.

2. Matthew 5:45, adapted.

3. *The Book of Common Prayer* (New York: Seabury Press, 1979), 133.

4. "We have seen that all real artists, as well as all pure mystics, are sharers to some degree in the Illuminated Life." Evelyn Underhill, *Mysticism: A Study in the Nature and Development of Spiritual Consciousness* (New York: Dutton, 1930), 236.

5. Underhill, *Mysticism,* 415.

6. Robert Davis Hughes, *Beloved Dust* (New York: Continuum, 2008), 373.

7. International Commission on English in the Liturgy, *The Roman Missal* (Washington, DC: USCCB, 2011), 529.

8. Psalm 82:6.

9. Matthew 18:3.

10. C. S. Lewis, *The Lion, the Witch and the Wardrobe* (New York: Collier Books, 1970), 185–86.

CHAPTER TWENTY-TWO: LIVING A MYSTICAL LIFE

1. 2 Corinthians 9:6.

2. Thomas Keating, *Invitation to Love* (London: Bloomsbury, 2011), 105.

APPENDIX B: A CONTEMPLATIVE READING LIST

1. Paulist Press's Classics of Western Spirituality series of great mystical books is an excellent resource for students of Christian mysticism, as well as Jewish, Muslim, and Native American spirituality.

APPENDIX C: THE CHARTER OF CHRISTIAN MYSTICISM

1. Many biblical scholars argue that this letter was not written by the same person who wrote most of the letters said to be by Paul. But for our purposes, the identity of the author is less important than the wisdom of the words, which after all have been accepted as inspired Scripture by Christians for many centuries now. If Paul didn't write Ephesians, we have no idea what the real author's name was, so for the sake of convenience, I'll go with tradition and call the author "Paul."

2. Ephesians 3:3–9.

3. John 10:30; 1 Corinthians 12:27.

About the Author

Carl McColman is an author, teacher, retreat leader, and spiritual director. He is the creator of www.anamchara.com, a blog devoted to contemplative living and mystical spirituality. He is a cohost of the *Encountering Silence* podcast.

Carl first explored Christian meditation and contemplation through the Shalem Institute for Spiritual Formation and received formation in lay Cistercian spirituality through the Lay Cistercians of the Monastery of the Holy Spirit. He is also a commissioned presenter of Centering Prayer Introductory Workshops.

He is the author of numerous books, including *Eternal Heart, Unteachable Lessons, Befriending Silence, An Invitation to Celtic Wisdom, The Little Book of Christian Mysticism*, and *Answering the Contemplative Call*.

Carl lives in Clarkston, Georgia, with his wife, artist Fran McColman.